D1524237

"Required reading! The Church *must* 'catch up'—and do it now! It's been nearly 50 years since the first 'Earth Day,' (1970) and the 1975 publication of the Appalachian Bishop's Pastoral. Deplorably, only in 2015 did the Church promulgate a Papal Encyclical on the *now*—'ecological crisis!' . . . This volume is a primer, showing the complexity of the crisis, but also the theological, moral, and spiritual grounding for an integral ecology at the heart of a sustainable world."

—DAWN M. NOTHWEHR, Chair in Catholic Ethics, Catholic Theological Union

"*Fragile World* takes seriously the notion of 'integral ecology' as described in *Laudato Si'*. Its chapters generate an informed, intelligent dialogue among a diversity of voices from around the planet to address the global ecological crisis. Seldom does a reader find in one volume both a clear, critical analysis of this issue as well as so many strong voices from the margins that have too often been ignored. This volume is required reading."

—DENNIS PATRICK O'HARA, Associate Professor, Elliott Allen Institute for Theology and Ecology, University of St. Michael's College

Fragile World

†

STUDIES IN WORLD CATHOLICISM

Michael L. Budde and William T. Cavanaugh, *Series Editors*

Karen M. Kraft, *Managing Editor*

Other Titles in This Series

Beyond the Borders of Baptism: Catholicity, Allegiances, and Lived Identities. Edited by Michael L. Budde. Vol. 1, 2016. ISBN 9781498204736.

New World Pope: Pope Francis and the Future of the Church. Edited by Michael L. Budde. Vol. 2, 2017. ISBN 9781498283717.

Scattered and Gathered: Catholics in Diaspora. Edited by Michael L. Budde. Vol. 3, 2017. ISBN 9781532607097.

A Living Tradition: The Holy See, Catholic Social Doctrine, and Global Politics 1965–2000. A. Alexander Stummvoll. Vol. 4, 2018. ISBN 9781532605116.

Forthcoming Titles in This Series

Love, Joy, and Sex: An African Conversation on Pope Francis's Amoris Laetitia *and the Gospel of Family in a Divided World.* Edited by Stan Chu Ilo. Vol. 6.

The Church and Indigenous Peoples in the Americas. Edited by Michel Elias Andraos. Vol. 7.

A Church with the Indigenous Peoples: The Intercultural Theology and Ecclesiology of JTatik Samuel Ruiz García. Michel Elias Andraos. Vol. 8.

Pentecostalism, Catholicism and the Spirit in the World. Edited by Stan Chu Ilo. Vol. 9.

Fragile World

Ecology and the Church

EDITED BY

William T. Cavanaugh

CONTRIBUTORS

Agnes M. Brazal
Daniel P. Castillo
Celia Deane-Drummond
Christopher Hamlin
Peter Hughes, SSC
Stan Chu Ilo
Emmanuel Katongole
Christie Klimas
Peter Knox, SJ
Germán Mahecha Clavijo

Michael S. Northcott
Edward Obi, MSP
Randy J. C. Odchigue
Michael A. Perry, OFM
Daniel F. Pilario, CM
Reynaldo D. Raluto
Bishop Luis Alfonso Santos Villeda
Rolando Tuazon, CM
Cardinal Peter K. A. Turkson

 CASCADE *Books* · Eugene, Oregon

FRAGILE WORLD
Ecology and the Church

Studies in World Catholicism 5

Cascade Books
An Imprint of Wipf and Stock Publishers
199 W. 8th Ave., Suite 3
Eugene, OR 97401

www.wipfandstock.com

PAPERBACK ISBN: 978-1-4982-8340-3
HARDCOVER ISBN: 978-1-4982-8342-7
EBOOK ISBN: 978-1-4982-8341-0

Cataloguing-in-Publication data:

Names: Cavanaugh, William T., 1962–, editor.

Title: Fragile world : ecology and the church / edited by William T. Cavanaugh.

Description: Eugene, OR : Cascade Books, 2018 | Studies in World Catholicism 5 | Includes bibliographical references and index(es).

Identifiers: ISBN 978-1-4982-8340-3 (paperback) | ISBN 978-1-4982-8342-7 (hardcover) | ISBN 978-1-4982-8341-0 (ebook)

Subjects: LCSH: Environmental responsibility—Religious aspects—Catholic Church. | Environmental responsibility—Moral and ethical aspects. | Catholic Church. Pope (2013– : Francis). Laudato si'. | Human ecology—Religious aspects—Catholic Church. | Ecotheology.

Classification: BX1795.H82 F72 2018 (print) | BX1795.H82 F72 (ebook)

Manufactured in the U.S.A.   MAY 16, 2018

English translation of "Extractive Industries, Destructive Industries: The Case of Honduras—A Fragile Country and Devastated Ecology" © 2016 by Karen M. Kraft. Used with permission.

English translation of "The Poor: An Endangered Species?" © 2016 by Karen M. Kraft. Used with permission.

Contents

PART SIX: Eschatology

Contributors

Agnes M. Brazal is associate professor of theology at De La Salle University in Manila. She holds a doctorate in theology from the Catholic University of Louvain. Among her various publications are the coauthored *Intercultural Church: Bridge of Solidarity in the Migration Context* (Borderless Press, 2015) and the coedited *Feminist Cyberethics in Asia: Religious Discourses on Human Connectivity* (Palgrave Macmillan, 2014).

Daniel P. Castillo is assistant professor of theology at Loyola University Maryland in Baltimore. He received his doctorate in systematic theology from the University of Notre Dame in 2014; his dissertation, "An Ecological Theology of Liberation," brings the work of Gustavo Gutiérrez into dialogue with contemporary research in both biblical studies and political ecology.

Celia Deane-Drummond is professor of theology at the University of Notre Dame where she also directs the Center for Theology, Science, and Human Flourishing. She holds a PhD in plant physiology from Reading University and also in systematic theology from Manchester University. Her numerous publications include *The Wisdom of the Liminal: Evolution and Other Animals in Human Becoming* (Eerdmans, 2014) and the coedited *Religion in the Anthropocene* (Cascade Books, 2017).

Christopher Hamlin is professor of history at the University of Notre Dame. He holds a PhD in the history of science from the University of Wisconsin, Madison. His publications include *Cholera: The Biography* (Oxford University Press, 2009) and *Public Health and Social Justice in the Age of Chadwick: Britain, 1800–1854* (Cambridge University Press, 1998).

Peter Hughes, SSC, is an advisor to the Instituto Bartolomé de las Casas (Lima) and to the Latin American Bishops' Conference (CELAM); he has spent five decades as a missionary based in Latin America. He holds a doctorate of ministry in pastoral theology from the joint ecumenical program shared by Catholic Theological Union, Lutheran University, and McCormick

Theological Seminary in Chicago. He has written widely in Spanish, and his publications include *Cuidado de la Creación en Aparecida* (CEP, 2007) and the coedited *Ser Iglesia en Tiempos de Violencia* (CEP, 2006).

Stan Chu Ilo is assistant professor of Catholic studies and a research professor in the Center for World Catholicism and Intercultural Theology at DePaul University. He holds a PhD in theology from the University of St. Michael's College at the University of Toronto and also in the sociology of education from University of South Africa. His publications include *Methods and Models for Doing Theology in Africa* (Paulines Africa, 2014) and *The Church and African Development: Aid and Development from the Perspective of Catholic Social Ethics* (Paulines Africa, 2013).

Emmanuel Katongole is professor of theology and peace studies at the University of Notre Dame with a joint appointment in the Theology Department and the Kroc Institute for International Peace Studies. He holds a doctorate in philosophy from the Catholic University of Louvain. A former visiting research fellow at DePaul University's Center for World Catholicism and Intercultural Theology (CWCIT), two of his many books are the result of this research: *Born from Lament: The Theology and Politics of Hope in Africa* (Eerdmans, 2017) and *The Sacrifice of Africa: A Political Theology for Africa* (Eerdmans, 2010).

Christie Klimas is assistant professor of environmental science and studies at DePaul University and a corecipient of a grant from the U.S. EPA as part of its P3 Program (People, Prosperity, Planet). She holds a PhD in environmental science from the University of Florida. Among her published journal articles are "The Importance of Ecological Economics in the Undergraduate Environmental Sciences and Sustainability Curricula" in *Environmental Practice* 16 (2014) and the coauthored "Soil Quality Assessment Is a Necessary First Step for Designing Urban Green Infrastructure" in *Journal of Environmental Quality* 45:1 (2016).

Peter Knox, SJ, is professor of systematic theology, deputy principal of Academic Affairs, and dean of the Jesuit School of Theology at Hekima University College (Nairobi), having previously taught at St. John Vianney Seminary in Pretoria and St. Augustine College in his native Johannesburg, South Africa. He holds an MA and PhD in theology from Saint Paul University (Ottawa). His publications include *Aids, Ancestors, and Salvation: Local Beliefs in Christian Ministry to the Sick* (Paulines Africa, 2009) and the chapter "Sustainable Mining in South Africa: A Concept in Search of a

Theory" in *Just Sustainability: Technology, Ecology, and Resource Extraction*, edited by Christiana Z. Peppard (Orbis, 2015).

Germán Mahecha Clavijo is professor of theology and director of the Eco-theology Research Group at the Pontifical Xaverian University in Bogotá. He holds a PhD in pedagogical science from the Central Institute of Pedagogical Sciences in Havana and a master's in environmental education from the Institute of Ecological Research in Málaga, Spain, as well as in environmental education and theology, both from the Pontifical Xaverian University. His publications include *Ecoteología* (Pontifical Xaverian University Press, 2016), coedited with Afonso Tadeu Murad.

Michael S. Northcott is emeritus professor of ethics in the School of Divinity at the University of Edinburgh and 2018 guest professor of theology at the University of Heidelberg. A board member of the International Society for the Study of Religion, Nature, and Culture, he has worked in the field of religion and ecology for more than twenty years. Among his many publications are *Place, Ecology, and the Sacred: The Moral Geography of Sustainable Communities* (Bloomsbury Academic, 2015) and *A Political Theology of Climate Change* (SPCK, 2014).

Edward Obi, MSP, is executive secretary of the Niger Delta Catholic Bishops' Forum as well as executive director of Gas Alert for Sustainable Initiative (Port Harcourt, Nigeria) and national coordinator of the National Coalition on Gas Flaring and Oil Spills in the Niger Delta. He holds a doctorate in moral theology and social ethics from the Catholic University of Louvain. His publications include the chapter, "The Exploitation of Natural Resources: Reconfiguring Economic Relations toward a Community-of-Interests Perspective," in *Just Sustainability: Technology, Ecology, and Resource Extraction*, edited by Christiana Z. Peppard (Orbis, 2015).

Randy J. C. Odchigue is vice president for Academic Affairs and Research at Fr. Saturnino Urios University (Butuan City, Philippines) and a guest professor at the Seminario Mayor de San Carlos (Cebu City). He holds a PhD in systematic theology from the Catholic University of Louvain. His publications include the chapter, "The Ecclesial Contribution to Sustainable Communities," in *Just Sustainability: Technology, Ecology, and Resource Extraction*, edited by Christiana Z. Peppard (Orbis, 2015).

Michael A. Perry, OFM, is minister general of the Order of Friars Minor since 2013. Previously, he served as vicar general for the Order, minister provincial of the Most Sacred Heart of Jesus Province in the U.S., and missionary in the Democratic Republic of Congo, and worked with Catholic Relief Services and the U.S. Conference of Catholic Bishops. He holds an MDiv in priestly formation, an MA in missiology, and a PhD in religious anthropology from the University of Birmingham.

Daniel F. Pilario, CM, serves as dean and professor of theology at the St. Vincent School of Theology (Manila). He holds a doctorate in sacred theology from the Catholic University of Louvain. His publications include *Back to the Rough Grounds of Praxis: Exploring Theological Method with Pierre Bourdieu* (Leuven University Press, 2005) and the coedited volumes, *The Ambivalence of Sacrifice* (SCM, 2013) and *Christian Orthodoxy* (SCM, 2014).

Reynaldo D. Raluto is the academic dean at St. John Vianney Theological Seminary in Cagayan de Oro City, Philippines. He holds master's degrees in theology and philosophy from the Ateneo de Manila University and obtained his licentiate in sacred theology as well as his theology doctorate from the Catholic University of Louvain. His publications include *Poverty and Ecology at the Crossroads: Towards an Ecological Theology of Liberation in the Philippine Context* (Ateneo de Manila University Press, 2015).

Bishop Luis Alfonso Santos Villeda is bishop emeritus of the Diocese of Santa Rosa de Copán, Honduras, which he served as bishop for twenty-seven years. He has also served as professor of Catholic social teaching and philosophy at the Instituto San Miguel in Tegucigalpa, and professor of philosophy at the Universidad Nacional Autónoma de Honduras. He is the founder and executive director of several national nonprofits, including Alianza Cívica por la Democracia and Fundación Polígono Industrial Copaneco, dedicated to the social, educational, and economic development of the poor. He holds a PhD in philosophy and theology from the Pontifical Salesian University in Rome.

Rolando A. Tuazon, CM, serves as rector of St. Vincent Seminary and as a professor of moral theology at St. Vincent School of Theology, both in Quezon City, Philippines; he is also administrator and project director of Santuario de San Vicente de Paul Shrine. He holds a licentiate and doctorate in moral theology from the Catholic University of Louvain. His publications include "Narrating Ethics from the Margins," in *Normativity of the Future: Reading Biblical and Other Authoritative Texts in an Eschatological Perspective*, edited by Reimund Bieringer and Mray Elsbern (Peeters, 2010).

Cardinal Peter K. A. Turkson is president of the Pontifical Council for Justice and Peace, since 2009, and archbishop emeritus of Cape Coast (Ghana). He also was appointed by Pope Francis in 2016 as prefect of the new Dicastery for Promoting Integral Human Development. He holds a license in Sacred Scripture from the Pontifical Biblical Institute in Rome and master's degrees in theology and divinity from St. Anthony-on-Hudson Seminary (New York). His publications include "Loving in Truth for the Sake of Humanity," in *Jesus Christ: The New Face of Social Progress,* edited by Peter J. Casarella (Eerdmans, 2015).

Acknowledgments

Authors often recognize that their books would be impossible without the help of many people, and that point is immediately obvious with an edited book of this nature, a collaboration of many different authors from around the world. My first thanks go to all the brilliant and inspiring authors gathered here. In any such volume with many authors, however, there needs to be one person to serve as focal point, one person to herd the cats and keep them all on task. That person, I am happy to acknowledge, is not me, the official editor, but Karen Kraft, who is in charge of publications for the Center for World Catholicism and Intercultural Theology at DePaul. Karen is the only true *sine qua non* of this volume. She has kept the authors mindful of their deadlines and style guides, and has worked through their prose line by line with a keen eye toward detail and readability. She has also translated two of the chapters from Spanish to English.

As if that weren't enough, Karen also worked side by side with Francis Salinel of the CWCIT to bring all of the authors (except Cardinal Turkson) to DePaul for the conference that served as the initial impetus for this volume. Francis and Karen were responsible for all the logistics and details that made the conference a success. In addition to their organizing skills, they are wonderful hosts, offering gracious hospitality to visitors from around the world. They were assisted by our very able student worker Anna Kreutz Beck, who had a hand in both the conference and this volume. I want to express my deep gratitude to all three of them, as well as to my faculty colleagues at the CWCIT, Michael Budde and Stan Chu Ilo, for their friendship and their work to bring the conference to fruition.

Final thanks go to Fr. Dennis Holtschneider, CM, in his final year as president of DePaul. The CWCIT was created under Fr. Dennis, and he has been a constant source of support and inspiration for our work.

William T. Cavanaugh
Director, Center for World Catholicism and Intercultural Theology
DePaul University

Introduction

WILLIAM T. CAVANAUGH

There has been an outpouring of theological reflection on ecology in recent years. What makes this volume different is that it is written by a team
of Christian scholars and activists from around the globe, not only North
America and Europe, but Africa, Asia, and Latin America, the "global
South." What is presented in these pages is not just a global angle on a crisis,
but a global angle on a global crisis. "The environment" is spoken of in the
singular for good reason: though there are many types of microclimates and
habitats and ecosystems on the planet, all are intertwined into one global
"the environment." What happens in any part of the world affects the rest
of the world; fossil fuel use in any part of the world raises the temperature
of the earth's atmosphere as a whole, for example. Even more pointedly,
the consumption patterns of the global North disproportionately affect the
poorer countries in the global South; so many of the extractive industries,
for example, wreak ecological destruction in the South for the benefit of the
wealthier North. Christians in the North have only begun to listen to the
testimonies and theological reflections of those in the South about the ways
in which their ecosystems have been disrupted by our consumption.

If there is one theme that unites the chapters in this volume, therefore,
it is that of interconnection. In his encyclical *Laudato Si'*, Pope Francis frequently uses the term "integral ecology" to call our attention to the ways in
which not only the physical environment but also human society, culture,
theology, and economics are all densely interconnected. Indeed, ecology is
not just one more issue for theology to take notice of and comment upon.
The ecological crisis is at its root a theological crisis, not only a crisis in the
way that humans regard creation and their place in it, but a crisis in the way
that humans think about God. An integral ecology demands that we think
deeply not only about humans and the physical environment, but also about
the God who not only created the world but sustains it in being. It is not
only that ecology must be thought theologically; it is that theology must be

1

thought ecologically. The modern neglect of creation comes from our neglect of God and God's Word, but it is also the case that our neglect of God
comes from the ways that our interaction with the physical environment
teaches us to relate to everything that is Other than ourselves. Theology and
ecology need to be thought and enacted together.

For Pope Francis in *Laudato Si'*, the ecological crisis has the same root
as the theological crisis: we humans have tried to put ourselves in God's
place. Francis quotes Pope Benedict XVI: "The misuse of creation begins
when we no longer recognize any higher instance than ourselves, when we
see nothing else but ourselves."[1] When there is nothing and no one above
our own desires, we see creation as something to be manipulated for our
own satisfaction. What Genesis identifies as the primordial sin—"eat of it
. . . and you will be like gods" (Gen 3:5)—is the heart of what Francis calls
the "technocratic paradigm," the gaze that sees all matter as inert, waiting
to be engineered for our own satisfaction. There is nothing wrong with
technology as such, and there may be some technologies—solar panels, for
example—that will help to ameliorate the ecological crisis. But neither the
problem nor the solution is solely technological. The real heart of the matter is theological, an anthropocentric worldview that puts humans in the
place of God. When Francis uses the language of a "deified market,"[2] he calls
attention to the way that human desires, especially the unfettered pursuit
of financial gain, are accorded god-like status, to be served no matter the
environmental consequences.

"We are not God."[3] According to Pope Francis, this simple fact, though
easily forgotten, is the answer to critics who accuse Christianity of promoting human "dominion" (Gen 1:28) over the earth in a domineering and destructive sense. As Genesis makes plain, we ourselves are dust of the earth,
not Creators but part of creation.[4] We are humus, soil, called to humility.
Our finite nature is not a condition to be regretted, though, because we are
called to live in communion with a good God and a good creation. In other
words, it is not simply that humans are not God, but the God we have is
also not a God of domination and exploitation. Any god that dominates
and exploits creation is a false god. We serve a God who calls a beautiful
creation into being through love, who sees that it is good. The Lord cares

---

1. Francis, *Laudato Si'*, 6.
2. Ibid., 56.
3. Ibid., 67.
4. Ibid., 2.

for and protects the earth, and we are called to do the same, nurturing the land (Gen 2:15).[5]

The interconnection of theology and ecology, and of God and humans, is complemented by the interconnection of all humans. We are all equally made in the image and likeness of God, so all share an equal dignity. Moreover, because it is God, not we humans, who own the earth (Ps 24:1), we are not entitled to regard the property under our control as our own.[6] Although Catholic tradition recognizes private property, "there is always a social mortgage on all private property, in order that goods may serve the general purpose that God gave them," in the words of Pope John Paul II.[7] The exploitation of the earth often goes hand in hand with the exploitation of the poor. Solving the ecological crisis will necessarily have a social dimension, such that the use of the earth will have to take into account those who suffer most when the land and water and air is degraded. Pope Francis furthermore recognizes that the earth is best cared for by small-scale producers who live close to the land and know it intimately, as opposed to large-scale agribusiness that manages the land from afar for the profit of anonymous shareholders.[8]

According to Pope Francis, "A fragile world, entrusted by God to human care, challenges us to devise intelligent ways of directing, developing and limiting our power."[9] The idea of limiting our power sounds negative to modern ears, a pessimistic shrinking back from the can-do spirit that embraces constant economic growth and technological progress as the ideal. But Pope Francis points to St. Francis of Assisi as a model for the way we should approach the world with reverence. St. Francis did not embrace voluntary poverty as a negation of the self, but rather as a "refusal to turn reality into an object simply to be used and controlled."[10] St. Francis lived in harmony with all creation and saw that "[r]ather than a problem to be solved, the world is a joyful mystery to be contemplated with gladness and praise."[11] The world is such a mystery because it is not simply inert matter, but a display of the inexhaustible beauty of its Creator. The ecological crisis is a spiritual, not merely material, crisis. It will only be solved by a

5. Ibid., 67.
6. Ibid., 89.
7. Ibid., 93.
8. Ibid., 94, 129.
9. Ibid., 78.
10. Ibid., 11.
11. Ibid., 12.

sacramental view of the world, in which the presence of a loving God is found radiant in all things.[12]

The essays in this volume can be seen together as reflections on the notion of interconnection that Pope Francis highlights in his encyclical. These essays are the finished product of discussions begun at the World Catholicism Week conference on ecology and the church in April 2015 at DePaul University. The conference brought together scholars and activists from around the world to discuss each other's research and to explore the interconnections among different places in the globe and different disciplines, all under the umbrella concern of how the church can respond to the global ecological crisis. Animating the conference was the conviction that building bonds of friendship among representatives of far-flung Christian communities across the globe can help to raise awareness of the global crisis and the catholic resources for responding to it. The conference was held in advance of Pope Francis's release of *Laudato Si'* in June 2015, but many of the participants have incorporated reflections on *Laudato Si'* in the final version of the chapters that appear in this volume. One of the essays, that by Bro. Michael Perry, OFM, Minister General of the Franciscans worldwide, contains an extensive analysis of Pope Francis's encyclical.

The volume begins with a section on Catholic social teaching on the environment, which serves as a primary touchstone for the reflections that follow. The first chapter, by Notre Dame historian Christopher Hamlin, unearths some of the antecedents to the Catholic environmental movement and emphasis on the environment in papal social teaching over the last few decades. Hamlin argues that Catholic concern for the environment did not simply tag along after the secular ecological movement; he traces a Catholic environmental tradition in patristic theology, in eighteenth-century natural theology, and most especially in the "Catholic Rural Philosophy" of the National Catholic Rural Life Conference in the 1930s and 1940s, the story of which Hamlin tells in fascinating detail. Cardinal Peter Turkson of Ghana, the president of the Pontifical Council for Justice and Peace and an important influence in the drafting of *Laudato Si'*, follows with a chapter that summarizes papal social teaching on the environment beginning with Paul VI, and concentrating on the pontificates of John Paul II and Benedict XVI. Cardinal Turkson then brings the story of Catholic social teaching on the environment up to date with a discussion of the intervention of the Holy See at the Rio+20 conference in 2012, and the more recent contributions of Pope Francis. Scientist and theologian Celia Deane-Drummond next analyzes papal social teaching on the environment not only for its promise

12. Ibid., 86, 234–36.

but also for its limitations, concentrating on the pontificates of Pope Francis's two immediate predecessors. Deane-Drummond is especially keen to identify those elements of papal social teaching that are most likely to gain a hearing in the global community more widely, beyond the boundaries of the church. The last chapter in this section of the book is an extended reflection by Michael Perry, on two Francises, the current pope and the saint whose name he took. Moving from Assisi to Buenos Aires, Perry shows how the current pope constructs his "integral ecology" from St. Francis's vision of an interconnected created order in which each individual thing on earth has a place and is loved and sustained there by God. In response to Pope Francis's invitation to ongoing dialogue, Perry closes with some principles to guide action to address the ecological crisis.

The second section of the volume, "Cry of the Earth," consists of testimonies and analyses of ecological destruction in the global South. Bishop Luis Alfonso Santos Villeda, a prominent activist for the environment in his native land, takes us to Honduras and shows us the havoc wreaked there by extractive industries from the global North, not only in terms of ecological destruction but also in terms of political corruption. Santos articulates a principled response and issues an impassioned plea for help from the outside world. Peter Hughes then examines extractive industries in the Pan Amazon, focusing on the dire consequences for the local indigenous people and for the whole world in the form of global warming. Hughes tries to overcome a sense of fatalism with a detailed analysis of signs of hope in church-based networks that seek to promote action in defense of the Amazon. Peter Knox next examines the concept of "planetary boundaries" with regard to his home continent, exploring Africa's particular points of vulnerability and resilience. Knox explains the recent scientific work which has tried to identify the ecological limits beyond which life on the planet cannot be sustained in its current form, and discusses theological resources for communicating this analysis to African people.

The third section of this book focuses on developing theologies for dealing with the ecological crisis. Stan Chu Ilo presents a creation story from his village among the Igbo people of Nigeria, and argues that African communities already have a deep eco-consciousness upon which to draw when constructing eco-theologies. African traditions recognize the sacred and interconnected nature of all life, human and nonhuman. Ilo shows how African theologians are bringing these insights with them when elaborating on God as Trinity, in whom mutuality and participation are expressions of the divine nature. In his contribution to this section, Dan Castillo argues that the church's response to the ecological crisis should take cues from previous attempts in Scripture and tradition to deal with situations of devastation in which it seemed that the world was coming undone. Castillo examines the tradition of prophetic mourning and lament following the Babylonian exile and argues that recovering these practices will help us focus not only on the devastation but on our sinful responsibility for the current crisis. Theological practices of mourning and lament can help us move from denial and despair to hopeful protest and action. Finally, Colombian theologian Germán Mahecha, who also has a degree in environmental sciences, considers the poor as an endangered species, and puts forth the provocative idea that the poor will be the only ones capable of surviving a global environmental collapse, because they have already adapted to living without regular access to good food, clean drinking water, health services, and more. The poor have also created structures of solidarity—in Christian terms, the church—that show the way forward for creating the altruistic relationships necessary to heal the planet.

The volume's fourth section highlights ethical responses to environmental degradation. Edward Obi critiques a human-centered ethic and examines its destructive effects in the oil and gas industries in the Niger Delta region of his native Nigeria. Obi argues that it is liberal individualism, not Christianity, that is responsible for the anthropocentric exploitation of the earth. Obi proposes a theological ethic that flows from the relational nature of the human person, which is based in turn on the biblical portrayal of humans as essentially related to both the earth and the Creator God, in whose image we are made. Rolando Tuazon's chapter argues that policy statements and ethical frameworks for addressing the ecological crisis often neglect the "ecology of everyday life" embedded in local cultures and traditions that helps to form ecologically conscious character. Tuazon brings virtue ethics theory into conversation with the life stories of three indigenous, Buddhist, and Catholic environmental activists in the Philippines, and shows how their activism is rooted in virtues like courage, wisdom, humility, and love that, in different ways, are learned within the context of their tradition-formed communities. Finally, environmental sciences professor Christie Klimas examines the environmental impact and ethical implications of consumer behavior during the Christmas season in the global North, especially with regard to wasteful spending associated with gift-giving. Klimas contrasts the birth of Christ, "born poor to serve the poor," with both the environmental degradation produced by gift-giving and the opportunities to serve the poor and the planet foregone in such giving. Klimas ends with concrete suggestions for charitable giving and responsible gift-giving at Christmas that are more in tune with the spirit of the holiday for Christians.

The fifth section of the volume offers pastoral resources for the church to deal with environmental calamity. Using his home village in Uganda as an example, Emmanuel Katongole shows how many Africans have become alienated from the land in pursuit of an illusory progress and moderniza- tion, with hunger, instability, and environmental degradation as the result. In response, Katongole offers not only a theological reflection on the fail- ure to acknowledge our deep connection to the land, but also a concrete pastoral response in the form of the Bethany Land Institute in Uganda, an educational program and experimental farm that brings together theology, ecology, and food production. In her chapter, Agnes Brazal examines the importance of cultural and religious discourses about natural disasters, an area of inquiry that has been neglected. Brazal examines discourses sur- rounding Super Typhoon Haiyan in her native Philippines, showing what kinds of discourse are helpful in disaster mitigation and what kinds are not. Brazal argues that the church has an important role to play in responding to disasters, not only in material ways but in helping to mediate among folk, religious, and scientific ways of conceptualizing what has happened. Randy Odchigue's contribution to this section of the volume argues that the fra- gility of ecosystems mirrors the fragility of communities. Odchigue argues that the church's pastoral response to the ecological crisis must draw on the wisdom and experience of indigenous communities, like the Manobo in the Agusan Marsh in the Philippines, for whom the land is sacred.

The sixth and last section of the book deals, appropriately, with the last things, or eschatology. Filipino theologian Daniel Pilario examines apoca- lyptic discourse concerning the ecological crisis. Apocalyptic language takes a variety of forms and can elicit reactions ranging from fatalism to a sense of immediate urgency to take action. Pilario outlines what he calls an "eco- apocalyptic spirituality" that gives hope and leads to responsible political ac- tion, drawing on the post-apocalyptic thought of James Berger, the theology of Johann Baptist Metz, and Pilario's own experiences with the victims of Super Typhoon Haiyan, who demonstrate resistance, resilience, solidarity, and compassion. In the next chapter, Michael Northcott traces the present ecological crisis to the worldwide privatization of common lands over the last few centuries for the benefit of a small capitalist class, who regards land as a commodity to be exploited. The cure must be an "Ecozoic" eschatology, a new and final era of human history in which the cosmic Christ and the sacred interconnectedness of all things are realized. Northcott is critical of Catholic resistance to birth control and the authoritarian structure of the Catholic Church, and argues that addressing the ecological crisis requires the kind of messianic democracy exhibited by Christ, who overturned our expectations of what power is. In the final essay of the section and of the volume, Reynaldo Raluto looks at the intersection of poverty and natural disasters in the Philippines, and offers a Christian eschatological vision of hope for a sustainable future. Christian eschatology drives us not to accept things as they are, but to look for a radical change, a utopia that the gospel calls the Kingdom of God, the divine ultimate destiny of all creation, in which a truly sustainable life can be lived.

The notes of resistance and hope sounded in these final essays, and indeed throughout the book, seem more urgent now than ever. As I write this, a new administration that appears generally hostile to ecological consciousness assumes power in the United States, threatening international environmental accords, inadequate though they are, that have been painstakingly crafted over recent years. If national governments weaken their support for action to protect a fragile earth, it will be even more urgent that the church—which is perhaps the only truly international grassroots organization—step up. That the church would do so illustrates not only its response to a crisis, but its response to the call of God, who has loved all of creation into being.

PART ONE

Catholic Social Teaching

1

Turning Over the Right Rocks:
Finding Legacies of Catholic Environmentalism

CHRISTOPHER HAMLIN

In 1985, when I began teaching at a Catholic university, the environment was no significant part of that university's mission.[1] A few years later, on the first day of my initial offering of an environmental history course (then a new field), I asked students what the environment had to do with Catholicism. Not only had they no clue, I saw signs that the question failed even to register, so remote were the realms of faith and nature. There was, by then, a Catholic side of the environmental movement that had begun two decades earlier. Catholic social teachings translated easily into sustainability, and environmental concerns appeared in encyclicals and bishops' letters. There were communities of various sorts, lay and religious, living sustainably, and issue- or place-oriented groups, including student groups at Catholic universities. And yet my students' bewilderment was certainly understandable. Environmental matters were scientific and secular. They were not at the core of parish life; they were absent from Catholic history (Catholicism, too, was largely overlooked in environmental history).

My own knowledge was sketchy, too, and I sought to broaden it. Though I have published little on the matter, much of my subsequent research has concerned the theologies of nature of many branches of Christianity, and, especially in the case of Catholicism, the institutionalization in

1. In its concern with Catholic higher education, an earlier version of this chapter was given as a lecture honoring the memory of Peter V. Byrne, CM, DePaul University's first president.

mid-twentieth century rural American parishes of an approach to sustainability that, to a striking degree, anticipates Pope Francis's recent *Laudato Si'*.[2]

By consolidating many elements of Catholicism, this new encyclical makes what was peripheral central. Pope Francis has broadened and transformed the domain of what may be called religious environmentalism, which, particularly in the United States, had hitherto conspicuously reflected a Protestant heritage, a matter I will explore below. But, as appropriate to an encyclical, concerned with principles valid to all times and places, he has not dwelt in details (with the exception of a sobering assessment of the current biogeophysical state of the planet). My hope here is to fill in some of that detail, particularly with regard to the vexed issue of how faith might inform practice.

Let me begin with three provisos:

- First, I do not mean to suggest that each religion *needs to* have a distinct approach to environmental matters; I shall suggest, however, that there are profound differences of orientation between *Laudato Si'* and most Protestant environmentalism.

- Second, I shall not assess Pope Francis as a theologian, an articulator of the most authentic Catholic theological response to the crises of the day. Such an assessment of a long and complex document would go far beyond my scope.

- Third, I do believe that an approach like that in *Laudato Si'* is much needed. Most importantly, it bridges the gap between concepts of personhood and states of nature, drawing in institutions and technologies in the process.[3] That vision is *not* well articulated elsewhere; it is hard to imagine another magisterium from which it *could* be. My concern is with how Catholics and others might find ways to live that vision, not in heroic defiance of prevailing institutions, but as modest alternatives to them. Here, precedents help. It is easier to do something when one knows it has been done. I will explore precedents of several sorts, but chiefly at what will be three critical sites of the reception/

2. The foundation of my work on these issues appeared in Hamlin and Shepard, *Deep Disagreement in U.S. Agriculture*. Later explorations are in the introduction and conclusion of Lodge and Hamlin, *Religion and the New Ecology*; and Hamlin and McGreevy, "The Greening of America." I would also like to acknowledge my work with Professor Steven Kolmes of the University of Portland with whom I co-led an Erasmus Institute summer seminar on Environment and Religion in 2004.

3. Francis, *Laudato Si'*, 5, quotes John Paul II: what is needed is an "authentic *human ecology*."

implementation of *Laudato Si'*: Catholic universities (and other forms of higher school), seminaries, and in the social and economic institutions of parish life.

First, however, it is important to explore the claim that Catholicism and Protestantism have developed different orientations toward environmental issues.[4] Pope Francis does not discuss the history of ideas about the relation of religion to environment. Christians in general have been on the defensive about such matters ever since 1967, when the eminent medieval historian of technology Lynn White Jr. charged Judeo-Christianity with responsibility for "our Ecologic Crisis" in an address to the American Association for the Advancement of Science.[5] There and elsewhere, White considered the convergence of several elements during the High Middle Ages: a *contempus mundi* that came through some strands of Augustinianism (even if Augustine was rejecting even stronger versions that circulated in the early church) and was exemplified in some forms of ascetic monasticism, and an unexpected consequence of Benedictine-style monasticism, the accumulation of capital (and thus, through re-investment, the emergence of a kind of capitalism) that came through transforming wildernesses into productive estates. Others had identified a medieval industrial revolution based on capital-intensive prime movers and the application to wealth-creating and nature-changing uses; White famously added the transformation of concepts of virtue from internal mental states to economically approved habits. He also amplified admiration for what were presumed to be more nature-friendly and less anthropocentric cultures—premodern cultures, ancient paganism, and "oriental" cultures. These were seen to acknowledge an equality in all things; they stressed cyclicity and balance in contrast to the Judeo-Christian linear cosmology of creation, sin, redemption, and consummation.[6]

As an afterthought, White suggested St. Francis as a model for a contemplative and biocentric form of Christian spirituality. In the eco-spirituality and eco-theology that blossomed in the aftermath of White's essay, St. Francis's Canticle addressing the birds and beasts as sister and brother would be often cited as writers sought to refute White and/or to redress the problem he had pointed to. The Canticle is prominent in *Laudato*

---

4. *Laudato Si'* does not emphasize those differences. While the document's foundation in Catholic theology is plain, parts of it sound themes that have historically been more conspicuous in Protestant circles.

5. White, "The Historical Roots of Our Ecologic Crisis," 1203–7.

6. White, *Dynamo and Virgin Reconsidered*; Whitney, "The Lynn White Thesis," 313–31; Whitney, "Changing Metaphors and Concepts of Nature," 26–52.

Si' (sections 10–12). And yet, however important as an expression of religious feeling, St. Francis's nature writings do not derive from, nor easily connect to, theological mainstreams beyond the maxim of the goodness of creation. Had White not called attention to it, it is unlikely that this overlooked aspect of the complicated Franciscan tradition would have the significance it now has.

Focused on medieval history, White overlooked a large scholarly literature developing in the early twentieth century, which assigned profound changes in views of nature to the early modern period, and the Reformation in particular: best known are the works of Max Weber, R. H. Tawney, Robert Merton, and Lewis Mumford. They stressed various aspects: the disenchantment of nature and triumph of a devitalized materialism; the replacement of communitarianism by individualism; and the emergence of new economic values in Calvinism. Tawney eloquently pictures the lonely Puritan, puzzling out his salvation on a cold, fallen dunghill earth, and taking material wealth as an indicator of election. Mumford sketched the dehumanizing aspects of what Pope Francis calls in section 112 of *Laudato Si'* "the dominant technocratic paradigm."[7]

Tawney's, in particular, was a Christian critique. Their assessments, and those of other non-Marxist analysts of industrialism and capitalism, often looked back to a medieval golden age of socioeconomic and religious unity, and their ideas resonated with the ideas of Catholic reformers. Most familiar are the English distributists, Chesterton and Belloc, who, like Francis (and like his predecessor Leo XIII, author of *Rerum Novarum*), would imagine a social order founded around the unit of the family rather than a cash nexus. Notably, none of these authors was addressing an environmental problem: instead, they were concerned with fundamentally religious questions of how humans understood themselves and the meaning of their existence, and, accordingly, with the social and economic institutions they established in light of those understandings. Those institutions affected the natural world, but nature's fate was secondary. But the heritage is important. From the standpoint of modern environmentalism, often preoccupied with the working of natural systems, Pope Francis's attention to personhood and institutions may seem digressive. Such matters may well be part of a pope's territory yet seem ancillary to the technical problems of climate change.[8]

7. Weber, *The Protestant Ethic and the Spirit of Capitalism*; Tawney, *Religion and the Rise of Capitalism*; Merton, *Science, Technology, and Society in Seventeenth-Century England*; Mumford, *Technics and Civilization*. More recent works which explore various of these themes include Gregory, *The Unintended Reformation*; Merchant, *The Death of Nature*; and Harrison, *The Bible, Protestantism, and the Rise of Natural Science*.

8. Francis, *Laudato Si'*, 49.

Such an assessment will seem especially tempting in North America, where there are historical and geographic reasons why environment has often been disconnected from social issues—e.g., inequality—or issues of personhood. A religious framework is central to that disconnect. As Mark Stoll has demonstrated in his insightful 1997 work, *Protestantism, Capitalism, and Nature in America,* Calvinist antitheses have dominated assessments of nature in America. To English and Scots-Irish settlers, the Americas are places without settled and sustainable communities.[9] Instead, they were a savage and savage-inhabited wilderness, a fallen world in which sinners struggled and an elect might thrive. Among them, however, a few would see that wild nature as unfallen. In it, we glimpsed the garden we had lost; through it, one might find solace if not redemption. Both positions, Stoll makes clear, were rooted in Calvinism—while John Muir, the sage most clearly associated with the second view, might think he was repudiating his father's extreme Presbyterian sectarianism, he was perpetuating its individualistic and polarized moral framework.[10]

The consequences of that polarization are with us still, so deeply entrenched in American culture that it has been impossible to recognize it as a contingent event of religious and cultural history, a peculiar theological framework being applied in a peculiar geographic situation—the invasion of a large land mass populated by persons with whom they shared no heritage and who quickly fell victim to imported infections. But consider the results: we all must function by using natural resources, but terms referring to that use—like "utility" or "environment" itself—are ideological brand markers. Nature, whether the Grand Canyon or Grand Tetons, has become significantly an aesthetic and transcendent entity—to visit, sanctify, admire in one's imagination. But it is "out there, not in here." Recognizing that one lives in it, and is somehow of it, has been more difficult. Moral confusion abounds as individuals calculate their "footprint"; Pope Francis notes the irony—"schizophrenia"—of this anti-human humanism.[11]

But another consequence has been the assumption that the condition-of-nature question is a discrete policy issue, a matter of finding political will and effective legal means for tweaking nature-management institutions, while social and economic institutions—and concepts of

9. Stoll, *Protestantism, Capitalism, and Nature in America.* See also Merchant, *Ecological Revolutions.*

10. Pointing to its moral imperiousness, some scholars have suggested that (American) environmentalism is best understood as a religion. If so, it belongs to the heritage of millenarian movements. See Dunlap, *Faith in Nature.*

11. Francis, *Laudato Si',* 117–18.

personhood—remain the same.[12] This view the pope has challenged, and yet *Laudato Si'* is itself in many ways a product of the profound global influence that American environmental institutions and ideas have had. Sensibilities toward matters of humans and nature have varied widely, but ecology was chiefly an American science and so, too, were exemplary environmental institutions like the national park where Progressive-era elites communed with nature.

Not only was the dominant framework Calvinist, those most conspicuous in its making were Protestant. Stoll finds that environmental scientists, particularly ecologists, usually came from Calvinist backgrounds and often from clerical families. Why were Catholics not involved? Again, consider contingencies. Geography, language, and ethnicity fragmented American Catholicism, but class was probably the most important factor. Few nineteenth-century American Catholic immigrants could afford the Adirondack immersions in nature, which were becoming popular with the Protestant elite: still today, "nature" often remains an expensive consumer good. Aspiration was probably important, too. For many Catholics, agriculture—where intersection with nature would be inescapable—was not an attractive option. Refugees from Ireland or from the latifundias of Calabria (less so for immigrants from Germany or Belgium, as I shall suggest below) would remember life on the land as one of misery: poverty and semi-serfdom or other economic victimization. In the new world, too, agricultural independence required capital; they had only labor. Often the countryside was already prominently Protestant—to extend an institution-dependent church into hostile confessional territory was no simple matter. America's Catholics remained mainly urban. And they made their own colleges and universities (usually in cities) rather than utilizing the land-grant institutions where the environmental sciences were beginning to be developed in the 1880s.

These differences have not only historical significance; many of them persist, and there are both theological and sociological dimensions. The following tentative impressions from my own research oversimplify but suggest both the depth and breadth of differences.

12. Ibid., 111–12.

	Protestant	Catholic
Social structure	Individualistic	Familial, communitarian
Exemplary site	Wilderness area	Family farm
Approach	Romantic transcendence of elite aesthetes (Muir, Thoreau)	Insights less important than embodiments
Concept of nature	The non-human—to look at and be redeemed by, or to use.	An aspect of our being, of our bodies and selves, as well as the place of our being
Eschatology/time	Central/apocalyptic	Not particularly important; more concerned with permanence
Texts: The Fall	An ongoing crisis and enormous tragedy to be forever mourned	OK, we need to work. It's good. Let's do it well.
Texts: Job	The essential crisis	Not especially important
Texts: Parable of the talents	Capitalism	Regenerative agriculture

In my view the most profound difference is how humans are to be conceived as natural. In this regard, *Laudato Si'* goes far to invert the central problem. White wrote of an *ecologic* crisis; Francis is concerned with a longstanding *human* crisis, which has recently manifested itself ecologically owing to ways of living that are both unjust and unsustainable.[13] The needed inversion is so hard because key terms like "nature," "environment," and "environmentalism" (and even the domain of environmental history itself) have often been predicated on a dualism: nature starts where the human domain leaves off. One is asked to side with nature or with people. For Stoll's alienated Calvinists, hoping to transcend themselves and their ugly society, "nature" would be pure and permanent while the human domain is artificial, transitory, and often sinful, materialistic, and selfish. From White on, "anthropocentric"—in opposition to "biocentric"—would signify moral error. Pope Francis recognizes that prevailing usage but makes clear that a criticism of species-based selfishness does not imply pervasive anti-humanism.

But how, then, might we come to see the reflective moral beings we take ourselves to be as part of this external order and thus see the flourishing of humans as consonant with the flourishing of non-human nature? Here, Pope Francis's stress on integration is central. Generally, modern

13. Francis, *Laudato Si'*, 106–10.

universities assume a distinction between the descriptive knowledge of fields known as sciences, and normative knowledge, confined to narrower fields of ethics and aesthetics. Given the enormous contemporary emphasis in such universities on beneficial application, the breakdown is absurd— outmoded and dysfunctional, as Pope Francis recognizes in *Laudato Si'*, sections 106–7).[14] Traditionally in Catholic higher education, the human sciences, especially anthropology, were significantly normative as well as descriptive, and the kind of integration Pope Francis imagines might well be built on that foundation. But even in Catholic universities it is not obvious how one would begin to build. Hence my exploration of precedents. A suffi- ciently holistic Catholic environmental tradition doesn't have to be invented but only uncovered—thus my title, "Turning Over the Right Rocks."

We should not be surprised. Questions of cosmic moral order are not products of recent environmental crises, nor are they dependent on the maturation of climate science. Always there will be questions of how things are supposed to be and how we should interact with the cosmos to make them so.

Pope Francis does make brief and general mention of my first source, the nine hexameral homilies of the fourth-century Cappadocian, St. Basil the Great.[15] Modern readers may be amused by Basil's selective moralizing from the natural histories of Aristotle and Pliny. But as the controversies over various forms of sociobiology reveal, we too cannot escape the tempt- ing translation of "is" into "ought," nor, since we regard ourselves in terms both of "is" and of "ought," should we. It can be done more or less well in conjunction with other moral maxims.

I want to highlight two features of Basil's treatment. The first is the genre of the homily. Basil is not writing a treatise for a learned philosophi- cal audience but addressing issues in real lives, though his parishioners, if that is the right term, are evidently already well versed in geography and natural history. The second is the depth of his ecological knowledge. What may seem his selectiveness might be better seen as efforts to generalize on ecological matters that have moral significance. Some of the analogies have specific theological contexts—i.e., insect metamorphosis as the model for

---

14. As an example of that incoherence consider the phrase "natural law." Hearing it as one walks by a classroom, one may not know whether it refers to descriptive regulari- ties of force and matter (as in a physics class) or to the normative issue of the conditions of human flourishing as espoused by a Thomistic philosopher. And yet, in the same university there will likely be research projects in which natural laws of the former sense will be applied without any serious attention to the flourishing of the human person.

15. Francis, *Laudato Si'*, 77.

resurrection[16]—but most, like the urge to care for offspring,[17] would be widely shared and uncontroversial. But Basil's moral-ecological gaze goes well beyond matters immediately applicable. He considers factors that control fish populations (preyed-upon species have high fecundity);[18] the distinct habitats of different fishes,[19] including migration;[20] the formation of corals;[21] the morality of sentinel animals (cranes),[22] a matter that would fascinate Charles Darwin; parenting among crows; and the instincts of vultures.[23] At a time when many read nature emblematically, he was interested in its material reality, in terms of self-acting natural systems. But accepting phenomena as natural did not interfere with addressing the components of nature in moral terms, an approach that would persist into the early modern period.[24]

If Basil opens the door to the history of homiletics, my second example does the same for schooling. Specifically, what did early nineteenth-century Catholic German youths learn about God, nature, and appropriate human aspirations and behaviors? My source is a bestselling, though now unknown, devotional almanac known as *Reflections on the Works of God and His Providence throughout all Nature for Each Day of the Year*. Though first published in 1772 by the orthodox Lutheran pastor Christoph Christian Sturm (1740–1786), the work appeared in innumerable translations and adaptations across the range of Christian denominations for more than fifty years, including an explicitly Catholic edition for use in German schools in 1803.[25]

Broadly, the genre of Sturm's work is natural theology, not in the theologian's sense of all non-scriptural theology (including logic and metaphysics), but in the narrower sense of design arguments—explicating the reasons and meanings of natural phenomena and, in doing so, establishing the existence and character of God. Usually the enterprise, prominent from

16. Ibid., 132.

17. Ibid., 135.

18. Ibid., 106–7.

19. Ibid., 109.

20. Ibid., 112.

21. Ibid., 115.

22. Ibid., 125.

23. Ibid., 131.

24. Harrison, *The Bible, Protestantism, and the Rise of Natural Science*. See also Glacken, *Traces on the Rhodian Shore*.

25. Sturm, *Christoph Christian Sturm's Betrachtungen über die Werke Gottes*. My quotations are from Christoph Christian Sturm, *Sturm's Reflections on the Works of God*.

1650 to 1850, is seen as Protestant, and Anglican in particular. In England, it is apologetic and political, an appeal to the works of providence to justify the political order. But exploration of French and German natural theology, barely begun, makes clear that it is not uniquely Protestant nor usually political. German natural theology—perhaps a thousand titles from the 1710s through the 1750s—is doxological, existential, and pastoral: it treats nature as the medium of our earthly dealings with God. Effectively, these works are expansions of various psalms and on the end of the book of Job, where God answers Job's laments with a series of rhetorical questions that may amount to divine endorsement of biodiversity.[26]

Sturm's almanac digests this large literature. Overall, his theme is humility. In every season are reminders of death, also exhortations to charity, patience, and acceptance. Aspects of nature have both systemic and symbolic importance. A common subject is the theology of thunderstorms: "brontotheology." They stir the air, purifying it of "noxious exhalations, and . . . increase . . . fertility." But they also exhibit God's grandeur.[27] Sturm is thankful for what fills human needs—for sheep, horses, silkworms (and for the grape, whose fermentation can "relieve . . . misery and solace").[28] But a century before ecology, he sees each species as having a "certain purpose." "Every thing is connected," he declares. "No creature is useless, or . . . placed there without an end, though we are ignorant" of the ends of what he estimates as 400,000 species of animals.[29] "Does anyone think that no rapacious animals should exist upon the earth? Let such people reflect that, by the beast of prey, the number of animals which would be troublesome to us is diminished."[30] Anticipating Rachel Carson in opposing eradication of agricultural pests, Sturm argues that God invests in bugs, too—look at their intricacy. Eradication would destroy whatever ecosystem services (our word, his concept) a species provides. We should not interfere with nature's equilibrating processes even where species appear "only [to] exist to torment mankind. . . . American colonists tried to kill jays, only to have their crops overwhelmed by worms and caterpillars."[31] Ecological reflections were self-cultivation, too. Sturm and his colleagues worried about how we engage with each other and with nature—practically, emotionally, and ethically. In

26. Lattimore, *The Book of Job*; McKibben, *The Comforting Whirlwind*.
27. Sturm, *Sturm's Reflections*, 286; 299.
28. Ibid., 45; 372–73.
29. Ibid., 200–203; 420.
30. Ibid., 346; 379–80; 381–82.
31. Ibid., 283; 288–89.

kindness to nature, we learn charity; in admitting that other parts of the world are significant to God, we learn humility.[32]

While we know little of Sturm's readers and the readers of the many volumes of natural theology concerned with human place in nature (and, incidentally, with human nature), we do know that there were many of them. Selfish anthropocentrism is not the only voice of the past; the need to integrate into the cyclical patterns of nature was well recognized.

My third example is the activities of the National Catholic Rural Life Conference (NCRLC), now known as Catholic Rural Life, in the upper Midwest in the 1930s and 1940s. Despite having received attention from several historians, its work remains largely invisible in Catholic history and in environmental history.[33] In my view, however, that work represents the fullest embodiment of the vision Pope Francis has outlined.[34] The movement's leaders thoroughly and thoughtfully explored the integration of the three foundations of sustainability: the institutional, the technical, and the personal. While particular practices and teachings were not unique, they were articulated in a contested and often hostile ideological environment, both for Catholics and for family farmers. Their views defy the dominant dichotomy of the history of American environmentalism—conservation versus preservation. They see no virtue in preservation for its own sake, but they are hardly utilitarians. A quarter of a century before *Silent Spring,* the Conference's leaders were writing of the "natural," "environment," "steward-ship," and the "organic," though not quite in the same ways we have since come to use those terms.

If the Conference's work is not well known, most of its themes—save the explicit spiritual dimension—are familiar in the work of an unknowing fellow traveler, the Kentuckian Baptist scholar-poet-farmer Wendell Berry, who is one focus of my early work with Phil Shepard. For four decades, Berry's essays about culture and agriculture have resonated widely, especially with Catholics. Most important here is "The Body and the Earth" from *The Unsettling of America* (1977), though his "Discipline and Hope" made most of the same points more bluntly. Berry holds that our relationship to the earth cannot be other than our relation to ourselves. He was explicitly challenging the pretense of an immature transcendence—that the admirer

---

32. Ibid., 185; 47; 104.

33. Hamlin and McGreevy, "The Greening of America"; Shapiro, "Catholic Agrarian Thought and the New Deal," 583–99; Woods, *Cultivating Soil and Soul;*. Bovée, *The Church and the Land.*

34. See especially Francis, *Laudato Si',* 94.

of nature need not acknowledge his or her own naturalness and the responsibilities that went with that embodiment.[35]

Literary scholar as well as farmer, Berry helps us dissect key words,
thus exposing the kinds of contradictions and disjuncts that concern Pope
Francis in *Laudato Si'*. Consider four such key words: "settle," "proper,"
"husband," and "fertile."

- Settle: Those who assumed *The Unsettling of America* would be simply
  concerned with demographic change—family farm to corporate agriculture—discovered that "settle" meant to feel oneself whole in one's
  place, abandoning fantasy lives for the joys of a real one.

- Proper: This word was linked to "propriety," "appropriate," and
  "property."[36] Berry's Jeffersonian agrarianism meshed with "dis-
  tributism." Private property was vital, but in family-sized units, for
  God's land must serve the godly ends of nurturing persons through
  nurturing families. For the family was not simply a reproductive unit;
  it was the foundational unit of society.[37]

- Husband: Dwelling on the link between "husband" and "husbandry"
  as the art of agriculture, Berry made clear that the family was also the
  foundational unit of sustainability. The *hus*-bond man was bonded
  to the *hus* (house) as well as to the *hus*-wife. The terms reflected the
  law of entail: a *hus*, distinct from a cottage, was—with its estate—a
  permanent structure, a renewable intergenerational family-producing
  resource that its life tenants must steward.[38]

- Fertility: We preside over life. The fertility we talk of when we empty
  bag into spreader and the fertility of human reproduction are not profoundly different, Berry insists. Neither is merely a matter of chemicals; both are matters of responsible personhood. "Material order"
  cannot coexist with "spiritual disorder . . . It is impossible to care for
  each more or differently than we care for the earth."[39]

Berry is eloquent but, like the Vanderbilt agrarians and others, also
nostalgic. One's yearning for a vital culture of settlement and faithful stewardship magnifies its absence. Coming down to us from Virgil, the tradition

---

35. Berry, *Unsettling of America*, especially 111; Berry, *Continuous Harmony*, 86–
168. See also Hamlin and Shepard, *Deep Disagreement*.

36. Berry, "Whose Head Is the Farmer Using?" 30.

37. Francis, *Laudato Si'*, 94.

38. Berry, *Unsettling of America*, 116–17. See also Francis, *Laudato Si'*, 157, 213.

39. Berry, *Unsettling of America*, 123, 131–33. See also "Oikos," in Hunt, *Surviving
Technopolis*, 78–92.

of philosophical agrarianism and of pastoral virtues more broadly is not only an ancient one, it is usually an aristocratic one. The poet or essayist can imagine and appreciate the authentic life on the land, but all too often those who live that life are too exhausted or inarticulate to express themselves. Berry writes to an educated and leisured elite who read essays. He may seem to force a choice: one can be a happy peasant or a pastoral poet (or consumer of such poetry). But both? Here, Berry's evident ignorance of Catholic agrarianism is tragic for, like Pope Francis, the agrarians of the 1930s and 1940s insisted that we could (and should) be both.

A generation before Berry's *Unsettling*, three Midwestern bishops, articulating what they were calling the "Catholic rural philosophy," had articulated exactly Berry's philosophy in writing that "human erosion is closely related to soil erosion."[40] They, and many German Catholics in the Midwest, were living what Berry preaches. Evidence comes from Sonya Salamon's 1992 book, *Prairie Patrimony*. Studying seven generations of land transfers in central Illinois, Salamon distinguished between a Yankee approach of Scots-Irish Protestants in which "farming . . . was a business and land . . . a commodity" and a German approach in which "farming . . . was a way of life and land . . . a sacred family possession."[41] In terms of sustainable stewardship, the latter—settling not speculating—was more successful. Though ostensibly national, the National Catholic Rural Life Conference founded in 1923 thrived in the so-called German belt—Missouri to Minnesota, Illinois to Kansas. Already Catholic, communal self-help organizations, united as the St. Louis-based Central Verein, had paved the way.[42]

I cannot do justice to the richness of this organization's work, nor do the several fine histories of it even do that fully.[43] The Conference was founded as an offshoot of the National Catholic Welfare Conference by Fr. Edwin O'Hara, an Oregon priest concerned with the viability of rural Catholicism. Outside heavily Catholic areas, some systematically colonized by ethnic groups, it was hard to maintain religious identity in majority-Protestant communities. The answer, O'Hara recognized, went beyond churches and priests; it required addressing all aspects of communities, including economic, educational, social, and even medical services. The Conference's mission would also include meeting the needs of the rural poor, including

---

40. National Catholic Rural Life Conference, *Manifesto on Rural Life*, 192.

41. Salamon, *Prairie Patrimony*.

42. Gleason, *The Conservative Reformers*.

43. For a more comprehensive treatment and fuller bibliography of the issues I treat here, see Hamlin and McGreevy, "The Greening of America."

farm workers; the resettlement of urban Catholics; and the spiritual en-
hancement of rural life.

Such matters were made pressing by the Great Depression. How
should the church respond to secular farm organizations (mostly concerned
with prices), to the complex of New Deal policies, to urban despair and
farm bankruptcies, but also to the extremism of far right and far left? Such
concerns would lead, in 1933, to articulation of the Catholic "green revolution." It referred not to high-yield crops as it does now, but to a Catholic
alternative to the communists' red and the fascists' black or brown.

Roughly speaking, the 1930s were occupied with working out a Catholic Rural philosophy, the 1940s with its implementation. That philosophy
had three legs: the institutional, the technical, and the personal, spiritual,
or cultural. Together, these constituted what Berry would call "solutions of
pattern": each must undergird the others in many ways and at many levels:
technologies, later called alternative and appropriate, must mesh with institutions, but also enhance the flourishing of the human spirit, which fed back
into technical practices and institutions.[44]

It is worth reflecting on the enormity of that challenge. Almost always, scholars who engage with environmental issues are experts in some
domain—science and technology, or policy, or ethics. Working out ideal
solutions in their domains, they expect others to accommodate. Often that
doesn't happen. Values, or the translation of scientific truths, just don't mesh
with institutions or the built environment in which we live. But here—and
this was crucial—the leaders, lay and clergy, were not specialists but rather
talented and thoughtful generalists, willing to borrow ideas and experiment,
and well-linked to the hierarchy through the rural life directors established
in the 1920s in each rural diocese.

The Catholic Rural Philosophy was complete at the end of the decade,
published in a *Manifesto* in 1939 under the names of three Midwestern
bishops and a companion *Rural Roads to Security* appeared in 1940 by the
Conference's new executive director, the voluble and indefatigable Monsei-
gneur Luigi Ligutti and the Jesuit John Rawe, its most militant prophet.[45]
Their work combines a pre-Berryan critique of the unsettlement with a
review of Catholic social experiments in alternative institutions, the most
important being the homestead community in Granger, Iowa, that Liguiti
had launched in 1935.

44. Berry, *The Gift of Good Land*, chapter 9.

45. National Catholic Rural Life Conference, *Manifesto on Rural Life*; Ligutti and
Rawe, *Rural Roads to Security*. For shorter versions of the program, see pamphlets by
Hynes, "'City Slickers' and 'Dumb Farmers'" and "Farm-Family-Prosperity."

Of the three legs of Catholic Rural Philosophy, the broadest was reform of economic institutions. A great threat to all rural families was monopoly. With regard to consumption, dispersed populations meant little
competition; with regard to production, the union of mechanization and
monoculture concentrated land holding, forcing farmers to leave or become
tenants (a situation that did not conduce to stability or stewardship). Their
answer was the same one Pope Francis[46] points to: cooperatives, for purchasing staples, marketing farm products, even possibly for owning tools
of production. Credit unions were important, too. These must be local and
embody Rochdale principles: voting was by member, not by size of investment. Such cooperatives were the mystical body of Christ, declared Bishop
McGavrick of Lacrosse in 1943 on the occasion of the centenary celebration
of the Rochdale principles by the Catholic Cooperative Committee.[47]

If the tradition of communal self-help came from the German Catholics of the Central Verein, the more immediate model was the Catholic-led
regional transformation of the Canadian Maritimes. Fishing and lumber-
ing supported the Scottish Catholic families that had settled around Antigonish, Nova Scotia, in the late eighteenth century, but post-World War I
mechanization-monopolization was threatening family integrity. Cooperatives and credit unions were the answer. The means to them would be adult
education orchestrated through the Extension Department of the Catholic
St. Francis Xavier University, a scheme initiated by the radical Fr. Jimmy
Tompkins and administered by his cousin, the consummate organizer, Fr.
Moses Coady. Its influence on the U.S. cooperative movement, Catholic and
secular, was enormous. Consider these titles: *The Lord Helps Those . . . How
the People of Nova Scotia are Solving their Problems through Cooperation*,
by Bertram Fowler, published by the Leftist Vanguard Press in 1938 and
Nova Scotia: The Land of Cooperation, by the Notre Dame sociologist Fr. Leo
Ward, CSC, published in 1942 by the Catholic publisher Sheed and Ward.[48]
The Coady Institute would become a center for Catholic missionary work
in economic development and remains a center for microfinance; in Nova
Scotia, a Tomkins Institute at Cape Breton University is concerned with ap-
propriate technologies for community-building.[49]

These were radical reforms, sometimes controversial. Some saw co-
ops as un-American, but co-ops were not collectives, conference leaders

46. Francis, *Laudato Si'*, 179.

47. Catholic Cooperative Committee, *Catholic Churchmen and Cooperatives*.

48. See St. Francis Xavier University, *How St. F. X. University Educates for Action*;
Ward, *Nova Scotia*; Fowler, *The Lord Helps Those*.

49. For more on the Coady Institute, see http://coady.stfx.ca/ and on the Tompkins
Institute, see http://www.cbu.ca/tompkins/content/history.

would insist. In "To Save the Farm," a story in the 1946 Faith and Freedom
Reader for Catholic School eighth graders, teenage boys, having heard from
their parents how hard it is to compete with corporate agriculture, start a
co-op with the aid of Fr. Vanhoeven, who is from Belgium and knows about
such things. Expect opposition, he tells them. Fr. Vanhoeven hopes to enlist
sympathetic Protestant clergy.[50] In the cases of Ligutti and the Canadians,
Catholic leadership extended to others in rural communities: institutional
interests were not faith-specific. The involvement of youths is also intrigu-
ing: their elders may be apathetic, Vanhoeven warns the boys. Inspired by
French and Belgian rural Catholic youth movements—chiefly, the *Jeunesse
Agriculturale Chretienne,* or *Jacistes*—American youths (mainly boys) were
beginning cells to spur reform. Members would recruit others, propagating
new cells in classic anarchist fashion.[51]

Their activism was liturgical, too. "Our pulpits in the rural areas must
interpret the life of the farm in terms of the life of Christ," asserted a bishop
in 1946.[52] Here, the leading figure was the Benedictine Virgil Michel of St.
John's in Collegeville, Minnesota, the focus of Fr. Woods' wonderful book.
Michel worried that communion had become individualistic, insufficiently
communal—hence, that extension of the mystical body of Christ to all manner of community institutions and activities. Included were celebrations ty-
ing the seasons of the church to the seasons of the land. Much was made
of St. Isidore, whose fields were plowed by angels while he concentrated
on devotion. Included were blessings of fields and flocks—even machinery—and the rogation procession circumambulating the bounds of the parish, thus celebrating the place of one's life. Borrowing from the emerging
Scandinavian tradition of folk high schools, there was much attention to
the preservation of rural Catholic, and even pre-Catholic, folkways. At the
Conference conventions' vast outdoor masses, youths would present the
priest with homegrown wheat and grapes for conversion to wine and host;
altar linens and candles were also homemade.[53]

Beyond these was the cultivation of a spirituality of rural domestic
life—of music, poetry, dramatics, artisanship, folk dance; of the celebration
of family and communal work; and of meditation that came through peace
of nature. Fr. Joseph Ettel, whose "Diary of a Country Pastor" began to appear in 1938, writes of the closeness to God that a Minnesota winter's night

50. Mary Charlotte and Synon et al., *These Are Our Horizons.*

51. Lohmer, "Keeping Them Up on the Farm."

52. See sermon by Peter Bartolome, coadjustor bishop of St. Cloud: Bartolome,
"The Land and the Spirit."

53. "Mass for Youth on Jocist Lines."

brings.[54] An Iowa farmer and cell member writes: "Out on the farm things are real. Life is real; living is real; horses, cows, soil, neighbors are real; everything a man sees and hears and feels is real. Things are there as God put them there; there man cares for what God has made, but never does he shape it into something grotesque and unnatural. . . . There are truth and beauty and goodness, but there is no mirage or imitation."[55]

Espousing a "Christian philosophy of the land," a bishop, anticipating Berry, notes the most "intimate" relation of body and earth—the land fashions, sustains, and ultimately assimilates the body. Assailing the scientism that makes that relationship a matter of chemistry and industry, he insists on a "moral and religious" engagement: "Of what good . . . to know the secrets of the soil, to have control of the productive powers of the land, if man has no control of himself." He goes on: "The greatest and most destructive error of our time is the belief . . . that science, mechanics, and legislation are the saving factors . . . It is this blind faith . . . the belief that knowledge alone saves" that has brought crisis. The church must teach that man is "steward . . . not . . . owner . . . Impress . . . the noble conception of the sacredness of the soil . . . responsibility to God for its right use. Show him how advantageously he can work out his own salvation and that of his family on the land."[56]

Especially as American agriculture lurched toward mega-farm and monoculture, a distinct philosophy seemed to require supporting science and technology. To find Catholics concerned with liturgy or communal institutions is hardly surprising, but compost, earthworms, and tractors? There was need for a Catholic agricultural science just as for a Catholic agricultural economics. The Catholic family farm must be a mixed farm, since its object was both family subsistence and modest cash income. It would have plentiful labor (family members) and would nurture the remarkable (but irreducible) skill and value needed for the stewardship of the land in perpetuity. Hence, as Berry and others have argued, book-learning and algorithms of efficiency were less important than, and even antithetical to, local wisdom and careful use of tools. If American farmers were skeptical of cow college learning, Catholic farmers would be more so: for them, farming would be mainly about living, not making a living.

It did not follow that Catholic farmers actually had the needed tools and know-how. The Conference was a clearinghouse for efforts of Catholic colleges to teach (and research) Catholic agriculture—most prominently at

54. Ettel, "I am a Country Pastor," 5.
55. Michaels, "Oasis."
56. Bartolome, "The Land and the Spirit."

St. John's but also at Creighton; St. Mary's seminary in Kansas; St. Bede's Abbey in Peru, Illinois; Trinity in Sioux City; St. Ambrose's in Davenport; St. Emma's in Virginia.[57] Here, too, were borrowings, mainly of the German-Swiss "biodynamic" agriculture, chief source of what the Rodales would popularize as "organic" agriculture. Catholics understood "biodynamic" both broadly (e.g., techniques that facilitated social and spiritual as well as biological sustainability) and narrowly (e.g., the precise composting processes Ehrenfried Pfeiffer had developed from the mystical teachings of Rudolph Steiner).[58] Similarly central was soil conservation. Under the Soil Conservation Service, communities fostered best practices; in some places, this achievement relied on the social capital of the parish. In Franklin County, Missouri, Monsignor "Alfalfa George" Hildner was a leader.[59] The mystical body of Christ was on the farm, too—farms might not be the cleanest of places, but they were sites of human production and should not be disorganized or dirty. Barn paint was a priest's business.[60]

What difference did the Conference make? It has been criticized as being a priest's movement. It the 1930s, it was. A farmer's newspaper, *The Christian Farmer,* failed within three years of its 1948 launch. But its impact went beyond memberships/subscriptions: we should include radio broadcasts, weekly press releases, and participation in its events: summer schools, retreats, and annual conventions.[61] Knowing what went on in homes, elementary schools, civic organizations, and church groups is harder, but the periodicals and archives give us indications of what was being attempted.

Having articulated a Catholic rural philosophy, the Conference's first task was to promulgate it to rural (and mostly young) priests. It did this through one- or two-week long summer schools. The first was at St. John's

57. Hamlin and McGreevy, "The Greening of America," 479; "A Catholic Agricultural College"; National Catholic Rural Life Conference, "Resolutions, NCRLC Annual Meeting, Jefferson City MO, October 1941." Often, the missions of these institutions have changed. For St. Mary's, see http://www.smac.edu/?TimeLine1931to1967; for St. Ambrose, see http://www.sau.edu/About_SAU/History.html; for Trinity, see http://www.trinityheights.com/trinity-college-high-school.htm.

58. Hamlin and McGreevy, *Greening of America,* 480.

59. Woods, *Soil and Soul,* 224. At Jefferson City in 1941, Hildner chaired a session entitled "Conserving Soil and Saving Souls." See National Catholic Rural Life Conference, "Program, NCRLC Annual Meeting, Jefferson City MO, October 1941." See also "'Alfalfa George' is a leader."

60. Koszarek, "Stewardship of the Land."

61. For weekly press releases, see the National Catholic Rural Life Records, NCRLC 6/9/12, Marquette Archives, Marquette University Raynor Memorial Libraries; for radio, see the October 17, 1933 *Milwaukee Journal* article in NCRLC Clippings File 11/1, Marquette Archives, Marquette University Raynor Memorial Libraries.

in 1940. By the mid-1940s, there were schools in the Northeast, the High Plains, the Deep South, and the Southwest. Each was adapted to regional social and technical issues—fifty-five and sixty schools in 1944 and 1945—teaching thousands of priests, sisters, lay leaders, and seminarians about co-op formation, leadership skills, and catechistics.[62]

They also taught science and sustainable technology. At St. John's in 1940, Fr. Henry Retzek, a priest-geologist from West Union, Minnesota, taught on "the Nature and Proper treatment of the Soil" and on "Climate and Climate Variations and their relation to the soil." At the 1943 summer school, Matthew Kiess, OSB, and Adelarde Thunte, OSB, conducted bio-dynamic farming workshops on the college's experimental farm. Sympathetic Minnesota Extension and USDA representatives taught, too—priests learned how to keep hogs worm-free.[63] Three years later, a meeting of school directors on best curricular practices considered how much science and technology to teach. Their answer: "general" coverage of "crops best suited to an area, crop rotation, soil conservation, fertilization," but the real foundation for sustainable agriculture should be seminary training. There, building on "general courses in chemistry and biology," future priests could "study up on the questions of scientific agriculture."[64]

By 1945, summer schools had led to retreats for Catholic farm family members to develop a "deep supernatural life," to comprehend their lives and work in terms of "Christian ethics," and to recognize their "duties as stewards of the land." One of the first, in Winona, Minnesota, drew eight hundred people.[65] A later broadside for farmers and ranchers listed the goals of a series of such two-day retreats in fourteen parishes across Montana:

- to "understand the meaning of life"; "[J]ust work, work to get ahead? Or is life really joyous and worthwhile?"

- to appreciate the dignity of the farmer and of the factors that degrade or dignify life;

62. Schirber, "An Open Letter to Sisters," 8–9. Figures were similar in 1945: 1,700 priests; 9,600 sisters; 9,900 lay persons; 775 seminarians; Schirber, "Rural Life Schools—Reconversion," 1–2.

63. National Catholic Rural Life Conference, "Rural Life Summer Schools: Program of the Collegeville Summer School." An extensive outline of the 1940 curriculum includes a highly technical guide to Steinerian biodynamic techniques (pp. 12–16), along with a bibliography of further readings on soils and fertilizers (p. 17), followed by a long discussion of catechesis.

64. National Catholic Rural Life Conference, "Rural Life Summer Schools: Meeting of the Directors."

65. Schimek, "Retreats for Farmers," 5–7; Schimek, Letter to Minnesota pastors.

- to hear Scriptural views on farming;

- to improve farm living so that descendants will want to continue the homestead;

- and finally, to acknowledge "the great responsibilities rural people have; the account they will give God in caring for the land, the animals, and the machinery entrusted to them."

The retreats were not just for Catholics but for all rural people, "the backbone of America." All "of good will . . . not afraid to think . . . work . . . or pray" were welcome. Conspicuous at the bottom of the broadside was the declaration that such retreats would be "very good for professional men and women—exceptional for business people."[66] Just as green business has become a nucleus of contemporary environmental change, the Conference also translated social capital into commerce.

We know, too, that at least some retreats passed on the biodynamic techniques taught to priests at the summer workshops—social and technical practices were intermixed with prayer and meditation, the spiritual agenda that one associates with retreats. In his detailed notes for a late 1940s retreat, the Wisconsin priest Fr. Thaddeus Koszarek (1912–2006) strikes themes and uses phrases generally associated with post-Lynn White ecotheology. On the first part of Genesis, for example: "subdue does not mean abuse." It was the "intention of God," writes Fr. Koszarek, "that land give life not to one man, one generation, but to all men for all time." We are not given "permission to mine the soil, misuse it, or sterilize it; e.g., denuding forests, pollution [sic] of streams and rivers, careless cultivation of soil for erosion to take place from wind and water." We have a duty to improve soil; we are to leave a farm better than when we came to it—that is the lesson of the parable of the talents (Matt 25:14–30).

Then, Fr. Koszarek becomes explicit, listing "practices of good stewardship." These include mixed farming, required by "Nature" and "according to the Divine plan of God," because a farm is a "biological unit." He is uneasy with the use of artificial chemicals, fearing that they will harm earthworms and the "bacteria needed for the building up of the soil. . . . Healthy, nutritious food comes from healthy soil having proper bacterial life. In fact, health of man depends greatly upon health of soil." He was concerned also with water-retaining tillage practices. Reviewing the fall of civilizations that had failed to care for the land, Fr. Koszarek quoted Xenophon: "The earth willingly teaches righteousness to those who can learn. He went on

---

66. National Catholic Rural Life Conference Records, NCRLC Clipping Files 11.1. This is an undated broadside, probably mid-1940s.

to consider the ethical treatment not only of farm animals, but of farm machinery and buildings, and to consider "art, beauty, order, and efficiency in
the house and home," but also the barn and its surroundings, a heading that
included everything from canning to fly control. So much for stewardship.
In his fifth and final conference, Fr. Koszarek considered "Catholic action,"
including the various forms of cooperatives.[67]

Here, we have the key themes of *Laudato Si'* long before Francis and
long before the post-Lynn White emergence of eco-theology. None of this
is idiosyncratic—both Fr. Koszarek's general views and technical particulars
represent NCRLC periodicals and pamphlets of the period. What seems
most important is the pastoral context. A priest has recognized that the
unity of good living requires addressing every aspect of it.

Last, the movement may be measured by attendance at the Conference's annual weeklong October conventions. One finds claims of 15,000
attendees in St. Cloud in 1940 and 30,000 in Columbus in 1949. On the
latter occasion, an essay contest on rural life elicited 3,800 submissions in
the Columbus diocese. A pageant at that convention, "The Golden Secret
of Green Acres," featured a cast of 1,200 and an audience of 5,000.[68] One
need not estimate the importance of these meetings from the Catholic press
alone—they were amply coverted by the general press. The Conference was
an important organization. The major farm organizations courted its con-
stituency; it was not uncommon for the delegates to be welcomed by the
host state's governor.[69] Within the church, many bishops—of dioceses like
Fargo, Crookston, or Winona—gave much time to it, even though it was
not directly under diocesan jurisdiction. It had a presence in Washington,
as well as an international reach (chiefly through the influential Jesuit, John
LaFarge, editor of *America*).

What happened to its vision? Over the long term, it declined owing to a
fundamental change in the structure of agriculture, with the disappearance

67. Koszarek, "Stewardship of the Land." Cf. Berry, *Unsettling of America*, 86–87.
On Fr. Koszarek, see Peerenboom, "Rev. Koszarek 'practiced what he preached.'" See
also his January 1, 2007 obituary, reprinted from the *Green Bay Press Gazette* on the
Sacred Heart Seminary Alumni website at http://shsoneida.com/Sacred_Heart_Semi-
nary/Fr._Tad.html. Fr. Koszarek was pastor of St. Hedwig's in Kewaunee at the time
these notes were probably composed. He was also the diocesan Rural Life Director.

68. "Tickets for Sale for Rural Life Pageant Nov. 6"; "Over 3,800 Catholic Students
in Diocese Submit Entries in Rural Life Essay Contest"; "The Golden Secret of Green
Acres."

69. See "Farm Future is Discussed," 1–2. The *Seattle Daily Times* ran six stories on
the weekend-long 1939 Spokane Convention, where Governor Martin welcomed the
delegates: "Two Thousand Catholics at Conference," 7, and "National Catholic Leaders
Assemble," 26; "Catholics Study Farm Problems," 20.

of the mixed family farm. While conference leaders had hoped that rural electrification and small and versatile tractors would make the family farm more viable, a new generation of chemical inputs—pesticides and fertilizers—and economies of scale made it harder for the mixed family farm to compete.[70] Nor was there yet any large market for organic or artisanal foods. As inflation made it harder to rely on farm income alone, the Conference turned to "two-footed living." Taking advantage of the automobile and the new parkways, Dad might work in the city, but the suburban home should remain a mini-farm. But while the code of the suburb might allow a modest vegetable patch, the home ceased to be a site of production: the Conference's leaders had not reckoned with the allure of the supermarket. The Cold War also transformed both ideology and priorities: co-ops were too red. Efficient large-scale production seemed necessary both to combat international communism and, more immediately for Catholics, to demonstrate that the world was not overpopulated. The rural church would retreat to its narrower duties leaving social, cultural, and environmental matters to take care of themselves. Once the environmental movement had begun in the 1970s, the Conference would reacquire a green focus, though by that time, its past had been largely forgotten. Its chief periodical (known earlier as *Landward* and *Land and Home*) would be called *Earth Matters* for a time. But, within certain constraints of geography and technology, that vision was and is viable.

Laudato Si' is an integrated geographic vision on a planetary scale addressed not just to Catholics but to all humans. But how will it be implemented? That the vision is well-precedented within Catholicism; that details of implementation were carefully worked out; and that it was once influential in parishes and regions as an alternative to a consumerist and technocratic paradigm is important—and should go far to convince skeptics that the vision is a realistic and attractive vision as well as a responsible one.

70. National Catholic Rural Life Conference, "Mechanization for the Small Farm."

2

Ecology, Justice, and Peace:
The Perspective of a Global Church

CARDINAL PETER K. A. TURKSON

Introduction

Dear participants of the "Fragile World: Ecology and the Church" conference, I bring you the greetings of the Pontifical Council for Justice and
Peace, and its prayerful wishes for a very successful conference.

In order to view ecology, justice, and peace from the viewpoint of our
global church, I will offer my remarks today in three parts. First, I will introduce Catholic social teaching and how it addresses the nature of ecology.
For this material, I will focus on the pontificates of St. Pope John Paul II
and Pope Benedict XVI. Both of these Holy Fathers have contributed significantly to a deepened understanding of the relationship between natural
and human ecology. Second, I will tell you about a practical application of
this teaching that occurred when the Holy See engaged in the International
Conference on Sustainable Development held in June 2012 in Rio de Janeiro. This was the "Rio+20" conference, so named because it took place
twenty years after the first Rio conference on the environment. Finally, I
shall introduce some contributions that the pontificate of Pope Francis has
made to the legacy of the church's teaching on natural and human ecology
to date.[1]

---

1. Editor's note: Cardinal Turkson wrote this paper for the CWCIT conference held
in April 2015, before the appearance of Pope Francis's encyclical on the environment,
Laudato Si', was published.

Ecology in the Social Teaching of the Church

It is customary to begin the account of Catholic social teaching with the encyclical *Rerum Novarum* of Pope Leo XIII, issued in 1891. While that encyclical focused on the conditions and rights of workers, it also contained some seeds of current ideas about our natural environment. For example, it stated that those who receive God's bounty in the form of natural resources or property should exercise their responsibility "as the steward of God's providence, for the benefit of others."[2]

Another milestone in Catholic social thought was the encyclical *Populorum Progressio* of Pope Paul VI. Issued in 1967, it treated many facets of the development of peoples. Two of its key ideas are that "development" is the "new name for peace," and that we need some *"effective world authority"* to cope with the scale of challenge in the environmental and financial realms.[3] And it includes this very positive remark: "By dint of intelligent thought and hard work, man gradually uncovers the hidden laws of nature and learns to make better use of natural resources. As he takes control over his way of life, he is stimulated to undertake new investigations and fresh discoveries, to take prudent risks and launch new ventures, to act responsibly and give of himself unselfishly."[4]

In his apostolic letter *Octogesima Adveniens* (May 1971), Pope Paul VI further addressed the inseparable relationship and interdependence between human life and the natural environment, saying: "Man is suddenly becoming aware that by an ill-considered exploitation of nature he risks destroying it and becoming in his turn the victim of this degradation. Not only is the material environment becoming a permanent menace—pollution and refuse, new illness and absolute destructive capacity—but the human framework is no longer under man's control, thus creating an environment for tomorrow which may well be intolerable."[5] Paul VI also expressed worries about how the concern to control nature through science could put the human dimension under parallel but inappropriate control;[6] about the "new positivism" of "universalized technology";[7] and about notions of "progress"[8] that embrace rampant industrialization that could turn persons

2. Leo III, *Rerum Novarum*, 22.

3. Paul VI, *Populorum Progressio*, 76–78.

4. Ibid., 25.

5. Paul VI, *Octogesima Adveniens*, 21.

6. Ibid., 38.

7. Ibid., 29.

8. Ibid., 41.

into "slave(s) of the objects" that they make.[9] The combination of themes in this letter makes it a true precursor of the focus on *integral* thinking of his successors.

In November of the same year and just before the Stockholm Conference (1972) launched the UN Program on the Environment (UNEP), Paul VI convoked the Synod on Justice in the World, which first gave prominence to the link between justice and ecology. Its line of thought suggested a close link between concern for the poor and a concern for the earth, essentially the cry of the poor and the cry of the earth, and adverted to the culture of waste of the rich.[10]

I offer you these historical touchstones to demonstrate that our recent and current popes have always built their contemporary perspectives on ecology derived from earlier foundations. Another reason is to assure you that Catholic social teaching offers a rich storehouse for further exploration of these topics.

Saint Pope John Paul II

In his first encyclical on the human person (*Redemptor Hominis*), John Paul II warned about the threat of pollution to nature.[11] Later, in his social encyclical *Sollicitudo Rei Socialis* (1987), on the twenty-eighth anniversary of *Populorum Progressio,* he focused on the nature of authentic human development and its moral character. In this regard, he centered on the need for individuals and communities to have full respect for the nature of the human person, whose origin and goal are found in God. He called attention to the need to respect the constituents of the natural world, which the ancient Greeks referred to as the "cosmos" (an ordered system with beauty). Such realities demand respect by virtue of three considerations that may be summed up in the three words "connection," "limitation," and "pollution."

The first consideration, he wrote, is the need for greater awareness, "that one cannot use with impunity the different categories of beings, whether living or inanimate—animals, plants, the natural elements—simply as one wishes, according to one's own economic needs. On the contrary, one must take into account the nature of each being and of its mutual connection in an ordered system, which is precisely the cosmos."[12]

9. Ibid., 9.

10. Land et al., *Justice in the World.*

11. John Paul II, *Redemptor Hominis,* 11.

12. John Paul II, *Sollicitudo Rei Socialis,* 34.

The second consideration is the realization that natural resources are limited. As we know, not all resources are renewable. If we treat them as inexhaustible and use them with *absolute dominion*, then we seriously endanger their availability in our own time and, above all, for future generations.

The third consideration reminds us of the effects of a certain type of development on the quality of life in industrialized areas—the sort of development that causes pollution of the environment, with serious consequences for the health of populations.[13]

When we take these considerations together, I believe they suggest a clear moral message from John Paul II: we readily understand that the demands of morality are a *sine qua non* for the well-being of humanity. We should extend our fundamental conception and application of morality to natural ecology—the use of the elements of nature, the renewability of resources, and the consequences of haphazard industrialization.

A few years later, on the hundredth anniversary of *Rerum Novarum*, John Paul II expanded further on this theme in his social encyclical *Centesimus Annus*. With regard to the nature of private property and the universal destination of material goods, he drew attention to what he termed "the ecological question" and its connection with the problem of consumerism. Here he referred to a widespread anthropocentric error: our failure to recognize that our capacity to transform, and in a certain sense re-create, the world through human work is always based on God's prior and original gift of all that exists. Man might imagine that he can make arbitrary use of the earth and subject it without restraint to his will. Rather than carry out his role as a co-operator with God in the work of creation, man sets himself up in place of God. The final outcome is a rebellion on the part of nature which is more tyrannized than properly governed by him.[14]

To correct these faulty ideas, John Paul II pointed out that all of us humans, as individuals and in our community, must respect the created world and be conscious of our duties and obligations toward future generations. Certainly, the things that God has created are for our use; however, they must be used in a responsible way, for man is not the master but the *steward* of creation.

The Holy Father did not stop at the natural environment when he drew attention to the ecological question. He focused as well on the destruction of the *human environment*. Here he introduced the concept of *human ecology*. Yes, damage to the natural environment is serious, but destruction of the human environment is more serious. We see people concerned for the

13. Ibid., 34.
14. John Paul II, *Centesimus Annus*, 37.

balance of nature and worried about the natural habitats of various animal species threatened with extinction. But meanwhile, too little effort is made to safeguard the moral conditions for an authentic *human* ecology. Not only has God given the earth to humanity, who must use it with respect for the original good purpose for which it was given, but the human being too is God's gift to us—indeed, it is the greatest gift. For this reason we must respect the natural and moral structure with which we have been endowed. The encyclical applies this thought to the serious problems of modern urbanization; it calls for proper urban planning which is concerned with how people are to live, and for attention to a *social ecology* of work.[15] With these teachings, John Paul II expanded the Church's social thought on the ecological question, leading to the teaching in the *Compendium of the Social Doctrine of the Church* that "the relationship of man with the world is a constitutive part of his human identity,"[16] and that the cry of the earth and that of the poor are related.[17] In fact, in his 1990 World Day of Peace message, he wrote: "The proper ecological balance will not be found without directly addressing the structural forms of poverty that exist throughout the world."[18] This message inspired the Canadian Conference of Catholic Bishops to teach that, "ecological harmony cannot exist in a world of unjust social structures; nor can the extreme social inequalities of our current world order result in ecological sustainability."[19]

To sum up the contribution of Saint John Paul II on our topic of ecology: in Catholic social teaching, respect for the natural environment and the human environment are inseparably and closely linked. On the one hand, man must respect the natural environment by not abusing it. On the other hand, the human environment receives the even greater respect it deserves when we respect the natural and moral structure with which we have been endowed. The more we respect our natural and moral structure, the more we respect others and also the created world. The natural environment and the human environment have a close relationship, and for the natural environment to be respected demands that the human environment be respected above all.

15. Ibid., 38.

16. Pontifical Council for Justice and Peace, *Compendium*, No. 452.

17. Ibid., Nos. 481–84.

18. John Paul II, "Message for the Celebration of the World Day of Peace," 11.

19. Social Affairs Commission of the Canadian Conference of Catholic Bishops, "A Pastoral Letter on the Christian Ecological Imperative," 17. Cf. also Pontifical Council for Justice and Peace and Keenan, *From Stockholm to Johannesburg*; Christiansen and Grazer, *And God Saw That It Was Good* (with pastoral letters of the USCCB and other conferences); McCarthy, "Catholic Social Teaching and Ecology Fact Sheet." Note the list of studies and pronouncements of other bishops' conferences and local churches.

Pope Benedict XVI

In the new millennium, Pope Benedict XVI recalled the teaching of his immediate predecessor and elaborated further on the nature of ecology. In his 2007 message for the World Day of Peace, he pointed to four variants of ecology: the ecology of *nature*, and alongside it, a *human* ecology which, in turn, demands a *social* ecology, and, finally, the ecology of *peace*. For peace to be effected in the world, we must be conscious of the relationship between natural ecology and human ecology. The ecology of peace is comprised of peace with creation and peace among men, which presupposes peace with God.[20]

The Holy Father provided the example of energy supplies to illustrate the close connection between natural ecology and the human ecology and the consequences for peace. Increased industrial production in recent years has led to increased energy needs. The subsequent unprecedented race for available resources has caused, on an overall basis, a rise in energy prices. Benedict XVI expressed serious concern for those affected, namely, for those suffering in the less developed countries who were excluded, as well as the injustices and conflicts that may be provoked by the race for energy resources. He affirmed the urgent need in international relations for a commitment to human ecology that can favor the growth of an ecology of peace, and he said that this can occur only when guided by a correct understanding of the human person, that is, an understanding not prejudiced by ideology or apathy.[21]

The following year, during his apostolic visit to Australia, Benedict XVI drew attention to the beauty of the natural environment created by God. But this natural environment now bears scars as well, including erosion, deforestation, and the effects of devastating drought. At the same time, the world's mineral and ocean resources are being squandered and water levels are rising.[22] He also drew attention to the human environment, the highpoint of God's creation, and the genius of human achievement such as advances in medical sciences, the wise application of technology, and creativity reflected in the arts. But the human or social environment also has its scars, such as alcohol and drug abuse, the exaltation of violence and sexual degradation, and the false notion that there are no absolute truths to guide our lives. He affirmed the true nature of human life that entails a

20. Cf. Benedict XVI, "Message for the Celebration of the World Day of Peace," 8.

21. Benedict XVI, "Message for the Celebration of the World Day of Peace," 9–11.

22. For example, strip mining, which reduces agricultural lands or forests to hillocks of rock waste and gaping craters, and contaminates rivers and springs with mercury, zinc, and cyanide.

search for the true, the good, and the beautiful, that to this end we make our choices, and that for this we exercise our freedom, knowing that there we find happiness and joy.[23]

In his landmark social encyclical, *Caritas in Veritate*, Benedict XVI dedicates the entire fourth chapter to the issue of the environment and human existence: "The Development of Peoples, Rights and Duties, the Environment." Because "the way humanity treats the environment influences the way it treats itself, and vice versa,"[24] Benedict XVI speaks of an inseparable relationship between human life and the natural environment which supports it as "that covenant between human beings and the environment, which should mirror the creative love of God, from whom we come and towards whom we are journeying."[25] This bond between man and his world paved the way for the Holy Father to teach that the Book of Nature is one and indivisible, and that it includes not only the environment, but *also individuals, family and social ethics*. Accordingly, as he goes on to teach, our duties towards the environment flow from our duties towards the person.[26] But, for Benedict XVI, the "decisive issue," in the relationship between man and his world, natural and human ecology, "is the moral tenor of society."[27]

During his apostolic visit to Germany in 2011, the Holy Father elaborated further on the importance of respecting both natural ecology and human ecology. There he drew attention to the fact that, in the ecological movement in Germany in the 1970s, young people had come to realize that something was wrong in our relationship with nature. Matter is not just raw material to be shaped at will; rather, the earth has a dignity of its own and we must follow its directives. As he said, "If something is wrong in our relationship with reality, then we must all reflect seriously on the whole situation and we are all prompted to question the very foundations of our culture. We must listen to the language of nature and we must answer accordingly."[28] He also underlined human ecology, namely, that man too has a nature that he must respect and that he cannot manipulate. His words were: "Man is not merely self-creating freedom. Man does not create himself. He is intellect and will, but he is also nature, and his will is rightly ordered if he respects his nature, listens to it, and accepts himself for who he is, as one who did

23. Benedict XVI, "Welcoming Celebration by the Young People: Address."

24. Benedict XVI, *Caritas in Veritate*, 51.

25. Ibid., 50. Cf. Benedict XVI, "Message for the Celebration of the World Day of Peace (2007)," 7.

26. Benedict XVI, *Caritas in Veritate*, 51. Cf. also Benedict XVI, "If You Want to Cultivate Peace, Protect Creation."

27. Ibid.

28. Benedict XVI, "Address to the Bundestag."

not create himself. In this way, and in no other, is true human freedom fulfilled."[29]

What Pope Benedict affirmed here is a mutual relationship between natural ecology and human ecology: that we must respect the created world and that we must respect the way in which the human person has been created, for only in this way will we be able to fulfill our freedom. Such an affirmation, moreover, is not a religious claim but the statement of a natural fact.[30]

Thus the Holy Father calls for an integral understanding of the world and the human person: one that respects both the created world and the highpoint of creation that is the human person. If we look at recent papal messages on the annual World Food Day, we see how natural ecology and human ecology are presented as being inseparably interrelated in order for integral development to take place. In 2011, for example, Benedict XVI called attention to the tragic famine in the Horn of Africa. Improvements cannot come unless "the agricultural sector has a level of investments and resources capable of giving stability to production and hence to the market."[31] But this will require changes in human behavior and decisions if the good of society is to be favored. In *Caritas in Veritate,* the pope spoke of the "moral tenor of society" as the decisive issue. Here, he calls for the cultivation of "an interior attitude of responsibility, capable of inspiring a different style of life, with necessary sobriety in conduct and consumption;" and this, he observes, is for the good of society and "also for future generations, for their sustainability, protection of the goods of creation, distribution of resources and, above all, the concrete commitment to the development of whole peoples and nations."[32] What is needed, in other words, is the interior transformation of persons in order to promote an integral development which respects the goods of creation and brings about authentic human development.

Social Teaching on Ecology in the Intergovernmental Context

Postponing momentarily the contributions of Pope Francis to the church's teachings on ecology, I wish to turn now to the United Nations Conference on Sustainable Development that took place in June 2012. Representatives of the international community came together to discuss many concerns regarding the environment and the need for common commitment on the

29. Ibid.

30. Cf. George, "Legislation Creating 'Same-Sex' Marriage."

31. Benedict XVI, "Message to Mr. Jacques Diouf," 3.

32. Ibid.

part of the international community to chart a course forward to address these issues in a sustainable manner. This process had begun in Stockholm in 1972 and had two high points: the first in Rio de Janeiro in 1992 at the so-called "Earth Summit" and the second at Johannesburg in 2002. These events, once again, came together at the Rio+20 Conference to discuss sustainable development and the interplay of the three acknowledged pillars of such development, namely, economic growth, environmental protection, and the promotion of social welfare.

During the initial preparations for the Rio+20 Conference, the Holy See noted that unanimous consensus had emerged in the international community on two points: first, that protecting the environment means improving people's lives, and second, that environmental degradation and underdevelopment are closely interdependent issues needing to be approached together, responsibly and in a spirit of solidarity.

It then focused on the first principle of the Rio Declaration on Environment and Development, which had been adopted at the 1992 conference—the principle that "human beings are at the center of concerns for sustainable development. They are entitled to a healthy and productive life in harmony with nature."[33] Expanding upon this fundamental theme, the Holy See called for the discovery of an art of living together—one that respects the covenant between human beings and nature, without which the human family risks dying out. The Holy See explained that there exists a stable and inseparable covenant between human beings and nature in which the environment conditions the life and development of human beings, while human beings in turn perfect and ennoble the environment by their creative, productive, and responsible labor.[34]

Indeed, the term *covenant* has a rich history in the Judeo-Christian tradition. In this context, *covenant* is not a contract between God and man, not a pact built on reciprocity; it is rather a gift given by God to man, a creative act of God's love.[35] For this reason, humans must use this gift for its purpose, not taking advantage of it, not abusing it, but using it wisely for integral human development and thus for the present and future generations.

During the negotiations of what would become the outcome document of the conference, the delegation of the Holy See regularly drew attention to principles that underpin the protection of human dignity. The seven principles are:

33. U.N. Department of Economic and Social Affairs, "Annex I: Rio Declaration on Environment and Development."

34. Cf. Holy See, "Position Paper," 2.

35. Cf. Ratzinger, "The New Covenant," 636.

1. responsibility, even when changes must be made to patterns of production and consumption in order to ensure that they reflect an appropriate lifestyle;

2. promoting and sharing in the common good;

3. access to primary goods, including such essential and fundamental
   goods as nutrition, education, security, peace and health, which stems
   from the right to life;

4. a universal solidarity capable of acknowledging the unity of the human family;

5. the protection of creation which in turn is linked to inter-generational
   equity solidarity;

6. intra-generational equity, which is closely linked to social justice and
   which requires taking into account the ability of future generations to
   discharge developmental burdens; and

7. the universal destination not only of goods, but also of the fruits of
   human enterprise.[36]

These seven principles were the contribution of the Holy See Delegation to
shaping the Rio+20 position; and they merit reflection and practical action
in pursuit of sustainable development.

Sustainable Development

The Rio Declaration on Environment and Development of 1992 did adopt
some important principles, such as the following: the polluter pays; responsibility for spill-over damage from one country to another; intergenerational equity; public participation; a precautionary approach; environmental
impact assessments; differential responsibilities; and healthy environments.
Nevertheless, some did not think that it had focused enough on environmental concerns.[37]

As we have seen, the Catholic Church affirms that there is an essential
relationship between natural ecology and human ecology and that ignoring
one will be to the detriment of the other. It also affirmed a link between
sustainable development and integral human development, because every
economic decision has moral premises and consequences. For this reason,
the Holy See Delegation argued that consideration must be given to the ethical and spiritual values that guide and give meaning to economic decisions

36. Cf. Holy See, "Position Paper," 3.
37. Cf. Callicott and Frodeman, "Rio Declaration," 201–2.

and to technological progress. Development must be considered not simply from an economic point of view but from an integrally human point of view, that is to say, one which necessarily takes into account the economic, social, and environmental aspects of development and is based on the dignity of the human person.[38]

It followed, for the Holy See Delegation, that any neo-Malthusian approach to development must be totally rejected. Such views hold that people are an obstacle to development. The solution to global poverty cannot be to eliminate the poor.[39]

Instead, people are the drivers of development. As the Rio Declaration had rightly pointed out in its first principle, *people* are at the center of concerns for sustainable development.[40] Accordingly, during negotiations, the delegation of the Holy See regularly drew attention to the inherent dignity of the human person and thus the role of the family in integral development and resisted efforts to impose language suggestive of population control.[41]

In the outcome document of Rio+20, entitled "The Future We Want,"[42] member states agreed to launch a process to determine a set of sustainable development goals. While much discussion surrounded what these goals would be like, agreement was reached during negotiations that they would be "action-oriented, concise, and easy to communicate, limited in number, aspirational, global in nature, and universally applicable to all countries while taking into account different national realities, capacities, and levels of development and respecting national policies and priorities."[43] The Holy See Delegation affirmed that whatever sustainable development goals are finally agreed upon by member states, they must not ignore, and rather must fully take into account, the dignity of the human person—from conception onwards to natural death—which includes the needs of the poor, the aged

38. Cf. Holy See, "Position Paper," 5.

39. Cf. Turkson, "Statement at the Summit."

40. Cf. also in this regard, U.N. General Assembly, "Declaration on the Right to Development," especially Article 1.1: "The right to development is an inalienable human right by virtue of which every human person and all peoples are entitled to participate in, contribute to, and enjoy economic, social, cultural, and political development, in which all human rights and fundamental freedoms can be fully realized"; and Article 2,1: "The human person is the central subject of development and should be the active participant and beneficiary of the right to development."

41. In this regard, the delegation of the Holy See and like-minded delegations successfully resisted efforts by some developed countries to insert in the text the term "reproductive rights," which can be interpreted to include abortion and artificial contraception.

42. Cf. U.N. General Assembly, "The Future We Want."

43. U.N. General Assembly, "Special Subjects."

and of future generations. This insistence is supremely significant because these sustainable development goals, or "SDGs," are quickly becoming the backbone of the United Nations post-2015 development goal process.

Green Economy

With regard to the subject of the "green economy," the fact that the concept had not yet been defined was much discussed. At Rio+20, member states chose not to provide a definition of the concept. However, they did agree to devote a section of the outcome document to the concept, and placed it within the context of sustainable development and poverty eradication. Accordingly, the document affirmed that the green economy "should contribute to eradicating poverty as well as sustained economic growth, enhancing social inclusion, improving human welfare, and creating opportunities for employment and decent work for all, while maintaining the healthy functioning of the Earth's ecosystems."[44] Moreover, in the light of human dignity concerns raised by various delegations including the Holy See Delegation, the document also accepted that however the concept of green economy might be defined, it should aim at

(a) reducing poverty,

(b) sustaining economic growth,

(c) promoting solidarity,

(d) improving human welfare, and

(e) promoting decent work for all.

Pope Francis on Integral Ecology

Lately, Pope Francis, rooted deeply in the teachings of his predecessors, has enriched the church's teaching on the relationship between natural and human ecology. He has mentioned and discussed care for creation, integral human development, and concern for the poor and the aged in

44. U.N. General Assembly, "United Nations Regional Centre for Peace and Disarmament in Asia and the Pacific."

his homilies,[45] addresses, and messages[46] at various audiences and events, and in his apostolic exhortation[47]—all of which culminates in his encyclical *Laudato Si'* on natural and human ecology.

We may synthesize Pope Francis's various pronouncements and treatment of the ecological question under four headings:

1. The call to protect (environment and life) is integral and all-embracing;

2. The care for creation is a virtue in its own right;

3. The moral conversion to care for what we cherish and revere; and

4. The call to dialogue and a new global solidarity.

Briefly considered,

1. The call to be protectors is integral and all-embracing: we are all called to protect and care for both creation and the human person. The threats that arise from global inequality and the destruction of the environment are interrelated, and they are the greatest threats to our human family today.

2. Compelled by the scientific evidence—but most importantly, by the real experiences of peoples—for climate change, we are called to care for humanity and to respect the grammar of nature as virtues in their own right. In responding to this combined threat, every action counts. We all have a part to play in protecting and sustaining what Pope Francis has called "our common home."

3. Binding regulations, policies, and targets are necessary tools for addressing poverty and climate change, but they are unlikely to prove effective without moral conversion and a change of heart. Our efforts at combating/mitigating/preventing climate change, global warming, poverty, and inhuman conditions require an integral approach to ecology. It cannot be limited to laws, policies, or merely scientific, economic, or technical solutions. To succeed, whatever is done must be undergirded by "ecology conversion"—a real conversion of mind, heart, lifestyle and solidarity.

45. Francis, "Homily for the Beginning of the Petrine Ministry"; Francis, "Homily for the Celebration of Palm Sunday," 2; Francis, "Homily on the Occasion of the XXVIII World Youth Day"; Francis, "Homily for 'Evangelium Vitae' Day."

46. For example, see Francis, "General Audience" (on U.N. World Environment Day in 2013), and Brooks, "In Brazil, Pope Francis Speaks Out on the Amazon, Environment, and Indigenous People."

47. Francis, *Evangelii Gaudium*, §6, 215–16.

4. Integral ecology thoroughly integrates the natural and the human. As the basis for justice and development in the world, integral ecology requires a new global solidarity, one in which everyone has a part to play and every action, no matter how small, can make a difference. At the center of this integral ecology and the call to dialogue and a new solidarity is a changing of human hearts in which the good of the human person, rather than the pursuit of profit, is the key value that directs our search for the global, universal common good.

In this, we have the core elements of an integral ecology that in turn provides the foundation for authentic and sustainable approach to human development. The "decisive issue is the moral tenor of society"[48] and an ecological conversion.

Helping Catholics Understand their Role Regarding Ecology in the United States

Within your own country of the United States, the Catholic Climate Covenant is working actively to respond to *Laudato Si'*.[49] I commend this group in particular for planning activities in three phases to maximize the impact of the encyclical on the consciousness of Catholics and of your nation. Very briefly:

1. Phase 1 includes press events and advertising. Local bishops and other high-profile Catholics speakers address the impact of climate disruption, draw out inspiration from the key messages of the encyclical, announce commitments by bishops to work towards reducing their diocesan carbon footprint, and press policy makers to take specific further action in supporting solutions that lead to positive climate change.

2. With the help of the United States Conference of Catholic Bishops (USCCB), local parishes receive gospel-based key messages addressing ecology that can be integrated into homilies; printed materials for distribution to both parishioners and the community; and short video messages that can be accessed through social media.

---

48. Benedict XVI, *Caritas in Veritate*, 51.

49. See http://catholicclimatecovenant.org, the website for Catholic Climate Covenant.

3. Study guides and curriculum are provided to parishes, schools, and other institutions to help Catholic communities understand the theology and the social implications of the pope's message.

The goal of these three phases is to maximize the impact of the encyclical by keeping it in front of your nation and your public officials; by reaching dioceses and especially parishioners; and lastly, by embedding the messages of ecology, including its relationship to justice and peace, within Catholic curricula for years to come.

In Conclusion

Here, as in the past, the church has a role to play. As Pope Benedict XVI wrote in *Caritas in Veritate*:

> In view of the threatening catastrophe, there is the recognition everywhere that we must make moral decisions . . . [But] how can the great moral will, which everybody affirms and everyone invokes, become a personal decision? For unless that happens, politics remains impotent.
> Who, therefore can ensure that this general awareness also penetrates the personal sphere? This can be done only by an authority that touches the conscience that is close to the individual and does not merely call for eye-catching events . . . .
> [Here the Church] not only has a major responsibility; she is, I would say, often the only hope. For she is so close to people's consciences that she can move them to particular acts of self-denial and can inculcate basic attitudes in souls.[50]

So I ask each of you, as you reflect on your discussions of our "Fragile World: Ecology and the Church," your own future, your own relationship to each other, and your own care for both *natural* ecology and *human* ecology: what will you do? How will you address ecology now and in the future? And how will you, as Catholics, Christians, or peoples of faith, bring the gift of the *covenant* given to you in sustaining our common home?

I encourage you to give great attention to what Pope Francis says about the themes mentioned above. As we confront the threat of an environmental catastrophe on a global scale, I am confident that a shaft of light will break through the many heavy clouds about ecology and bring us what Pope Francis describes as the warmth of hope! Most importantly, as we become

50. Benedict XVI and Seewald, *Light of the World*, 45, referring to the World Climate Conference in Copenhagen, December 2009.

revolutionaries of tenderness, overcoming the world's pervasive inequities, this period can indeed initiate a millennium of respect for life, of our care for God's creation, of solidarity and justice, and particularly of peace.

With my blessings and prayerful good wishes for your conference,
Cardinal Peter K. A. Turkson

3

Catholic Social Teaching and Ecology: Promise and Limits

CELIA DEANE-DRUMMOND

I am intending in this chapter to chart out different facets of why, in the context of an increasingly fragile world, Catholic social teaching on the environment is worth careful review. I will discuss its slow emergence over the last half century, while also indicating how the resources for such teaching are very ancient and are found in the early church. However, it is important to probe such teaching not just for its promise, but also for its limitations in the light of the specific challenges facing the global community. I will also examine those aspects that are likely to gain more general assent in the wider global community beyond those limits. My focus will be on the writings of Pope John Paul II and Benedict XVI. I will offer some comments on the contribution of *Laudato Si'* to this ongoing discussion.

Promise

Historical Emergence

Benedict XVI has, in the past, been named in the media as the inaugural "green pope," perhaps because under his leadership, the Vatican became the first carbon neutral state in the world.[1] But to suggest that he offered anything radically new, or that Pope Francis has done something radically different in his so-called environmental encyclical, *Laudato Si'*, is to misunderstand how Catholic social teaching (CST) builds on its prior history,

1. This chapter draws on Deane-Drummond, "Joining the Dance," 193–212.

while weaving in emphases that are appropriate for a given historical period in accordance with the "signs of the times." A developmental movement, such as it exists, is certainly there, but it is very subtle and it takes a keen observer not to jump to the wrong conclusions. Pope Francis, perhaps more than his predecessors, is prepared to take ecological science seriously and sweep away some of the lingering doubts about how far the Catholic Church might be able to come to terms with climate change. But to discuss this without looking at the context, especially that internal to Catholic social teaching, would be to miss the point.

Historically, the publication of Rachel Carson's book *Silent Spring* in 1962[2] was something of a watershed in marking the beginning of a more self-conscious awareness of environmental problems facing humanity; in her case, the most pressing issue was pollution, whereas arguably the one facing us in the twenty-first century is climate change. CST started to concern itself with environmental issues as far back as 1971, at the same time that a field of theological reflection loosely known as "eco-theology" had started to emerge among lay theologians and more progressive priest-theologians such as Columban priest and missionary Sean McDonagh. McDonagh started his missionary career in the Philippines in the early 1970s by engaging in land-use projects.[3] Around this time historian Lynn White, in the widely circulated scientific magazine *Science* in 1967, blamed Christianity for being responsible for the ecological crisis.[4] Although this term is rarely heard today, it was understood as an escalating, almost *apocalyptic* destructive pollution of the planet rather than any more specific focus on climate change. White's charge, very well known to those of us who have worked in this field for the last quarter century or longer, was that Christianity, both by being human-centered and by removing nature from the sphere of the sacred, opened the door to oppressive attitudes in a way that many other religious traditions do not. His solution was to turn either to the Eastern Church or to recover the sensibility of Saint Francis.

As expected, his work spawned a host of reactions among (mostly) Protestant writers from the 1970s onwards wishing to expunge the blame attributed to Christian religion. How far this defensiveness is justified depends on how one might interpret the command in Genesis to "have

2. Carson, *Silent Spring*.

3. McDonagh published a number of significant works in eco-theology that were written in an accessible style and so designed to shift public and lay opinion in the Catholic Church and beyond. His book, *The Greening of the Church* was particularly important. He was one of the advisors to Pope Francis as he developed his encyclical, *Laudato Si'*.

4. White, "The Historical Roots of the Ecological Crisis," 1203–7.

dominion over the earth." Historically, at least, some Christian interpreters have used the Genesis text as a license for subsequent exploitation, even if biblical scholars quake at the validity of such a reading.[5]

In searching back for the first inklings of environmental[6] awareness in CST, perhaps the best place to look is the writing of Pope Paul VI and his Apostolic Letter of May 14,1971—*Octogesima Adveniens*—dedicated to the eightieth anniversary of *Rerum Novarum*.[7] While the main point of this letter is directed to social problems of urbanization and the social justices that emerge in this context, there is a short section on environmental issues, described as "the dramatic and unexpected consequence of human activity," which amounts to an "ill-considered exploitation of nature." The main threat, nonetheless, is the eventual impact on human lives, so such activity leads to human beings becoming "the victim of this degradation," so that "the human framework is no longer under man's control."[8]

What seems to be recognized here is not just the dangers of environmental destruction but the shared responsibility to do something about it. At this stage, there is little concrete suggestion as to what environmentally responsible actions might entail, or the theological basis of this concern.

In the same year (1971), however, the World Synod of Catholic Bishops in Australia produced a statement entitled *Justitia in Mundo* where the blame for environmental degradation is laid firmly at the feet of the richer nations of the world, both capitalist and socialist.[9] They call for the acceptance by the richer nations of a simpler life, with less waste, in order to avoid the destruction of the earth, seen as a common heritage for all members of the human race.[10] Romans 8 is also cited here as a way of reinforcing the suffering of creation and the vocation of Christians to bring about a better world, reflecting the fullness of creation.[11] It took, however, the papacy of Pope John Paul II to work out a consistent theological basis for such a view, as well as to build in an ethical basis grounded in an interweaving of ecological issues and questions about development. Running through such an

5. Peter Harrison, for example, notes that the exploitative strand in the interpretation of dominion as domination was evident in some Calvinist groups. See Harrison, "Having Dominion," 17–30.

6. For a discussion of the differences between environmental science and ecology, see Deane-Drummond, "Environmental Sciences," 71–84.

7. Paul VI, *Octogesima Adveniens*.

8. Ibid., 21.

9. World Synod of Catholic Bishops in Australia, *Justitia in Mundo*, 11.

10. Ibid., 70.

11. Ibid., 75, 77.

unt, we find references to the particular virtues that need to come into play: wonder, compassion, mercy, hope.

Building a Theological Mandate for Poverty and Ecology

(a) Christ in Cosmological Perspective

Pope John Paul II in his first encyclical *Redemptor Hominis*, written in 1979, showed an acute awareness of the importance of ecological concern. Early on in this text, he takes the profound step of linking the original creation with the incarnation of Jesus Christ, so that Christ acts to restore not simply broken humanity, but a broken earth as well. So, "[i]n Jesus Christ the visible world which God created for man—the world that, when sin entered, 'was subject to futility'—recovers again its original link with the divine source of Wisdom and Love."[12] Other subsequent encyclicals reinforce this idea of the cosmic scope of Christ, so "[t]he incarnation of God the Son signifies the taking up into unity with God not only human nature, but in this human nature, in a sense, of everything that is 'flesh': the whole of humanity, the entire visible and material world."[13]

There is here, then, *a Christological mandate* to restore brokenness in its personal, social, and ecological dimensions. It reflects, in other words, what might be termed a cosmic Christology, or what some contemporary theologians have termed *deep incarnation*.[14] The cross links different aspects of social devastation, ranging from destruction of the natural environment through to nuclear war and lack of respect for the life of the unborn, alongside the unbridled use of new technologies.[15]

The basis for going back to Genesis and to a Christological reading of that text is a focus on *right relationships*, what dominion over the earth *should* entail. This is a mandate given to both men and women together, as made in the image of God.[16] Exploitation of any kind is ruled out.[17] But it would be a mistake to see any leaning towards biocentrism in that the human vocation to "subdue" the earth is still intact, but now it is mirrored after

---

12. John Paul II, *Redemptor Hominis*, 8.

13. John Paul II, *Dominum et Vivificantem*, 50.

14. Noted Catholic writers in this vein include, for example, Denis Edwards, such as his *Ecology at the Heart of Faith*. The most recent volume on this theme is Gregersen, *Incarnation*.

15. John Paul II, *Redemptor Hominis*, 8.

16. Ibid., 9.

17. Ibid.

the pattern of Christ's kingship, which consists in "the priority of ethics over technology, in the primacy of the person over things, and in the superiority of spirit over matter."[18] And following from this is a radical criticism of the current financial and political systems, viewing them as not solving global problems, but instead contributing to a deepening of environmental damage. These "structures make the areas of misery spread" along with dilapidating material and energy resources.[19] *Laborem Exercens* applies an ecological mandate to the sphere of work, so in as much as the earth is subdued, it is also carried out in "justice and holiness," mirroring the work of the Creator.[20]

(b) Structural Sin

Another very important aspect of CST is the way environmental issues are woven into development questions in a way that was not, until much later, characteristic of the secular literature, where there was (and still is, to some extent) a greater sense of division. One reason for this is the focus on creation and Christology in CST, named above, so that different areas of life are thought of as interlaced with each other. So, in *Sollicitudo Rei Socialis* (1987), we find "superdevelopment," where goods were used to excess, embedded in "structures of sin" that discriminated most against the newly developing nations.[21] Environmental issues need to be recognized and taken into account in planning development projects.[22] The basis for structural sin is, however, theological, so *Sollicitudo Rei Socialis* (SRS) claims that, following human disobedience, what should have been an exercise of right relationships becomes instead "difficult and full of suffering."[23] The inspiration for this comes from reflection on Genesis 3:17–19; the Fall of humanity described in Genesis 2 is one that has repercussions much more widely and in an escalating sense. The root of ecological destruction is "an anthropological error," because human beings forget that their power to create "is always based on God's prior and original gift of the things that are." Human beings must, therefore, respect the requisites embedded in the natural world

---

18. Ibid.
19. Ibid.
20. John Paul II, *Laborem Exercens*, 25.
21. John Paul II, *Sollicitudo Rei Socialis*, 28.
22. Ibid., 26.
23. Ibid., 30.

and its God-given purposes, "which man can indeed develop but must not betray."[24]

So, the task of humanity becomes one that recognizes the interweaving of human activity with environmental responsibility: "A true concept of development cannot ignore the use of the elements of nature, the renewability of resources, and the consequences of haphazard industrialization—three considerations that alert our consciences to the moral dimension of development."[25]

(c) Image Bearing and Integral Human Development

The image of humanity as the gardener portrays what human development should be like. In this sense, the concept of sustainable development that has become more fashionable today is found much earlier in CST. The sociality of human beings, as reflected in the Genesis account, where men and women work together in complementary ways, becomes the basis for a wider perception of human flourishing that is inclusive in relationship with all living things, rather than exclusive. It is the right exercise of human dominion over the earth "within the framework of obedience to divine law" that is the means of human "perfection."[26] In other words, this is not simply an optional extra in terms of Christian discipleship but the *very means through which humans become perfect* and express the image of God. Here we find a theological anthropology that is grounded in the way we treat the natural world, the special *task* assigned to humanity, using texts from Genesis as well as Wisdom 9:2–3.

This theological basis becomes the platform for Pope John Paul II's development of *human ecology*. In commenting on the value of preserving the natural habitat of other species, he writes that "too little effort is made to *safeguard the moral conditions for an authentic human ecology*."[27] He draws on this term that was originally developed by social scientists[28] in order to stress the importance of considering what he believes are the *ontological* conditions needed for human flourishing. In this way, he can claim that

24. John Paul II, *Centesimus Annus*, 37.

25. John Paul II, *Sollicitudo Rei Socialis*, 34. For a discussion of the concept of collective conscience in the light of climate change, see Deane-Drummond, "A Case for Collective Conscience," 5–22.

26. John Paul II, *Sollicitudo Rei Socialis*, 30.

27. John Paul II, *Centesimus Annus*, 38. Italics in original.

28. See, for example, Hawley, *Human Ecology*; Catton, "Foundations of Human Ecology," 75–95.

"man too is God's gift to man. He must therefore respect the natural and moral structure with which he has been endowed."[29] John Paul II is therefore reinforcing one of the traditional aspects of CST, namely, that there is an ontological basis for moral law that is rooted in the doctrine of creation, and it is the violation of this law that is the most fundamental reason behind the ecological crisis. And the link between human and social ecology is one that Benedict XVI also picks up in his writing.[30]

(d) Perspectives on the Earth

While there are occasional references to the idea of domination of the earth in some places in the earlier CST documents, in *Sollicitudo Rei Socialis* there is an edging towards something more radical theologically. So, if human beings refuse to submit to the rule of God, then "nature rebels against him and no longer recognizes him as its 'master' for he has tarnished the divine image in himself."[31] Similar ideas come to the surface in *Centesimus Annus*, so "[i]nstead of carrying out his role as a co-operator with God in the work of creation, man sets himself up in place of God and thus ends up provoking a rebellion on the part of nature, which is more tyrannized than governed by him."[32]

Such ideas are reminiscent of the Gaian theory of James Lovelock, whose provocative writing on the earth as a closely interlocking system where life systems help regulate conditions necessary for that life has captured the attention of liberation theologians such as Leonardo Boff. Boff pushes this boundary far further compared with anything that might be evident in CST; for him, concern for the earth becomes primary over and above considerations of poverty. His argument is simple: without a functional earth, all humans are doomed, rich and poor alike.

Benedict XVI is, as one might expect, far more cautious about any edging towards pantheism or referring to the natural world in terms that give it agency, while also resisting what he sees as dangerous naturalistic forces arising from the modern project of science. For him, "nature, including the human being, is viewed as the result of mere chance or evolutionary determinism."[33] He is critical, then, of scientism or forms of naturalism that

---

29. John Paul II, *Centesimus Annus*, 38.

30. Benedict XVI, "If You Want to Cultivate Peace, Protect Creation."

31. John Paul II, *Sollicitudo Rei Socialis*, 30.

32. John Paul II, *Centesimus Annus*, 37.

33. Benedict XVI, *Caritas in Veritate*, 48.

reduce the worth of nature "to a collection of contingent data."[34] Scholars who have picked up the environmentalism latent in Pope Benedict XVI's thought have generally selected those aspects that can be built on in order to affirm environmental activism, rather than viewing his position as a step away from the thought of Pope John Paul II.[35] My own position is that going back to Pope John Paul II is rather more fruitful, especially given the way the importance of environmental issues have flowered in the writing of Pope Francis.

The important concept of the earth as *gift* to all of humanity without discrimination is spelled out in *Centesimus Annus* (1991) in a way that provides a foundation for the concept of the common good. Given this, it is remarkable how relatively little attention has been paid to ecological issues in subsequent episcopal statements drawn up about the common good. In this sense, *Laudato Si'* provides an exception, since here the climate is explicitly identified as a common good.[36]

(e) Ecological Conversion

Given the theological roots of this discussion, the problem of environmental destruction is interpreted in CST as rooted in distorted relationships in relation to God, humanity, and the natural world, both individual and collective. A movement towards an alternative, therefore, takes its bearing from the concept of *ecological conversion,* or *metanoia*, a view shared with the ecumenical patriarchate Bartholomew I. So, Pope John Paul II does not mince his words and insists that "[t]here is a need for *ecological conversion*, to which Bishops themselves can contribute by their teaching about the correct relationship of human beings with nature. Seen in the light of the doctrine of God the Father, the maker of heaven and earth, this relationship is one of 'stewardship:' human beings are set at the center of creation as stewards of the Creator."[37] Ecological conversion is, in the first instance, conversion to Christ, based on the cosmic Christology mentioned above.

Limits

Often when CST is discussed, those engaging with it seem to avoid critical remarks based on the authority of the Magisterium. But no documents are

34. Ibid.

35. Schaefer and Winright, *Environmental Justice and Climate Change.*

36. Francis, *Laudato Si'*, 23.

37. John Paul II, *Pastores Gregis*, 70; italics in original.

perfect this side of heaven, so it is important to be aware of potential weakness, especially in the context of global ecological issues.

It is important to identify some of the limitations to CST as discussed so far:

1. There is a lack of consistency, even in one encyclical, as to the status of the natural world mentioned above, including what it means to be in right relationship with it; is it domination/subduing the earth, or stewardship/management of the earth, or a more passive sense of communion, or some combination of them all? Such inconsistencies reflect, no doubt, multiple authorship. *SRS* speaks about the need for cooperation between different peoples so that all can "dominate the earth," thus edging uneasily towards a view of the earth that is subject to human control. The assumption in this text is that as long as that domination is perceived as in accordance with God's will, it is licit. What is illicit is an unbridled consumerism, particularly prevalent in Western economies that put more emphasis on a "desire to have and to enjoy rather than to be and to grow," and in this way, humanity "consumes the resources of the earth and [their] own life in an excessive and disordered way."[38] Clearly the idea of the earth as gift is incompatible with such a notion, thus highlighting another inconsistency.

2. There is also a naïve approach to the way the world works at a sociopolitical and economic level. For example, the importance of restraint in polluting the earth or overuse of resources found in the early encyclicals such as *Laborem Exercens* will not necessarily take on the pattern of holiness and justice in the way that this document implies. Further, negative and positive trajectories of development are spoken about in very general terms, so it is not clear precisely in what social or political contexts such attitudes might prevail, or what social or political contexts might be preferable. The concrete examples, such as the hoarding of nonrenewable energy resources by some nation-states or companies and the need for more regulation[39] is still generalized in that it does not seem to demand a more radical restructuring of economic and political systems that allow such practice to proliferate. Again, suggestions that advanced societies must lower their energy consumption, either through alternative energy or greater restraint in use,[40] still keeps the market systems basically intact. Benedict XVI sprinkled *Caritas*

38. John Paul II, *Centesimus Annus*, 37.
39. Benedict XVI, *Caritas in Veritate*, 49.
40. Ibid.

in Veritate with the concept of an economy of gratuitousness, but this seemed to lack teeth in relation to advocating any real change. Related to this is a loose and uncritical use of concepts such as sustainability or development, without critical reflection on the political and ethical presuppositions in the way such concepts are used.

3. The idea of co-creation that appears on occasion is also one that can easily slide into a mandate to do anything within human capacities.

4. In all encyclicals so far, there is a tendency to focus on big-picture global problems and their perceived moral roots, with vague reference to local issues. For example, it is mooted that food insecurity might be approached through "involvement of local communities in choices and decisions that affect the use of agricultural land."[41] Now while the intention is that such generalized issues could be appropriated in local contexts, it is difficult to avoid the criticism that any such application could be avoided.

5. There is a lack of attention to issues of gender. Women in particular are given stereotypical roles couched in terms of complementarity, rather than engaging with the reality of facing the huge burden that falls on women in particular in deprived social, economic, and political contexts, including situations of environmental injustice.

6. Climate change is not tackled in a way that reflects current knowledge of science, and there seems to be some nervousness in current CST about addressing this problem. While dominant societies such as the U.S. have made climate change a political football, this is not true of the majority of the rest of the world. Ask Filipinos if climate change exists, and they are likely to stare in disbelief. The shift to the claim of uncertainty about the causes of such climate change is based on weak scientific evidence that has been over-manipulated by a media hungry for controversy.

7. Some critics such as Donal Dorr have found CST too wedded to an anthropocentric philosophy.[42] While there is certainly a leaning in this direction, in some ways that may prove an advantage in reaching a wider audience. Seemingly innocuous phrases such as "creation care" or even "stewardship" can give the (wrong) impression that humans are actually capable of looking after the planet. But this is manifestly not the case.

41. Ibid., 27.
42. See, for example, Dorr, *Option for the Poor and for the Earth.*

8. An idealization of global government hinted at in documents such as *Caritas in Veritate* will be interpreted as a bias towards centralization that is likely to sound too doctrinaire for many Catholics.

9. The documents raise controversies related to population and family size. While the encyclicals are all consistent in their traditional stance on contraception, Benedict XVI opened the possibility of responsible *parenthood* in the context of discussing environmental and other limits in *Caritas in Veritate*. The Catholic Church has never supported the idea of natality; that is, having as many children as possible. Rather, natural fertility cycle family planning methods are condoned.

How far does *Laudato Si'* measure up in relation to the limits identified in CST more generally? The first issue—lack of consistency—does appear in this encyclical, though rather less so. For example, at times Pope Francis is prepared to talk of the natural world as providing "ecosystem services" to human beings, while at the same time affirming its intrinsic value in other places in the document. This may be because of the sources he is using; the scientific community will have no truck with romanticized notions of the natural world or those that find spiritual value in it. As a scientist and as a theologian, Pope Francis is capable of looking both ways, but he does not face the dilemma that this causes in his writing. Yet, his openness to insights from science, social science, and other works is remarkably refreshing compared with those of his predecessors. What about the second point about a naïve approach to economics and politics? Yes, these limitations are still present, and this is especially true in a North American context, but at the same time, if his encyclical inspires a groundswell of public opinion, then politics will need to wake up. The global reach of encyclicals and a lack of attention to local issues is rather less in evidence here; the mark of spending time with liberation theologians shows forth. Guidelines such as coming off the use of coal are given as moral injunctions, rather than worked through in terms of practical impact. The issue of women and gender is still problematic, even though men and women are referred to repeatedly. He has, far more than his predecessors, taken account of science, at a rich and more detailed level. The charge of anthropocentrism is also much harder to level at this encyclical even though, like all other papal documents, he puts a high priority on human dignity. There is also less idealization of global government compared with Pope Benedict XVI, for example, though it is clear that one of his intentions is to have an impact on international law and politics. On the matter of population growth, the encyclical is clear; "To blame population growth instead of extreme and selective consumerism on the part of some, is a way of refusing to face the issues."[43] He is right, of course, that issues of food waste, consumption, and distribution need to be tackled, but the trajectory of exponential population growth won't go away; whatever the consumption rate, the earth has a given carrying capacity that is reaching its limits. He is also prepared to admit that attention has to be paid to "population density" without spelling out what that means.

Beyond Limits

In spite of these caveats, and especially in the light of Francis's encyclical *Laudato Si'* that serves to reinforce the following themes, it seems to me important to stress the particular aspects of CST that cannot so easily be refuted theologically and are likely to have wider appeal even across different religious traditions or among secular groups such as humanists.

1. In the first place, attention to particular virtues. These include contemplation and wonder, mercy, compassion, humility, respect, wisdom, faith, and hope; these virtues draw from the roots of Christian moral insight and can be recognized by those in or outside the household of faith. Added to this, the ascetic tradition in relation to material resources that calls for the virtue of temperance and chastity is particularly relevant to the Western world, bent as it still is on an economy of growth without limits. And mercy applies not just in our relationships with those who are suffering hardships, including the impacts of environmental damage, but also towards the natural world itself. So, "[t]he word and the concept of 'mercy' seem to cause uneasiness in man, who, thanks to the enormous development of science and technology, never before known in history, has become the master of the earth and has subdued and dominated it. This dominion over the earth, sometimes understood in a one-sided and superficial way, seems to leave no room for mercy."[44]

2. Attention to peace making and solidarity. This is also a very important strand in the tradition and is relevant to all aspects of human relationships, including those with the earth. That such peace making has spiritual roots gives reasons for hope in the future, including steps towards resilience as climate impacts start to become more acute.

43. Francis, *Laudato Si'*, 50.
44. John Paul II, *Dives in Misericordia*.

3. Justice as virtue and as social theory. This is also extremely important to consider, and in spite of the caveat that different societies will understand justice differently, so in the face of extremes of climate, adjudicating the just distribution of basic commodities such as sufficient fresh water, health care, and education are likely to be extremely important.

4. Collective community conscience. How do we know what justice and love entails? I suggest that collective community conscience is important to consider in the way it can inform decisions that relate to social structures. Given the social and political place of the Catholic Church in the global community, how it acts collectively has important impacts. So, it is not enough just to discuss climate change; steps must be taken towards collective ecological responsibility.

5. The relationship between conscience informed by magisterial teaching and the individual conscience inspired by the work of the Holy Spirit. I suggest that this is a crucial dynamic, and the hardening of stress on magisterial teaching has softened under the leadership of Pope Francis. He speaks of a hardening of consciences towards the most deprived sectors of the global population.[45] Conscience is also linked with responsibility, though it is a wider notion of responsibility rather than that related to explicit magisterial teaching. This is deliberate, as Pope Francis wants his encyclical to appeal both within and beyond the Catholic Church.

6. The healing aesthetic value in the natural world. While this thread was begun by Pope John Paul II,[46] who was known earlier in his pre-papal ministry for his "nature" retreats, the power of such studied attention is likely to get an increased hearing.

7. A message of joy and hope in a world that is on the verge of despair. Pope Francis indicates this in his apostolic exhortation, *Evangelii Gaudium* (*The Joy of the Gospel*), the message of Christianity is fundamentally a hope-filled one based on the power of the resurrection. So, God will restore all creation through Christ and in the power of the Holy Spirit. Can this message of hope and joy still make sense in the context of climate change, ecological devastation, and numerous and compounding social injustices? Pope Francis insists that it can, that the last word for Christians has to be one of faith in the providential care of God alongside ultimate hope in the power of the resurrection

45. Francis, *Laudato Si'*, 94.
46. John Paul II, *Peace with All Creation*, 14.

and restoration of all things. Deeper contemplation on the Eucharist can provide a first step through which prayer is united to action, a transformation of the basic material of the natural world into the body of Christ. It is significant that Pope Francis is prepared to enlarge the scope of the mass to a cosmic scale on a par with the thought of Teilhard de Chardin.[47] There are, of course, some intermediate steps along the way between the eschatological future and the feast of the coming reign of God and the real difficulties that we find in the present. These steps represent our particular human responsibilities and how to act in the world.

---

47. "In the Eucharist fullness is already achieved, it is the living Center of the universe, the overflowing core of love and of inexhaustible life." Francis, *Laudato Si'*, 236.

4

From Assisi to Buenos Aires:
The Cry of the Poor and the Cry of the Planet

MICHAEL A. PERRY, OFM

The gospel is about the Kingdom of God; it is about loving God who reigns in our world. To the extent that he reigns within us, the life of society will be a setting for universal fraternity, justice, peace and dignity.[1]

Setting the Context

Universal fraternity, universal justice, universal peace, universal dignity, and the common good: these are the central elements that guide the recent reflections of the Holy See on the critical issues related to the plight of the poor and the plight of the planet.[2] They also are constitutive to an integral understanding and living out (ortho-praxis) of our faith as disciples of the risen Lord Jesus, and not simply nominal and unconnected appendices to be randomly selected or excluded from our Christian lives.[3] This is the argument that I will pursue in the analysis of the life and teachings of St. Francis of Assisi and the most recent popes, as they relate to the poor and

1. Francis, *Evangelii Gaudium*, 180.

2. See *Compendium of the Social Doctrine of the Church*, "Principles of the Church's Social Doctrine," 91–120.

3. See Christiansen and Grazer, *And God Saw*, 2: "The appeals by Pope John Paul II, the U.S. Catholic bishops, and other Catholic religious leaders mean that the Catholic community needs to take up the challenge to see environmental concerns not just as emerging political or economic issues, but as concerns intimately related to their faith life."

the planet. Special attention will be given to the central themes of the first encyclical of Pope Francis, *Laudato Si'*, as they relate to an integral Catholic approach to care for humanity and the planet.

The trajectory for this reflection will lead from St. Francis and the city of Assisi to Pope Francis and his hometown of Buenos Aires. In the case of the former, St. Francis was awarded the distinct title of "heavenly Patron of those who promote Ecology" by Pope John Paul II in 1975 because of his keen insight into the inherently divine beauty and dignity of all people and all elements within the universe. St. Francis progressively found himself being drawn into a new vision of humanity and of creation, one that embraced all as brother and sister, and excluded no created thing. His embrace of the lepers of Assisi provided St. Francis an opportunity to discover the presence of God in all people and creatures, irrespective of their pedigree or external form. In God's eyes, all are related, all are connected, all belong; nothing is out of place. St. Francis even went so far as to honor the sun, the moon, the wind, and other realties in the environment by speaking of them in personal terms, naming them brother and sister: "brother Sun, sister Moon."[4]

This vision of the created universe promoted by St. Francis of Assisi is the opposite of the vision that emerges from the globalized and secularized modern age. Recently canonized Pope John Paul II, reflecting on the consequences of a contemporary assault on the dignity of human beings and the environment, is convinced that a spirit of conquest and exploitation controls the modern age. This spirit leads to the subjugation of human beings and the natural environment, with very destructive consequences for both. The pope writes: "In our day, there is a growing awareness that world peace is threatened not only by the arms race, regional conflicts, and continued injustices among peoples and nations, but also by a lack of *due respect for nature*, by the plundering of natural resources and by a progressive decline in the quality of life. The sense of precariousness and insecurity that such a situation engenders is a seedbed for collective selfishness, disregard for others, and dishonesty."[5] Thus, what transpires in one arena, the human community, has a direct impact on quality of life in the other, the environment, and vice versa. Nothing is separate; all is connected. Thus, we must develop a new approach and a new awareness, one that is interdisciplinary, inclusive, and integral.[6]

4. Armstrong et al., *St. Francis of Assisi*, 113–14.

5. John Paul II, "Peace with God the Creator, Peace with All of Creation," 1.

6. Boff and Nguyen Van Si, *Sorella Madre Terra*, 8. The authors call attention to the need for a more holistic approach to the integral relationship between society and culture and the natural environment: "Ecology embraces not only nature (natural ecology) but also culture and society. This concept of ecology initiates for us a new

The direct consequences of degrading exploitation of the environment, guided by unbridled exploitation of resources and bolstered by the myth of unlimited economic development, spoken of by Pope John Paul II and also by Pope Francis in *Laudato Si'*,[7] are the reduction of the "environment's hospitable aspect," and decreasing prospects for the survival of the planet and its future inhabitants.[8] Similar conclusions have been reached within the scientific community, with particular reference to the work of the United Nations Intergovernmental Panel on Climate Change (IPCC), which was established in 1988.[9] The most recent reports (2013 and 14) make eminently clear that global warming is occurring at an alarming rate. The scientists conclude that humanity is playing a significant role in climate change, with anthropogenic emissions of greenhouse gases at their highest level in history.

The global climate system is undergoing radical changes that could be irreversible unless immediately and substantially addressed. Even with the best of mitigation efforts, the impact of global warming will most probably continue for centuries, leading to further extreme changes in weather patterns that could disrupt human and ecological life throughout the world, most especially among those who are economically marginalized, the poor. Immediate decisions and clear steps must be taken to reduce carbon emissions and move towards their elimination. Reduction of carbon emissions could provide additional time for the climate system to make necessary adaptations. It would also provide additional time for the creation of new and more energy efficient technologies that could help further mitigate the impact of greenhouse gases on the climate system. These efforts will require tremendous political will on the part of governments, businesses, local communities, and individuals, with increased investments in alternative forms of energy. It also will require a profound ethical engagement on the part of all people in order to initiate and sustain the changes necessary to achieve the goal of reducing the anthropogenic impact on the climate system.

The agreement of the Paris climate conference in December 2015 (COP 21) is a positive move in the direction of gaining political commitment on

---

awareness, a new sensitivity for perceiving the dimension of what is real. If all things exist in relationship with all (with one another), in a synchronic manner, there is need for a sensitivity to understand that separate knowledge [of things], at first fragmented and atomized, must now be [approached] in an interdisciplinary manner."

7. See Francis, *Laudato Si'*, 109–10 et passim.

8. John Paul II, "Address to Conference on Environment and Health," 2–3 et passim. See also John Paul II, *Centesimus Annus*, 37–38.

9. See Intergovernmental Panel on Climate Change, *Climate Change 2013* and *Climate Change 2014*.

the part of the member states to seek a reduction in greenhouse emissions. Pope Francis's encyclical *Laudato Si'* and the direct involvement of the Holy See Mission at the Paris conference demonstrates the serious commitment of the Catholic Church to working with the community of nations to reduce greenhouse gases and to protecting the environment. Such reduction of emissions could help to avoid dangerous climate change by limiting global warming to well below the critical point of two degrees Celsius.[10] Much work remains if these goals are to be achieved, including the development of a set of instruments for measuring compliance with promises made through the Intended Nationally Determined Contributions (INDCs).[11] Even should nations follow through on their commitments made in Paris, the damage that has already been done to the environment will more than likely require the human community to abandon the planet in the coming millennia, as renowned British scientist Stephen Hawking argues.[12] What difference can we make?

For many ordinary citizens living around the world, one of the first questions that might arise in discussions about the future of the human community and the natural environment is rather simple and straightforward: what difference does it make to my life if the popes and scientists and so many others are correct in saying that the environment—all the elements of the created world—are in serious peril? What does it matter that the consequences of our current lifestyle and of our use of the earth's resources place in jeopardy the life and well-being of future generations of human beings and place at risk the planet?

A second question arises immediately when trying to give answer to the first: What can I or we do about global change and global greenhouse emissions? In trying to respond to the second question, three serious challenges emerge. First, there is the tendency to minimize what is actually happening within and to the climate systems, leaving the problem to future generations to solve. A second risk is that of the "paralysis of analysis." In seeking to understand the complexity of what might be occurring, something that is "overwhelming" in its scope, there is the temptation to wait and see, without making any changes to lifestyle that might actually make a positive contribution to reducing our human impact on the environment. A third tendency of which Pope Francis speaks in *Laudato Si'*[13] is that of denying the human impact on global warming and climate change. This

10. European Commission on Climate Action, "Paris Agreement."

11. World Resources Institute, "What is an INDC?"

12. Knapton, "Professor Stephen Hawking."

13. Francis, *Laudato Si'*, 60, et passim.

temptation, promoted by some Christians, politicians, and even a very small number of scientists, fails to take seriously the changes occurring in the natural environment, de-linking faith and responsibility, ethics and daily life.

The Poor and the Planet: The Search for an Integral Vision

In my current role as minister general of the Order of Friars Minor, my previous service as a missionary in the Democratic Republic of Congo (DRC), my position as policy adviser to the United States Conference of Catholic Bishops and Catholic Relief Services, and my policy work at the New York office of Franciscans International (our Franciscan NGO at the United Nations), I have had many occasions to witness firsthand the devastating consequences of the unbridled and irresponsible exploitation of the planet's resources as described by Pope John Paul II in his writings on the environment, and in the IPCC's report, *Climate Change 2013: The Physical Science Basis.*[14]

It is my contention, and that of successive popes, that there is a direct link between uncontrolled and ethically irresponsible exploitation of the natural environment and a worsening of conditions for the world's poorest—the "bottom billion" spoken of by Professor Paul Collier.[15] A clear example of this can be found among those who suffered most from such cataclysmic events as Hurricane Katrina, the Indian Ocean Tsunami of 2004, and Typhoon Hagupit—those who were poor. In the case of Katrina, fifteen million people were affected, with an economic impact of over $150 billion. The poorest lost not only their homes but also their stability. They continue to suffer the consequences of this catastrophe more than ten years later.[16] For those living in Asia, one has only to reflect on the Indian Ocean Tsunami of 2004, which left more than one hundred and fifty thousand dead or missing, and millions more homeless in eleven countries.[17] The poorest of the region's most affected lost everything. They continue to live in temporary housing and are totally dependent on meager support from their respective governments and on international donors and religious groups for survival. In the case of the Philippines and Typhoon Hagupit, thousands perished; property was destroyed; at least 1.7 million people were displaced;

14. See Intergovernmental Panel on Climate Change, *Climate Change 2013.*
15. See Collier, *The Bottom Billion.*
16. Eaton and McWhirter, "An Unfinished Riff."
17. *National Geographic News*, "The Deadliest Tsunami in History?"

and more than one million others were severely affected.[18] According to many recent scientific studies, these "natural" catastrophes will increase and will affect most directly the poor unless immediate and decisive actions are taken to address underlying causes.[19]

Another area of the natural environment's exploitation that is particularly troubling is related to mineral extractions by multinational mining conglomerates and involving national, regional, and local government officials. Mineral extraction is having devastating consequences on both the human and the natural environments, and two cases in particular bear examination since they demonstrate what is at stake for both. The first is drawn from personal experience, from my time as a Catholic missionary in the DRC and, later, in my role as vicar general of the Order of Friars Minor. In the case of the DRC, and more specifically the region of Katanga and the localities of Funguruma/Tenke, methods employed for extracting copper have left in their wake toxic chemical "tailings," rivers of toxic sludge. As a consequence, these toxic flows have penetrated the underground aquifers, polluted local water supplies, and turned vast expanses of formerly arable land into toxic wastelands.[20] The social consequences have been devastating, as the local inhabitants have reported increasing respiratory difficulties, skin disorders, and blood and other abnormalities among the younger populations. Due to soil poisoning, farmers increasingly have abandoned fields in close proximity to the mines. In addition, there has been a noticeable decrease in annual rates of rain and an increase in the heat index throughout the region of Katanga. These same mining consortiums tout the significant steps they have made to deepen their corporate social responsibility, providing medical and other services to affected communities and guaranteeing forms of control to mitigate potential damage to the physical environment.[21] Despite these lofty promises, field studies on social and environmental impacts from the mining paint a very different story.

Local inhabitants and people brought in to work in the mines have complained of serious respiratory and other health problems. Reports

18. Silva, "Philippines Typhoon Haguput Update 2014."

19. Cf. Environmental Defense Fund (EDF), "Climate Change's Effects Plunder the Planet."

20. A clear example of the impact of mining activities on quality of life of people in Katanga is found in Kashimbo Kalala et al., "Impact of Liquid Tailings," 448–64.

21. See "Tenke Fungurume Copper Mine DRC." It is important to note that Freeport-MacMoRan Copper and Gold, Inc. sold its controlling interest in the Tenke Fungurume copper mine to a Chinese conglomerate in August 2016, effectively shielding itself from potential liabilities and responsibilities to the Congolese people. See Brophy, "DRC's Largest Mine Was Just Sold."

indicate that infiltration of tailings of dangerous chemicals used to clean the copper and cobalt have been found in concentrations in water sources. Serious concerns remain as to whether these have penetrated the underground aquifers in the region, which would have a long-term negative impact on the quality of human life and on the environment.

A second example comes from the Indonesian village of Serise in Flores where, beginning in the 1980s, a mineral exploitation license was granted by the government to a major mining company to begin exploitation of manganese mineral deposits. Representatives of the mining company met with local village representatives to discuss their project, offering the promise to revive economic activity, provide jobs, and care for the environment. The project was initially well received by this impoverished village community, even though the people did not understand the full implications and potential impacts that it might have on their social and natural environments. Soon after the mining activities began, people began to experience very negative social and environmental consequences. Siprianus Amon, a local social activist, offers the following description:

> After the agreement, the villagers of Serise slowly discovered how they had lost sovereignty. Their land had been taken over by the company and they could no longer farm it. The mining industry began to clear trees to build processing plants for the manganese. Women were hired for about U.S. $2 per day, and the men for about U.S. $2.50. The wage was not enough to meet basic needs. Compensation for their land and its produce, destroyed by the mining process, was by any standards unjust. Promises for economic advance and social development never materialized.
>
> The following account is based on eyewitness testimony found in a private February 2015 report to the Order of Friars Minor (OFM)'s Justice, Peace, and Integrity of Creation (JPIC) Commission of Indonesia. During the rainy seasons, an increase in the number of landslides threatened their lives, their farms, and their houses. People came to realize that the exploitation practices of the mining company had reduced the quality of their physical health, their lands, their water systems, and their sovereignty. Early protests by the people were met with violence and illegal detentions on the part of government officials who benefitted from bribes by the mining companies. Continued efforts by the people, supported by Franciscan friars and the

local Catholic Church, eventually convinced the government to impose a ban on mining activities.[22]

The Church's Efforts to Defend our Sister, Mother Earth

Beginning with Pope Paul VI, successive popes have criticized models of development that believe in absolutizing human technological progress without giving sufficient attention to the human/social community and the natural environment. In *Octogesima Adveniens*, Paul VI makes clear that "Man is suddenly becoming aware that by an ill-considered exploitation of nature he risks destroying it and becoming in his turn the victim of this degradation."[23] Pope John Paul II, following upon the contributions of Paul VI, speaks out strongly in his encyclical, *Redemptoris Hominis*, on the vices of a misguided development, driven by a liberal capitalist system that permits—worse, even encourages and rewards—a system of unbridled exploitation, consumption, and waste in the name of progress and profit.[24] He demands that a responsible system of verifiable controls be established that might limit the exploitation by humanity of the natural environment. "What else can be the essential meaning of this 'kinship' and 'dominion' of man over the visible world," asks the pope, "than the priority of ethics over technology, in the primacy of the person over things, and in the superiority of spirit over matter?"[25]

Three pillars—the primacy of ethics, the human person (human ecology), and spirituality—form the nucleus of John Paul II's thinking and efforts to elaborate an ethics of sustainability. He was most concerned with what the destruction of the natural environment revealed about the spiritual state of humanity, and the impact of unbridled destruction of the environment on the plight of the poor and marginalized. Thus, human dignity, human rights, and human development were at the center of his reflection. Less clear is John Paul II's understanding of the specific dignity of the created universe, the environment, and its specific and autonomous value independent from any utilitarian role it plays in support of "integral" human development. It appears that John Paul II's vision was more focused on the human person, leaving nature to be appreciated principally for its instrumental role in service to humanity.[26]

22. Amon, Eyewitness testimony in private report to JPIC-OFM Indonesia.
23. Paul VI, *Octogesima Adveniens*, 21.
24. John Paul II, *Redemptoris Hominis*, 15.
25. Ibid., 16.
26. See Dorr, "'The Fragile World.'"

Pope Benedict XVI builds on the foundations laid by John Paul II, emphasizing the primacy of "human ecology" in the promotion of an "environmental ecology" capable of respecting and protecting other creatures. "Men and women," writes Benedict XVI, "will be capable of respecting creation to the extent in which they have a full appreciation of life; otherwise, they will be inclined to condemn themselves and their surroundings, to respect neither the environment they live in nor creation. Thus, the first ecology that is in need of defense is 'human ecology.'"[27] Already in his Message for the World Day of Peace of January 1, 2007, Benedict lays the foundation for his argument on the relationship between humanity and creation:

> Alongside the ecology of nature, there exists what can be called a "human" ecology, which in turn demands a "social" ecology. This means that humanity, if it truly desires peace, must be increasingly conscious of the links between natural ecology, or respect for nature, and human ecology. Experience shows that disregard for the environment always harms coexistence, and vice versa. It has become more and more evident that there is an inseparable link between peace with creation and peace among men. Both of these presuppose peace with God. The poem-prayer of Saint Francis, known as "The Canticle of Brother Sun," is a wonderful and ever timely example of this multifaceted ecology of peace.[28]

Benedict goes a step further than John Paul II in his understanding of the essential dignity of creation and our responsibility for its care. He declares, in the language of one of his intellectual mentors, Franciscan theologian St. Bonaventure, that "Nature expresses a design of love and truth."[29] Nature has a vocation, to act in partnership with humanity. "The natural environment is more than raw material to be manipulated at our pleasure; it is a wondrous work of the Creator containing a 'grammar,' which sets forth ends and criteria for its wise use, not its reckless exploitation."[30] He proposes the adoption of a new lifestyle "capable of generating an authentic human search for truth, beauty, and communion."[31] He calls upon the international community, singular governments, and the business sector to do all they can to help reduce the impact of unbridled exploitation and the destruc-

27. Benedict XVI, "Message to Brazilian Bishops for the 2011 Brotherhood Campaign."

28. Benedict XVI, "If You Want to Cultivate Peace, Protect Creation."

29. Benedict XVI, *Caritas in Veritate*, 48.

30. Ibid.

31. Ibid., 51.

tion of the environment, and to be guided by ethical standards, not only by economic interests of the few, powerful, and most wealthy citizens.[32] He also highlights the importance of intergenerational justice, intergenerational solidarity, and a solidarity embracing space and time. This theme is taken up and expanded by Pope Francis in *Laudato Si'*.[33]

Despite the tremendous attention given to the issue of the environment by Benedict, and his specific actions within Vatican City to convert conventional forms of energy to green energy,[34] he was not able to overcome a tendency to dichotomy, the separation of human/social from environmental "ecologies," creating distinct and seemingly autonomous categories. Neither John Paul II nor Benedict XVI successfully articulated a theological vision that recognized the inherent dignity of nature *per se*, independent of its instrumental role in promoting integral human development. Nature, in the end, is valued for promoting human and social ecology. Pope Francis will move in a new direction, incorporating this dimension of the inherent dignity of nature as part of his integral ecological vision of the relationship that God intends for humanity and the natural environment, working together in partnership, giving glory to the same Creator God.

St. Francis of Assisi:
Proposal for Integrating Human and Natural Communities

The vision proposed by St. Francis in his *Canticle of the Creatures*, while not articulated in the contemporary language of human/social versus ecological, goes beyond these seeming dichotomies, proposing an integrated and integrating understanding of the essential and inseparable relationship between humanity and nature because of the grace and love that each of these contain and are called to share one with one another. Each has its proper vocation, divinely created, and each is to act within a field of ethical care one towards the other. The question here is one of companionship, complementarity, reciprocity, and sacrifice or self-donation for the sake of God and for love of the other. Nature partakes of the same dignity owing to its participation in the life of the Creator God. St. Francis does not appear to argue in terms of "equality of dignity" but rather a "communion through cooperative participation" by the divine origin of its nature, and also through its service to humanity.

32. See Benedict XVI, "General Audience: Safeguarding of Creation."
33. Francis, *Laudato Si'*, 159–62.
34. Singh, "Vatican City Crowned the 'Greenest State in the World.'"

St. Francis's practical understanding of the nature of the relationship between the human and natural environments—a vision expressed by way of "communion through cooperative participation"—provides a new way forward for the articulation of an integrated and unified theological vision. Trees, fire, rain, wind, sun, plants, animals, and all other creatures animate and inanimate possess within themselves a dignity that flows from the fact they have been created by the Supreme and Most High Creator. They participate in life with God and are invited to give thanks to God through participative service to and together with the human community. This co-operation with humanity does not reduce creation to a mere object to be exploited without limits or responsibility. Creation is essential to the life of the human community, and for this reason, Francis believed we have a special responsibility and duty to honor and care for the created universe. Whatever places in danger the created universe also places in danger humanity. There is no separation between human ecology—the protection and dignity of human beings—and environmental ecology—the protection and dignity of creation. The "cry of the poor" and the "cry of the planet" are mutually interrelated. A threat to one or the other, to the poor or to the planet, is an act of sinfulness, a desecration of the beauty of God's creation. Creation contains within itself the capacity and the vocation to collaborate with humanity, but it also retains its right to be treated with respect and not threatened or exploited.

St. Francis of Assisi was not born with an innate awareness of the inter-connectedness of all living things, human and natural. He came to this slowly, through an interior conversion of mind and heart. This conversion was not only or exclusively religious, but spirituality was central to the process. The experience of St. Francis reveals the heart of a troubled man, someone who had witnessed the violence of conflict and war in the name of God, in the Crusades, and who most probably participated actively in the killing of others, in defense of his hometown of Assisi. His social status in the evolving city state of Assisi in the twelfth and thirteenth centuries provided him with privilege and protected him from experiencing contact firsthand with the marginalized and excluded of the town and its environs. Francis makes clear in his writings that God played a central role in changes to his thinking that he would progressively experience. However, it also is clear that the poor and excluded peoples of Assisi as well as the natural world would come to play a decisive role in shaping his ethics of inclusion, founded upon an ever-expanding awareness of and commitment to an understanding of participation in a universal fraternity that embraced all of humanity and creation without exclusion.

When speaking of his "conversion," St. Francis immediately and simultaneously speaks about a series of events that led him to discover a new
vision of God and God's role in the human and natural communities. His
spiritual encounter with the Son of God, Jesus, in the dilapidated and abandoned Benedictine church of the Portiuncula located outside of the walls
of Assisi is a decisive event leading to a radical choice in his life. There,
through the suspended wooden crucifix of San Damiano,[35] he experienced
a personal call to go and repair the church. God was speaking through an
object of nature, an image carved in wood, upon which was superimposed
the image of the Son of God, surrounded by a cloud of human witnesses,
and even a rooster! The emerging theme of this encounter was one focused
on the poor, crucified Christ who became poor for the sake of the poor and
marginalized, for all human beings, and for all of creation. Thus, the plight
of those who were poor and excluded took center stage in St. Francis's vision
of God and God's plan for the world.

His encounter with a poor beggar of Assisi, a man who bore the physical wounds of Hansen's disease (leprosy), would play another decisive role in
his development of an integrated understanding of the moral responsibility
he bore towards all human beings. It also contributed to his protest against
an emerging mercantile mentality in which the value of human beings, and
most explicitly the poor, was based on their capacity to contribute to wealth
production for the more powerful groups in Assisi: wealthy landholders,
the emerging merchant class, and even Catholic religious authorities. For
Francis, his embrace of a new vision of God and a new vision of humanity
would create within him one of the pillars upon which he would construct
his ethical practice. This pillar was two-fold: a recognition of the inherent
and inalienable divine dignity of each and every person created in the image of the Creator and the moral responsibility that each human person
bears because of his or her participation in God's plan for humanity and the
created universe. This disturbing insight led St. Francis to the conviction
that he could not participate in the money economy and the social system
that dominated medieval Italian society. The aristocracy—the *maiores*—and
the merchants who aspired to this class increasingly dominated the poor
and marginalized classes—the *minores*. St. Francis abandoned all aspirations to enter into the class of *maiores,* stripping himself of title and even
the very clothes provided by his father, and embraced the social position
of *minores.* For St. Francis, the refusal to participate in the dehumanizing
socioeconomic structures of his time was the only way for him and for all

35. For a fuller description of the crucifix of San Damiano, see Scanlan, *The San
Damiano Cross.*

human beings to recover their dignity as creatures of a loving and merciful Creator God. Francis understood that not only are the poor progressively robbed of their dignity, but that those who participate in a market system of exploitation and dehumanization become victims of the same process. Thus, St. Francis chose the way of evangelical poverty, living simply so that others could simply live, refusing to receive coins for work because he knew the coins were constantly devalued, thus ensuring that the poor would remain perpetually poor.[36]

The life of evangelical poverty was not, for Francis, an exclusively spiritual matter. He did not choose a life of material simplicity and self-denial in order to dignify the material poverty generated by the existing economic system that produced social inequality, exclusion, and dehumanization. Rather, Francis chose his specific form of life, I believe, for two motives. The first is laid bare in the early Franciscan sources, which speak of his desire to live the same spirit of non-possessiveness as did the poor and crucified Christ. However, I also believe that in following this spiritual intuition, Francis found himself standing with God on the side of the poor who were relegated by their social condition to live in absolute dependence on providence, through the sweat of their brows.

As a consequence of this spiritual insight, Francis refused to participate in the economic structures of his time. This provided Francis with an opportunity to live a newfound freedom, one necessary if he were to pursue the exploration of a new model of society, one based on the principles of human dignity, the common good, the right to participation by all in the economic, social, and political life of the society to which they belonged.[37]

As St. Francis grew in understanding of the Creator's intention, and as the fundamental "divine" dignity of human beings and their vocation to become one in God deepened, he increasingly found himself pushing against social, political, and even religious barriers. After multiple failed attempts to travel to the Holy Land, where the Fifth Crusade was raging, St. Francis managed to arrive in Damietta, in Egypt, in 1219. What he found was a land of death and destruction. The religious leaders of Christianity and Islam were locked in a protracted and perilous war that led to the progressive dehumanization of all involved. There are no written accounts of the encounter between St. Francis and the Muslim sultan and military commander Al-Malik al-Kamil. What we have are a series of interpretations reflecting different religious and political understandings (ideologies)

36. See Carney, "Naming the Earthquake," 83–84.

37. See Warner, "Retrieving Franciscan Philosophy for Social Engagement," 401–21, especially 413 and following.

at different moments in history.[38] Some writers see reflected in Francis's visit
to one of the sites of the Fifth Crusade his desire to be martyred for his faith.
St. Bonaventure, seeking to defend the Franciscan Order from its critics,
presents Francis as a global evangelizer who sought to convert the Muslims
to the Christian (true) faith. Still other writers argue that Francis's mission
was much more sympathetic and involved the promotion of respect, peace,
and reconciliation. The latter interpretation was presented in 2000 by then
Cardinal Ratzinger who argues that St. Francis held the conviction that the
crusades and religious warfare were not the solution to differences between
Christianity and Islam. Cardinal Ratzinger found in the experience of St.
Francis a model for the church in our times. "Let us walk down the path
towards peace, following the example of Saint Francis."[39]

> The same cardinal, who later became Pope Benedict XVI, ex-
> tended the understanding of the dignity, rights, and responsi-
> bilities linked to human relationships and human ecology, to
> an understanding of environmental ecology. Ratzinger's study
> of St. Bonaventure, a thirteenth-century Franciscan cardinal
> and theologian, led him to the conviction that the created world
> contains within it the image and purpose of the Creator God.
> He subsequently made efforts to establish a strong connection
> between human ecology and environmental ecology. This is re-
> flected most clearly in Benedict's message for the World Day of
> Peace, January 1, 2010: "If you want to cultivate peace, protect
> Creation. Respect for creation is of immense consequence, not
> least because "creation is the beginning and the foundation of all
> of God's work,' and its preservation has now become essential for
> the pacific coexistence of mankind. Man's inhumanity to man
> has given rise to numerous threats to peace and to authentic and
> integral human development . . . Yet no less troubling are the
> threats arising from the neglect—if not downright misuse—of
> the earth and the natural goods that God has given us. For this
> reason, it is imperative that mankind renew and strengthen 'that
> covenant between human beings and the environment, which
> should mirror the creative love of God, from whom we come
> and towards whom we are journeying.'"[40]

The final barrier that St. Francis confronted and overcame was that
which separated human beings and the environment. As has been argued, St.

---

38. See Tolan, "The Friar and the Sultan," 115–26. See also Tolan, *Saint Francis and the Sultan*, and Moses, *The Saint and the Sultan*.

39. Ratzinger, "Lo Splendore della Pace di Francesco."

40. Benedict XVI, "If You Want to Cultivate Peace, Protect Creation."

Francis progressively came to a deeper awareness of the interconnectedness of all human beings leading to an ethics of global responsibility and global solidarity. This same process of spiritual, philosophical, and social conversion would lead him to a further and necessary step, that of an "ecological" conversion that was not distinct from but rather the direct consequence of a prior "human and social" conversion. His expanding understanding of fraternity led St. Francis to embrace the inherent dignity and value of all created things, human/social and natural.

In one of his prayers, the *Praises of the Virtues*, Francis makes clear that the human person, living in right relationship with the Creator, submits his or her will in obedience to another person, "to one's brother, so that it is subject and submissive to everyone in the world."[41] St. Francis does not stop with submission of one's will to every person, however, but extends it to include submission to the natural world, "not only to people but to every beast and wild animal as well."[42] Thus we see clearly the results of St. Francis's ecological conversion, which was grounded in his appreciation of and commitment to living as a "lesser brother" to all of humanity (social conversion) and all of creation (ecological conversion). Submission is related to the quality of relationship that should exist between creatures who have been created by the same God, and who share a common vocation of giving glory, praise, and thanks to God, through a reciprocity of respect and care. It is here that we discover the conversion of the social and the ecological into a unified vision and practice, an "integral" ecological vision.

In 1226, as St. Francis lay dying, he transmitted to one of his faithful friars what is considered to be one of the best examples of early Italian religious poetry, *The Canticle of the Creatures*. This text reflects in a most profound manner Francis's conception of the integral nature of the social and natural environments. For this reason, I would call this his "Magna Carta" of an integral Christian theology of ecology. Let us examine briefly the different elements of this song/prayer.

According to "The Assisi Compilation (1244–1260)", St. Francis makes clear the intention of the *Canticle:*

> I want to write a new *Praise of the Lord* for his creatures, which we use every day, and without which we cannot live. Through them the human race greatly offends the Creator, and every day we are ungrateful for such great graces, because we do not praise, as we should, our Creator, and the Giver of all good."[43]

41. Ibid. 165.
42. Ibid.
43. Armstrong et al., *Francis of Assisi: The Founder*, 186.

The Canticle of the Creatures can be divided into three sections, each revealing a facet of Francis's vision of God, humanity, creation, and the human soul. In the first section, up to the phrase "who produces various fruit with colored flowers and herbs," Francis gives thanks to the Creator for all of creation and for all creatures. He recognizes the dignity of each and every creature, which "bears the likeness" of God. Francis also recognizes the spiritual vocation which each of the created forms is called to celebrate and fulfill. What is most clear is the sense of co-participation and cooperation to which all of God's creatures are called without distinction.

Thomas Stratman, writing in a Dominican publication, argues that it was Francis's respectful attitude towards creation that kept "the *good of being* primary over the *good of use* . . ."[44] Francis does not condemn the use of these creatures. Rather, he argues that they be allowed the freedom (*from* threat, *for* service) to fulfill their "vocation":

> Fire lights the night, a useful and beautiful trait. And the canticle praises God for Sister Water who is very useful, it says, and lowly or submissive. But she is also *pretiosa* (sparkling like a jewel) and *casta* (pure, clear, chaste). Francis appreciates both kinds of goodness but keeps the *good of being* as primary. Water, after all, becomes less useful when she loses her appealing clarity.[45]

Following upon this central insight of St. Francis of the dignity of the created elements, Franciscans Keith Warner, Ilia Delio, and Pamela Wood explore the nature of the relationship between the human/social and the natural, which can be discerned in the *Canticle of the Creatures*:

> The Canticle reminds us that we humans are as dependent on the elements of creation as they are dependent on us. With his marvelous respect for creatures of all kinds, for sun, moon, stars, water, wind, fire and earth, Francis came to see that all creation gives praise to God . . . As we see in the life of Francis, union with God is union with all other beings, whether humans, animals, plants or the elements.[46]

The second part of the Canticle speaks of pardon and is a reference to a specific crisis that emerged in Assisi. He rebukes his Franciscan brothers for their refusal to intervene in a serious conflict between the bishop and the mayor of Assisi. He composes the verse about pardon and instructs his brothers to summon the bishop and the mayor to the center of the city,

---

44. Stratman, "St. Francis of Assisi, Brother to All Creatures," 224; italics mine.

45. Ibid.

46. Delio et al., "Creation Care."

where the brothers are to sing the new verse. According to the early sources, the two litigants were greatly moved by the message, having been reminded of the dignity each shared because of God's creating grace and their responsibility to fulfill their vocation as promoters of peace and reconciliation.[47]

What emerges from the second section of the *Canticle* is a vision of solidarity and communion that deposes humanity from its pretended domination over creation and that proposes a type of democracy in which all of God's creatures participate. Boersema goes as far as to argue:

> With [St. Francis] the ant is no longer simply a homily for the lazy, flames a sign of thrust of the soul toward union with God; now they are Brother Ant and Sister Fire, praising the Creator in their own ways as Brother Man does in his . . . All things animate and inanimate [are] designed for the glorification of their transcendent Creator, who, in the ultimate gesture of cosmic humility, assumed flesh, lay helpless in a manger, and hung dying on a scaffold.[48]

The third part of the *Canticle*, which speaks of death, reveals the depth of St. Francis's understanding of his total dependence on the Creator and the freedom that comes from allowing this vision to guide his life. It is possible to speak of his life as a continuous chain of events that progressively and cumulatively brought him to a new understanding of the dignity of human life and the dignity enjoyed by all of creation. It is because of this interior freedom that St. Francis is able to let go even of his earthly life. He recognized that to let go of one's life is to embrace all of life, all peoples, and all of creation for who and what they are in the sight of God. Reflecting on St. Francis's vision of life beyond social and historical boundaries, Delio argues, "The second death, the death of the body, then becomes a complete participation in the cosmic community of life."[49]

The *Canticle of the Creatures* is more than an elaborate, poetic display of the brilliance of its author and his mystical vision of the world. Rather, the *Canticle* is a summons to all of life, all humanity, and all of creation to recognize our most authentic identity as beloved creatures of the Most High God. This awareness gives birth to the responsibility we bear towards one another and towards the created universe. Just as we have been loved and cared for by the Creator God, so too are we to do the same towards all created beings. The *Canticle of the Creatures*, much like what Pope Francis articulates in his encyclical *Laudato Si'*, is a wake-up call to all of us to

47. See Armstrong et al., *Francis of Assisi*, 187–88.

48. Boersema, "Why is Francis of Assisi the Patron Saint of Ecologists?" 53.

49. Delio et al., "Creation Care."

assume our common responsibility to reverence and care for one another and for the created universe. This, according to Pope Francis, could help set the parameters for charting a very different course for the future of the planet and our life on it. In order for this to happen, for us to develop ethically directed models for sustainability, we must assume responsibility for the current plight of humanity and the planet and implement change at all levels, beginning within our individual lives.[50]

To Buenos Aires:
Pope Francis and the Search for a New Ethical Synthesis

The encyclical *Laudato Si'* of Pope Francis was one of the most anticipated documents inside and outside of church circles in modern history.[51] In its opening paragraph, Pope Francis makes clear his desire to connect the social teaching of the church on the environment to the integral vision of the inherent dignity and interconnectedness of human life and the created universe exemplified in the life and writings of St. Francis of Assisi. "St. Francis," writes the pope, "reminds us that our common home is like a sister with whom we share our life and a beautiful mother who opens her arms to embrace us."[52] Because our sister or our mother earth is under attack, and faces the risk of being exploited beyond her capacity to respond or recover from the assault, the pope seeks to create an open dialogue with the entire human community.

This dialogue is not simply to generate a new discourse on the environment, although this is clearly one of Pope Francis's intentions. Rather, he is concerned with raising awareness and generating a new energy among political leaders, religious leaders, scientists, university professors and students, and ordinary citizens of the global human community in order to avoid a potential "ecological catastrophe under the effective explosion of industrial civilization," stressing the "urgent need for a radical change in the conduct of humanity"[53] towards both the social and the natural environments. Dialogue is thus framed in the context of an imminent danger to the

50. See Francis, *Laudato Si'*, 148–49.

51. A very special thanks to Bro. Joseph Rozansky, OFM, and Walter Grazer for their invaluable insights and assistance on the following section, revised (ollowing the May 2015 release of the encyclical *Laudato Si'*) from what I originally presented at the April 2015 "Fragile World" conference at DePaul University in Chicago.

52. Francis, *Laudato Si'*, 1. See also Latin American Bishops' Conference (CELAM), "Concluding Document: Aparecida," 125.

53. Francis, *Laudato Si'*, 4.

human community and the natural environment for which human beings must assume their share of responsibility. Dialogue seeks to deepen awareness and provoke a reaction that is simultaneously ethical and technical, leading to a change of perspective and to a radical change in the manner by which human beings interact with one another and with the environment. Dialogue is also about providing a voice to those who are poor, and especially the poorer nations who most often are deprived of their voice and relegated to the margins. They are the ones who suffer the most from the consequences of unbridled exploitation, and from the destruction of ecosystems and global warming. Pope Francis insists that we must no longer speak of the interests of the human community in isolation and independence from the interests of the environment. "Everything is connected . . . genuine care for our own lives and our relationships with nature is inseparable from fraternity, justice, and faithfulness to others (the human community)."[54]

Buenos Aires, Welcome to Assisi: *Laudato Si'* and Integral Ecology

The subtitle of the encyclical makes clear Pope Francis's underlying concern: On Care for our Common Home. Our sister, Mother Earth, is crying out because of the harm done to her due to our lack of responsibility and abusive methods of exploitation, and a lack of personal awareness of the costs for maintaining an unsustainable lifestyle. It is here where the pope seeks to establish a clear link between social justice and care for the environment, between the poor and the fragility of the planet. This link echoes the central message of the original version of *The Canticle of the Creatures* composed by St. Francis of Assisi. Buenos Aires, welcome to Assisi!

Brief Overview of Central Themes of *Laudato Si'*

One of the characteristics of the encyclical is its emphasis on reading the signs of the times.[55] "We need only take a frank look at the facts to see that our common home is falling into serious disrepair,"[56] writes the pope. He

54. Ibid., 70, 139.

55. This same approach is present in the Aparecida document of the Latin American Bishops' Conferences (CELAM), where the bishops reflected on the crushing political, economic, cultural, and other conditions and the impact of these on the quality of life for the people of Latin America. See Latin American Bishops' Conference (CELAM). "Concluding Document: Aparecida."

56. Francis, *Laudato Si'*, 61.

then goes on to name six major areas requiring careful analysis. These include (1) pollution and climate change;[57] (2) overexploitation and access to fresh water resources;[58] (3) threats to a loss of biodiversity;[59] (4) decline in the quality of human life and a breakdown of societies;[60] (5) increasing global inequality;[61] and (6) a weak response and lack of political will to address our urgent environmental problems.[62] These "conditions" have placed both the human community and the natural environment at grave risk.

At the heart of Pope Francis's argument in the encyclical is the theological and scientific premise that all of us living creatures are dependent on one another. Whatever happens to one living thing has a direct impact on all other living things. The pope, quoting a text from his Apostolic Exhortation *Evangelii Gaudium,* writes that "God has joined us so closely to the world around us that we can feel the desertification of the soil almost as a physical ailment, and the extinction of a species as a painful disfigurement."[63] One of the clearest examples of where the disfigurement of creation is taking place is, according to the pope, in the world's urbanized centers where there is, on the one hand, a simultaneous and exponential destruction of conditions for normal, healthy social life, and on the other hand, overuse and abuse of water sources, excessive and wasteful use of fossil fuels, release of pollutants and toxic emissions, and a lack of "green spaces," all contributing to both a social and an environmental malaise.[64]

According to Pope Francis, the current paradigm of infinite progress,[65] which governs political, economic, technological, and social programs and decisions related to exploitation of the world's peoples and resources, has let those who control the mechanisms of this paradigm conceive of themselves as demigods. This in turn has provided justification for perverting what God envisioned from the very beginning of creation as the type of relationships that should exist between the Creator and all of God's creatures. "Human life is grounded in three fundamental and closely intertwined relationships: with God, with our neighbour, and with the earth itself," writes the pope.[66]

57. Ibid., 23–25.
58. Ibid., 27–31.
59. Ibid., 32–42.
60. Ibid., 43–47.
61. Ibid., 48–52.
62. Ibid., 53–60.
63. Ibid., 89; See also Francis, *Evangelii Gaudium*, 215.
64. Francis, *Laudato Si'*, 44–46.
65. Ibid., 106.
66. Ibid., 66; see also 67.

When this fundamental moral vision of relationships is not respected, human beings grant themselves permission to exploit one another and the natural environment without any consideration for the impact this has on the dignity of people and of creation.

These often unregulated and unbridled assaults on human dignity and the dignity of the planet and the planet's capacity to sustain this onslaught, lead to deep social inequalities. The poor become poorer and increasingly disenfranchised. Inequality also leads to a gradual "dumbing down" of our ability to appreciate and critically analyze the consequences of the current models of development on human societies and the environment. Disenfranchisement also takes the form of political exclusion. The richer nations together with multinational corporations set the conditions for any and all rules aimed at redressing the situation of abusive exploitation, disproportionate responsibility for greenhouse gasses, destruction of biodiversity, and other human created threats to the environment. In many instances these rules or strategies—including proposals to internationalize environmental costs, the carbon exchange credit system, and other such proposals for the reduction of greenhouse emissions—do very little to reduce the impact. Such rules and agreements work to the disfavor of poorer nations who are least responsible for the current global ecological disaster.[67]

Moving from a more scientific, technological, and sociological analysis of the current plight of human communities, Pope Francis develops his theological vision for an integral ecological approach to the cry of the poor and the planet. Drawing upon more than a century of Catholic social teaching, Pope Francis reminds us that human beings are part of God's plan for creation and are meant to live in loving relationship with God, with each other, and with the natural world.[68] One of the greatest failures of humanity is that of pretending to take the place of God and dis-ordering the nature of the trifold relationship that exists between God, humanity, and creation. While the pope makes explicit use of the biblical term for "dominion" found in Genesis 1:28, he goes on to argue that this word is a call not to exercise uncontrolled exploitation over all created things, using and discarding at will. Rather, we are called to assume very serious responsibility for the respect and care of the created universe. Our vocation is one of responsible stewardship.[69] As stewards, we are called to recognize the interconnectedness of everything. All things that exist function in a network of mutually supporting relationships, each bearing its own particular vocation, each

67. Ibid., 170–71.
68. Ibid., 65.
69. Ibid., 67–69.

meriting respect and honor, each making its particular contribution in a way that does not threaten the existence or vocation of the other.[70] Quoting from the Catholic Bishops' Conference of Japan, Pope Francis reminds us "[t]o sense each creature singing the hymn of its existence is to live joyfully in God's love and hope."[71] In this way, we are called to celebrate and honor the Creator. "Praise be you, my Lord, with all your creatures,"[72] who invites us to participate in the universal "fraternity" of all that God has created. For Pope Francis, as is the case for St. Francis of Assisi, there is no separation between "human" and "natural" ecologies. All are one and must be approached in a unified, consistent, and holistic manner. But in order to arrive at this awareness, we must educate ourselves, entering into a conversion of mind and heart, one that implies a renewal of our humanity. "There can be no ecology," writes Pope Francis, "without an adequate anthropology."[73]

Pope Francis is convinced that the renewal of an anthropological vision of humanity is vital to the development of an integral ecological approach. In chapter four of his encyclical, he calls attention to the intersection of various "ecologies" that must somehow be integrated into a unified, integral vision. These "ecologies" include the environment, economic and social activities, and experiences of daily life where we are called to express the values of the common good and demands for intergenerational justice, namely, our responsibility for caring for the environment for the sake of future generations of human beings. For this to be achieved, the pope acknowledged the need to develop and commit to a new, integral ecological vision and guiding principles that can respond to the complex crisis affecting the human community and the planet. "We are faced not with two separate crises, one environmental and the other social," writes the pope, "but rather with one complex crisis, which is both social and environmental. Strategies for a solution demand an integrated approach to combating poverty, restoring dignity to the excluded, and at the same time protecting nature."[74] Our response must not only provide technical solutions. They also must provide reasons for the birthing of a new hope for the future of humanity and our common home, the planet.

70. Ibid., 70 et passim.

71. Ibid., 85, quoted from Catholic Bishops' Conference of Japan, "Reverence for Life."

72. Ibid., 87.

73. Ibid., 118.

74. Ibid., 139.

Cultivating an Ecological Spirituality

In the final chapter of the encyclical, Pope Francis seeks to promote an eco-logical conversion by way of two interconnected methods capable of "awak-ening a new reverence for life, the firm resolve to achieve sustainability, the quickening of the struggle for justice and peace, and the joyful celebration of life."[75] The first of these methods involves a pedagogy that is capable of communicating accurate, scientifically-based information about the causes of the ecological disaster, including what the pope calls the "myths" of a modernity grounded in a utilitarian mindset (individualism, unlimited progress, competition, consumerism, the unregulated market)."[76] This ped-agogy must include an ethical reflection on the perils of the ecological crisis while creating opportunities for people to make what Pope Francis calls "the leap towards the transcendent, which gives ecological ethics its deepest meaning."[77] This transcendence is grounded in the event of the Incarnation, and more specifically, in the person of Jesus Christ who is the model *par excellence* of a unified, integrated ecological spirituality. St. Francis is pre-sented as a second model, expressing a "selfless ecological commitment"[78] capable of transforming the world. This ecological awareness will necessar-ily lead people to embrace a greater simplicity of life, thus opening them to a similar experience as that of St. Francis of Assisi. In this way, they might find themselves as fellow travelers on the road towards reconciliation, com-munion, and peace, preconditions for an authentic spirituality of integral ecology.[79]

Assisi, Buenos Aires, and Beyond: Essential Elements for Ethics-Based Sustainability

The poor and the planet are crying out, beseeching all of humanity to listen deeply, and to open itself to imaging a world where basic material needs are satisfied, where rights are respected, where the contribution of those who

---

75. Ibid., 207. Pope Francis once again reaches beyond the traditional methods employed in official church pronouncements, engaging the reader in a larger dialogue about establishing an ethical framework promoting a more just, sustainable, and peace-ful global community. For this reason, he recognizes the values proposed in the 2000 Earth Charter initiative, and their contribution to specific forms of education that en-gage individuals, families, local communities, and even the faith communities.

76. Ibid., 210.

77. Ibid.

78. Ibid., 211.

79. Ibid., 228.

are poor and marginalized is sought, and where the dignity and physical limits of the environment are safeguarded. St. Francis of Assisi listened to these cries and undertook a journey of faith and of humanity, which created within him an unlimited capacity to accept and welcome all as "brother" and "sister." This relational sense of hospitality and fraternity helped him to expand dramatically the double command of love of God and love of neighbor.

In a similar way, the historic encyclical of Pope Francis urges us to leave aside the notion that the world "as is" is the world "as it ought to be," and asks that everyone answer the challenge of restoring our common home. For this reason, he drops his "bombshell proposal," inviting the entire human community to substitute without delay alternative forms of energy for fossil fuel.[80] As with Francis of Assisi, so too with Francis of Buenos Aires: it is the discovery of the interrelated nature of all things, their connectedness, that enables—even requires—all people to assume full responsibility together for the fate of our common home.

I would like to offer a response to Pope Francis's invitation to participate in the dialogue about the plight and future of our common home. It takes the form of a proposal to further the "dialogue," one that argues for an ethics-based model of sustainability rooted in six rather humble principles. First, I believe there is a need to develop what might be called an "ethic of companionship," grounded in a relational anthropology, to replace an ethic of individualism and the pursuit of self-interest that betrays the common good. It entails developing what Pope Francis calls "a loving awareness that we are not disconnected from the rest of creatures, but joined in a splendid universal communion."[81] Second, there is need to expand our understanding of the "common good" to include the environment, as proposed by Pope Francis when speaking about the embrace of an "integral ecology." Third, the human community has need of a charter of fundamental rights that apply to the environment, which must be discussed and agreed upon by members of the world community. The climate agreement signed at COP 21 in Paris is a step forward in this direction.

Fourth, it will be important to develop a charter of "best practices" agreed upon by the major contributors to global climate change, the transnationals, multinationals, other non-state actors, working together with the states. While enforcement could prove extremely difficult, the charter would serve as a tool for advocacy, for "naming and shaming" those companies and governments that fail to incorporate best practices for promoting

80. Ibid., 165.
81. Ibid., 220.

integral human development and safeguards for our common home. Fifth, efforts must continue to be made to educate all citizens of the earth to become active partners in dialogue for the sake of the human community and the environment, to respond immediately and decisively to the urgent plight of the poor and the planet. All educational institutions, beginning with the first years of primary school and continuing at all levels of instruction and research, should initiate programs of specialized study of the plight of the poor and the planet and engage administrators, professors/teachers, students, and their families in the pursuit of a vision promoting care for our common home and that leads to concrete action. And sixth, those who profess to be believers in God must commit to the development of a spirit of contemplative action, grounding concrete action in meditation and discernment so that "we [might] feel [more deeply] the working of God's grace within our hearts, and . . . in creatures outside ourselves,"[82] and make our necessary contributions for care of one another and for the environment. Joint study and action by members of the different religious traditions could help bring believers closer together, overcome prejudices, and create new avenues for respect and dialogue, thus making a contribution to world peace and stability. In these ways, we might move away from what we want to what God's world truly needs.[83]

A Return to Assisi

The city and hill areas of Assisi continue to beckon pilgrims from around the world who come in search of peace, of meaning, of forgiveness, and of hope. It is here where St. Francis received his call to bind his future to the fate of the poor and of the planet. The insights he continues to offer to the world derive from the experience of being a mystic, one who caught hold of God's vision of a harmonious universe wherein all work together for the good of all. Both St. Francis and Pope Francis invite us to open our eyes and our hearts—individually and collectively—and perceive the spiritual community to which all living things belong and in which they participate. There are no "we" and "they," "inside and outside." All is connected. All are one, sharing in the same originating dignity and grace of the creator God. Thus we, like St. Francis of Assisi, might recover a spiritual vision of the world, one capable of creating within us a longing for the mystical, which recognizes and celebrates beauty and dignity within each and every creature. It is this mystical awareness that will allow us to humbly journey

82. See Francis, *Laudato Si'*, 233, quoted from St. Bonaventure, *II Sententiae*.
83. Francis, *Laudato Si'*, 9.

along the sands of time, walking in partnership with our fellow human beings—brothers and sisters—and with all of creation, building together the
necessary conditions for the safeguarding of our common home.

PART TWO

Cry of the Earth

5

Extractive Industries, Destructive Industries: The Case of Honduras—A Fragile Country and Devastated Ecology

BISHOP LUIS ALFONSO SANTOS VILLEDA

Augustine of Hippo wrote that, in every cognitive act, the Holy Spirit is present. You are dedicated to knowledge. You are fortunate to have the Holy Spirit as a companion in everything you come to know. Before coming to this conference, I asked the Holy Spirit for his light so that you might enjoy the presence of the Spirit in everything that I am going to say and you are going to hear. May it all be for God's greater glory and for your own benefit, and so that Honduras may maintain a friendly relationship with the environment. Let us ask God that the strength of the Holy Spirit may triumph over the ambition of those who, destroying the earth, also destroy humanity.

I come from Honduras, a country that still is 67 percent agricultural. I was born in a farming area, a mountainous region with a pleasant climate and ecological niches of extraordinary natural beauty like the Guisayote Biological Reserve, the Celaque Mountains, and Santa Barbara National Park. Some of these mountains reach six thousand feet in height, with fresh water springs and abundant vegetation. The people who live there have, for centuries, cultivated the earth, raised cattle, and maintained an ecological balance. In these mountains, at the required altitude, they cultivate coffee which has won international awards for its quality. I love the area where I was born, and I love Honduras because it is my homeland. Honduras is a small country with a surface area of 112,600 square kilometers (approximately seventy thousand square miles), but it is a land full of natural riches and great beauty. Honduras's coast, on the Atlantic, has beautiful beaches that make tourism attractive. And near the island of Roatán, in Honduras's Bay Islands, lies the second largest coral reef in the world. Among other tourist attractions, there are classical temples that recall the Spanish colonization and vestiges of ancient, extinct cultures such as the recent discovery in Mosquitia, and the world-famous Ruins of Copán, declared a World Heritage Site by UNESCO.

However, all the beauty described above is being threatened by the extractive industry: metal mining and hydrocarbons. One hundred and twenty-two years ago, a U.S. mining company, then called the New York and Honduras Rosario Mining Co., started exploiting minerals. It began in the town of San Juancito, in the department of Francisco Morazán, where it left three hundred kilometers of tunnels (approximately 186 miles), and since 1949, it has been extracting ore in the village of Mochito, in Las Vegas of the department of Santa Bárbara. Recently, this company sold everything to an Australian mining company by the name of Nystar. They say in Honduras that these companies have so much money that they can decide which political party will win the elections. In the 1990s, Canadian mining companies arrived: first, the Greenstone mining company, followed by Minosa, Yamana Gold, and now, Aura Mineralis. Their mining operations are located in the villages of Platanares, San Miguel, San Andrés, and Azacualpa, in the municipality of Unión, Copán. They are using the extraction method of open-cut mining, and they use cyanide, which contaminates the ground, the air, and the water but gives them great profits because it separates 97 percent of the gold particles. All of these companies are protected under the Central American Free Trade Agreement (between Central and North America) called CAFTA. Under this treaty, they feel that they have the right to destroy the environment in our country. They systematically use corruption to influence the communications media and finance soccer teams, and they have taken ownership of the Honduran government in its three branches: executive, legislative, and judicial.

In 1998, they wrangled the elected representatives in the National Congress into abolishing the previous mining code, enacting a new decree that increased the mining companies' profits at the expense of Honduran profits. In 2013, a new law which is in force today was promulgated, completely favoring foreign miners while providing the State of Honduras a mere 0.21 percent profit per $0.01 USD, in addition to the $0.25 USD/hectare territorial tax (*canon territorial*) paid annually by mining companies for a new "concession," or legal land title. As you can see, the mining companies make off with most of the wealth. Moreover, half of that 0.21 percent is allocated to the Honduran Department of Security—in other words, to the National Civil Police and Military Police. According to confidential reports, they have budgeted billions of *lempiras*[1] for the security of companies that come to invest in Honduras but not for the security of the people. Between 2010 and 2013, the government approved twelve laws to hand over seashores, forests, mountains, and water and biodiversity resources to foreign companies, and to guarantee the impunity of enterprises that were violating environmental and human rights. With the full support of a Honduran government completely dominated by foreign companies, the arrogance of such companies has grown. They subdue people by means of the armed forces, destroying churches and entire villages, even removing the dead from cemeteries in order to obtain the gold found in those areas. These companies bribe municipal boards with donations of money, vehicles, expensive trips, and overpriced goods.

Besides this corruption, we must speak about the pollution that mining companies produce. In 2006, there was a spill of 29 million gallons of water tainted with cyanide in the San Andrés Mine in Unión, Copán. This spill reached the rivers, killing aquatic species, poisoning the beef cattle that drank the water, and even killing the birds of prey that ate the dead cattle. All this has been duly documented. An Italian biologist, using his own laboratory equipment, detected heavy metals in the water of the Lara River, a tributary of the Higuito River; the city of Santa Rosa de Copán, with a population of about fifty thousand, takes its drinking water from this river. And now we know, through unofficial information, that acid water from the San Andrés Mine in Unión, Copán, has been spilling into the environment for five years.

We formally denounced all of the above in due time and form, because we had legal and medical illustrations of the mines' pollution damage. Because of these complaints, we were brutally repressed by the National Preventive Police, which at the time was receiving fuel from the mines for its patrols. In one particular incident, lay people and priests were beaten, among them Father Reginaldo García Vásquez, the diocese's vicar general. That day, the repression was directed from a helicopter by an army officer who was a former member of Honduras's notorious Battalion 316, a special forces unit of military repression responsible for the assassination or disappearance of 184 people.

In these last fourteen years, the greediness of mining companies has increased; they are attracted by the price of gold on the international market and its cheap purchase price in Honduras, plus the cheap price of corrupting authorities at all levels, considering that Honduras is the most corrupt

---

1. The *lempira* is the Honduran currency; in November 2016, one *lempira* equals $0.043 USD. XE Currency Converter, "HNL to USD."

country in Central America and the second most corrupt in Latin America. With what I mentioned before, we can prove the truth of the saying that mining in a poor country only serves to produce enormous profits for the exploiting companies, cause environmental pollution, increase corruption, and ignite social upheaval.

For more information on the topic of this conference regarding extractive industries and intercultural theology, I would like to include some conclusions of the Latin American Bishops' Conference in which, as bishop, I represented Honduras at a meeting held June 14–16, 2011, in Lima. This meeting was titled "Extractive Industries (Mining and Hydrocarbons): The Problem of Nonrenewable Natural Resources in Latin America and the Mission of the Church."[2]

(A) According to the Christian faith, our Earth is the creation of God. Therefore, we must treat it with respect. Human beings, created in the image of God (Gen 1:26), are called to be responsible stewards of the goods of creation. We do not have the right to exploit the earth's resources, "irrationally demolish[ing] sources of life."[3] God created life in great diversity (Gen 1:11-12, 20), and our Latin American continent has one of the greatest varieties of flora and fauna in all the world.[4] This is the gratuitous and fragile heritage "that we receive to protect."[5]

(B) A substantial basis for the care of the goods of creation is the Creator's alliance with all living beings (Gen 9:17). The social doctrine of the church emphasizes that "[a] correct understanding of the environment prevents the utilitarian reduction of nature to a mere object to be manipulated and exploited."[6] Rather, the intervention of the human being in nature should be governed by respect for other persons and their rights as well as respect toward other living creatures.[7] This also implies the responsibility to leave a habitable planet for future generations to inherit.

(C) We reaffirm the necessity of preserving planet Earth as the "common home" of all living beings. Saint John Paul II warned us of the risks

2. Latin American Bishops' Conference, "Documento Conclusivo: Industrias Extractivas (Minería e Hidrocarburos)."

3. Latin American Bishops' Conference, "Concluding Document: Aparecida," paragraph 471.

4. Ibid., paragraph 84.

5. Ibid., paragraph 471.

6. Pontifical Council for Justice and Peace, Compendium, 463.

7. Ibid., 459–60, 464.

associated with considering the planet as only a source of economic revenue: "the environment as 'resource' risks threatening the environment as 'home.'"[8] For this reason, it is necessary to evaluate the long-term environmental cost of extractive activities, along with licit activities like ranching, agriculture, and aquaculture or illicit enterprises like coca and poppy cultivation for drug trafficking.

(D) Jesus announced, in words and deeds, that God is the God of Life. Fidelity to the gospel requires us to contemplate life in all of creation as a gift of God. This comprehensive and interdependent dimension of all that is created obliges human responsibility.

(E) There exists a close link between following Jesus and the mission of the church. The mission must be at the service of the life of the Latin American people. This is particularly highlighted by the bishops in the concluding document of Aparecida: "the mission of evangelization cannot proceed separated from solidarity with the poor and the promotion of their comprehensive development."[9] Thus, "the living conditions of many of those who are abandoned, excluded, and ignored in their poverty and pain stand in contradiction to this project of the Father and challenge believers to greater commitment to the culture of life. The Kingdom of Life that Christ came to bring is incompatible with such inhuman situations. If we try to close our eyes to these realities we are not advocates of the life of the Kingdom and we place ourselves on the path of death."[10]

(F) Living according to the Spirit of Jesus calls us to reaffirm the option for the poor, the favored recipients of the Kingdom and the first victims of the negative effects of the current socioeconomic model and natural disasters generated as a consequence of global climate change.

(G) In our search for an integral development born of solidarity, we are inspired and assisted by the spiritual experience of indigenous and Afro-descendant peoples who, since ancient times, have felt themselves to be part of "Mother Earth" and relate with the planet as the "womb of life." In the native cultures, there is a spirit that discovers the wisdom and power of God in creation. This motivates them to search for *buen vivir*.[11] Recognizing this reality, all of the world's nations that were

---

8. Ibid., 461.

9. Latin American Bishops' Conference, "Concluding Document," paragraph 545.

10. Ibid., paragraph 358.

11. Translator's Note: Loosely translated as "living well," *buen vivir* is a much more complex and all-encompassing concept. As stated in Hicks, "Buen Vivir": "[It]

convened in the UN General Assembly in April 2009 unanimously approved a resolution to designate April 22 as International Mother Earth Day.[12]

(H) With respect to the activities of extractive industries and the use of nonrenewable natural resources, it is necessary to bear in mind the principle of the universal destination of the goods of creation, especially of vitally important resources like water, air, and land. This is the fundamental principle of all ethical-social order.[13]

Faced with the destruction of the environment due to the pollution caused by the mining companies, I can only launch an appeal to the world for help, in defense of the poor indigenous peoples who are forced to abandon even the bones of their dead to the hands of the mining companies.

---

has existed as a worldview for millennia and, at its core, is about communities living sustainably with mother nature. . . . Maria Estela Barco Huerta of DESMI [Social and Economic Development for Indigenous Mexicans] . . . eloquently described *buen vivir* as being based on a concept of deep, great respect, or *Ich'el Ta Muk* in the Mayan language, that each person has for the spirit, or *Ch'ulel*, of every other living being, which includes humans, animals, nature, and the spiritual realm. . . . Professor Mauricio Phélan of the Central University of Venezuela . . . explained three distinct harmonies which exist within communities practicing *buen vivir*: (1) Harmony within yourself: physical, mental, and spiritual components; (2) Harmony between communities: between yourself and your family, your community, your neighbors, your colleagues, institutions, and markets; (3) Harmony with nature: mutual balance between human activities and environmental health. When harmony with and amongst individuals, communities, and the natural world are achieved, then *buen vivir* is achieved."

12. United Nations General Assembly, "General Assembly Proclaims 22 April 'International Mother Earth Day.'" See also Pontifical Council for Justice and Peace, *Compendium,* paragraph 461, and John Paul II, "Address to Conference on Environment and Health."

13. Pontifical Council for Justice and Peace, *Compendium,* paragraph 172.

6

The Pan Amazon, Extractive Industries, and the Church

PETER HUGHES, SSC

Introduction

On Pope Francis's first visit to Latin America in July 2013, in his address to the Brazilian bishops, he challenged the church to give priority to the defense of the Amazon. He underlined dramatically the rate of destruction of the rain forest and its precarious state, declaring that over 20 percent has now been irrevocably lost because of increasing investment in the extraction and exportation of its natural resources. The planet's climate as well as the indigenous peoples, their territories, and their culture are the big losers in the wake of the increasing onslaught of corporative extractive industries in this region.

The consequences and implications due to the gravity of the situation mean there is a major impact not only on the life of the region, but also on the planet, especially in relation to the world's climate. The destruction is taking place at an accelerated pace, and it is incumbent on us all to seriously assume our collective responsibility to effectively halt the process. The plight of the inhabitants of the region—the original indigenous inhabitants—is particularly frightening. They are now being forcibly obliged to flee from their lands, their original habitat where they have lived and developed their cultures over thousands of years. These people practically have little or no defense in the face of the gigantic onrush of the earthmoving equipment of the corporate extractive industries' operations. These operations increasingly exploit the rich natural resources of the region with total disregard for the health of people and the preservation of the rain forest and the biosphere. As we become more aware of climate change, both the Amazon and Congo basins take on more importance because of their direct impact on the planet's climate. For example, of every five glasses of water a person drinks and every five breaths that person takes, one of each is provided by the Amazon basin. Its destruction will mean much less water and oxygen, the basic requirements for life; it will literally take our breath away.

For many years, there have been a myriad of initiatives and serious efforts implemented to protect the rainforest. Measures have been taken on the local and national levels, as well as the international level through the operation of networks dedicated to the specific needs of the rich and unique flora and fauna. Obviously, these efforts are both praiseworthy and valuable and, in some cases, have achieved notable success. However, taken as a whole, they do not amount to an overall solution to the gravity of the problem. In real terms, we need a more thorough examination and a cultural mind change—a change of heart—that addresses the pulse of our very civilization, particularly the dominant economic component, if we are to implement more significant and effective change. The present state of play points to the fact that we are losing the battle. The major institutions and resources—academia, mass media, environmental movements and above all, political decision makers—will have to work together to have a much more collective and powerful influence.

It may be helpful if we take stock of the current attitudes that unconsciously affect general public opinion in relation to the task of saving the Pan Amazon. Most will say that the situation is grave and even tragic, but immediately we succumb to a general sense of helplessness in which we are forced, against our best wishes, to admit that nothing really effective can be done about it. We are faced with something that has an air of permanence, an ongoing reality, in which nothing really changes for the better. Our perception is invaded by an overall stalemate in which we realize that the critical situation of the Pan Amazon both questions and calls out to us for help, and we in turn are forced to accept an unwelcome recognition of our inadequacy. At the same time, our attention is absorbed by other major issues: faltering economies, increasing global insecurity, armed conflicts, the advance of ISIS, and massive migration dominate the airwaves and establish the agenda which seems to be never-ending, leading to fatigue of compassion. Powerlessness rules the day.

The New Moment

Recent events on different fronts have also opened new horizons where we can affirm the emergence of important developments which appear to create the beginnings of a new agenda. Now, climate change is universally recognized and accepted. The science debate has ruled in favor of the International Panel of Climate Change reports' findings. The empirical evidence is having an increasing impact as witnessed by record levels of flooding, droughts, irregular and more destructive cyclonic activity, all of which leave in their wake swaths of irreparable damage, of human tragedy and destruction as well as major loss of livelihood. It is now clear that climate change and global warming are the result of humankind's own doing and can only be halted and subsequently reversed by humankind's concerted efforts.

The UN COP 21 summit on climate change held in Paris in November 2015 was a milestone for the political process which eventually achieved major agreements on decisions to be implemented by the nations regarding reducing toxic emissions in the atmosphere to avoid global warming exceeding more than 4 degrees Celsius by the end of this century. A more equitable costs-sharing mechanism, as well as the agreed timeframes and evaluation methods, are grounds for hope that this moment can also be a new beginning for more urgent shared responsibility to protect life on the planet from increased global warming.

Pope Francis, on choosing the name of Francis of Assisi, made his priorities clear: to care for both the poor and the earth, our common home. After his election, on his first trip abroad to Brazil in July 2013, he focused in his address to the Brazilian bishops particularly on the church's need to assume a new role in caring for the Pan Amazon region. He stressed the urgency for a new beginning, a clear focus on shared objectives, using a forceful colloquial Argentinian expression: we must be *corajudos,* courageous, even bold. He promised that the church would play its part with renewed presence and commitment in the task that will be demanding and arduous. Francis's commitment to save the Pan Amazon from further destruction is a commitment to caring for life in an integral sense, life that is God's gift expressed in the wonder of creation, the beauty of the regions with its myriad treasures of species, all under threat. The pope believes that the church's commitment in this region strikes at the heart of the gospel message to give witness and protect life, especially where it is most endangered. Francis lays down the gauntlet by stating this will be the challenge for the church in Latin America, the test (*proba*) we have to face. This theme was further made explicit by Cardinal Claudio Hummes on the occasion of the foundation of the Red Eclesial Panamazónica—REPAM, or in English, the

Pan Amazon Church Network—in September 2014: "the Church here must have an Amazonic face . . . a mission to become incarnate, inculturated in the indigenous population here, in this particular reality of creation."[1]

The call to action by Francis follows on the concerns expressed by the Latin American Bishops' Conference (CELAM) in Aparecida in 2007. The bishops denounced the proposals to make the region a special zone to be entrusted to the highest bidders and placed under a joint international administration.

> The growing assault on the environment may serve as a pretext for proposals to internationalize the Amazon, which only serve the economic interests of transnational corporations. Pan-Amazon society is multiethnic, multicultural, and multireligious. The dispute over the occupation of the land is intensifying more and more.[2]

In his recent encyclical on the environment, *Laudato Si'*, Francis underlines what the bishops stated, specifically drawing attention to the protection of

> those richly biodiverse lungs of our planet which are the Amazon and the Congo basins, or the great aquifers and glaciers. We know how important these are for the entire earth and for the future of humanity . . . for we cannot overlook the huge global economic interests which, under the guise of protecting them, can undermine the sovereignty of individual nations.[3]

The bishops declare it necessary to save the Pan Amazon, promoting awareness about its importance for all humanity and establishing joint pastoral action in the countries that share the Amazon basin to create a development model that prioritizes the poor and the common good.[4]

It is important to point out that Francis challenges the international community in his encyclical. His address is directed to the great human family, not just to Christians and the church. The reason is obviously the urgent universal need to care for and protect the earth and human existence whose survival is threatened by the ecological crisis. The encyclical is also the result of scientific review, research, dialogue, and discussion with notable representatives of the scientific community, the Academy, and the ecological movements that have engaged in interdisciplinary investigation on

1. Pan Amazon Church Network (REPAM), *Memoria*, 107.
2. Latin American Bishops' Conference, "Concluding Document," para. 86.
3. Francis, *Laudato Si'*, 38.
4. Latin American Bishops' Conference, "Concluding Document," para. 475.

these particularly complex transcendental issues. Pope Francis's approach is from the faith perspective and the experience of pastoral theology from the field. He assumes the responsibility with evangelical freedom and offers his insights and opinion as a service for peace building in the defense of God´s great gift of life.

The Pan Amazon Basin: Era of Change

The Pan Amazon territory is home to the world´s largest rain forest, one of the richest geological and most complex biospheres on the planet. It contains one third of the world´s biodiversity and genetic stock. Geographically, the territory extends in varied measure over nine South American countries, including the three smaller Guyanas which claim 0.1 percent of the region. Brazil occupies 67 percent, Peru 13 percent, Bolivia 11 percent, Colombia 6 percent, Ecuador 2 percent, and Venezuela 1 percent. The use of the term "Pan Amazon region" is a more accurate form to express the communal sharing by these nation states that covers a vast area: 7.8 million square kilometers, the heart of the South American subcontinent. It contains 34 percent of the planet's virgin rain forests necessary to maintain the cycle balance of carbon and 20 percent of the planet´s oxygen and fresh water. The region stores 110,000 million tons of carbon dioxide (CO_2), 50 percent of the CO_2 of the planet's tropical forests. The Amazon River itself is nearly 7,000 kilometers long, the world´s largest navigable river.

The Pan Amazon is home to great human diversity: 2,779,478 indigenous people from 390 ethnic groups, 137 of which are still isolated. There are 240 spoken languages belonging to forty-nine linguistic families; among the better known are Aruak, Karib, and Tupi-Guarani. In recent decades, the area has witnessed the massive arrival of migrants and colonists from other Brazilian regions as well as neighboring Andean countries and the Caribbean. Manaus and Belém, in Brazil, are now major cities while Iquitos (Peru) and other fast-growing urban centers are expanding. The population of these new urbanizations is calculated at close to thirty million.

Human habitation is largely confined to the river banks. From time immemorial, transport, communication, and travel have been conducted on the great rivers like the Amazon, Madeira, Putumayo, and Tapajós, and the myriad of lesser fluvial connections. The changing face of the region has also witnessed the construction of major transoceanic highways that open and connect the interior for transportation of raw materials for export from the Pacific ports. What was once an immense, unknown, and unexplored world has now become a focus of mega capital investment drawn to the exploitation of the vast resources of raw materials, minerals and metals, oil and timber. Mega hydroelectric projects appear overnight to fuel Brazil's burgeoning economy. Rivers are harnessed to build giant dams to the detriment of lands and the destruction of the delicate balance of the ecosystems. Indigenous peoples are forced to flee from the land that has been their life for millennia and is now claimed for agribusiness and monocrop cultivation, where high yields and monetary return are the imperatives that obliterate all other considerations.

Amidst the vast rain forests and rivers, the cacophony of the jungle's wildlife sounds has diminished and the majestic flora's wonderful blaze of color is beginning to vanish as the wheels of so-called development and progress grind relentlessly towards the lure of high dividends, where stock markets are king. In this context, the region and its peoples can be described as a global frontier, the guardians of one of the ecosystems that is important for the well-being of the planet. Access and control of its resources have become a strategic geopolitical and economic priority. The mosaic of millennial culture that binds the ancestral inhabitants to the environment, interwoven in a tapestry of respect and balance, and rooted in a profound sense of the sacred, is rapidly becoming lost. The poorest and most vulnerable, their dignity and rights trampled upon, are caught in the crossfire of an economic power struggle. Big business is exterminating the Pan Amazon and its peoples to fuel the voracious consumer appetite created by and dependent on the dominant liberal economic model of development. The Pan Amazon that once was a backwater has now become a major plaza of the new El Dorado.

Development or Destruction?

The price of commodities has become the currency of international trade. The emergent Asian markets of China and India, as well as Korea and Taiwan, are major importers of raw materials, especially minerals and precious metals, the material base for the production of the artifacts of information technology. While prices reached a high in 2012, production levels of extractive operations have not decreased in Latin America. What has increased is the amount of socio-environmental conflict due to increased labor restrictions and further deteriorating working conditions.

The development model of using natural resources as raw materials for export is accepted and unquestioned in the economic policies implemented by Latin American states.[5] Slight corrections have been introduced

5. For a good example of a more extensive treatment of the debate about the

by Evo Morales's government in Bolivia, which succeeded in renegotiating oil contracts with the big corporations more in favor of the state. The current sad situation of Venezuela, with its vast oil reserves, is a classic example of how an economy based on commodity exports is not a good recipe for authentic national development, strengthening democracy, or nation-building. It evokes the withering verdict of Felipe Huamán Poma de Ayala, the first indigenous writer of the colonial period, who named mines and mining *el estiércol del diablo*: the devil's excrement!

The current practice of implementing concession agreements between nation-states and corporative extractive groups guarantees exploration and extraction rights in large areas and is accepted as the way forward to national economic development. In this context, it is enlightening and frightening to review the current map of the Pan Amazon and witness how most of the region is now colored in concessions to foreign extractive interests.[6] The practice of granting concession rights has been exacerbated by the forceful implementation of free trade agreements championed by the U.S. This policy, a product of the Washington Consensus, continues to be controversial.

The above-mentioned trade agreements are imposed on the previous traditional rights of indigenous peoples to their lands. This is more striking when taking into account the indigenous cosmic vision: land is viewed as sacred, a gift to be respected, cultivated, and protected. As such, it cannot be reduced solely to an object of possession and ownership. Humans and land are integrated in a harmonic relationship of mutual dependency and respect. The non-recognition of this culture is more serious when it is taken into account that most states have recently legislated in favor of indigenous rights to their land, sanctioned by UN charter and accepted by international trade agreements. The pathetic juridical construct from colonial times—giving the original landowner rights only to the surface soil and simultaneously granting the newcomer rights of use below the ground—is often invoked to the detriment and exclusion of the indigenous.

A major issue of contention is the reticence and often the refusal by governments to implement the right of previous consultation with local and indigenous groups prior to their making concession contracts for exploration and subsequent exploitation. This universal right is sanctioned by No. 069 of the International Trade Organization and is often the cause of

---

region's economic development from the perspective of the current economic model favoring extraction and exportation of natural resources, see the *El Comercio* articles written by Alan García during his presidency: "El Síndrome del Perro del Hortelano"; "El Perro del Hortelano contra el Pobre'" and "Receta para Acabar con el Perro del Hortelano."

6. Cf. Dourojeanni et al., *Amazonía Peruana en 2021.*

conflict between the parties. A most important issue is the damage done to the water supply in rivers and lakes and the poisoning of the soil. Mining is highly destructive of these basic needs of the local community; when lands are destroyed, crops cannot be cultivated, animals cannot survive, and people are forced to leave.

The conflict should not simply be couched in terms of winners and losers, between powerful economic interests and environmental and human degradation in the region. This would be both short-sighted and missing the point. *The core issue is that environmental destruction—the disconnection with nature—is the base of the economic construct, the link to production, marketing, and consumption that prioritizes profits over human needs.* This leads to injustice, violence, and a culture of waste where both the poor and the environment are the victims. The developed North is *the other jungle* economically linked, geographically separated. We are the Pan Amazon. The well-being of society becomes divorced from the well-being of the environment. In the Pan Amazon world, the challenge is how the territory can be reclaimed, rescued from its neocolonial degradation, and restored to its authentic healthy well-being. As the pithy question of Luis Ventura encapsulates, "How can the territory be rescued for the territory?"[7]

The earth is our common home, a shared inheritance, in the words of the Latin American bishops in Aparecida. We are obliged to continually rediscover and implement new forms of corresponding responsibility. One of our civilization's tragedies is the loss of a common sense of care for creation in favor of a relationship governed by conquest and domination. The challenge we now face is how to reverse this aggressiveness towards creation and replace it with a harmonious relationship with nature of which we ourselves are an intrinsic part. Francis reminds us what it means to till and keep the garden of the world.[8] "'Tilling' refers to cultivating, ploughing, or working, while 'keeping' means caring, protecting, overseeing, and preserving. This implies a mutual responsibility between human beings and nature."[9] The inheritance of rights, a valued legacy of the Enlightenment, must be revisited and reexamined in the light of the destruction taking place in the Pan Amazon. Rights not only pertain to the individual; they must also become the truthful expression of self-understanding in an integrated and interdependent relationship with the environment—Francis of Assisi's concept of brotherhood and sisterhood with the natural world.

---

7. Ventura, "El Clamor de los Pueblos y la Tierra Amazónica."
8. Cf. Gen 2:15.
9. Francis, *Laudato Si'*, 67.

The Pan Amazon territory is a special scenario where destruction and degradation caused by extractive corporations' mega capital investment is a visible consequence of the techno-economic paradigm of development and the environment. The realistic possibilities for self-defense by the victims are weak. The Pan Amazon region and its inhabitants belong to the more marginalized sector of the different nation-states and, as a result, they neither have strong organizations to defend their rights nor the political strength in their governments' national institutions. The needs of indigenous peoples are, by and large, relegated by the state to ineffective rhetoric. Ethnic and labor organizations are fragile or nonexistent, while the reality of great distances and physical isolation also weaken effective leadership, decision-making, and action. Defense organizations are also severely handicapped by the legislation that now considers protest illegal. The criminalization of defense means that local leaders are not taken into account for dialogue or conciliation at the time of conflicts; they are more often imprisoned, denied their rights, and subjected to various forms of abuse.

At the present time, institutions such as the Catholic Church and the Inter-American Commission on Human Rights (ICHR) are being called upon to represent indigenous peoples and their rights in the face of the abuse perpetrated against them. An emblematic case in La Oroya, Peru, concerns the impact on the local population's health due to the negligent operation of an American-owned smelter plant for copper and iron ore. With the collaboration of a prestigious university's medical faculty, it became possible to monitor, over a five-year period, the health and blood counts of women and children who suffered high rates of cancer and whose blood samples showed high levels of toxins such as mercury, lead, and arsenic from the smelter. It became clear that the levels of illness became higher and more dangerous when the plant was in operation and lowered significantly during lengthy stoppages of operations due to labor disputes. In this case, the bishop of the local diocese of Huancayo, Msgr. Pedro Barreto, in representation of his people, took the case to the U.S. State Department and Congress. In June 2013, a congressional hearing during which victims gave their testimony based on medical evidence found the company negligent in complying with minimal health and safety regulations as well as international environmental standards. The company was subsequently forced to cease operations. As yet, no compensation has been paid to the victims.

On March 19, 2015, the Catholic bishops of Latin America were joined by their counterparts in Canada and the U.S. in a public audience of the Inter-American Commission on Human Rights to present a petition on the abuse of human rights in mining conflicts where local members of the church were direct witnesses. The petition, prepared and submitted by the bishops, gave testimony of cases of different forms of human rights abuses in mining conflicts in Mexico, Guatemala, Honduras, Brazil, Colombia, Ecuador, and Peru. These abuses included damage to the local population's health through pollution of air, water, and soil; negligence in health and safety standards, which resulted in the injury and death of miners; and imprisonment of leaders and abuse of their human rights because of the criminalization of protest. The hearing ended on a very positive note where the Commission was enabled to call to account the collusion of governments with international corporations in not defending the human rights of its citizens. In her opening address, the president, Marie Rose Antoine, noted that history was being made; it was the first occasion that representative bishops of the Americas together presented a joint petition to the Commission. At the end, the Commission expressed its desire that this would be the beginning of close cooperation between the church and the ICHR, natural partners in the common task of defending human rights.

Signs of Hope

The evidence is overpowering for the need of a new paradigm of sustainable development that will protect people's lives and care for the planet. The techno-economic development model is bankrupt, bereft of ideas that can offer hope for the needs and aspirations of the world today.[10] In the words of Pope Francis,

> The first task is to change the economy, place it at the service of the people. Human beings and nature should not be at the service of money. Let us say NO to an economy of exclusion and inequality where money rules instead of being a service. That type of economy kills. That economy excludes. That economy is destroying Mother Earth . . . let us say it aloud without fear: we demand change, real change, a change of structures. This system cannot last anymore; the peasants cannot put up with it, neither can the workers tolerate it, neither can neighborhoods and the different peoples of the world . . . the earth, our sister, the Mother Earth of Saint Francis, cannot survive in this system.[11]

In our effort to participate in the debate about a new approach towards joint responsibility in the Pan Amazon, it will be helpful to retake some of Pope Francis's perspectives in *Laudato Si'*. The pope adds his voice to the

10. Cf. Hardoon, "Wealth: Having It All and Wanting More."
11. Francis, "Address at Second World Meeting of Popular Movements."

plea made on numerous occasions for the urgent need to join together and replace the irrational culture of an economy whose sole focus is profit and consumerism with little regard for the real needs of people, thereby destroying the future possibility of life on the planet. Important milestones on the same journey were the 1992 UN climate summit in Río de Janeiro; the 2002 Kyoto agreement; the 2000 Earth Summit in The Hague; and the 2015 COP 21 in Paris.

Francis encourages us to think in terms of integral ecology. He speaks of the need to integrate different disciplines, interests, and spheres of action with a view towards contributing steps for protecting the life of the rain forest and its peoples. We must review together the conditions needed to protect the life and the survival of society which is now seriously threatened. Honesty and openness are called for, to question the dominant model of economic development where production feeds a questionable culture of consumer patterns. Francis continually returns to the same starting point with his insistence on the conviction that all things are connected; he says, "it cannot be emphasized enough how everything is interconnected."[12] We need to pause, reflect, dare to break our society's accepted codes, and enter the realm of wonder and the life of the spirit. To affirm again that everything is interconnected and interdependent is to reenter the deepest level of understanding, scientifically, how the natural world with all its beauty and marvel has evolved before time and from time immemorial. We are challenged to engage in reintroducing the sense of our spiritual selves with a genuine scientific conversation with, and about, the world we live in, are part of, and for which we are responsible.

Christians are invited to revisit our spiritual tradition that has developed through ages in different parts of the world. We become further enriched by listening to other cultures, traditions where we find such solid agreement on the same affirmation that all things are connected. Our human story is woven from a common starting point. The Lautoka people greet each other with the reminder that everybody is "my cousin." Celtic culture is infused with the conviction that survival is rooted in connectedness; people flourish when we share the same shadow. Buntu and Quechua have stubbornly insisted that the community, life shared together, is the real subject, prior to individual decision. The legacy of modernity can become enriched by another conversation with our ancestors, including the people of the Pan Amazon.

Francis reminds us that we are part of nature; we cannot survive apart or separated from the natural world. He says, "when we speak of the

12. Francis, *Laudato Si'*, 138.

'environment,' what we really mean is a relationship existing between nature and the society which lives in it."[13] We are reminded to listen to the natural world, appreciate its beauty, become aware of its wounds, and be sensitive to its pain. The world we have forgotten, relegated—the Pan Amazon—must be allowed to come forward and become an equal partner in the conversation. The economic dimension of our society is important; we hardly need to be reminded of the obvious. Our task is to review and renew, place it in the context of a more complex web of other strands present in our world with a view towards creating a more sensible fabric of life and living. Real hope for the future consists in working together, inspired by the conviction that we can change the world in which we live for the better.

Culture is the relationship between human beings and the environment. It is never static, aloof, or apart from the fabric of our lives. We visit museums to bring into the present the memory of our shared story with our predecessors. We revisit and learn, widen our perceptions and understanding, see things in a new way and in a different light. Culture is a living, dynamic, and participative reality. Our connection to a tree, a hill, or other creature of the natural world can have the same effect, widening our perceptions and understanding. Knowledge is continually growing, flexible, dynamic, and integrated to *know how;* method is the way forward to becoming more human. Care for the world is caring for one another and looking after our common home. Culture is treasure, accumulated wisdom, the legacy we inherit that provokes and promotes us to begin again, make new options and decisions. Francis tells us of "a need to incorporate the history, culture, and architecture of each place, preserving the original identity. Ecology involves protecting the cultural treasures of humanity in the broadest sense."[14] He also reminds us that the "disappearance of a culture can be just as serious, or even more serious, than the disappearance of a species of plant or animal."[15]

Culture is imbued with a sense of the sacred. The touchstone of spirituality will be how it enriches and enhances our living, its importance or place in our evolving story and history. Spirituality is communication, soul-sharing. Language opens doors, and libraries can be life- giving museums. The language of people who live on the margins, the periphery of society, may not be recorded but it is nevertheless a treasure of lived and reflected experience, wisdom wrought together in good days and bad, accumulated and handed on to others. Let us appreciate the cost and loss of losing the

13. Ibid., 139.
14. Ibid., 140.
15. Ibid., 145

story of the Amazon peoples, developed over thousands of years in a special and unique habitat, losing the riches of their sustained and sustaining mutual relationship with the great world of the Pan Amazon.

Pan Amazon Church Network (REPAM)

Francis's challenge to the church to be more responsible and do something that will be effective has coincided with the creation of REPAM. The church has a long presence in the Pan Amazon region; it is a story of service and generous commitment, of light and darkness, of both achievements and martyrdom, errors and failures.[16]

Through the Latin American Bishops' Conference (CELAM), the church is concerned with how to renew its mission and become more effective in using its available resources. Following a period of reflection and search, it became clearer in meetings held in 2013 in Puyo (Ecuador), Lima, and Manaus that there was a need to create a networking relationship of the different actors, missionaries, and institutions working directly or in a supporting role in the region. The need is to integrate the church's role, taking into account the economic, political, social, and cultural dimensions to have a more faithful presence of witness to the gospel of life, God´s gift of love for creation and people, especially the poor in the Pan Amazon region. A network was decided on as the way forward.

In September 2014, REPAM was founded in Brasilia by the joint action of the bishops (CELAM and CNBB), Caritas of Latin America (SELACC), and Confederation of Latin American Religious (CLAR) with the active support of Rome's Pontifical Council for Justice and Peace. The birth of REPAM is a response to the felt need for confluence of the church in the Pan Amazon's nine countries; a service of communication and integration; effective shared action; a place of encounter, communion, and fullness of life.

---

16. Note the strong condemnation of Pius X in his 1912 encyclical *Lacrimabili Statu* of the abuse and conditions to which the indigenous slaves were subjected at the time of the rubber boom, specifically in La Casa Arana, Putomayo, on the Colombia-Peru border. On the occasion of the centenary in 2010, Benedict XVI sent a special message of renewed commitment to the indigenous to Cardinal Rubén Salazar, Archbishop of Bogotá. In 1912, Sir Roger Casement, the English consul based in Iquitos and commissioned to investigate the same reality, sent his report on the same abuse to Westminster. The impact was such that Casement renounced his allegiance to the Crown and became a leader of the 1916 Irish Easter Rebellion. He was imprisoned and hanged for high treason by the British but is considered an Irish patriot. Casement is also the central character in Mario Vargas Llosa´s *El Sueño del Celta* (2010).

REPAM promotes a more effective church based on the real-life experience of immersion and insertion in the life of the Pan Amazon territory and its peoples in order to empower and have the necessary means for effective presence in wider and more universal spheres of organizations and institutions. This is a process that begins in the territory and goes forward, connecting the territory to the wider world.

The first, or micro, level is the territory and the missionaries who work with the people on the ground in coordination with the leaders of the local church in vicariates or dioceses. The second is the relation with the nine countries' national bishops' conferences. The next is strategic integration in relation to the Pan Amazon, CELAM, SELACC, CLAR, CNBB, and then, finally, the relationship with the Pontifical Council for Justice and Peace and Pope Francis.

The following are REPAM's strategic objectives and action areas:

- Cultures and life proposals of indigenous peoples
- Social and political action and promotion of human rights
- Strategic communication and visibility of REPAM
- Articulation with members and groups active in the territory
- International support networks
- Pastoral training for missionaries
- Investigation and research
- Models of development, indigenous culture, and climate change

Some of the achievements to date of these objectives include

- The organization and presence of REPAM in the public audience in the Inter-American Commission on Human Rights in Washington DC, in March 2015, as described above.

- The April 2016 inauguration of the school of human and environmental rights for twenty-six indigenous leaders from thirteen conflictive flashpoints in the region of Coca, Ecuador. The first module took place over a six-week, intensive live-in period with a roster that included professors, pastoral leaders, and lawyers, all of whom contributed their time *ad honorem*. The second module will take place in Washington, where the leaders will have the opportunity to have direct access to the different institutions of the ICHR's Organization of American States, to learn how to proceed in the defense of their lives and the Pan Amazon.

- Coordination with superiors of religious congregations and Vatican representatives in Rome in March 2015.

- The November 2015 meeting of representative bishops of the Pan Amazon in Bogotá.

- National organization of REPAM is underway throughout the nine countries.

- Meetings of the international support networks in Washington (2015 and 2016), New York (2015), and Madrid (2016).

- Publication of REPAM bulletin and the virtual networking of leaders.

The world cannot continue to have ears deaf to the cry for help from the great expanse of the Pan Amazon in the plight of its inhabitants, the destruction of the rain forest, the myriad expression of the serious threat to flora and fauna. The stakes are too high, both for the survival of the region itself and the ecological balance and climate of the planet. The present onslaught by extractive industries must stop. They must be subjected to a rigorous review that encompasses industrial, technical, political, and ethical dimensions so we can radically change the present grossly misnamed "development" to an alternative sustainable model of relation to nature and its dwindling resources.

Awareness of the gravity and complexity of the situation is not enough; it must be accompanied by concrete action and the political will to ensure effective implementation. The international community must convoke an immediate summit to forge the agreements that must be implemented by the nation states. A helpful reference can be the overall process on climate change through the COP Summits ending in Paris 2015. Pope Francis has thrown down the gauntlet, calling us to action so that we can learn to rename nature as our brother and sister and truly care for the Earth as our common home.

7

Planetary Boundaries:
Africa's Vulnerabilities and Resilience

Peter Knox, SJ

In 2009, scientists from the Stockholm Resilience Centre and a number of leading research institutes in Scandinavia, the US, UK, Netherlands, Germany, and Australia brought the term "planetary boundary" to the world vocabulary. The object of this paper is to consider how these nine planetary boundaries impact the peoples of Africa. What are Africa's particular points of vulnerability and resilience? It will become evident that the tradition of Catholic social teaching may make an important contribution to help Africans to understand their vulnerability.

From Limits to Sustainability to Capitals to Boundaries

Since the publication in 1972 of the seminal *The Limits to Growth*,[1] the world has been aware that unlimited growth is neither feasible nor desirable. For this work, four MIT scientists led an international "team [that] examined five factors that determine, and therefore, ultimately limit, growth on this planet—population, agricultural production, natural resources, industrial production, and pollution."[2] The scientists examined whether it is possible to discover a sustainable feedback pattern among these five variables by altering their growth trends. Using mathematical modelling with the WORLD3 computer program to simulate various growth patterns in a

1. Meadows et al., *Limits to Growth*. The report was not well received in certain Catholic circles, because it strongly recommends limits to population growth.
2. Ibid., 11.

world of finite resources, they produced twelve scenarios, which predicted overshoot and collapse of the global system by the mid to late twenty-first century. A final simulation predicted "a controlled, orderly transition from growth to global equilibrium."[3] This scenario obviously requires a concerted global vision and sufficient worldwide political commitment.[4]

The Limits to Growth spawned an entire industry in futurology, but importantly it was a major impetus to the "sustainability" movement.[5] On the international stage, its publication coincided with the UN conference on the Human Environment, which "brought the industrialized and developing nations together to delineate the 'rights' of the human family to a healthy and productive environment."[6]

In 1987, the United Nations World Commission on Environment and Development published the fruit of four years of work, *Our Common Future*[7] (alternatively known as *The Brundtland Report,* after its author and chair of the commission, Gro Harlem Brundtland). It gives the seminal definition:

> Sustainable development is development that meets the needs of the present without compromising the ability of future generations to meet their own needs. It contains within it two key concepts: the concept of "needs," in particular the essential needs of the world's poor, to which overriding priority should be given; and the idea of limitations imposed by the state of technology and social organization on the environment's ability to meet present and future needs.

One of its observations is that "environmental degradation, first seen as mainly a problem of the rich nations and a side effect of industrial wealth, has become a survival issue for developing nations."[8] This obviously applies to Africa, and has been the starting point of much of my theology in the past ten years. The report optimistically says that "[h]umanity has the ability

3. Ibid., 184.

4. More radical economists actually advocate a "post-growth economy." See, for example, the interview with Professor Nico Paech in Werner, "Weg mit dem Überfluss."

5. Three of the original authors were involved in twenty- and thirty-year updates: See Meadows et al., *Limits to Growth: The 30-Year Update.* In 2012, for the fortieth anniversary, the Club of Rome published online the multimedia *What Was the Message of "The Limits to Growth."* See http://www.clubofrome.org/flash/limits_to_growth. html. That same year, they published a prediction for the next forty years: Wijkman and Rockström, *Bankrupting Nature.*

6. United Nations World Commission on Environment and Development, *Our Common Future,* 6.

7. Ibid.

8. Ibid., 7.

to make development sustainable to ensure that it meets the needs of the present without compromising the ability of future generations to meet their own needs."[9] It recognizes that limits are imposed "by the ability of the biosphere to absorb the effects of human activities."[10]

Jumping forward twenty years, we have the Forum for the Future writing in terms of five interconvertible "capitals" of sustainable organizations.[11] The thesis is that the five capitals—natural, manufactured, social, financial, and human—are constantly interconverted, and this can be done in a sustainable manner. This was popularized in Jonathan Porritt's *Capitalism as if the World Matters.*[12] Porritt has the rather disheartening (in my estimation) prognosis: "Whether capitalism really is capable of delivering a genuinely sustainable, equitable economy is by no means clear. But it had better be. It is the only game in town, and will be for many years to come."[13] The "it had better be" is a wish statement for a sustainable and equitable economy, rather than a statement of fact. I see no reassuring concrete evidence that capitalism and capitalists have the discipline to remain within the boundaries of sustainability. Thus, while Porritt and the Forum for the Future take seriously the fact that there are real limitations to the resources of the planet, and that natural capital is not an endless resource, they seem to be promoting "business as usual" but with a more responsible approach, "emphasizing enlightened self-interest and personal well-being of a different kind."[14]

That is why it was important to be confronted in 2009 with the sobering work of Rockström and his colleagues, many of whom are associated with the Stockholm Resilience Centre.[15] Their work on planetary boundaries has given fresh impetus to the conviction that the earth is a vulnerable, limited system, with a precarious ability to sustain human life. This has been a wake-up call to anyone who might have been lulled into a sense that all we need to do is manage flows of the five capitals.

9. Ibid., 16.

10. Ibid.

11. Forum for the Future, *The Five Capitals Model.* This is applied to organizations, with the implication that it might also be applicable on the global scale. But it fails to convince.

12. Porritt, *Capitalism as if the World Matters.*

13. Porritt, "Capitalism as if the World Matters."

14. Ibid.

15. Rockström et al., "Planetary Boundaries"; Rockström et al., "A Safe Operating Space for Humanity"; Rockström et al., "Supplementary Information."

Taking a Step Back: Thresholds and Boundaries

In their collaborative work "Planetary Boundaries: Exploring the Safe Operating Space for Humanity," the twenty-nine authors "define nine planetary boundaries in which [they] expect that humanity can operate safely. Transgressing one or more planetary boundaries may be deleterious or even catastrophic due to the risk of crossing thresholds that will trigger nonlinear, abrupt environmental change within continental- to planetary-scale systems."[16]

In language that a layperson might understand: in order to survive, humans need very specific conditions of climate, nutrition, atmosphere, etc. Altering the conditions in which we live has potentially catastrophic implications for the survival of the species. Many of the processes, flows, and chemicals of the planetary system have highly complex interactions with others, all of which combine to support human life. But the interactions can equally produce conditions harmful for human life.

While many people believe they have been making their local environment more liveable or comfortable, the overall interactions of this activity, particularly since the Industrial Revolution, have in fact made the planet as a whole (the "Earth system") a potentially less secure environment for humanity. Human activity during the most recent centuries of the Holocene—the geological era that has supported human life on the Earth—has had such significant impact on overall environmental conditions that it warrants the ascription of "Anthropocene."

There are physical conditions for the planet outside of which human life is not possible. Each of these physical conditions has some thresholds or tipping points at which a major, potentially calamitous, change occurs to the living conditions of the planet. The importance of the work of Rockström, et al., is the recognition that it is a political, economic, and ethical decision where boundaries should be set so that anthropogenic changes to the environment remain at a safe distance from these thresholds or tipping points. This application of the precautionary principle is a prudential determination that needs to be made, and then adhered to by the whole of humanity.

The authors acknowledge that it is a very difficult task to quantify the boundaries precisely, since they are influenced by so many variables, which in turn influence other, sometimes unknown, variables. Some boundaries are even quite difficult to conceptualize. But for the purposes of this paper, I accept the notion of boundaries, and that the authors and their colleagues are doing their very best to quantify them. When the best scientific minds

16. Rockström et al., "Planetary Boundaries," abstract.

in the world are saying that we are in danger of transgressing some of the boundaries, then we should sit up and take notice.

In subsequent work, the original nine boundaries have been somewhat refined, reformulated, and regrouped, as an entire industry of research, correspondence, and controversy[17] has begun to advance the concept of the initial boundaries articles. It is important to note that much of the work since 2009 has been about defining and refining the boundaries, and less about the imperative of identifying and then adhering to boundaries as such. The following table compares the boundaries identified in 2009 with those identified at present (May 2015):[18]

Planetary Boundaries Identified in 2009	Planetary Boundaries Identified in 2015
Climate change	Climate change
Chemical pollution	Novel entities (e.g., radioactivity and nanoparticles)
Stratospheric ozone depletion	Stratospheric ozone depletion
Atmospheric aerosol loading	Atmospheric aerosol loading
Ocean acidification	Ocean acidification
Biogeochemical flows (mainly nitrogen and phosphorous cycles)	Biogeochemical flows (mainly nitrogen and phosphorous cycles)
Global freshwater use	Freshwater use
Change in land use	Land-system change
Biodiversity loss	Biosphere integrity (functional and genetic diversity)

17. Rockström, "Addressing Some Key Misconceptions."
18. Stockholm Resilience Centre, *Planetary Boundaries Research.*

Transgressing Boundaries and Denialism

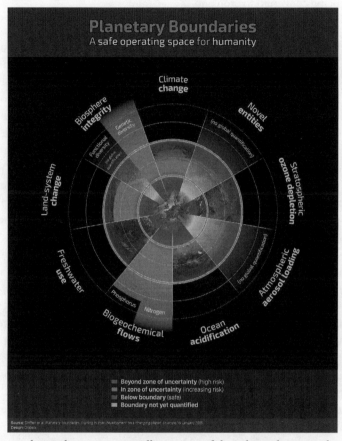

Figure 1 shows the most recent illustration of these boundaries, at the time of writing (May 2015), and how humanity has transgressed several of them. It illustrates that human activity has certainly already caused the transgression of the safe limits of

(1) biosphere integrity, with more than ten extinctions per year per million species, and of

(2) nitrogen flows, with fixation of more than thirty-five megatons of atmospheric nitrogen per year.

We are in the uncertain, potentially hazardous zones of

1) climate change, with a concentration of more than 350 ppm CO_2 in the atmosphere, and a radiative forcing of more than 1 watt per square meter, and of

2) land-system change, with 15–20 percent of global ice-free land surface being converted to cropland.

It ought not to be necessary to wait until scientists have more or less agreed on boundaries to propose targets to politicians and world decision-makers.[19] However, so long as there is no unanimity among scientists (regarding climate change, for example), vocal climate change denialists will have space to argue that the evidence is not conclusive. Their political representatives will take their arguments seriously, rather than "bite the bullet" to legislate costly alternatives to their countries' current dependence on fossil fuels. We have seen this take place in a series of "COP" meetings where countries that are most heavily reliant on sources of energy that generate greenhouse gases are not prepared to commit themselves to alternative sources of energy. They argue (quite reasonably) that poorer or developing, yet heavily polluting countries must make similar changes to their energy profiles.[20]

Similar inertia was largely overcome when the balance of scientific evidence demonstrated that CFCs, HCFCs and HFCs—used as propellants, coolants, fire suppressants, industrial solvents, etc.—were largely responsible for the thinning of the earth's protective ozone (O_3) layer above the poles. The layer lessens the entry of harmful and potentially carcinogenic ultraviolet B radiation. The UN's Montreal Protocol on Substances that Deplete the Ozone Layer was agreed in 1987, even before there was absolute consensus among all scientists about what was causing the depletion of the O_3 layer. The protocol has subsequently been universally ratified, with all parties agreeing to phase out production of, and eventually eliminate the use of these damaging substances. Rockström, et al., use this as an example of a planetary boundary which has been identified and agreed upon, and where the political will existed for humanity to step back from a threshold beyond which the earth system might not be able to support human life

---

19. This will bring us to the principle of precaution, which we will discuss in a later part of this paper.

20. Very interestingly, on March 13, 2015, the International Energy Agency reported that the "global energy-related emissions of carbon dioxide stalled in 2014." The subtitle of the article is "IEA data point to emissions decoupling from economic growth for the first time in forty years." The article states further that this is "the first time in forty years in which there was a halt or reduction in emissions of the greenhouse gas that was not tied to an economic downturn." The downturn is attributed to the changes in the way China and OECD countries source their energy, using more renewables, and less coal, and to a more efficient use of the available energy. It remains to be seen whether this is a "blip" or the beginning of a trend. Further analysis was to be made available on June 15, 2015. See International Energy Agency, "Global Energy-Related Emissions of Carbon Dioxide Stalled in 2014."

safely. "On balance, the case of stratospheric ozone is a good example where concerted human effort and wise decision making seem to have enabled us to stay within a planetary boundary."[21]

Implications of Planetary Boundary Theory

The most obvious implication of planetary boundary theory is that it is not sufficient to tackle threats to the hospitability of the earth in isolation from each other. There are multiple environmental factors that could potentially make this planet a very uncomfortable place for human habitation. One cannot be a "climate warrior" and ignore the burgeoning use of nanoparticles, or the acidification of the oceans, or threats to biosphere integrity, or the deforestation of Gabon or Mozambique. Efforts must be made on all fronts to avoid transgressing planetary boundaries. The theory speaks of the "Earth system" in which many of the boundaries are interlinked. It states that, if environmental conditions approach one threshold, this is likely to have chain-reaction effects on other thresholds.

Obviously paying more attention to some planetary boundaries than to others is urgent, and priorities have to be set. As the theory is still in its infancy, its proponents don't claim to have tuned it into an exact science yet. Many boundaries are best guesses using the limited information and understanding available. However, this is no reason to dismiss or to ignore the warnings that we should be hearing from the boundaries theorists.

Nor is it acceptable to maintain that the theory should not begin, even now, to inform policy. In 2012, it was included in the draft negotiating text of the Rio+20 conference in Rio de Janeiro. The precautionary principle compels us to begin to take all of the boundaries seriously and compels policymakers to avoid any potential further damage to our Earth system, even when not all of the science is conclusive.[22] Galaz, Cornell, Rockström, and Persson argue that much misunderstanding or obfuscation of the original planetary boundaries work has taken place in order to dismiss its implications for policy making.[23]

21. Rockström et al., "Planetary Boundaries."

22. Notably two U.S. administrations under George W. Bush did not exercise the precautionary principle and did not begin to wean the world's largest economy off fossil fuels. On the contrary, they promoted conditions to facilitate the use of petrochemical energy and did not ratify multilateral instruments like the Kyoto Protocol. For this, their names are entered in the global history of notoriety.

23. See Galaz et al., "Planetary Boundaries Are Valuable for Policy."

Implications for Africa—Some of Africa's Vulnerabilities

Mainland Africa is home to approximately 1.033 billion people in 2014.[24] There are some forty-eight countries and nine territories spread over 30.2 million square kilometers, between the latitudes of 37.3° N and 38.4° S.[25] In addition, there are some six island nations. Given such a vast area and diverse population, it would be foolhardy to claim that all of the continent is uniformly vulnerable or resilient. With this important caveat, I will venture some generalizations: the size of the continent and its altitudes between sea level and 5895 meters (Mt. Kilimanjaro) means that it has many different climatic zones and areas which have been more or less affected by anthropogenic change. This suggests that no planetary boundary will have a uniform effect on the entire continent. The continent thus has some inherent resilience to conditions that may make some regions of the continent uninhabitable. However, most of the populations of Africa would be highly threatened if some of the planetary boundaries were transgressed. Using the most obvious example for the purpose of this paper, I will deal mostly with climate change.

Relying so heavily on small-scale agriculture, the people of the continent are most vulnerable to climate change. Peasant farmers don't have the same resilience as commercial agro-industrialists to ride out "bad weather" events. Small-scale farmers are not insured against losses or adverse conditions. In addition, their recovery time is great, since they rely on growth from agricultural inputs. For example, if all one's livestock dies in a drought, then it takes careful husbanding over several generations to raise a new herd or flock. More drought- or pest- or rust-resistant plants might enable a farmer to survive adverse conditions.[26] But with little or no financial backup, subsistence farmers are not able to change the varieties of livestock or crops they raise. Thus, financial constraints compel farmers to make do with the varieties and techniques that they have used for years.

We are all familiar with images of famine-struck areas of Africa and Asia, where subsistence agriculture makes no provision for the stockpiling of grain or foodstuffs. Most of our governments are not gifted with the charism

---

24. World Population Review, *Africa Population 2014*.

25. By comparison, the contiguous U.S. has a population of 307 million people. The forty-eight states and one territory are spread over 7.94 million square kilometers between the latitudes of 49° N and 25.9° N.

26. There is a whole debate about GMOs which I am not going to enter here. But heirloom plants and landrace domesticated animals are less and less common in the global South as industrialized agriculture seeds and breeds penetrate even down to the lowest levels of agriculture.

of planning, and are thus insufficiently far-sighted to keep adequate reserves of staple provisions. So, one or two bad seasons can mean the difference between life and death for millions of our citizens. We swing through cycles of feasting and fasting—hardly different to the hunter-gatherer lifestyle of our forebears.

Traditionally, people build the kind of shelter they need to survive with a degree of comfort in normal weather conditions. Weather patterns are changing in unpredictable ways. Even though this might not be ascribable to global climate change, we are already experiencing "rare weather events." The trouble is that these events are becoming less rare and more severe.[27] In these rare weather events, traditional shelters are inadequate to protect people from searing heat or rampant floods.

Growth in Africa may have implications for two other planetary boundaries. Firstly, growing populations mean that there are more mouths to feed.[28] Needing to feed more mouths will push Africa closer to the boundaries of land-system change and of biogeochemical flows: more land will have to be converted to cropland. And in order to enhance food production on land that is already under crops, African farmers will inevitably use more nitrogen- and phosphorous-based fertilizers, the effluent from which increases the risk of eutrophication of lakes, rivers, and ultimately the oceans.

Secondly, economic growth leads to higher material aspirations. As more people enter the middle classes,[29] they will want to drive automobiles and have larger houses and all the trappings of the middle classes. Unfortunately, the paradigms for these trappings are often from the global North, and therefore not always appropriate for Africa. While one does not want to deny our people the convenience of time- and labor-saving technology, said technology is often harmful to the environment and inches us toward planetary boundaries. "Emerging markets," regarded by some as the salvation of the industrialized world, are often dumping grounds for much of the wasteful technology of the industrialized nations. A prime example of this is the stream of secondhand automobiles unloaded weekly in the ports of Eastern Africa. Regarded as obsolete or too polluting, Japanese vehicles more than three years old are resold in Africa and ply the already congested streets, adding to the atmospheric aerosol loading of African cities.

27. At least that is what oral history and some weather records are showing.

28. The *World Population Review* estimates that "[i]n most countries in the continent, the population growth is in excess of 2 percent every year." Put another way, the population of Africa has doubled in the past twenty-seven years.

29. See Standard Bank, *Rise of the Middle Class in Sub-Saharan Africa*.

An Epistemological Problem

Planetary-boundary theory requires every citizen of the planet without exception to modify his or her use of modern conveniences. However, the above-mentioned higher material aspirations present a particular epistemological problem: how to explain to people in Africa, with their understandable aspirations for comfort and convenience, that these are potentially harmful to the planet and to the common good. Would they consider forgoing the trappings of modernity they see their counterparts enjoying in industrialized countries?

For many Africans, nature is sacred. Various cultures have developed taboos and traditions to protect sacred spaces. Often these have arisen to prevent the destruction of a forest, the erosion of a mountain, or the overexploitation of a species. As an obvious example, in many traditions a leopard skin, or the feathers of a particular species of bird, may only be worn by a chief. John Mbiti, a Kenyan theologian, has written: "Africans are notoriously religious and each people has its own religious system with its set of beliefs and practices."[30] From a theologian's point of view, this is a highly commendable reason for notoriety. But it has proven frustrating when trying to impart Western scientific understanding, or to replace a religious or spiritual metaphysic of causality with an impersonal, "scientific" metaphysic.

Specifically, in traditional religion widespread over many parts of the continent, misfortune, crisis, danger, harm, or threat to a person or clan are attributed to the displeasure of the ancestors of that person or clan. Most frequently, the ancestors have withdrawn their protection because they feel that they have not received the homage or attention that is their due. However,

> while they may have traditionally lived in a world of magic and spirits, this is no longer invariably the case. Many Africans have accepted the Western scientific paradigm and no longer situate themselves in a cosmos containing divinities, spirits, totems, familiars, and mythical creatures. However, when Western science fails, as it does in times of crisis and social stress, many Africans return to traditional religious discourse to make sense of the situation and hopefully to gain strength and meaning out of a traditional worldview.[31]

Better colleagues than I have pondered how one communicates the dangers imposed by a "hole in the ozone layer" to people who have no

30. Mbiti, *African Religions and Philosophy*, 1.
31. Knox, *AIDS, Ancestors, and Salvation*, 101.

concept of ozone, little understanding of cancer, and not the first clue about UVB, CFCs, HCFCs, and HFCs. If Africans are going to be truly on board with programs of avoiding planetary boundaries, then we need scientists who have a foot in both epistemological camps, who can explain the planetary boundaries, and more importantly, encourage our compatriots to embrace the necessary changes in values and behavior. We have too few scientists with this kind of expertise. Many of our top scientists and academics are lured away to greener pastures and end up in the industrialized world. It is said that the most critical export from the continent is grey matter—our "brain drain."

This is not to say that African scientists are entirely absent from the field of planetary boundaries. Some *are* engaged in bringing home the message of planetary boundaries. For example, working for the Council for Scientific and Industrial Research in Pretoria, biodiversity scientist Belinda Reyers writes:

> From a South African or developing country perspective, the important message about the planetary boundaries is not that we must stop developing our economies and societies, but rather that we need to carefully choose possible pathways that can deliver inclusive and sustainable development within these boundaries. The current pathways of global development risk transgressing these boundaries, which will reduce the options for fair and just pathways in future—especially in regions most in need of development.[32]

Where to Find Appropriate Teaching?

I have looked to Catholic social teaching for some indicators of how to bring the ethics implied in the planetary boundary theory home to fellow Africans. Relevant to general concerns about the environment, the tradition teaches about love of one's neighbor,[33] the global good, the universal destination of all creation, global solidarity and interdependence, stewardship of God's creation, respect for human dignity, the pursuit of peace, etc. This growing and changing body of writing, preaching, and magisterial teaching[34] has only relatively recently started addressing strictly environmental

32. Council for Scientific and Industrial Research, "Scientists Say Four of Nine Boundaries that Make Earth a Safe and Stable Place to Live, Crossed."

33. In a global world, neighbors might be at the other side of the planet, and one's action has an effect on him/her.

34. Catholic social thought is considered to have begun with Leo XIII in *Rerum*

issues. Notably, in *Caritas in Veritate*, Benedict XVI addresses the ecological issues, "the energy problem," nature expressing a design of love and truth, "solidarity and inter-generational justice," "responsible stewardship over nature," the church's responsibility towards creation, etc.[35]

In his landmark encyclical on the environment, *Laudato Si'*, Pope Francis echoes most of the concerns of planetary boundaries theory.[36] Of the nine boundaries, Pope Francis specifically refers to climate change (23–26), biosphere integrity (32–42 [biodiversity]), freshwater use (27–31, etc.), land-system change (39, 41 [deforestation and agricultural monoculture]), ozone depletion (168), and ocean acidification (24). After announcing the sacredness of all creation, his major point is that disrupting systems so vital for human life causes untold suffering to the poorest in society, and is thus immoral.

> Specific social teaching about the environment in Africa first appeared in 2011 at the Second Special Assembly for Africa of the Synod of Bishops.[37] Of the propositions sent to the pope by the synod "fathers," three concerned resources and the environment. Proposition 22 was about environmental protection, sustainable exploitation, and reconciliation with creation. Proposition 29 concerned natural resources, and Proposition 30 concerned land and water. It is clear that during the synod the participants thought deeply about the threat to the survival of ordinary Africans who are being more and more marginalized in terms of access to resources they need for their survival—the most important of which are land and water. Not surprisingly, the discussions did not focus on the nine planetary boundaries as such, but the propositions do allude to climate change, pollution, land system change, biodiversity loss, freshwater use, and threats to the survival of mankind. In a single paragraph of his postsynodal apostolic exhortation, Pope Benedict XVI wrote specifically about pollution, biodiversity loss, and land system change: Some business men and women, governments, and financial groups are involved in programs of exploitation which pollute the environment and cause unprecedented desertification. Serious damage is done to nature, to the forests, to flora and fauna, and countless species risk extinction. All of this

---

Novarum: Encyclical on Capital and Labor.

35. See Benedict XVI, *Caritas in Veritate*, 48–52.

36. Francis, *Laudato Si'*. The encyclical does not cite planetary boundaries theory as such.

37. See Knox, "Theology, Ecology and Africa."

threatens the entire ecosystem and consequently the survival of humanity.[38]

Importantly, Pope Benedict writes in terms of what *persons* are doing: "some business men and women, governments, and financial groups." This is more suited to an African personalist epistemology than impersonal, physical forces, and chemical interactions.

While planetary boundaries theory is potentially very helpful at the level of informing scientists who might be able to influence policies of their respective governments, much work must still be done to popularize the insights of Rockström and his colleagues. The basic insights of *The Limits to Growth* are more easily communicated in popular African settings and may help to moderate the aspirations of citizens on the cusp of the "African Century."

38. Benedict XVI, *Africae Munus*, 80.

PART THREE

Theology

8

Fragile Earth, Fragile Africa: An African Eco-theology for Human and Cosmic Flourishing

STAN CHU ILO

Introduction: An African Creation Story

Since the earliest times people have honored water, worshipped water, granting it a special place in their language, myth, and rituals.

—MAGGIE BLACK

My ancestral community, Adu Achi, in eastern Nigeria has a stream, Ahuruma, where fishing is forbidden. This tradition is as old as human history can go. This stream was venerated until recently when many Christians started to defy some of the religious traditions, practices, and rituals surrounding the stream. The late chief priest of this stream, Nwano, told me in 1999, when I sought a deeper cultural understanding of why fishing was forbidden in the stream, that Ahuruma is like a mother to the community. He shared the origin myth of Ahuruma this way: Many years ago, when the whole earth was wet and there were no animals and fish which could inhabit the swampy water, clean water was very scarce. People from my community were trekking great distances in search of clean water. Many people died from water borne diseases since they relied only on rainwater, which was not well preserved and sanitized.

One hot evening, Mother Ahuruma, an elderly weak woman who dwelled with God and had supernatural powers, came down from heaven for an excursion on earth. She journeyed across many towns and villages, and after several days was very thirsty. She went from house to house begging for water from many communities and across many hills and deserts, but no one was generous enough to give her a cup of clean water to quench her thirst. Many people looked down on her and none offered her hospitality. She walked for days, weeks and months and was at the point of expiring when she strolled into the house of another woman in Adu Achi and begged her for water. This woman gave her a glass of water and also a can of water for her journey. Mother Ahuruma drank the water, and could have died of contamination from it, but her supernatural strength prevailed over the dirty water. She was, however, impressed by the generosity of this Adu Achi woman who gave her water from her scarcity. She was also concerned about the unsanitary water that this generous woman, along with many sons and daughters of Adu Achi, were drinking--which was a leading cause of death--and decided to do something about it. Mother Ahuruma then proceeded to ask God to turn her into water so that she could become clean drinkable water for this generous community. She strolled to a nearby mangrove forest and turned into water and soon men and women who were going to their farm the next day saw this miraculous water and stopped by to drink from it. The story goes that the water tasted like water from heaven, pure and uncontaminated!

This was how the Ahuruma stream was born, hence the name, "ahuruma" which literally means "the beautiful body which turned into a long-lasting gift of life for the people." It can also translate as "see and reverence this beautiful body." The myth goes on that the stream also gave birth to fish and green vegetation, and all kinds of other sea creatures like crocodiles, sea weeds, sea lions, etc. It was out of reverence for this stream which is a "living" creature from heaven that the community decided that no one should fish in the water. Ahuruma is alive. It was forbidden for anyone to do their laundry in the stream, as the chemicals from the soap and detergent were considered unhealthy for the water and aquatic life in it. People were also punished if they stepped into the water with their shoes or slippers, as it was believed that the dirt from their footwear was wounding the stream. Everyone was required to leave their footwear on the shores of the stream.

According to the tradition, there are two weeks in the year when no one is allowed to fetch water from this stream. It was said that Mother Ahuruma decreed that twice every year, she should be given some time to rest and replenish herself. In these two weeks, sacrificial gifts are made to the shrine by the entrance of the pathway to Ahuruma. The sacrificial gifts include food items and drinks which were usually left at the shrine so that she (Ahuruma) could eat and be refreshed after her sleep. I was always amazed as a little kid at the beauty of the shrine and the symbolism of white chicken (sign of purity and life), white cloth (sign that creation is sacred and pure and that Ahuruma is vulnerable and naked and needed to be clothed from danger), and the drinks left for the spirit of Ahuruma to drink in order to relax and sleep.

This story which I learned from the chief priest more than twenty years ago did not make much sense to me then even though I appreciated the morals of the story. Jacob Olupona has argued that the "ritualization of the environment or nature" is a central element of African traditional religions. There is a profusion of this ritualization in Africa—the Chisumphi cult of the Chewa and the ritual managers of natural resources under the guardian "spirit wife"; the rain-calling ceremonies of the Lovedu people in South Africa among many others. There is a double movement in this process according to Olupona. First, the ritual is a way of establishing a relationship of control over the environment, and second, the environment serves as the medium through which the essences of the rituals are realized. Therefore, he sees the ritualization of the environment and nature in African traditional religions as offering a possibility of "an indigenous hermeneutics" for understanding the African worldview on ecology, spirituality, nature and their roles in understanding the narratives which African religious ideals offer on how this worldview affects notions of the dynamics of human-nature relationships.[1] This is particularly so with regard to water in African religious thinking because "water serves as a tangible manifestation of divine essence"; it is "'held to have miraculous properties'"; "rivers are propitiated as holy, with shrines and temples along the bank"; "life is viewed as a transitory process of moving from being wet to being dry."[2] Olupona concludes that in African mythologies the earth is the home of humans, vegetation, and animals which emerged from a huge ocean of chaos following the orders of the Supreme Being that the world should emerge.[3]

Thus, in my academic life, as I studied the creation stories in Genesis and the myths of origins like the *Enuma Elish*, I came to appreciate this story of Ahuruma even at a deeper level. This was particularly illuminating for me when I read these words from Pope Francis's *Laudato Si'* on the importance of stories of creation: "these ancient stories, full of symbolism, bear witness to a conviction which we today share, that everything is interconnected, and

1. Olupona, "Religion and Ecology in African Culture and Society," 268–74.
2. Ibid., 277.
3. Ibid., 277–78.

that genuine care for our own lives and our relationships with nature is in-separable from fraternity, justice and faithfulness to others."[4] I also came to appreciate that human stewardship of the earth and eco-spirituality in sub-Saharan Africa could be gleaned from the wisdom of Ahuruma and many African stories of the origin of creation. The point here for this discourse is that *African communities have a deep sense of eco-consciousness and care which should be appropriated in proposing and promoting an ecological ethics both in Africa and outside Africa.* Ecological consciousness and a sense of moral responsibility for issues such as climate change and environmental decline are late arrivals in Western societies; however, in Africa, they were a spiritual and daily reality, part of the warp and woof of many African societ-ies and religions.

African Eco-spiritual Consciousness and Our Fragile Earth

In addition to the myth of Ahuruma, my community also has a special respect for the tortoise as a totem of great significance and the source of communal wisdom. Many stories told in our community begin with the wisdom of the tortoise and are often woven around the daily realities of the tortoise. Each story of the tortoise is filled with scenes of this sacred creature meeting with human beings, eating with them, engaging them in debates and teaching wisdom, especially to women who are often presented as the ones who preserve creation. The tortoise was regarded as a sacred animal because of the mythical belief in the community that the tortoise passed on her wisdom to the community so that it can make the practical decisions re-quired in decisive times and in times of adversity. This way, the most ancient species of African tortoise are found in Achi in eastern Nigeria.

But the tortoise is also present in many stories of origin in traditional Igbo folklore. One point which I wish to underline in this regard is that the framing of wisdom in traditional Igbo society around the tortoise is not only a mere cultural accident or narrative device; it is inherently grounded in the cultural knowledge that animals can teach humans wisdom, and that other creatures have something to teach us as humans about how to live in a world in such a way as to promote, preserve, and protect human and cosmic flourishing.

There are numerous communities in the Igbo ethnic nation of eastern Nigeria who regarded some species of snakes, birds, and animals as sacred and did not kill them and would not eat their meat. These creatures were allowed to move freely in the community as members of the community,

4. Francis, *Laudato Si'*, 70.

and were also respected as divine emissaries. There are many ancestral groves and fertility groves in many communities in sub-Saharan Africa where trees are not felled. Rather, they are allowed to grow and die naturally, and even when some of them die there is a ritual of homecoming for them. This is because of their link to the spirit of the living, the dead and the not-yet-born. Trees in the ancestral groves were usually planted on top of the umbilical cord of a newborn baby to show this intimate bond. In my traditional society, people's ages were counted through the cambium layer of the trees planted where their umbilical cords were buried. These practices underscore the belief that every being created has life. There is an intrinsic relationship between all things, and they mutually share and participate in a covenant of respect and reverence for a sustainable planet.

Today, some of these African sacred groves and streams like Ahuruma have been "desecrated," as traditional eco-consciousness and the law of participation of all reality in vital union have been abandoned in many African communities as a result of industrialisation, modernisation, and increasing scarcity of means. One of the reasons for this abandonment is poverty, which has pushed many people in Africa to the point of desperation to kill some of these protected species for food and meat. In many cases, the protected animals like tortoises, pythons, and elephants, are seen as having supernatural powers and are used for ritual sacrifices, and to make amulets and charms. Some of the sacred groves and trees have been destroyed by road construction, and urban or rural development. In a few instances, some religious avant-gardes have also led the campaign to break these practices which they consider as fetishistic and pagan.

What is at issue here for me is the worldview behind these practices in terms of developing an ecological ethics. As Pope John Paul II wrote in *Ecclesia in Africa*, "In this time of generalized social upheaval on the Continent, the Christian faith can shed helpful light on African society. *Catholic cultural centers* offer to the church the possibility of presence and action in the field of cultural change. They constitute in effect public *forums* which allow the church to make widely known, in creative dialogue, Christian convictions about man, woman, family, work, economy, society, politics, *international life, the environment*."[5] *Ecclesia in Africa* affirms that there are multiple sites for gaining wisdom, places where we can learn to listen, respect and embrace insights which can help us to achieve the triple bottom line of people, planet and prosperity.

What, then, are the aspects of the wisdom from Ahuruma with which one can dialogue in the search for ecological ethics for Africa and the world?

5. John Paul II, *Ecclesia in Africa*, 103.

There is much that can be debated about how mythical tropes like *Ahuruma* could be appropriated through a Christian understanding and how they can be interpreted in the light of the received faith traditions which now dominate Africa over the inherited African traditional religions. However, one cannot fail to appreciate the ecological spirituality and morality behind these practices. *First*, it reveals a world in which human and the non-human life forms have a sacramental and mutual relationship that is mimetic of the divine. As Pope Francis highlights in many places in *Laudato Si'*, the earth is our planetary homeland; humanity shares an interconnected homeland with all creation.[6] In Africa, every member of the created world is regarded as having life. Life here is not understood as simply living—sensitive, vegetative, or intellectual—existences, for instance, we can say with regard to humans, animals, and plants in their own degrees. Rather, *life is seen as a force, a causative spiritual dynamic which inhabits creation in general and is translated and transmitted through every reality.*

Second, in African traditional thinking, there is an intimate bond of mutuality among all creatures. Nature and humans share a relationship of equality and regenerative interaction governed by respect, care, and reverence in order to bring about human and cosmic flourishing. The activity of every member of the cosmos has diverse consequences for the survival of all members of the cosmos. The possession of vital force by all created reality means that any harm to any member of creation is a wound to the rest of creation. However, the human being is the one whose moral agency is decisive, because the rest of creation exercises a spiritual agency in a natural pattern which it follows in obedience to the rhythm of creation. This is why, ultimately, it is human beings in the natural cycle of life who must constantly reappraise their moral agency in the exploitation of the earth, evaluating how they are promoting or imperilling human and cosmic flourishing. African creation myths are filled with such stories of human destruction or punishment, reflected metaphorically through the collapse of the order of things resulting from wrong choices made by humankind.

Third, mutuality of all creation can only come about in a healthy way through the respectful and equal participation of nature and humanity in a common web of life that is divine and spiritual. No creature can flourish by dominating the other or doing violence to the other. Thus, the entirety of creation is wounded through the indiscriminate abuse of nature, pollution of streams and other water sources, destruction of animals, fish, and their natural habitat without respect for the rhythm and rhyme of life.

---

6. Francis, *Laudato Si'*, 164 and 21.

Fourth, nature is inherently divine and spiritual. That which is divine and spiritual is not simply that which is outside of the world; there is a *theandrocosmic dynamism and harmony* in creation (theos-anthropos-cosmos). What this means in the light of the interpretation of the Ahuruma myth is that the divine is not something removed from the natural ordering of creation's forces and energies incarnate in every creature; every reality has a vital principle which confers on it the intrinsic power to bring beauty and order to creation if there is healthy and respectful interaction. In this traditional African eco-spirituality, the survival of the human race is predicated on the survival of the rest of the created world.

Fifth, African traditional eco-spirituality and morality hold that human activity is governed by certain natural laws, orders, and cycles all of which work together for the good of all creation of which the human is only a very tiny though important member. The human must respect and reverence this natural cycle of creation in order to survive here on earth and maintain the sustainable evolution of the creation cycle for future generations.

At a deeper level of cultural understanding, what the wisdom of Ahuruma reveals to me is that the infinite majesty of creation is underlined by the truth within various African ethnic groups' mythical traditions of the late arrival of humans into an infinite and sacred universe. Human beings are the weakest members in the cycle of life, and their vulnerability is heightened by the fact that they cannot sustain life on earth except by a dependent relation on other creatures and nature.

Furthermore, human beings do not define the world process but are defined by the mysterious and sacred hand, which holds everything in care through a dynamic vital principle of participation, regeneration, renewal, and sustainability. Thus, holding creation in care is a reciprocal act of gratitude by the human person. In African ecological spirituality, the present climate change is seen as evil. It is an evil, because it is not an inevitable phase in an evolutionary process, but rather because it is caused by failed human choices and the failure of the human race to become a good participant in creation's regenerative and sustainable cycle and order. This cycle and order should be governed by what could be called a regenerative participatory ethics of communion, friendship, mutuality, and care. Thus, African ecological morality will agree with the consensus among scientists that climate change is human induced, or anthropogenic, and will impose severe difficulty on human and cosmic life if nothing is done to address it. Ecological ethics is seen within African traditional thinking as essential to the vitality and fecundity of humans in their orientation toward being a participant in creation. Humans will suffer and even die if they fail to act in such a way that creation can be sustained in care by the multiple hands which African traditional thinking sees in the cosmos; this failure is also somewhat "self-ish" on the part of humanity.

On a recent visit to the Ahuruma stream, I was shocked at her gradual death. The group of Engineers Without Borders–USA who visited the stream with me (and helped the Canadian Samaritans for Africa to provide a comprehensive water project for my community) attributed the drying of Ahuruma to climate change. For many in my community who do not understand the logic and science of climate change, Ahuruma's affliction and inevitable death are signs of the terrible things which could come upon humanity if we continue to violate the sacredness of the earth. If we do not preserve the earth, the earth will not preserve us. We must embrace a *civis* of nature and the human—and all creation.

Christian theology must play an important role in articulating an ecological ethics which draws wisdom from diverse cultural settings and traditions like the African worldview on the life force mutually shared among all creation. Central to this will also be some concrete steps toward living out an eco-spirituality that respects the integrity of creation and the right of all creation to flourish. This is what I wish to offer in the rest of this essay, particularly showing how Africa's fragility in the face of the variability in weather patterns and climate change is challenging the continent, especially given its current vulnerable economic and social realities. I shall conclude with some indications of the conversations going on in Africa among theologians and Christian activists on the path to a new eco-consciousness that can help Africa develop steps towards adapting to and mitigating the effects of climate change and the ecological crisis facing our world.

Fragile Africa in a Fragile Earth

The variable and unpredictable weather patterns resulting from climate change pose a major threat to Africa, as they do to the rest of the world. However, they also result in different levels of vulnerabilities in Africa. As defined in Article 2 of the UN Framework Convention on Climate Change (UNFCCC), vulnerabilities refer to the impacts of "dangerous anthropogenic interference with the climate system"[7] as a result of greenhouse effects. Such impacts are judged based on the level to which such interference "allows ecosystems to adapt naturally to climate change, to ensure that food production is not threatened, and to enable economic development to proceed in a sustainable manner."[8] The key vulnerabilities identified in Article

7. *UN Framework Convention on Climate Change Handbook*, 92.

8. Ibid.

2 are those associated with many climate-sensitive systems including food supply, infrastructure, health, water resources, coastal systems, ecosystems, global biogeochemical cycles, ice sheets, and modes of oceanic and atmospheric circulation. Vulnerabilities are not universal but are specific to particular regions based on other variables like the reversibility or persistence of the effects; the severity of the impacts; adaptation and mitigation factors; and the distribution of the effects among others.[9] In terms of Africa's vulnerabilities, ten key areas were identified by the Intergovernmental Panel on Climate Change (IPCC) in its "Special Report on Managing the Risks of Extreme Events and Disasters to Advance Climate Change Adaptation."[10] This report also identified the nature, causes, and seriousness of Africa's vulnerability: "High vulnerability and exposure are generally the outcome of skewed development processes, e.g. environmental mismanagement, demographic change, rapid and unplanned urbanization, failed governance, and a scarcity of livelihood options. This can result in settlements in hazard prone areas, the creation of unsafe dwellings, slums and scattered districts, poverty, and lack of awareness of risks."[11]

In this paper, when I write about fragile Africa, I am thinking of the specific aspects and manifestations of Africa's vulnerabilities to the effects of climate change in light of her already unstable socioeconomic and political systems. But vulnerability has an even deeper meaning here for me in terms of Catholic social ethics, and Pope Francis brings this out so clearly in *Laudato Si'* with regard to the poor. I will mention two points rather briefly here among many: creation as vulnerable and the poor as vulnerable and how this affects Africa.

Catholic theological anthropology affirms a God-centered universe. God is designated as creator. This is the central Christian affirmation which is the first article in the profession of faith. But this God who is creator is also a Trinity whose being is prior to creation. Creation is not a necessity on the part of God. As Pope Francis teaches, it did not emerge as a result of "arbitrary omnipotence, a show of force or a desire for self-assertion."[12] Creation is the result of God's free love to bring creation into being as Pope Francis writes in *Laudato Si'*: "creation can only be understood as a gift from the outstretched hand of the Father of all, and as a reality illumined by the

---

9. See *UN Framework Convention on Climate Change Handbook*, 111.

10. Climate and Development Knowledge Network, *Managing Climate Extremes and Disasters in Africa*, 2.

11. Ibid., 4.

12. Francis, *Laudato Si'*, 77.

love which calls us together into universal communion."[13] The beauty of
creation reflects the beauty of God; the glory of creation is the glory of God
because creation images God in all its beauty, splendor, and order.

When we enter into the inner life of God and the internal divine relations—mutuality, participation, love, solidarity, sociality, respect, exchange
of gifts, cooperation, and collaboration—we can see how this Trinitarian
identity and character becomes a model for governing human agency. The
world already bears within itself the very logic for its sustainability if human beings discover and embrace the Trinitarian image of creation and its
dynamic and harmonious functionality. God did not make a vulnerable and
fragile earth; like God, creation has a stable base. The root of vulnerability
is not simply then to be understood as how the interruption of the laws of
nature through anthropogenic factors has brought creation to the verge of
collapse but also in terms of how human responsibility fails in giving to
creation and to fellow humans the tenderness and love through which God
brought creation into being. Creation is not vulnerable in itself; it is vulnerable because human freedom and responsibility, which should embrace it
with tenderness, have not always respected the integrity of creation which
gives it solidity and makes it sustainable. That is the wisdom of Ahuruma.

It is also further highlighted in the defunct anthropocentric notion
of stewardship in which human beings made themselves the center of the
universe, the acme of creation, as if creation were for humanity rather than
humanity for creation. Pope Francis rejects the anthropocentric notion of
stewardship by arguing that climate and nature are common goods.[14] Following the teaching of Pope Benedict, he argues that "the book of nature is
one and indivisible" and includes all of creation;[15] and that the earth "is a
shared inheritance."[16] This is why he calls for a new way of seeing creation
in which the fragility of the earth drives human beings to "devise intelligent
ways of directing, developing, and limiting our power."[17]

The second point on vulnerability is the condition of the poor and how
it affects Africa. In many passages of *Laudato Si'*, Pope Francis writes of how
climate change affects the poor in terms of poor governance, international
economic and political systems,[18] and subtle local and global structures of
exploitation which continue to harm the poor. He notes that the needs of

13. Ibid., 76.
14. Ibid., 23.
15. Ibid., 6.
16. Ibid., 93.
17. Ibid., 78.
18. Ibid., 94 and 172–75.

the poor, the weak, and the vulnerable as highlighted in the 2001 document of the United States Conference of Catholic Bishops are being dominated by the economic interests of powerful nations, corporations, and businesses.[19] In Africa, according to Pope Francis, global inequality harms millions of people because of poverty.[20] This is why he calls for "ecological debt" to be paid to Africa and social debt[21] to be paid to the poor who lack clean water and sanitation. He argues rather forcefully on this: "the warming caused by huge consumption on the part of some rich countries has repercussions on the poorest areas of the world, especially Africa, where a rise in tempera-ture, together with drought, has proved devastating for farming. There is also the damage caused by the export of solid waste and toxic liquids to developing countries, and by the pollution produced by companies which operate in less developed countries in ways they could never do at home."[22]

One aspect of Africa's vulnerability that Pope Francis points out con-cerns the issue of water: "the habit of wasting and discarding has reached unprecedented levels"[23] in industrialized countries to the peril of poor countries. On this, he writes: "Water poverty especially affects Africa where large sectors of the population have no access to safe drinking water or ex-perience droughts which impede agricultural production. Some countries have areas rich in water while others endure drastic scarcity."[24]

There is much evidence for Pope Francis's argument about the way climate change severely affects the poor. Let us take, as an example, water scarcity in Africa. In its 2007 Fourth Assessment Report, the IPCC noted that Africa is one of the continents most vulnerable to climate change and climatic variability. The report predicts that, by 2020, between 75 and 250 million people will be exposed to increased water stress due to climate change.[25] The growing demand for water and scarce resources within and between African countries will lead to increasing competition in some places between communities and different countries. Under certain politi-cal conditions, as a result of failed or failing government and internal ethnic divisions, this competition may turn to violence and war.[26]

19. Ibid., 52.

20. Ibid., 51.

21. Ibid., 30.

22. Ibid., 51.

23. Ibid., 27.

24. Ibid., 28.

25. Pachauri et al., *Climate Change 2007: Synthesis Report*, 11.

26. Moran et al., "Climate Change and Security in Africa," 9–10.

In an article on the relationship between climate change and poverty in Africa, Kempe Hope points out that the scarcity of water will be very deleterious to African development in the areas of agriculture, hydroelectric power, and health and well-being. Africa is witnessing unstable weather patterns that threaten its future. Some of these threats include the climate-induced rise in sea level along coastal zones; droughts occurring since the 1960s in the Sahel, southern Africa, and the Horn of Africa; and flooding in many regions caused by heavy rainfall (Mozambique, Ethiopia, Mali, north and eastern Uganda, etc.).[27] Hope makes the following conclusion: "Among the future potentially devastating impacts of climate change in Africa will be changes in water availability. Changes in precipitation will ultimately affect the availability of water which, in turn, may lead to decreased agricultural production . . . Changes in precipitation and evaporation translate directly to deficits in water supply. Some analysts suggest that the population at risk of increased water stress in Africa is projected to be 75–250 million by the 2020s and 350–600 million by the 2050s."[28]

The All Africa Conference of Churches (AACC) agrees with this dire situation. It contributed to a 2007 statement issued in Entebbe, Uganda, as part of the conference "Churches for Water in Africa," which stated that "in rural Africa 65 percent of the population still lack access to adequate water supply."

There are several other examples of empirical evidence showing that the people who suffer most from the effects of climate change are the poor. According to Robert Bailey, "while climate change increases people's exposure to disasters, it is their vulnerability to them that determines whether they survive, and if they do, whether their livelihoods are destroyed. People's vulnerability is inextricably linked with poverty. In rich countries, an average of 23 people die in any given disaster, in least-developed countries, the average is 1,052. Poor people live in poorly constructed homes, often on land more exposed to hazards such as floods, droughts, or landslides, and in areas without effective health services or infrastructure. They have fewer assets to use or sell to cope in the aftermath of a disaster. Climate change is a human tragedy."[29] Bailey argues further that developing countries are the most exposed to climate-related disasters and that the poor in these countries suffer a double jeopardy as a result. The injustice borne by the poor is clearly evident in the fact that they are the least responsible for climate change, but the most affected by it. It is long established that responsibility

27. Hope, "Climate Change and Poverty in Africa," 456.

28. Ibid.

29. Bailey, "Oxfam Background Paper," 3.

for climate change lies with the industrialized countries that became rich burning fossil fuels. Despite accounting for only 20 percent of the world's population, developed countries are responsible for over 60 percent of industrial emissions since 1990.[30]

Writing in this same vein in *Laudato Si'*, Pope Francis highlights the values and wisdom of indigenous knowledge and cultural ecological values[31] in developing ecological ethics which can make a difference, because they "instill a greater sense of responsibility, a strong sense of community, a readiness to protect others, a spirit of creativity, and a deep love for the land. They are also concerned about what they will eventually leave to their children and grandchildren."[32] This is why he calls for dialogue[33] which will involve different approaches to meeting the challenges of climate change between rich and poor countries, the weak and the powerful. Dialogue is needed, because questions of economic and environmental development will require diverse approaches geared towards addressing the contextual nature of the challenges we face. However, while affirming the importance of local action and local knowledge, Pope Francis emphasizes the need for a global consensus in addressing these challenges, because the problems we face cannot be met simply through the unilateral actions of individual countries and communities.[34]

The UN's 2012 Human Development Index reveals that the twelve countries at the lowest levels of development are in Africa—namely Niger, Democratic Republic of Congo, Mozambique, Chad, Burkina Faso, Mali, Eritrea, Central African Republic, Guinea, Burundi, Sierra Leone, and Guinea-Bissau.[35] In the UN's 2015 Human Development Report, thirty-four of the countries in the low-development index are in Africa.[36] According to this report, even though the number of people living in low human development fell by nearly 2 billion, human deprivations are still widespread and much human potential remains unused. For instance, there are 795 million people who suffer from chronic hunger worldwide; eleven children under five die every minute; thirty-three mothers die every hour; and about thirty-seven million people live with HIV and eleven million with tuberculosis; 103 million young people between the ages of fifteen and

30. Ibid., 3–4.

31. Francis, *Laudato Si'*, 143–46.

32. Ibid., 179.

33. Ibid., 176–81.

34. Ibid., 62–64, 164.

35. Jahan, *Human Development Report 2015*, 212.

36. Ibid., 214.

twenty-four are illiterate and there are seventy-four million young people based on formal data who have no job. These statistics refer especially to Africa where two-thirds of her countries fall in the lowest rungs of the human development index.[37]

However, it must be noted that Africa's poverty is not natural; it is the result of a combination of many historical factors. It is therefore difficult and sometimes untenable to justify the designation of Africa as poor. In *The Bright Continent: Breaking Rules and Making Change in Modern Africa*, Dayo Olopade argues strongly that African development is following a different trajectory which does not fit into the clinical development graph of the UN or the World Top Incomes Database (WTID). According to her, there are a different convergence of interests, creativity, local initiatives, and significant victories and positive stories of young people, women, and civil societies which are all changing the face of Africa. These do not, however, show up on some of the analyses which inform and sustain the economic and social policies of many Western governments and international organizations like the UN, World Trade Organization (WTO), International Monetary Fund (IMF), etc. She therefore argues that, "when you're thinking of Africa in the context of the wars you've seen, the poverty you assume, or the government you've given up on, you're likewise missing the point."[38]

In *The Fortunes of Africa*, Martin Meredith argues that

> the lure of Africa's riches remains as strong in the twenty-first century as in the past. As well as the activities of Western corporations, new players have entered the field. The rising economic might of China and other Asian countries has stimulated a boom in demand for Africa's oil and mineral resources. Land, too, has become a prized commodity once more. . . .
>
> But much of the wealth generated by foreign activity flows out of Africa to destinations abroad. Africa's ruling elites further drain their countries of funds, stashing huge sums in bank accounts and properties abroad.[39]

Meredith argues further that Africa has its own peculiar problems like unreliable rainfall, frequent droughts, harsh and variable climate, challenging terrains, and human and animal diseases, but in all these what is so evident to everyone on the continent is its vast and rich resources.[40] But to understand how to reverse the poverty in Africa, one needs to pay attention

37. Ibid., 3 and 29–30.
38. Olopade, *Bright Continent*, 13–14.
39. Meredith, *Fortunes of Africa*, xvii.
40. Ibid.

especially to the non-formal sectors—women groups, local and grassroots economic activities and social entrepreneurship, social innovation and social capital within churches and third-sector organizations. These groups combine local knowledge, sound eco-ethics, and strong and robust participatory practices which are helping to create alternative communities of hope and belonging and community-based adaptation (CBA) to the effects of climate change.

Beyond the theological attribution of the earth's fragility to human agency, scientists point to the damaging effects of climate change in Africa. Oli Brown and Alec Crawford argue that Africa's vulnerabilities arise from the complex climate system and its interaction with socioeconomic challenges like endemic poverty. In addition, they say that poor governance, limited access to capital and global markets, ecosystem degradation, complex disasters, and conflicts and urbanization are also contributing to weakening the capacity of African communities to adapt to the effects of climate change. They identify three main factors which make Africa particularly vulnerable to these effects. The first is Africa's position on the globe, being already a warm climate exposed to inconsistent weather patterns that are affecting large areas characterized by poor soils or flood plains. Second, most of Africa's economic activities revolve around sectors like agriculture, fishery, forestry, and tourism which are susceptible to the fluctuation in climatic conditions. Third is the structural framework-governance, limited human and institutional platforms for sustainable practices, and weak financial capacities, poverty, and other factors which make it impossible for Africa to find pathways toward mitigation and adaptation to the effects of climate change.[41]

However, Africa's fragility is worsened by international development groups and Western nations which sustain practices that stymie African economic development and weaken the capacity for mitigation and adaptation in the face of climate change. Climate change has been described as "an 'out of Africa' problem crying out for 'made in Africa' solutions."[42] In the light of these, it is obvious that Africa faces a major challenge with regard to climate change in terms of what Lloyd Timberlake calls "livelihood security."[43] According to Timberlake, this scenario has resulted in two reali-

41. Brown and Crawford, "Climate Change and Security in Africa," 11–12.

42. Edwards, "Global Problems, African Solutions," 4.

43. Timberlake, *Africa in Crisis*, 10. Timberlake argues that Africa's crisis is caused by environmental bankruptcy which is characterized by the misuse and abuse of the rich natural resources of the continent and the failure of the government, international donors, and Western business interests in Africa to work towards sustainable development that leads to livelihood security. He writes: "The famine suggests a breakdown

ties among ordinary Africans in many resource-rich areas of the continent: people seek short-term responses to "get by" in the midst of smothering, extreme poverty without consideration for the environmental or ecological impacts. For instance, in the 1970s and 1980s when the people in the African Sahel were suffering from extreme drought (which led to the death of over three hundred thousand Africans), people resorted to different coping strategies which offered them possibilities for survival—migration, logging, poaching, etc. Thus, coping patterns as a response to the increasingly volatile ecosystems of sub-Saharan Africa have become a way of locally inventing patterns and practices to maintain a modicum of modest livelihood. How these coping strategies could lead to a system of living that guarantees long-term sustainability is yet to be seen.

The other tendency, according to Timberlake, is that the range and diversity of livelihood strategies are increasing, both in response to adversity and the widening range of choices offered by the effects of economic globalization, which have affected African societies whether in times of adversity or with regard to resource management.[44] A 2012 study conducted by the U.S. National Academy of Sciences supports the claims of "Climate Change and Security in Africa" while reinforcing the fact that climate change is leading to more conflict in Africa, which is regarded as particularly vulnerable to the effects of sharp shifts in temperature and precipitation.[45]

Whereas there are inconclusive arguments as to how climate change has contributed to numerous conflicts in East Africa and other parts of Africa, the late Kenyan environmentalist and Nobel Prize winner, Wangari Maathai, argues that there is strong evidence that climate shocks are increasing the risk factors for conflicts between and within countries.[46] She also argues further that millions of Africans may become environmental refugees in this century. She points out that climate change is weakening the capacity of Africans to generate wealth, decreasing the GDP, and leading to migration, creating widespread drought and desert encroachment in the African Sahel, the Rift Valley, Ethiopia, Eritrea, and the West African subregion, especially Chad, northern Nigeria, and Niger.[47] Maathai concludes this way: "Given these realities, it continues to baffle me that African leaders do not educate their people so they understand the enormous threat likely

in the relationship between people and the environmental support systems that could lead Africa into a crisis of historic dimensions—one that goes far beyond short-term emergency food relief."

44. Baro and Batterbury, "Land-Based Livelihoods," 65.

45. Kelley, "U.S. Study Links Climate Change to Violent Conflict in East Africa."

46. Maathai, *The Challenge for Africa*, 252.

47. Ibid., 251.

to face them and how important it is for them to use the resources within their borders to mitigate this threat and adapt to the inevitable changes in climate."[48] But what are theologians in Africa doing? What is the church in Africa doing?

The Contribution of African Theologies to Ecological Ethics

Conversations among African theologians about responding to the continent's ecological crisis have gone on at three levels of critical engagement. These three pathways, in my thinking, will define the trajectory of eco-theology on the continent for the foreseeable future.

First, African theologians connect the cries of the earth to the cries of Africa for a place in the world. The writings of African theologians in this area present climate change as part of a broader search on the continent for a distinctive African approach to solving the African predicament. Climate change and its effects in Africa reveal all the complexities and challenges of African social, political, economic, cultural, religious, and spiritual life. There is a strong link between climate change and its effects on every other aspect of African life. This total picture approach offers African theologians the hermeneutical tools to identify and interpret the causes of climate change in Africa and identify the solutions that are working. African Christian models of ecological ethics thus are emerging as holistic integral eco-theologies. They engage the African predicament at multiple levels of historical analysis using tools from biblical theology as well as African cosmology and African religious-cultural worldviews, especially those on life as a participation of both nature and humans in sacred communion and relationship.

Viewed in this light, the emphasis on local approaches to ecological ethics like the wisdom of Ahuruma resonates in many eco-theological writings in Africa. The argument here is that the mechanistic, deistic, and dualistic Western worldview that gave birth to an anthropocentric conception of creation—the main cause of the patterns of living that led to climate change—cannot bring about a new ethics for environmental sustainability. This Western worldview is in need of conversion, because the ecological crisis is also a result of a predominantly Western epistemological crisis regarding how the world is seen and the relationship between humans and nature. In the search for a new ethical framework for integral ecology, African theologians are developing alternative pathways for eco-theology in conversation with other worldviews.[49] In addition, many African theolo-

48. Ibid., 254.

49. See Ndung'u, "Environmental Management," 69: Ndung'u points to some of

gians are linking Africa's suffering, which is caused by climate change and environmental pollution, to the continuing pattern of exploitation of Africa both by the West and African religious, economic, and political elites.[50]

Second, African theologians are linking the ecological crisis to the suffering of the vulnerable, especially women, ethnic minorities, and those on the margins of society. They link the destructive anthropogenic factors at the heart of the ecological crisis to the rough edges of patriarchy and male dominance of women in many African cultures. In most African myths of origin, the earth, or nature, is considered a mother which not only gives life to all creation including humans but also nurtures it. But the motherhood of nature is exercised through the agency of multiple creatures of which the woman occupies an important place. However, just like nature itself, the feminine genius cannot fulfill this creative and nurturing function when male domination, like the human domination of the earth, works against the flourishing of the gift which God has given to women. Like nature, women themselves are not passive participants in the web of life; they are not simply functional and disposable agents to be exploited and discarded. On the contrary, like Mother Nature, women play a dynamic, active, and indispensable role in the mediation of the gifts that God offers freely for cosmic and human flourishing in a world governed by a moral universe.[51]

Margaret Gecaga proposes that the intimate link being made in feminist theology between humanity, nature, and the interdependence of all life forms offers theologies—especially in Africa—new pathways for developing

---

these resources present in African Christian theological reflection when he writes: "We need to rediscover African wisdom concerning the management of natural resources. Africans traditionally adopted an all-inclusive approach, emphasizing the attitude of partnership between humanity and nature. Furthermore, they viewed nature as God's gift which must be treated with care and love. This sacramental view of the universe counters the value-free scientific approach to the human-nature relationship."

50. For instance, see Sindima, "Community of Life," 137–47, where the author calls for "the African hermeneutical process" in the appropriation of an African ecological ethics that sees the whole of creation as held together in a bond of life and community over and above the mechanistic worldview of the West and the mentality of dominion of humans over the rest of creation.

51. Magesa, *African Religion,* 41–46: Magesa shows, through an analysis of many African myths, that natural disasters like drought, starvation, and death are viewed through a moral prism in the light of how human agency conspires in reducing or increasing life and the life force. When linked, for instance, to the question of earth's vulnerability or the vulnerability of the poor and women in Africa, theological thinking in Africa would see the consequences of these negative practices as the result of human failure to embrace a moral universe which defines the rhythm and rhyme for environmental sustainability and promotion and protection of the common good.

new approaches to an integral ecology.[52] In this light, she shows the values being developed in Africa for an ecological ethics—the values of life as an ongoing process in which women, men, and nature are active participants; a God-centered ethics of care; and engaging in ecological conversation, new languages of discourse which are able to convey a sense of mysticism about creation, harmony among all creatures, and an understanding of creation as a common life interwoven in a common destiny.[53] African theologians show that when these values are not in place, as is the case in Africa today, there is insuperable suffering for the poor who are the greatest victims of what Lloyd Timberlake says is Africa's environmental bankruptcy in the continent's failed attempt to modernize following an exogenously imposed historical trajectory.[54]

Third, African theologians explore the link between poverty in Africa and its fragile social, economic, and political structures. The link is often made through the identification of Africa's underlying causes of poverty and its failure to undertake a comprehensive continent-wide environmental consciousness to develop mitigating structures that can meet the challenges of climate change. There are four main issues discussed by some African theologians which will be permanent features in the analysis of poverty, climate change, and the search for new pathways and alternate communities of hope outside of the political structures and mainstream ecclesial models:

(1) Whether Africa's poverty is a result of its population explosion, and whether its population is an asset or a liability. Linked to this are the many contending arguments, especially in African Catholicism, around birth control, family structures, and patterns of dependency within the family and communal relationships.

(2) Food security and agriculture in the face of unpredictable weather patterns and occasional natural disasters. This reveals many dimensions of the challenges of leadership in Africa and how churches and governments in Africa are helping to find the answer to the Lord's mandate, "you yourself give them something to eat."

(3) How African theology can account for natural disasters, diseases, poor healthcare systems, and failing leadership in many African ecclesial and political settings in such a way as to not reinforce some prevailing worldviews of African traditional religions that see every evil upon the earth as a result of the anger of God or the ancestors. In a sense,

52. Gecaga, "Creative Stewardship for a New Earth," 43–44.
53. Ibid., 44–46.
54. Timberlake, *Africa in Crisis*, 4.

there is the need to strike a balance between scientific evidence in explaining the negative effects of climate change in Africa and the ethical judgment as to the praxis that can meet the challenges of mitigation and adaptation as well as how to strengthen cultural, political, social, and ecclesial structures to help overcome these challenges.

(4) How to bring about healing and restoration of the earth ravaged by climate change. Added to this is the healing of divisions and conflicts in Africa, as well as the semi-permanency of the refugee crisis in many parts of the continent resulting from war, terrorism, natural disasters, locust invasion, etc. African theologies speak of healing the earth in terms of removing evil and sin wherever they exist. This highlights the decisiveness of human agency, especially in light of the worldview that the human being—more than any other creature in creation—is the only moral participant whose choices are most determinative in disrupting creation's rhythm. This human agency in preserving the earth is also called forth to preserve peace and order in communities and nations. However, this is not simply some reversal which will come about through prayer vigils, prophetic pronouncements, and predictions. Rather, it will require a new way of being church, or what Emmanuel Obeng calls churches that are "creation awareness centers."[55]

As creation awareness centers, African churches are being challenged to become sites for a praxis of hope, places of education where environmental education and ecological ethics are shared in a collective palaver, communities of dialogue where various approaches to healing and restoration are discussed in the light of the Christian faith, African wisdom, and the fruits of scientific evidence which can help translate into concrete daily practices what is revealed and accepted in faith. Churches as creation awareness centers become "a new heaven and new earth." They become a place where the narrative of good neighborliness and solidarity in meeting some of the ills of society (like tribalism, corruption, and ecological sins—e.g., not disposing of refuse, contaminating water sources, etc.) become a daily which people are challenged to live in their daily lives.

Arguing strongly to examine and reject theology in Africa that aggravates the poverty and suffering of people while papering over the causes of and cures for climate change and poverty, Obeng writes,

> At any faith-healing session, it is the devil who is blamed for all the diseases which afflict our bodies. He is cursed and driven out of bodies to ensure healing, but we forget that no amount of

55. Obeng, "Healing the Groaning Creation in Africa," 20–26.

penance or prayers will be of use to a person suffering from an environmental-related disease like cholera, cerebrospinal meningitis, malaria, and typhoid fever if the conditions which cause these diseases are not removed. Some Christian denominations have faith healing "clinics" where "patients" are expected to stay and undergo a course of treatment, mostly prayers sessions. I have visited some of these "clinics" in Ghana and the living conditions there are deplorable. The "clinics" are characterized by poor sanitation, lack of good drinking water, poorly ventilated rooms. These are suitable conditions for the spread of ailments. They are not conducive for healing.[56]

One of the most successful African creation awareness centers is the Association of African Earthkeeping Churches (AAEC) in Zimbabwe. This was a novel approach to ecological theology which combined traditional African religious values and ethics of creation and sustainability with biblical theological understanding of human stewardship and the science of climate change. Each of these three components was supplied by one of the three partnering groups in this significant initiative—members of government and the scientific academy, African traditional religions, and African Independent Churches. The Zimbabwean Institute of Religious Research and Ecological Conservation (ZIRRCON) provided the science on climate change and environmental degradation caused by the unethical cutting of trees and devastation of the forest especially in Zimbabwe. The Association of Zimbabwean Traditionalist Ecologists (AZTREC) provided the world-view and wisdom from African traditional religions, while the African Initiated Churches (AICs) and other Christian churches joined together as the AAEC to provide an African theological perspective on what came to be the most extensive ecumenical green movement in sub-Saharan Africa.[57]

This initiative succeeded in sensitizing over half of the population to the dangers and threats of climate change and environmental degradation. First, it combined African traditional narratives and myths of creation and stewardship with reinterpreting the biblical creation myths, while incorporating scientific evidence to create a consistent and integral message to help the people understand the issues around the crisis they faced. Second, it integrated this message into every aspect of the daily life, beliefs, practices, and liturgy of the church. For instance, there were ecological prayers said at the beginning of religious worship; Sunday worship services as well as

56. Ibid., 20–21.

57. For the history of this green movement, see Daneel, *African Earthkeepers*, vol. 2; Daneel, "African Initiated Churches as Vehicles of Earth-Care in Africa"; and Darr, "Protestant Missions and Earthkeeping in Southern Africa, 1817–2000."

special religious ceremonies were woven around a particular ecological theme and followed by ecological action like tree planting. Third, because of the centrality of healing in African religious consciousness, the three partners integrated healing into eco-consciousness and eco-responsibility for all the membership showing how the worthy reception of the sacraments is tied to daily actions for the healing of the earth. Fourth, small communities of solidarity were created to support each other in implementing specific ecological action; they were characterized by the involvement of every member, a clear administrative and organizational structure, and a harmonization of messages such that there was a strong and active participation of all members. This green movement was termed a second *chimurenga*—liberation of the earth from ecological threats in a way similar to the liberation of Zimbabwe from racism and colonialism.

What is obvious from the AAEC's success is that, in developing ecological ethics as an integral part of African theology, different voices and religious traditions in Africa are engaged in conversation with scientists, governments, and traditional leaders. Indeed, African eco-theology is not being developed as a separate branch of theology but rather is being integrated into all branches of theology—moral, systematic, pastoral, ecclesiology, dogmatic, liturgical, canonical, etc. Another characteristic of African eco-theology which one can glean from the AAEC is that eco-theology must be interdisciplinary, as it requires a very extensive understanding of the issues and how to address them.

The final lesson learned from the AAEC is that African eco-theology is the fruit of the "creation awareness centers" which are sites of hope, praxis, daily practices, and healing. It validates the view among many African theologians that we can harvest both indigenous and biblical knowledge to create some alternate communities of hope that offer praxis for problem-solving in the many challenges facing Africa, including climate change.

This approach points to the success of an African solution to an African problem. By way of conclusion, we must note that African eco-theology, like African Christianity, is just budding forth and offers multiple new approaches to meeting the challenges of climate change. Patience and experimentation will be needed throughout many parts of Africa in discovering and birthing such practical approaches like the one discussed here. What I have done here is to offer some pointers as to why Africa will be increasingly fragile on a fragile earth as well as offer the theological and cultural resources that can help address these vulnerabilities, not only for Africa but for the rest of the world.

9

Between Exile and the New Jerusalem: Prophetic Mourning, Lament, and the Ecological Crisis

DANIEL P. CASTILLO

I have seen the earth, and here [it is] wildness and waste
and [I look] to the heavens—and their light is gone.
I have seen the mountains, and here, they are wavering,
and all the hills palpitate.
I have seen, and here, there is no human being,
and all the birds of the heavens have fled.
I have seen, and here, the garden-land is now the wasteland,
and all its cities are pulled down.

—JEREMIAH 4:23–26[1]

Introduction

Contemporary discussion regarding the ecological crisis tends to emphasize the unprecedented scope of the social and ecological upheaval that the world now faces as a result of massive and accelerating ecological degradation. To be sure, there is good reason to highlight the singularity of this situation in human history. However, as the above passage from the prophet Jeremiah indicates, this is not the first time within the life of the church that the people of God have been exposed to catastrophe. For example, many of

1. This translation is from Davis, *Scripture, Culture, and Agriculture*, 10.

the Christian communities in Augustine's time would have experienced the sacking of Rome as an event of radical decimation. Indeed, one can note that the apostles likely perceived the crucifixion of Jesus in a similar manner. In cases such as these, it would have appeared that the world was being threatened with dissolution.

Therefore, as the contemporary Church considers how it is called to respond to the complex and harrowing realities of the ecological crisis, it would do well to examine the Christian tradition, scrutinizing the manner in which the people of God have understood their relationship to God in the midst of previous experiences of decimation. This examination should be carried out for the purpose of discerning how these earlier responses might shape the imagination and praxis of the church today. Such an analysis can help to inform the church as to how it might best realize its vocation to be a "sacrament of salvation"[2] for the world at a time when it must confront the potentially catastrophic effects of the ecological crisis.

In this essay, I begin by drawing attention to parallels between the contemporary context, particularly that of the global North, with respect to the ecological crisis and the experience of Judah leading up to the Exile in 587 BCE. The latter was perhaps the most catastrophic event in the Old Testament, and its specter shapes the context of Jeremiah's ministry. My purpose is to elucidate how the prophetic imagination that was active in Judah in the time leading up to and during the Exile can inform the thought and action of the present-day church. In particular, while drawing on the work of biblical scholar Walter Brueggemann, I argue that the praxis of prophetic mourning is essential to the Church's public and political response to the pressing realities of the ecological crisis. Furthermore, I maintain that this praxis must be cultivated in concert with the practice of lament—prayers of exhortation and protest to God. In considering lament, I turn briefly to the Book of Revelation in order to highlight the implications of this form of prayer for the Christian life. I assume throughout my argument that the tasks of mourning and lament should be focused not only on the potentially devastating effects of the ecological crisis but also on the manner in which human sinfulness has shaped the current context. As I begin my argument, I first consider in closer detail the current situation with respect to the ecological crisis so that when I turn to Brueggemann, the similarities between our historical moment and that of Judah at the dawn of the Exile will become clear.

2. Vatican Council II, *Lumen Gentium*, 48.

The Global (North's) Context

As I just noted, the world is now facing unprecedented societal and ecological destabilization. To many educated observers, it appears that if human society continues on its current trajectory the probable effects of the crisis should be couched in catastrophic if not apocalyptic terms. Indeed, the work of noted environmental scientist Johan Rockström suggests that given the nonlinear manner in which the dynamics of the earth-system function and given the multiple boundaries of the earth-system that are currently being transgressed, the collapse of human society at a global level is becoming an increasingly real possibility.[3]

In view of this, numerous atmospheric scientists have warned against adopting a "business-as-usual model" with respect to economics and politics for addressing the ecological crisis. As Will Steffen and his colleagues point out, while a business-as-usual approach normally is thought of as conservative, in this case such an approach appears increasingly reckless.[4] In view of the risks portended by massive ecological degradation, a safer approach would actually be one that is proactive in reconfiguring the structures of society. Yet, as the failures of numerous international summits on climate change indicate, the business-as-usual model continues to be the overriding response.[5] Pope Francis laments this state of affairs in *Laudato Si'*, writing that, from the global powers of the world today, "the most one can expect is superficial rhetoric, sporadic acts of philanthropy, and perfunctory expressions of concern for the environment, whereas any genuine attempt by groups within society to introduce change is viewed as a nuisance based on romantic illusions or an obstacle to be circumvented."[6]

The reasons why this model remains regnant are, of course, complex. Here, I would like to focus briefly upon the ideological dimensions underlying this stasis by turning to the work of sociologist Leslie Sklair. In his work, Sklair seeks to provide an account of the structural and ideological dynamics of the global social system—what he labels "global capitalism."[7] According to Sklair, globalization should be understood as a distinct moment in economic and political history, one that is marked by the rise of transnational corporations as well as by the advent of what he terms the

3. Rockström et al, "A Safe Operating Space for Humanity," 472–75.

4. Steffen et al, "The Anthropocene," 739–61.

5. Jamieson, *Reason in a Dark Time*, especially 34–59.

6. Francis, *Laudato Si'*, 54.

7. Sklair, *Sociology of the Global System*.

transnational capitalist class.[8] While it is outside the parameters of this essay to examine these categories in any detail, it must be observed that Sklair locates the roots of the ecological crisis within the structural elements of the global system. In other words, it is the global economy, informed by the logic of continuous growth, that is the primary driver of the ecological crisis.[9] Having acknowledged this point, it is a third dimension of Sklair's analysis of global capitalism that is most pertinent to my argument. According to Sklair, the structures of the global system are reliant upon the spread of what he terms, "the culture-ideology of consumerism."[10] It is this concept that I now consider.

The Culture-Ideology of Consumerism and Faith in Progress

In describing the culture-ideology of consumerism, Sklair asserts that the dramatic growth in advertising and communication technologies over the last century have allowed transnational corporations to create and promulgate the fictive persona of the consumer as the ideal person.[11] In describing this persona, Sklair writes, "The culture-ideology of consumerism proclaims, literally, that the meaning of life is to be found in the things that we possess. To consume, therefore, is to be fully alive, and to remain fully alive we must consume."[12] Moreover, he argues that today the culture-ideology of consumerism has become virtually hegemonic, colonizing the life-world of any society tied to the global economy. The fictive persona of the consuming person thus appears to be on the verge of becoming an unrivaled global ideal.[13]

Importantly, Sklair observes that the ideal of person-as-consumer is essential to the life of global capitalism. This is because the functioning of the system is predicated upon the continuous accumulation of capital, and it is the act of consumption that drives the process of accumulation. Thus, he comments, "Without consumerism, the rationale for continuous capitalist accumulation dissolves."[14] The culture-ideology of consumerism, then, is

---

8. Ibid., 8–9.

9. Sklair, *Transnational Capitalist Class*, especially 198–254.

10. Ibid., especially 255–94.

11. Sklair, *Sociology of the Global-System*, 47–48.

12. Ibid., 48.

13 This persona can be understood in terms of the concept of *homo consumens* first postulated by psychoanalyst Erich Fromm. See Fromm, *On Being Human.*

14. Sklair, *Globalization, Capitalism, and its Alternatives*, 116.

the "glue" that holds the system together—a system, it must be emphasized, that continues to accelerate the pace of ecological degradation.[15]

It is also important to observe that Sklair detects an implicit faith in progress built into the culture-ideology of global capitalism. According to this worldview, the act of consumption not only promises the good life, *it also promises an increasingly better life.*[16] Here, faith in progress is tied most strongly to the innovative items and technologies that are created and consumed. However, this faith also extends to human ingenuity in general.[17] Thus, one finds that those who have been socialized within the culture-ideology of consumerism maintain a belief—when faced with the apparent threats posed by the ecological crisis—that human ingenuity will be able to adequately remedy these threats.

In order to understand the dangers inherent in an uncritical faith in progress—which will allow us to see more clearly why the business-as-usual approach remains regnant—it is helpful to turn to the thought of theologian Johann Baptist Metz. At the dawn of postmodernity, Metz argued that a false metaphysics of progress still colored the collective imagination of the West. As he saw so perceptively, this ideology engenders a mode of existence for the human person, which relieves her of the responsibility to act. Among the reasons this is so is that, under the influence of this ideology, political and ethical life have been eclipsed by technical reason and a faith that efficiency and market logic will produce the best of possible worlds—the human person need only go along with the formulae of the planners.[18] Thus, Metz finds that the cult of progress which affirms humanity's omnipotence in its ability to manage its own destiny, gives way to a "cult of apathy and [to] the apolitical life."[19] Accordingly, Metz sums up the spirit of contemporary society by quoting Bertolt Brecht, writing: "When atrocities happen, it's like when the rain falls. No one shouts 'stop it!' anymore." This, it seems to me, continues to capture the *zeitgeist* of our situation today. Under the influence of the culture-ideology of consumerism, human persons have been able to ignore the ethical and political imperatives that the ecological crisis presents to us as a global society. Thus, even as the "business-as-usual" approach

15. Ibid., 115.

16. Sklair, *Transnational Capitalist Class*, 5.

17. It should be noted that Pope Francis criticizes this mentality throughout *Laudato Si'*.

18. Here, I am referring to what the Frankfurt School has termed the "dialectic of the Enlightenment." For a helpful outline of this concept, see J. Matthew Ashley's introduction to Metz, *Faith in History and Society*, 11–14.

19. Ibid., 157.

continues to steer the world in perilous directions, no one shouts "stop it!" anymore.

Thus far, I have asserted that the contemporary situation with respect to the ecological crisis is such that a break from the business-as-usual approach to politics and economics appears necessary. At the same time, such a break has proven to be elusive. A key reason for this elusiveness is the fact that human beings are increasingly beholden to the culture-ideology of consumerism. This culture-ideology leads us to direct our energies towards consumption as the means for expressing the fullness of our humanity; it leads us to affirm a faith in progress that vitiates any imperative for ethical or political action, and, at the same time, it leads us to continue to fuel the very structures and mechanisms that are at the root of the anthropogenic-ecological crisis.

Royal Consciousness at the Time of the Exile

The contemporary situation described above, characterizing much of the global North in particular, bears a striking formal resemblance to the socio-political atmosphere of Judah on the eve of the Exile. As Brueggemann describes it, in the years leading up to the Exile, Judah had truly become a nation "like all the nations" (1 Sam 8:20). Under the monarchy, Judah's programs of governance came to approximate the type of imperial regime from which God had delivered the Hebrews through the Exodus.[20] As such, the monarchy of Judah maintained and expanded its wealth and power through the exploitation of the poor and the abuse of the land.[21]

At the same time, the monarchy gave rise to an ideology that sanctioned Judah's exploitative power arrangements. According to Brueggemann, this ideology, which he dubs the "royal consciousness," maintained that the sociopolitical order established by Judah was in fact a Divine order.[22] Thus, the royal consciousness permitted no talk of alternatives—one's only option was obeisance to the wisdom of the monarchy.

Importantly, Brueggemann observes that in sanctioning the status quo, *"The royal consciousness leads people to numbness, especially to numbness*

20. Brueggemann finds this to be especially true of the Solomonic regime, which, in his view, reverses the radical egalitarianism of the Mosaic communities. On this point, see Brueggemann, *Prophetic Imagination*, 21–37.

21. Ibid., 26–28. See also, Brueggemann, *The Land*, especially 85–100. More recently, Ellen Davis has masterfully drawn out the manner in which the imperial excesses of Egypt exhaust not only the poor but the land as well. See Davis, "Scripture, Culture, Agriculture," 66–72.

22. Brueggemann, *Prophetic Imagination*, 28–37.

about death."[23] This is because in order to affirm the exploitative regime of the monarchy, one must become desensitized to the deaths and sufferings upon which the monarchy is built. It is this culture of numbness and denial—endemic to the royal consciousness—that allows the monarchy to maintain its claims of legitimacy. Since there is a denial of unjust suffering and of sin, there is no impetus for change—nothing new must or can be birthed into history.

The Exile, of course, shatters the monarchy's presumption. Moreover, when the Exile does occur, decimating Judah's social and theological order, the royal consciousness has nothing to offer. Since this ideology was so deeply interwoven with the maintenance of the dominant order, when the dominant order collapses, the royal consciousness cannot imagine something new emerging, it cannot find reason to hope. As Brueggemann writes, "the same royal consciousness that could not imagine endings and so settled for numb denial is the one that could not imagine beginnings and so settled for hopeless despair and a grim endurance of the way things now are."[24] From the perspective of the royal consciousness, "history is ended."[25] Thus, those who had been colonized by this ideology can only give themselves over from denial to despair.

It is in these times of pending and realized catastrophe—times in which the impotence of the royal consciousness was most clearly revealed—that Brueggemann observes Judah coming to rely upon the vision and imaginations of its prophets. Within the alternating situations of seemingly timeless hegemony (be it the monarchy or global capitalism) and ruin (the Exile or the ecological crisis), it is the prophet who has the ability to see the most fearful aspects of reality and nevertheless imagine a new future. Thus, the prophetic imagination has at its disposal the power to counter the royal consciousness. Indeed, both in times of the status quo and in times of radical destabilization, it is the prophet who calls the people of God and, indeed, the whole world to conversion.

In view of our current situation with respect to ecological degradation and the culture-ideology of consumerism, I would suggest that an especially important task of the church today is the cultivation of its prophetic imagination. In appealing to the need for the prophetic within our present day context, however, my claim is somewhat more specific. In particular, I believe that it is the prophetic task of mourning that must be fostered with the greatest urgency in the church today. As Brueggemann observes, an

23. Ibid., 41. The italics are Brueggemann's.
24. Ibid., 62
25. Brueggemann, *The Land*, 103.

essential task of the prophet was to express the pathos that had been collectively denied by a culture under the influence of the royal consciousness
and, in so doing, make present symbols of grief within the public and political spheres; symbols that are able to capture the terror of current and future
realities; symbols that, when presented rightly, lead us to mourn.[26]

The question, of course, is this: why grief? What is the purpose of
embracing or even cultivating a praxis of mourning? To these questions
Brueggemann suggests that the numbness, denial, and despair fostered by
the royal consciousness can only be broken, "by the embrace of negativ-
ity [and] by the public articulation that we are fearful and ashamed of the
future we have chosen."[27] The task of mourning, therefore, is the work that
permits the person or community to see reality in all of its severity and not
be overcome by the darkness. Mourning is the praxis that allows one to
break through the cycle of denial and despair, thus permitting the possibilities of conversion, consolation, and hope to emerge.

Brueggemann's argument finds support in the contemporary work
of systems theorist and psychoanalyst Joanna Macy. Macy has worked at
length with individuals and communities in uncovering and working
through their latent environmental guilt and despair. She observes that
this despair, when not confronted, tends to hold the person or community
captive, vitiating one's ability to respond to the crisis in meaningful ways.
When the information that we have regarding the ecological crisis is not
met with corresponding grief, Macy argues, persons tend to be driven into
deeper denial or become even more overwhelmed by a sense of futility.[28]
Simply put, information alone is often either ineffectual or counterproduc-
tive. However, in her practice, Macy has found that through honest and
painful mourning—what she describes as "despair work"—the person or
community can find not only the power to confront the realities of ecological and social devastation, the person or community can also uncover the
generative power that allows one to imagine a new future and in so doing
enter into deeper forms of solidarity with the world.

---

26. As Brueggemann writes, the prophetic task of mourning "has three parts: (1) To
offer symbols that are adequate to confront the horror and massiveness of the experience that evokes numbness and requires denial. . . . (2) To *bring to public expression
those very fears and terrors* that have been denied so long and suppressed so deeply that
we do not know that they are there. . . . (3) To *speak metaphorically but concretely about
the real deathliness that hovers over us and gnaws within us* and to speak neither in rage
nor with cheap grace, but with the candor born of anguish and passion." Brueggemann,
Prophetic Imagination, 45.

27. Ibid., 56.

28. Macy, "Working through Environmental Despair," 252.

From Mourning to Lament

It is possible that the pathos Brueggemann and Macy describe can be understood simply as an emotional catharsis emanating out of one's own experiences of powerlessness and/or guilt. There is, of course, something to be said for catharsis if it helps a person to face honestly the pain of limitation and culpability. Nonetheless, here, a fair question to ask is this: what prevents a generative act of mourning from simply collapsing back into the type of stultifying despair that both Brueggemann and Macy wish to overcome? In my view, the answer lies most fundamentally in the virtue of hope. The cultivation of hope in something beyond oneself and one's own power appears an important safeguard against despair.

Iris Murdoch powerfully captures something of this view in a scene from her novel *The Good Apprentice*. There, a young man named Stuart attempts to comfort his stepbrother Edward who is overwhelmed with despair at his complicity in the death of a friend. Finding Edward despondent, Stuart pleads,

> Try to sort of pray, say "deliver me from evil," say you're sorry, ask for help, find some light, something the blackness can't blacken. There must be things you have, things you can get to, some poetry, something from the Bible, Christ, if he still means anything to you. Let the pain go on but let something else touch it like a ray coming through from outside, from *that* place outside.[29]

Note that Stuart's exhortation resists the temptation toward denial (of pain and guilt), even while attempting to move his stepbrother beyond despair. The pain can persist for Edward. However, it is imperative that he open himself to something beyond the pain. This movement to look for something beyond the pain—particularly when one is in the midst of it—is fundamentally an act of hope.

Within the Christian imagination, of course, the ultimate ground of all hope is the faithfulness of God. Likewise, "*that* place outside," which "the blackness can't blacken," is most fully identified with the eschatological realization of God's reign—the time when all tears will be wiped away (Rev 21:4), when righteousness and peace shall kiss (Ps 85:10). From faith's perspective, the move beyond despair while in the midst of suffering is most properly realized through turning—indeed, crying out—to God. This cry

---

29. Murdoch, *Good Apprentice*, 47. Patrick Miller cites this passage in arguing that lament is both pain and prayer. See Miller, "Heaven's Prisoners," 17.

to God is the act of lament; a prayer that, in its exhortation, holds together anger, suffering, mourning, and hope.[30]

The catalysts of biblical laments are varied.[31] Innocent suffering, most obviously in the book of Job, occasions this form of prayer. In the Book of Revelation, it is the persecution faced by the holy ones for their faithfulness to Christ that prompts them to cry out to God. In the time of Exile—a focus of this essay—it was the community's experience of collective guilt that incites lamentation. These differing provocations help to illuminate how lament can function as a proper response of the global church today as it faces the ecological crisis. At the risk of gross overgeneralization, the churches of the global South—having contributed relatively little to climate change for example—find themselves in a position proximate to that of Job. Theirs is largely an innocent suffering. On the other hand, the context of the churches in the global North, as I stated at the outset of this essay, bears a distinct resemblance to that of the Exile.

If these distinctions point to particularities within acts of lament, then it must be observed that what gives this form of prayer its universal character is its material content. In every case, prayers of lament exhort God to be faithful to God's promises.[32] Lament, then, can be rightly characterized as a form of apocalyptic prayer. Come Lord, and wipe away the tears from our eyes! On the surface, this presents a conundrum. After all, the genre of apocalypse, especially in the United States, is closely associated with a view that champions the destruction of the earth.[33] Given this, would not prayers of lament stand in diametrical opposition to a spirituality and ethos that mourns the contemporary ecological crisis and seeks to resist the forces that perpetuate and intensify the crisis?

---

30. This anger can be, perhaps most notably, directed at God. For this reason, Eva Harasta and Brian Brock point out that the German word for lament, *Klage*, is actually more effective at capturing the biblical sense of the term because it connotes a sense of accusation. "Why have you done this God?" the lamenter cries, "How long will you allow this to happen?" See Harasta and Brock, "Introduction," 4. Nevertheless, distinctive of the character of lament is that even as it raises an accusation against God, it continues to call out in faith and hope. As Patrick Miller observes, in considering lament in its relationship to Jesus Christ, the cries "My God, my God, why have you abandoned me?" and "Father, into your hands I commend my spirit" can be understood as two dimensions of the single act of lament. See Miller, "Heaven's Prisoners," 22.

31. See Eklund, "Empires and Enemies," 26–28.

32. As Rebekah Eklund writes, "The fundamental problem of every lament—whether the symptom of that problem be sickness, slander, or exile—is a rupture in that relationship, a threat to the integrity of God's own character and promises." Eklund, "Empires and Enemies, 27.

33. Here, I am thinking specifically of the *Left Behind* series.

While it is not possible to enter into a thoroughgoing discussion of apocalyptic discourse here, a point that Barbara Rossing makes in her work on the Book of Revelation—that most apocalyptic of texts—can help to move us beyond this apparent impasse. As Rossing observes, "Contrary to current popular apocalyptic thinking, there is no 'rapture' in the Book of Revelation, no vision of people snatched from the earth. Instead, God is 'raptured' down to Earth to take up residence and 'tent' (*skene*, skenoo) with us."[34] Importantly, this downward "rapture" occurs only after the "great city of Babylon"—a symbol in the text for the Roman Empire—has fallen. The apocalyptic hope narrated within the Book of Revelation, therefore, does not long for the end of the world so much as it longs for the ending of the *world-system* of Roman imperial power. As Revelation tells its readers, it is the forces that destroy the earth that will be destroyed (Rev 11:18).

It is wholly appropriate, therefore, to cultivate prayers of lament when mourning the ecological crisis and facing the ways in which humanity (to varying degrees) is culpable for the crisis. Indeed, Brian Blount finds that in the Book of Revelation, lament is seen as a catalyst for witnessing against the destructive powers of the world. Lament, Blount maintains, "breeds fury" at the injustices and abuses of the world, which "drives those who lament to resist."[35] Blount's claim returns us to the thought of Metz, for whom the shortest definition of religion was simply, "Interruption!" Lament, in effect, is the cry of "stop it!"

However, this cry, and the interruptive acts of resistance accompanying it, must not be understood simply as *witnesses against* the powers of the world. Instead, these interruptive acts—if they are not merely to flame out and give way to despair—must be *witnesses to* the hoped-for reality of God's reign, or, in Revelation's terms, the New Jerusalem—the ecotopian "city" in which humanity is fully reconciled with God and creation. Lament, then, through the power of God's grace, can help to move the church from a situation characterized by denial and despair (especially in the global North) to one of hopeful protest and solidarity with the earth and with those persons most vulnerable to the effects of ecological degradation. This, it seems to me, is needed now more than ever.

Conclusion

Amidst the specter of anthropogenic sin and its effects, and within the seemingly universal culture-ideology of consumerism, it appears that if the

34. Rossing, "River of Life," 214.
35. Blount, "Breaking Point," 149.

church is to realize its vocation as a sacrament of salvation it must become a site of mourning, or in Macy's terms, a conduit for "despair work." However, for despair work not to collapse into mere despair it should be grounded in hope in the faithfulness of God. Thus, essential to the despair work of the church is the practice of lament. It is this practice, among many to be sure, that can help the people of God find the courage to bear the weight of reality—the weight of *salvation*—within the context of the ecological crisis and, in so doing, begin to imagine and witness to the possibility of another world—on earth as it is in heaven.[36]

36. This terminology comes from the liberationist philosophy and theology of Ignacio Ellacuría. For an illuminating introduction to Ellacuría's thought, see Lee, *Bearing the Weight of Salvation*.

10

The Poor: An Endangered Species?[1]

GERMÁN ROBERTO MAHECHA CLAVIJO

With the widespread dispersal of information about the consequences of pollution, increasing greenhouse gas emissions, deforestation, loss of biodiversity, and soil deterioration, the ecological topic has become more relevant not only to experts in that field, but it also has challenged the essence of a broader range of disciplines, such as theology.

An example of this is the magisterium of Blessed Paul VI, Saint John Paul II, and Benedict XVI, who can be considered the pioneers of this theological reflection, and of course, our Pope Francis who issued his encyclical *Laudato Si'* on May 24, 2015. However, the best example of this migration of ecology into other fields is the event where I first presented this paper: the conference, "Fragile World: Ecology and the Church," which demonstrates that the dialogue between theology and ecology is possible and relevant. It has also been presented as a sign of the times.

"World," "fragile," "ecology," and "church" are not merely four categories, concepts, or notions found within the conference title and elaborated throughout the course of the event. Rather, they reveal themselves as part of the discourse that fosters ecology and theology, amalgamated as "eco-theology," that offers a different look depending on the particular interest each might be concerned about.

Addressing all four concepts during this presentation would be a quixotic enterprise; therefore, I shall limit myself to a minimum common denominator of the four. I have found that the poor provide the possibility of developing an idea that will serve as a common thread for me to connect

1. Translated from the Spanish by Karen M. Kraft.

my thoughts.[2] Let me share with you some of my personal history, not out of vainglory, but as a way of testimony that has allowed me to make sense of my life.

Introduction

When I was asked to participate in this event, the first thing that came to my mind was the line, "We live in a broken world," the famous title of *Promotio Iustitiae* (No. 70) published in 1999 by the Social Justice and Ecology Secretariat of the Society of Jesus's General Curia. The reason? It is a text that came to me the very year my son Miguel Ángel was born and served as a pretext for me to reflect on what it meant to bring a child into a world which, by that time, was broken in every way. First, scientists had already announced that, up to an altitude of 25 km, the ozone layer over the North Pole had a hole which had enlarged to a size equivalent to the area of the United States.[3] Moreover, social problems involving education, politics, and economics, among others, were stressing communities even more and evidently rupturing social ties. At that time, education in general—and, in particular, environmental education—was asked to implement procedures that could contribute to modifying human behavior and thereby establish a new type of relationship with natural resources, a term I find problematic.[4]

In that moment, I began to question my academic training, as I observed that all of the theoretical and practical knowledge acquired in the study of biology (as part of my master's in sanitation and environmental development) and throughout my environmental education master's had not helped to modify the behavior of those human beings with whom I interacted. I have to confess that I even thought it was a matter of pedagogy and didactics, and that's why I did my PhD in educational sciences; I was seeking a way to sensitize those who passed through my classrooms each semester.

---

2. See Francis, *Laudato Si',* 10, 16, 20, 25, 27, 30, 48, 52, 71, 94, 152, 162, 172, 190, 201, 214, 232, 233, 237, 241, and 243.

3. Tovar, *La Última Esperanza.*

4. The word *resource* refers to something one could use and even abuse. Hence, referring to water as a resource makes it possible for us to think of its use without any limits and thus, squander and even pollute it. One can speak similarly of soil, forest, or air among others. And the controversy deepens when this pattern of thought leads to the anthropological level and begins to talk about human resources. As an alternative, we might talk instead about the goods the planet offers—or for believers, the gifts of creation.

But it was outside of academia that I recalled an experience I'd had twenty years before, making the Scout Oath promise on February 22, 1985:

> On my honor I promise that I will do my best
> To do my duty to God and my country
> To help other people at all times and
> To obey the Scout Law.

And then it came to my mind as a diaphanous idea, the sixth point of the Scout Law: "the Scout sees in nature the creative work of God and seeks its conservation and development." At the same time, I contrasted this with what Howard Gardner, who developed the theory of multiple intelligences, claimed in his book *Flexible Minds*: "After examining various definitions of spirituality, I have come to the conclusion that it does not meet the criteria of intelligence."[5]

And it was at this point that I started a master's in theology, and with it, a way in which I could look into a dimension of the human being that my natural sciences training had not allowed up until that moment; I had not bothered to explore (that is to say, I had ignored) spirituality.

This exercise allowed me to write my thesis, entitled "An Approach to the Features of an Ecological Spirituality,"[6] and thereby initiate a search which has led me to reflect on the relationship between theology and Ecology, while coordinating the Eco-theology Research Team for the Department of Theology at the Pontificia Universidad Javeriana in Bogotá. And it is in this reflection process we have carried out, as a team, over thirteen years that I have discovered—and am increasingly more convinced—that, to modify the relationship between human beings and nature, "theologians need to address the issue of environmental values and to include them in religious teaching."[7]

Here again arises a call to education[8]—and this time, religious education in particular—to embark on an initiative typically begun on the "shores" of ecology, starting with environmental education: to propose a discussion that generates a change in the relationship between humanity and nature, but this time beginning on the other "shore," theology.

---

5. Gardner, *Mentes Flexibles*, 58.

6. The title of my monography for my MA in theology in the Department of Theology at Pontificia Universidad Javeriana. I later published it as an article in *Theologica Xaveriana* 169 (January–June 2010) 105–32. Compare with Francis, *Laudato Si'*, chapter 6, "Ecological Education and Spirituality."

7. Caduto, *Guía para la Enseñanza de Valores Ambientales*, 16.

8. Compare with Francis, *Laudato Si'*, 210 and 211.

Thus, the best place to begin this discussion and possible approach is Sacred Scripture, because it is recognized "as the soul of Sacred Theology."[9] It is therefore the starting point and the axis on which all reflection and theological endeavors turn, including the deliberations of this conference.

The Poor Will Inherit the Earth[10]

There are many definitions of "poverty," among which cultural, intellectual, and moral aspects are highlighted. However, they who have traditionally been regarded as poor are those who "lack material goods."[11] This is the classic concept of European origin which has been used to judge as a particular way of being a man and woman in the world.

In this view, "being poor is a disgrace, it's something negative, it is to be less;"[12] and although certain values such as solidarity, compassion, or charity are recognized, it has been seen as a condition that must be removed, deleted—in other words, extinguished.[13] For this reason, today many people do not recognize it as their own condition.

But, when does one feel or recognize oneself as poor? "A person may not know how to define what it is to be poor, but he certainly knows how to distinguish a poor man from a rich one, merely by the outward appearance of a deficiency, or not, of material goods."[14]

However, it should be clarified that people do not generally talk about material goods nor about those that could be considered essential.[15] Thus it follows that, if people *do not perceive* themselves to be lacking something, they will not consider themselves poor.[16]

9. Vatican Council II, *Dei Verbum*, 24.

10. Matt 5:4.

11. Carrasquilla, *Escuchemos a los Pobres*, 31.

12. Ibid.

13. In Colombia, there is a popular saying, *Soy pobre pero honrado* ("Poor, but honest"), which fosters the idea that it is bad to be poor. And it is reinforced by another proverb, *Todo lo del pobre es robado* ("A poor man can have nothing unless he steals it").

14. Carrasquilla, *Escuchemos a los Pobres*, 31.

15. This concept is relative, because what may be needed for one person may not needed for another.

16. A survey conducted by Colombia's National Bureau of Statistics (Departamento Administrativo Nacional de Estadística—DANE), which included six hundred questions on various topics, found that one in five heads of household in Colombian cities had lost jobs in the last five years, and in nearly a million of those families, one member had stopped eating one of the three daily meals at least once a week. However, 50 percent of the 24,090 heads of household interviewed for the "Survey of Quality of Life" responded that life was good or very good, a result that experts credit to the

That is also why in the frontline fight to eliminate poverty—and consequently, the poor—some universal parameters[17] have been established for everyone. The following is an example of such parameters in Colombia:

> The concept of poverty applies to families with an average of four members and a monthly income falling between $400,000.00 COP [$156.50 USD][18] and $1,000,000.00 COP [$391.26 USD]. This amount is spent on food, housing, clothing, and basic services. The concept of indigence [extreme poverty] applies to families whose monthly income is less than $400,000 COP ($156.50 USD) and which is spent only on food.[19]

From July 2013 to June 2014, the extreme poverty line in Colombia increased 0.7 percent nationwide to $92,312.00 COP from July 2013 to June 2014. That means that a four-member household with an income below $369,248.00 COP[20] was nationally classified as extremely poor (indigent). According to this approach, what can then be said of those people who find themselves condemned to live on less than a dollar a day? The data reveals that there are many people who must live this way.

Such is the case of a student—whose name is kept private out of respect—in the Department of Sciences at the Pontificia Universidad Javeriana in Bogotá. She presented this testimony regarding her family's economic situation during a class where the issue was addressed:

> I get up to go to school, shower, get dressed, and have breakfast. Since I have no break [she has classes all morning], I don't eat anything else until lunch, which is a ham and cheese sandwich that costs $1,200.00 COP [less than $0.50 USD]. However, sometimes I'm lucky, because some charitable friend will treat me to a complete meal.
> During the afternoon, my friend shares a small package of cookies with me. I do my readings directly from books in the library to save money on photocopies. Even though the only

---

increase in energy, aqueduct, sewage, and education services in big cities. García, "Economía-Colombia."

17. See Colombia's Law 1259, Article 6, paragraph 6 (passed December 19, 2008) which, among other provisions, introduced a national environmental subpoena against those who violate hygiene, cleanliness, and trash collection standards.

18. The peso (COP) is the currency of Colombia; the exchange rates given are accurate as of August 2015.

19. "Colombia le ganó más terreno a la pobreza."

20. National Administrative Department of Statistics of Colombia (DANE), "Pobreza Monetaria, Año Móvil Julio 2013–Junio 2014."

thing I spend daily is my roundtrip TransMilenio[21] bus ticket
[$3,000.00 COP], the question I ask myself is this: If so far, I
have spent $4,200.00 COP, how would my dad who is unem-
ployed pay for the apartment mortgage, utilities, and our food,
and—on top of that—go out to look for a job with less than
$1.00 USD a day, when the exchange rate today is $2,485.00
COP per dollar?

In light of such testimony, we must reflect on the title of Leonardo
Rodriguez's article published in the Colombian newspaper, *El Espectador*:
"The gap between rich and poor in Colombia is no longer concerning; now,
it is frightening."[22]

In the year 2000, Colombia's foreign debt was $16,561 million USD. It
is estimated that, by the year 2015, it will be close to $48,367 million USD.[23]
With the previous data, it is evident that "poverty" has been increasing,
which means that the number of poor people is increasing, too. Although
this fact contradicts the title of this chapter, we find that "the poor" are so
unfamiliar, so ignored, that they are not even taken into account. There is a
tendency to separate ourselves from them, to exclude them from the figures,
eliminate them, extinguish them.[24]

Accordingly, it could be argued that there are fewer poor. First, because
the reality is that some are dying, but also because now—by decree—no one
earning minimum wage[25] can be considered poor.

Given this picture, hope is the only thing left, which according to conventional wisdom, "is the last thing to lose." Because even though the phrase
which is attributed to Jean Paul Getty is true—"The meek shall inherit the
earth, but not its mineral rights"[26]—so is the principle of natural selection—or, survival of the fittest[27]—formulated by Charles Darwin in 1859.

Paradoxically, when the prophecies of ecologists and environmentalists are fulfilled—when the greenhouse effect finishes off the glaciers; when,
as a result of the butterfly effect, droughts at one end of the planet lead to

21. TransMilenio is the bus rapid transit system of Bogotá.

22. Rodríguez, "La Desigualdad entre Ricos y Pobres."

23. Banco de la República, "Deuda Externa de Colombia."

24. See also Francis, *Laudato Si',* 52: "The foreign debt of poor countries has
become a way of controlling them, yet this is not the case where ecological debt is
concerned."

25. Cfr. Decree 2731, issued December 30, 2014 by Colombia's Ministry of Labor, whereby the monthly legal minimum wage beginning January 1, 2015, was set at
$644,350 COP.

26. Midgley, "Kidnap of the Tycoon's Tragic Grandson."

27. Darwin, *On the Origin of Species,* 135.

rains and floods at the other; and finally, a crisis ensues that leads to the suffering of new diseases, hunger, and thirst—that will be the day that witnesses the full triumph of the strongest.

Thus, the poor and impoverished who today are considered the weakest—those who were subjected to indifference, abandonment, misery, and mistreatment[28] (including plants and animals), in other words, the entire planet—will be the ones able to survive in an inhospitable world into which they were forced by a selection process that, although artificial, was seen by many as something natural.

It is there, where only they will be able to survive to become heirs of a planet destroyed as they themselves are, but with the hope of emerging resilient, despite adversities, to finally proclaim the victory of life over death.[29]

Thus, the hope—if not, certainty—is that the poor are definitely the only ones fit to survive the fullness of the environmental crisis. The reason is that they are the only representatives of the human species who have been able to endure hunger, drink dirty water, withstand inclement weather with only newspaper, and live without basic health services. And they have even overcome, with courage, the lack of solidarity among their fellow citizens.[30]

A Non-conclusion

"World," "fragile," "ecology," and "church" are the four categories, concepts, or notions implicit throughout this presentation, but they become explicit (not necessarily in that order) when one is able to understand—and on occasion, accept—that the term "world" refers not only to the planet, or even the men and women who inhabit it, but to the "the whole of all created things,"[31] to the whole, including the animate and the inanimate.

28. Cfr. John Carr's comments in "Los Pobres, Víctimas del Cambio Climático."

29. "In physics, resilience is a material's ability to resist pressure of any kind. One can bend a rod up to a certain limit, but just barely exceeding that margin, the rod breaks," in Ángel, *The Challenge of Life*, 36. In this way, the concept is not only used in ecology to refer to the power that allows a forest to recover after a fire, but it also applies to humans, allowing them to overcome any peril, because they can "generate their own resources to adapt and emerge from conflict with unsuspected strengths," in Rodriguez, *Resiliencia*, 77.

30. In *Laudato Si'*, 227, Pope Francis "reminds us of our dependence on God for life; it strengthens our feeling of gratitude for the gifts of creation; it acknowledges those who by their labors provide us with these goods; and it reaffirms our solidarity with those in greatest need."

31. First meaning, *Diccionario de la Real Académica Española de la Lengua*. [Translator's Note: This was the first meaning given when the author originally accessed the online version of this dictionary in 2014. However, by December 2016, this first

And including everything acknowledges the ecosystems where all those created things mentioned in the above definition coexist. It is therefore relevant to talk about ecology, however, not in the way that great treatises do,[32] but in a much more precise way, as originally conceived by the German biologist Ernst Haeckel in 1866 in his *General Morphology of Organisms*.[33]

In other words, we must acknowledge that, when talking about ecology, we are talking fundamentally about relationships. This way of understanding corroborates the need to chart a new course for the concept, to propose a new paradigm where, from an anthropological and biocentric stance, the human being is to be part of the unfolding of evolution, integrated into God's plan in His continuous process of Creation.

In this way, ecology is no longer limited exclusively to the field of natural sciences—in particular, biology—but instead it opens onto a wider horizon, where dialogue between different disciplines is relevant and necessary. And it is there where theology has not only an opportunity but the moral obligation to offer a word of hope.[34]

This is where the notion of church emerges. "Church" is traditionally understood as "the congregation of faithful Christians by virtue of baptism," or "the whole body of clergy and people of a country where Christianity has followers."[35] However, a broader view enables us to understand that *ekklesia* translates from the Greek as "assembly" or "community."[36]

So thought Solon of Athens—one of the Seven Sages of Greece—who used this concept to establish a new social order that favored economic

---

meaning had changed to "conjunto de todo lo existente," or "the whole of all that exists"; this meaning still serves, though, the author's purpose.]

32. "Specialized discipline of biology that deals with the study of the interrelationships of organisms with their environment," in Odum, *Ecología*, 1. "Ecology is the biology of ecosystems," in Margalef, *Ecología*, VIII.

33. "We understand ecology as the corpus of knowledge that deals with the economy of nature: the investigation of the total relations of the animal with its inorganic and organic environment, including above all especially their friendly or hostile relations with animals and plants with which it establishes direct or indirect contact. In short, ecology is the study of all the complex relationships that Darwin referred to as the conditions of the struggle for existence. This science of ecology which, often inaccurately, is referred to as 'biology' in a narrow sense, has so far been the main component of what usually is called 'Natural History.'" Haeckel quoted by Foster, *Marx's Ecology: Materialism and Nature*, 298.

34. To understand and expand upon the idea that there is no contradiction between evolution and creation, see Edwards, *El Dios de la Evolución*. and Francis, *Laudato Si'*, chapter 4, "Integral Ecology."

35. First and second meanings, *Diccionario de la Real Académica Española de la Lengua*.

36. Cfr. Francis, *Laudato Si'*, 7, 67, 112, 126, 146, 148, and 214.

growth and promoted the direct relationship between the citizen and the state in Greece between 594 B.C. and 591 A.C.[37] Currently, it is also defined as "an assemblage of organisms of different species inhabiting a common environment and interacting with one another."[38]

And contextualizing the phrase attributed to St. Cyprian, *extra Ecclesiam nulla salus,* what Darwin claimed acquires its full meaning: "any form represented by few individuals will . . . run a good chance of utter extinction."[39] Thus, our fragility is made explicit. For one who departs from the herd, from the group, from the community, becomes weak and will not be saved. We see the best example in the *National Geographic* documentaries where the lioness is chasing a zebra, or in the poor man who drifts away from his family and is lost in the streets of the big city. Additionally,

> The creation accounts in the book of Genesis contain, in their own symbolic and narrative language, profound teachings about human existence and its historical reality. They suggest that human life is grounded in three fundamental and closely intertwined relationships: with God, with our neighbor, and with the earth itself. According to the Bible, these three vital relationships have been broken, both outwardly and within us. This rupture is sin. The harmony between the Creator, humanity, and creation as a whole was disrupted by our presuming to take the place of God and refusing to acknowledge our creaturely limitations.[40]

Here it is evident that eco-theology has important work ahead in trying to promote an altruistic culture. Though not regarded as a good strategy for evolution,[41] an altruistic culture nevertheless takes on a different meaning in the process of humanization. In this process, the believer, living in a broken world, enters into relationship—ecology—directly with a God who invites us to "gather the fragments left over, so that nothing will be wasted" (John 6:12).

37. Ruiza et. al., "Solón," *Biografías y Vidas.*

38. Curtis and Barnes, *Invitation to Biology,* 811.

39. Darwin, *On the Origin of Species,* 102.

40. Francis, *Laudato Si',* 66.

41. An example of this is that the lioness hunting a zebra cannot feel bad that the zebra's offspring will be left without a mother to feed them, because otherwise, she and her own offspring would die. The situation is the same situation when seen from the perspective of the process of humanization.

PART FOUR

Ethics

11

Fragile Ecosystems and the Pressures of *Anthropogenia*: Recovering a Theo-ethic of Relationality in Our Common Home

Edward Obi, MSP

Introduction

There is plenty of reason to believe that a profound shift is occurring, even now, in the relationship that human beings have with other creatures. Experts worry that Earth's ability to provide the ecosystem services required to maintain viable human civilizations is being put into doubt. This, they say, is largely the result of "human-driven alterations" of what could be considered Earth's fundamentals, namely, its biological fabric, the stocks and flows of many elements of the planetary machinery and the energy balance on the surface of the earth.[1] What is more disturbing is the fact that these largely human-driven alterations are affecting not just other creatures but human beings as well, in a rather negative way. While adaptation to the natural environment remains a key faculty of human reason, one which has preserved our species through millions of evolutionary years, adapting the natural environment to suit our needs is a more recent attitude, perhaps no more than two hundred years in development! It comes from our very rapid advancement from roaming hunter-gatherers to settled communities of scientific and technological beings. Thanks to technology, our quality of life has greatly improved in all aspects, and we are the better for it. At the

---

1. See Steffen et al., "The Anthropocene."

same time, elements from the material world have always been sourced to foot the bill for new inventions and interventions. There is, therefore, a constant depletion of the natural world that keeps expanding and fostering a perceptible gap between us and the rest of Earth's inhabitants.

I wish to argue that human activity is putting undue pressure on the earth system, and thereby exacerbating the limitations of the earthly household. In order for the earthly household to survive the onslaught and reach its full potential, there is need for a revamping of house rules and understandings. This shall be based on a new ethical formation: a theo-ethic of relationality, built from the earthiness of human persons to our spiritual likeness to the Creator God. In traversing this theo-ethical maze, my path begins with problematizing present *anthropogenia* and the high-speed consumption of both what we immediately need and apparently do not. I shall then present the concrete case of the ecological deficit of oil and gas exploration in the Niger Delta region before interrogating what, in my opinion, is the flaccid and age-worn supposition that Christianity is somehow responsible for humanity's aggressive attack on nature's artifacts, namely, the environment. My theological argument is grounded in a proper accentuation of the relational nature of the human person, whose adequate consideration is the basis of this ethic.

Anthropogenia

What I have chosen to refer to as *anthropogenia* (human *be*-ing [*esse*] and *act*-ing [*agere*]) is the cumulative impact of an apparent hegemony of the *humanum*, in which everything is subjected to and determined by human beings and *our* need, or the value *we* place upon it. While nature will always be called upon to provide what our species needs for survival, our belligerent *be*-ing and voracious *act*-ing in the natural environment is what constitutes *anthropogenia*. This hegemonic intent is born of a false sense of freedom of the technologically astute person to dominate and manipulate other species, in the manner of an *imperator furioso*! Functioning with this intent, the technological person undermines moral restraint and assumes that just because something *can* be done, it *should* be done. Unfortunately, however, this creates a gap, a shift, a veritable and ever-expanding relational *di*-stance between human beings and other earthly creatures.

Let us, for a moment, rehash the question as to what the ultimate goal, end, or perfection (*telos*) of human *be*-ing and *act*-ing is. The short answer to this would be the attainment of happiness. But this answer is deceptive in its simplicity, because what human beings really crave is not happiness

in the momentary or fleeting sense in which one is happy in the morning
and unhappy in the evening, but rather a fulfilment that is surfeited by the
highest goodness that life can give us, in an ongoing and permanent way.
In the Aristotelian sense, this is what *eudaimonia* (*eu* means "well"; *daimon*
means "divinity or a spirit") consists of; and one was *eudaimon* when one
was living in a way that is well favored by a god.[2] Thus, *eudaimonia* means "a
life well lived in every respect, but particularly lived in a way that enables us
to achieve the excellence proper to human beings."[3] It is this excellence that
we crave in the totality of our *be*-ing and *act*-ing, that is, in all the activities
and relationships that collectively lead, direct, and enable us to prosper as
human beings. Now, both Aristotle and Aquinas agree that human beings
achieve their most fitting excellence through the development and exercise
of all the virtues, because the virtues are "qualities of character and habits of
being and acting through which we reach what is truly good for us by per-
fecting our most distinctive capacities."[4] In fact, for Aquinas, the moral life
did not consist merely of avoiding sins or wrong acts but rather of getting
into some healthy habits that would make life richer.[5] Far from limiting our
functional capacity to enjoy, in the fullest measure, the goodness that life as-
sures, the virtues expand these capacities while at the same time instructing
us on how to enjoy them in a balanced and intelligent way. *Anthropogenia*
is precisely the abandonment of virtue in ecological *be*-ing and *act*-ing, especially the attitude of the modern person of science and technology who
forsakes the relational balance between humans and other creatures.

This attitude is now constituting a problem, not only with regard to
our relationship with Earth's *others* but also with regard to human relations
as well.[6] The heightened entropy around the earth system bodes a future
that may be literally unbearable, a situation in which we would have become victims of our own success. Thus, *anthropogenia* as described above
is irresponsible at best, for there are practical and moral consequences of
our actions that we cannot ignore. The unassailable fact is that there is only
one Earth, and human beings are fated to live on its surface. This exposure
makes us quite vulnerable to the elements and limits us to scarcity of everything necessary for survival. Living in the limitations of scarcity paradoxically draws us into the vicious frenzy of exploiting and consuming more at

---

2. Center for the Study of Language and Information at Stanford University, *The Stanford Encyclopedia of Philosophy*, "Aristotle's Ethics."

3. Lamoureux and Wadell, *The Christian Moral Life*, 112.

4. Ibid., 114.

5. Keenan, *Virtues for Ordinary Christians*, 12.

6. Muzaffar, "Conclusion," 154–72.

a faster rate than we ever have and wasting much more in the process, all in the name of growth.[7] Now, having severely depleted Earth's fundamentals in the fury of *anthropogenia*, the final assault seems to be directed at our own species!

A Difficult but Necessary Conversation

Pope Francis's encyclical, *Laudato Si'*, and his call for a "new dialogue" on our dysfunctional common home[8] includes, but is not limited to, an interrogation of our "throwaway culture" that "quickly reduces things to rubbish" without "moderating their consumption, maximizing their efficient use, reusing and recycling them."[9] I consider this a poignant example of the voice of religion intervening in the public sphere, seeking and forming new transformative partnerships between the secular and the theological for the preservation of all that we hold dear, not least our common home. This "reterritorialization in the city" by reason of our earthy issues "may represent crossover narratives around which post-secular partnerships can converge around particular ethical precepts and practical needs."[10] Global warming and the "power geometry of time-space compression"[11] that is often implicated in its fallouts are such practical needs. Impoverishment of the majority of human persons, migrations of human beings and animal species, and global threats to security are all practical needs arising today from this power geometry—and demanding attention!

The volume, extent, and intricacy of connections in international travel is a case in point. The numberless interlinkages of communication networks and their satellite constellations in orbit may have led to the globalization of economies and greater interconnectedness of cultures, but it has also significantly heightened global *entropia*, with no ostensible opposite pull to maintain Earth's original equilibrium. The following scientific study of Earth's responses to atmospheric pollution is instructive: "A one-third increase in atmospheric CO_2 from pre-industrial levels of 270 parts per million (ppm) to 400 ppm in 2013 has provoked a globally averaged warming of 0.8 Celsius and significantly elevated warming in the Arctic region and in North Africa. . . . Whereas atmospheric CO_2 levels rose at 1.5

---

7. Cf. Obi, "The Exploitation of Natural Resources," 225.

8. Francis, *Laudato Si'*, 14 and 61.

9. Ibid., 22.

10. Cloke and Beaumont, "Geographies of Post-Secular Rapprochement in the City," 27.

11. Massey, *Space, Place, and Gender*, 149.

ppm per decade from 1750, from 1950 to 2010 they rose at an average of *14 ppm per decade*."[12] In my opinion, this is the cumulative result of unbridled, profit-motivated industrial-scale and indiscriminate logging that denudes the landscape; mining and oil exploration that pollutes rivers and oceans, poisoning the air and threatening aquatic breeding grounds for fish, mollusks, sponges, and algae; and so-called urban "development" that disperses mammal, bird, and insect populations, among other human activities. All of these have become common place with burgeoning corporate enterprise, and have made some claim emphatically that, during the last fifty-odd years, "humans have changed the world's ecosystems more rapidly and extensively than in any other comparable period in human history."[13]

What is more, there is stiff resistance in many quarters to the suggestion that we could or should cut down on, and better manage, our consumption of fast-depleting resources. Underlying this resistance is the stated view of some that "the needs and desires of humankind represent the crux of our assessment of the state of the world."[14] In other words, humankind remains the index of measurement for the worth of other species, and whether this worth is upheld or not. Rather than reduce, reuse, and recycle, some think that developing more technological capacity to absorb our wastes is *sine qua non* for the future prospects of mankind's survival on Earth. The pressures of *anthropogenia* are, thus, affecting and turning to waste quite a significant amount of our natural ecological endowment. Waste that remains wasted upon the earth and is not made useful for some other purpose remains but a burden on the earth. Unless science and technology are deployed to care for and restore health to the earth organism, the survival of the human species and all other cohabitants of the earth hangs at a precipice, precariously. Indeed, the survival of the planet will depend increasingly on the deliberate effort of all who are in a position to stem the tide of environmental degradation and effectively repair and roll back the damage that has already been done. The tragedy of the environmental pollution of the Niger Delta region in Nigeria, occasioned both by legitimate oil and gas industry activities and associated criminality, is one that is worth sharing.

Contextual Snapshot of the Niger Delta

The Niger Delta Region in Nigeria is undeniably a composite part of the global ecosystem architecture from which the world benefits a great deal,

12. Northcott, *Political Theology of Climate Change*, 5. (Emphasis original.)
13. Steffen et al., "The Anthropocene," 617.
14. Lomborg, *Skeptical Environmentalist*, 11.

by reason of its rich and diverse mangrove vegetation. Mangroves, in their varied species and distribution worldwide, are known to be great absorbers of greenhouse gasses (GHGs) like methane and CO_2 and provide rich nesting and feeding areas for diverse aquatic species, among other ecosystem benefits.[15] This is why I believe that the global atmospheric balance suffers a major deficit with the rate of damage being done currently to the environment of this region. The unnecessarily destructive oil and gas industry and associated criminality in that region are fast rendering the ecological zone a wasteland and, as a consequence, compromising the livelihoods of ordinary local residents. Poverty and its degrading and dehumanizing consequences cannot be tackled effectively unless human actors consciously reestablish the intersubjective relationship between us and the natural environment.

The Niger Delta is one of the world's largest wetlands, covering an area of approximately seventy thousand square km. Geographers locate the region between a latitude of 4 degrees and 6 degrees north of the equator and between a longitude of 5 degrees and 7 degrees east of Greenwich. Although it can be roughly categorized into four ecological subzones—coastal barrier islands, mangrove, freshwater swamp forest, and lowland rainforest—the mangrove is by far the largest and more dominant of these.[16] In fact, these mangrove forests are said to be the "largest in Africa and third largest in the world after India and Indonesia,"[17] and therefore constitute an ecological resource of global significance. It is obvious from this that the region's natural endowments more than make up for the disadvantage of a precarious topography. I have written elsewhere that, on account of the evenly distributed tropical, seasonal rainfall, and sunny spells, the Delta was a major natural habitat and breeding ground for a rich biodiversity. The land was rich, fertile, and arable, and the inhabitants alternated among farming, hunting, and foraging on the land, and fishing in the teeming creeks. There was carbohydrate and fiber, meat and fish, and lots of vegetables and fruits for their food.[18] The Delta had such economic benefits to its inhabitants that attachment to the land was unquestionable, which is why the precarious topography alone was not enough to discourage continuous habitation of the land. In Jack Doyle's vivid description, "[T]he fertile soils supported the cultivation of rice, sugar cane, cassava, palm oil, yams, and beans for decades. Thanks in part to its rich mangrove breeding grounds, it has more freshwater fish species than any other coastal system in West Africa."[19] But

15. See Koné, "Dynamics of Carbon Dioxide and Methane."

16. Cf. Benard, "Status of Mangrove Forest in the Niger Delta."

17. Oyebade et al., "Quantitative Review and Distribution Status," 84.

18. Obi, "Oil Corporations' Private Ownership in South-South Nigeria," 8.

19. Doyle, *Riding the Dragon*, 161.

that was before oil exploration in the region peaked during the boom period of the 1970s.

At present, this region is a shadow of itself, due to the environmental destruction occasioned by the legitimate oil and gas industry on the one hand and the criminal access by third parties to industry facilities on the other. Among other reasons usually given for this unauthorized engagement is the apparent lack of access by local communities to the value-chain of the industry. Now, anyone who is familiar with the process of exploration and extraction of oil and gas knows how intrusive this industry can be to the lives and livelihoods of ordinary people. For the same industry to so exclude them, as is the case in the Niger Delta region, is provocative in a real sense. For instance, apart from large crews needed for the operations, flora is cleared, trees are felled, holes and trenches are dug and flushed with water, usually from the creeks. Explosives are also usually laid and detonated in order to record seismic signals. All of this is carried out just as part of the process of prospecting, and when commercial quantities are found, equipment and machinery are brought in for extraction to begin. One writer who was in a position to know the facts, since he was employed to work directly in the trenches, so to speak, estimated that the oil giant Royal Dutch Shell, working through its Nigerian subsidiary, Shell Petroleum Development Company (SPDC), had cut a total of thirty-seven thousand miles of 2D seismic lines in the period before it adopted the new 3D method. And since adopting the new method, it had added another nearly twenty thousand miles, of which eleven thousand were in the mangroves. Furthermore, based on the one-meter-line width used in the industry, approximately thirty-five square miles of land had been cleared for seismic surveys by the time of his report twenty years ago. Of this amount, twenty-two square miles was made up of prime mangrove forests.[20] Now, oil exploration and production in the Niger Delta did not end then, and Shell is not alone in this business. Other members of the Delta's "Big Five" include Total-Fina-Elf from France; Agip, a subsidiary of Eni, from Italy; and Exxon-Mobil and Chevron from North America. It is the combined global output of these Big Five companies that put Nigeria on the map as Africa's biggest producer. Ironically, it is also the cumulative impact of their exploration and extraction/transportation activities that has rendered the Niger Delta the shadow it has become of its former self.

In addition to the misadventure of corporate swashbuckling described above, there is a more recent trend of oil theft and artisanal refining by third parties, which threatens to be even more injurious to the local ecosystem

---

20. See van Dessel, "The Environmental Situation in the Niger Delta."

than the organized oil and gas industry. This comes from a warped sense of
ownership by some community members and their collaborators from all
around the west coast of Africa and elsewhere, which, as they claim, gives
them the right to hack into pipelines and steal oil. According to this warped
logic, the oil was in the ground before the foreign companies came to exploit
it and now that the flourishing industry bypasses the original owners and
rather fuels the engines of a national government that cares nothing for the
ordinary person in the creeks, they are entitled to take back what is theirs
and use it while it is there. I may never do justice to this (*mis*)understanding
of ownership, snippets of which one gets in statements accredited to militant
leaders and their followers. Nevertheless, one thing that is often overlooked
is the sheer profligacy of the local political elite: whether this is justified or
not is the basis for another discussion, but the criminal activity, organized
and unorganized, associated with this underground counter-economy has
in the recent past shaken the very soul of the socioeconomic viability of
the Nigerian nation. A Chatham House report on this specific issue details
that oil thieves interviewed "justified their actions as part of the struggle for
greater Niger Delta 'resource control.'"[21]

While a huge and indeterminable quantity of this stolen oil is exchanged with criminal networks over international waters, sometimes for
arms and ammunition, the small quantity that gets into the hands of local
players and is further exchanged with local artisanal refiners in the Niger
Delta gives cause for grave concern. The so-called *kpo-fire* technology (a
type of fractional distillation) is crude, basic, and highly explosive. The
yield-per-barrel of oil depends both on the refining methods used and geological properties of the particular crude. A typical barrel of oil might yield
about 2 percent kerosene, 2 percent petrol, 41 percent diesel and 55 percent
wastes (including bitumen).[22] It is this waste, or "residue," that gets dumped
into the surrounding environment. Until now, the half-hearted efforts of
the Nigerian government to contain and possibly roll back the access that
these oil thieves have to the resource—the brazen acts of sabotage and crude
refining that fuels the underground diseconomy—has proved ineffectual.
Ordinary citizens watch helplessly, with dismay, how the military and other
security agencies deployed to track down and arrest culprits end up exacerbating the environmental problem by emptying the products from these
illegal refineries unto the ground and setting them ablaze! The cumulative
impact of all of these activities is seriously undermining the ecosystem of
the region.

21. Katsouris and Syne, *Nigeria's Criminal Crude*, 2.
22. Cf. Stakeholder Democracy Network (SDN), *Communities Not Criminals*, 18.

Whether it is in the Niger Delta, the Congo Basin, Didipio in the Philippines, or the Amazon Rainforest, questions have been arising in many resource-rich areas of the world where resource extraction in mining, logging, fishing, etc., are now putting increasing pressure on human persons as well as Earth's other inhabitants. Corporations as fictive personalities often demand to be treated as persons but lack the moral capacities that *real* persons normally possess. As a consequence, they "will not learn ecological virtue absent of legal and regulatory reform and the ecological education of business leaders and owners."[23] This ecological education should, in my opinion, begin with an examination of the origins of the individualism that is the soul of liberal market economics. Perhaps the obvious place to start is with the time-worn question of whether Christianity has a role in initiating and sustaining the ecological crisis.

Is Christianity to Blame for the Ecological Scourge?

This is a difficult question, because it raises the question of ethical formation. For instance, how do people get the moral values and convictions that govern their *be*-ing and *act*-ing? With particular reference to ecological being and acting, what is the genesis of the values and convictions that brought postmodern humans to this critical point in our relationship with the Earth? Without much nuance, ecological thinking often blames Christianity for the historical roots of the ecological problem, and Lynn White's famous indictment of the religion is not yet forgotten.[24] But Northcott blames White for omitting the fact that it was Francis Bacon's influential association of domination of nature with Christianity that spurred the conquest of matter on Earth. The idealist, Bacon, he says, was the originator of the secular narrative of human salvation, which has become the dominant eschatology of the modern era. Bacon believed that "progress in dominating nature—through scientific discovery and technological invention—is the means to redeeming the original fall from Paradise."[25] Implausible as this may sound today, there is a hint of a reason to believe that some in the Christian world not only believe but, perhaps, still live by that narrative.

The individualist one-upmanship of our consumerist market civilization may rightly be blamed for so-called Enlightenment liberty, especially in the manner in which it is said to have taken root in the New World. Northcott avers that without the limitations of monarchic power and

23. Northcott, "Artificial Persons against Nature," 104.
24. See White, "The Historical Roots of Our Ecological Crisis."
25. Northcott, *Political Theology of Climate Change*, 105.

aristocratic claims to landholdings, "[A]merican ideas of liberty, property, and rights take more individualistic and atomistic directions than those of many Europeans."[26] Central to this organizing idea of liberty was a dualism (Cartesian in origin) that disjointed nature from culture, and mind from body. Because there were always two distinct realities, this philosophy paved the way for modernity's de-spiritualization of nature. In itself, this created a dramatic new narrative of humanity's exalted and exceptional place in a cosmos increasingly perceived as having no other moral significance or divine purpose than its material value to humans. Approaching the rest of creation in this utilitarian way effectively deifies, idolizes, and, consequently, absolutizes the *anthropos* (human being), one out of the many different species on earth. This is idolatry! For idolatry really is "the root of all moral deviance, not only of deeds but also of the attitude."[27] Herein lies the hegemonic instinct that sustains *anthropogenia*, humanity's rapacious relationship with the rest of created reality.

This all-consuming "warfare" is now at the brink of consuming its perpetrator as well, for wherever and whenever one member of the household is rarefied, exclusion and exception is imposed, with detrimental effects. Thus, what faces us is not merely an ecological crisis; it is a rupture in our original relationship with the earth, where the human person had the responsibility of tending and keeping even as s/he tilled the earth for her/his sustenance. In the words of the Ecumenical Patriarch Bartholomew, our inhuman and godless attitudes towards our planet are "because we fail to see it as a gift inherited from above . . . . [thus] our obligation to receive, respect, and render this gift to future generations."[28] This is unjust, because for the patriarch justice means that we can see "the perfect relationship of all things to one another."[29] Similarly, Celia Deane-Drummond commented on Benedict XVI's deployment of the term "gratuitousness" in *Caritas in Veritate* to describe how foundational relationships in the reign of God need to find expression in the earthly city. She suggests that receiving the gift of creation as our own depends on God's mercy, and the goal is full communion.[30] With this understanding and application of gratuitousness, therefore, it should be possible to build relationships of whatever kind with freedom, in the assurance that we are part of the excess of gift that comes from God and is God.

---

26. Ibid., 239.

27. Poorthuis, "Prohibition of Idolatry, 56–57.

28. Chryssavgis, *On Earth as in Heaven*, 127.

29. Ibid., 163.

30. Deane-Drummond, "Technology, Ecology and the Divine," 151.

Roger Burggraeve says, "In Adam, every human receives a mediatory role to be fulfilled between God and the rest of creation, whereby the distance between God and creation is not so much annulled but rather bridged."[31] This mediatory role imposes a foundational responsibility to accept and treat the earth as a "gift" worth tending or shepherding, as it were. This is affirmed by Benedict XVI when he blames original sin on humanity's refusal to accept and live in this foundational relationship with God and other creatures, preferring rather to live in a self-destructive autonomy.[32] This relationship must be properly understood. There are few that would absolutely deny the instrumental value of nature for human subsistence, because almost everything that humans need for survival is sourced from the natural world. Pope Francis is forthright and point-blank in his assertion, "[W]e are not God. The earth was there before us and it has been given to us. . . . This implies a relationship of mutual responsibility between human beings and nature. Each community can take from the bounty of the earth whatever it needs for subsistence, but it also has the duty to protect and to ensure its fruitfulness for coming generations."[33] As far as I understand, the pope is saying that mutuality between us and nature was God's intention in creation *ab initio*.

The value that the biosphere has does not only relate to man's need and use. There is more, surely. Richard L. Fern suggests that, even at this most humble level where nature is simply a pool of resources to satisfy man's needs, it is already an "*indirect* object of moral concern relative to the good of humans."[34] This means in effect that its devaluation, depletion, or unfair distribution to present or future generations is already an ethical provocation. But even more than this is the demand that nature, wild and tame, makes on humans in that excess of being that nature's grandeur represents. Are we not struck by the awesome beauty and ferocious power of nature left to its own devices, how small we sometimes feel in the face of it, and how it beckons us to a reality beyond itself? The human being, because s/he is endowed with reason, has a moral responsibility to do all in his/her power to preserve the integrity and balance of the whole community or restore it where it has been compromised by human activity. Wherefore the pope wonders why "we seem to think we can substitute an irreplaceable and irretrievable beauty with something which we have created ourselves."[35]

32. Cf. Benedict XVI, *Caritas in Veritate*, 34.
33. Francis, *Laudato Si'*, 67.
34. Fern, *Nature, God and Humanity*, 14.
35. Francis, *Laudato Si'*, 34.

Human Persons Restoring Life to Creation

The rupture that we have established so far in the relationship of human beings with the created world is not irreparable, and our ecosystem losses are not irretrievable. Paradoxically, however, healing and restoration can only come about—apart from the earth's own incredible resilience and its capacity to self-repair—by deliberately recovering and restoring the dignity of the human person, both theoretically and didactically. This is the dignity in which God created her/him in the first instance, the inviolability of which is absolutely necessary for the full realization of the destiny of the human person both in him/herself and within society. What liberal individualism had achieved in systematically discarding human *personhood* in preference to human *individuality*[36] can be healed by a positive reappropriation of personhood and all the relational responsibility that the notion inspires and entails. I suggest that we begin with Jesus of Nazareth, the perfect *anthropos*, in whose incarnation the creator God (in Greek, *pneuma* means "spirit") is reunited with his creation (in Greek, *sarkikos*; in Latin, *materia*, which means "earthly, carnal, material, thing") in a virtuous *anthropogenia*, without *di*-stance or separation, yet distinct and distinguishable from what he created. It is this privileged divine mingling with creation that imposes upon human beings (the only ones created in the image and likeness of God and endowed with *nous*, i.e., a rational mind) the responsibility to protect and sustain life in the rest of creation, even as s/he reciprocally receives life-giving sustenance from the earth. Jesus, the perfect image of the invisible God, metaphorically assumes and dedicates full responsibility for the created order as when a shepherd assumes complete responsibility for the welfare and well-being of the sheep. Unlike the thief who comes to steal, kill, and destroy, He the Good Shepherd says, "I have come that they may have life, and have it to the full" (John 10:10, NIV). Giving life and sustaining life in both human and other species appears, therefore, to be the most responsible *be*-ing and *act*-ing of those persons who are redeemed by, and are in, Christ.

Now, the moral person is responsible not only in the indicative but also, and more importantly, in the imperative, for "human beings are not merely neutral, ontological beings, one kind of being among others. Rather, human beings are made responsible. They are not simply responsible for their responsibility also receives a certain content and direction."[37] Their responsibility, well-conceived, can only be in the context of freedom. In this sense, we subscribe to the consensus that freedom and responsibility are

36. Cf. Michel, "Ownership and the Human Person," 155.
37. Burggraeve, "Responsibility Precedes Freedom," 120.

two sides of the same ethical coin. The ideas that "the human person can lead a good life because God has called him or her into life out of love" and that "human dignity depends on freedom, as does the idea that the human person is made in the image of God"[38] must remain central to Catholic ethics. The priority of God's loving action in creation is what dignifies and energizes it, and the human person is the greatest beneficiary of this prior love. Human fidelity and virtue, ecological or otherwise, proceed from out of that excess of love. Following Emmanuel Levinas (1906–95), Burggraeve refers to responsibility as "the negative reverse side of freedom," a veritable "weight of the task that is stuck to the being of the 'I.'" According to this thinking, freedom is literally a "work" that "needs to be done,'" and by reason of which "freedom is transformed into fate."[39] Yet, unlike a horse that is bridled and controlled by its rider to go one way and not another, human freedom is truly free except, of course, for the "unspoken injunction" of responsibility that hangs about it, ineluctably, to moderate it.

It is important to point out here that I am not referring to the metaphysical (ontological) *freedom of fact* but to the moral (teleological) *freedom of development*.[40] Rational human nature is self-reflective and is equipped with moral antennae that perceive, deliberate, and freely pass judgment on possible courses of action. Only beings that are internally free with the freedom of development, which opens up to fresh new possibilities for growth in intellectual and moral virtues, can sufficiently possess this self-control or dare to take up the responsibility of restoring life to the earth. The license that is fixated merely on the metaphysical level of fact, on the other hand, simply impels one to uncontrolled and unrestrained action, without consideration of moral consequences. It prompts the agent, for instance, to action in all cases: if something *can* be done then it *should* be done, especially if one can get away with it! This favorite philosophical stance of liberal individualism eventually "ended in the enslavement of man (*sic*) to his (*sic*) impulses and his (*sic*) environment."[41] Where human freedom is genuine and not just a form of license, it lends itself to "rational self-control which is in turn opposed to any absolute freedom taken in the sense of totally uncontrolled and unrestrained action."[42]

38. Marx, "Archbishop's Perspective," 277.

39. Burggraeve, "No One Can Save Oneself," 24–25.

40. This distinction was well made in Michel, "Ownership and the Human Person," 161–62.

41. Michel, "Ownership and the Human Person," 160.

42. Ibid., 161.

I have belabored this point because our understanding of the human person is key to making sense of the maze of moral and ethical issues we are confronting now, and at any given time. It affords us a moral compass with which to navigate our world without crashing over the precipice. In *Gaudium et Spes*, the Council Fathers insist that "objective criteria must be used, criteria drawn from the nature of the human person and human action."[43] That is why Michel infers that one of the great achievements of Christianity lies in the development of the notion of the human person. He could see even then that "the history of Christianity is the history of the gradual recognition of the inviolability of the human person by men and by society, of the sacredness of man's right to freedom of self-determination in the exercise of his conduct."[44] Because modern civilization failed to place this freedom in the context of the whole person, it created a world in which individuals became self-referring atoms with no external reference points. The result of this is the development of liberal anthropologies that negate the intrinsic connection of the individual to community or society. This connection, it turns out, is indispensable to the full realization of his/her potentialities, even with regard to tending the earth.

Furthermore, because ethics arises from conceptions of the human person, some liberal ethical positions tend to "posit the human person as an isolated, singular, *suppositum* of rights" (ontological) while excluding the (teleological) "dimension of intersubjectivity as well as the engendered aspects of human existence."[45] This understanding of the human person, no doubt, grounds and directs the way we come to think of human society and its political and economic functioning. Gregory Beabout, et al., explain that *suppositum* denotes individuation as captured in a specific species or nature, and restricted to matter or substance, but without the rational quality that constitutes personhood. The human person, however, is not just material substance, s/he is also a spirit, and by that token, capable of relation subjectively with God in a transcendent way and intersubjectively with other persons and with nature. Perhaps at this point we should give an adequate consideration to the human personhood under review.

Adequately Considered Human Persons

I cannot fail to credit the Belgian moralist Louis Janssens (1908–2001) with influencing present magisterial teaching on the human person with his

43. Catholic Church, *Gaudium et Spes*, 51.
44. Michel, "Ownership and the Human Person," 156.
45. Beabout et al., *Beyond Self-Interest*, 9.

groundbreaking article on the subject of artificial insemination,[46] in which he articulated eight fundamental dimensions of the human person. The human person, he said, is (1) a subject; (2) an embodied subject; (3) part of the material world; (4) interrelational with other persons; (5) an interdependent social being; (6) historical; (7) equal but unique; and (8) called to know and worship God. Though these dimensions can be delineated and analyzed individually, they cannot be separated one from another, because they "belong to one and the same human person: they are interwoven and form a synthesis because each is proper to the integrity of every person."[47] Thus, when we take these essential dimensions together, they constitute what Janssens refers to as the human person integrally and adequately considered. According to this objective criterion enthroned by the Council Fathers, whatever promotes the good of the human person considered in this comprehensive way is good, and whatever violates it is bad. Perhaps we need to interrogate our present rapidity in exploiting the resources of the earth, and whether that has not somehow diminished the human person as such. Pope Francis has just reemphasized the vital connection between the sufferings of human persons and the depletion of the environment in such a way that we cannot any longer separate them one from another, or radically differentiate their origin.[48]

Prospects for a Theo-Ethic of Relationality

Throughout this essay, I have endeavored to balance the dignity of the human person on the one hand and her/his responsibility on the other hand, to recognize and promote the intrinsic value of non-human nature. In doing this, I have refrained either from rehashing an outright anthropocentrism or enthroning an "undifferentiated biocentrism." My approach has been informed by Simone Morandini who admonishes that we "concentrate on *responsibility*, which is a typically human trait, namely, the capacity to assess the consequences of one's actions over a wide space of time without yielding to the temptation of looking only at the present day."[49] The pursuit of virtue is a more positive expression of responsibility, and it involves, *inter alia*, living a life that honors and respects our most basic needs and desires, and all the goods that make for human well-being. Virtue opens the way to the

---

46. Janssens, "Artificial Insemination."

47. Ibid., 4.

48. Francis, *Laudato Si'*, 90–91.

49. Morandini, " Ecology and Theological Ethics," 76.

enjoyment of all these, though in an ordered, reasonable, and joyous way.[50]
Exercising due and appropriate restraints in our relationships—political,
economic, and ecological—is part of being virtuous.

According to the Jewish biblical creation narrative, the human person was created last of all. By this token, perhaps, s/he inherits the original
burden of building relations with all that preceded her/him, each in their
distinction. The personal maturation of any individual involves coming to
accept oneself as a distinct person, and also recognizing that other persons
and things are really *other*, and not just extensions of oneself.[51] This is what
Burggraeve means when he reads the content of the creation narrative as
one "movement from indistinguishability to separation and difference."[52]
He further speaks of the creator God as "the One who creates in order not to
let his creatures disappear in his own bottomless, dark depths, but in order
to make them 'come to be' as independent beings with their specific individuality. . . to make them live as distinct beings who precisely out of their
separateness can commit themselves to God as partners."[53] In like manner,
the relationship of human beings with the rest of nature is commissioned to
be mutually supportive and mutually upholding in such a way that nature is
not absorbed or dissolved into naught by human tech-ingenuity. Being the
rational and responsible one, it behooves him/her naturally to uphold these
distinctions, albeit, at the risk of making these others into creation's outsid-
ers in a tribalistic instinct which is the hallmark of original sin.[54]

The view of the human person as individual and distinct could tempt
us to adopt individualist anthropologies that exclude the equally valid emphasis on the social nature of the person. In saying this, it is not my intention to discount the appropriate self-love that recognizes the individual's
personal worth. This loving response to, and "recognition of one's own value
as a person is not only not at odds with love of others but is the only feasible base for such love."[55] Self-love is, therefore, neither always egoistic nor
self-indulgent, but recognizes value in sharing with other selves in a kind
of "participated glory," out of which agapeic self-sacrifice, "a mysterious response to the person-related values,"[56] of community can result. So, there is

50. See Lamoureux and Wadell, *Christian Moral Life*, 115.

51. Cf. Kelly, *New Directions in Moral Theology*, 43.

52. Burggraeve, "To Love Otherwise," 17.

53. Ibid., 15.

54. See Edwards, "Humans and Other Creatures."

55. Maguire, *Moral Choice*, 93.

56. Ibid., 93 and 94.

no necessary conflict between individual subjectivity and the social nature of the human person, even extending to community of nature.

Conclusion

Catholic social thinking has always maintained a creative balance between individuality and openness to the human or biotic community, because relation is at the core of Christian understanding of life.[57] Creation "in his own image" implies a constitutive relationship between the creature and the creator, the fruit of which relationship graces the communal bonding of creatures between and among themselves. This two-tier relationship of the human subject with God and with his/her earth-fellows is the basis of community—political, economic, or ecological. We cannot exclude ecological relations from this system, because this is the tissue upon which the *humanum* lives or dies. This fundamental relationality "as existing in communion with God and with others, leads to a very different perspective than a view of the person as autonomous, independent and separate from others, a perspective that puts primary importance on the good of the individual."[58] It is my belief, therefore, that recovering relationality as a central pillar of ethical living may be the access point we require to a full recovery of our appropriate place in creation and, consequently, to the much desired peace in our common home.

57. Congregation for the Doctrine of the Faith, *Catechism of the Catholic Church*, 2415.

58. Stabile, "CST 101," 2.

12

Becoming Stewards of Creation: Ecological Virtue Ethics from the Perspective of Otherness

ROLANDO A. TUAZON, CM

If the simple fact of being human moves people to care for the environment of which they are a part, Christians in their turn realize that their responsibility within creation, and their duty towards nature and the Creator, are an essential part of their faith.
—POPE FRANCIS[1]

Introduction

The environmental crisis has been addressed with comprehensive scientific analyses, complex theories, and global agreements, policies, and protocols, along with either deontological or utilitarian ethical frameworks.[2] Such may prove to be quite important in the responsible management of our natural environment. Yet, there may be an equally necessary resource, too often forgotten, in environmental discourses which is found in the "ecology of

1. Francis, *Laudato Si'*, 64.

2. For example, the Climate Change Convention (CCC), Kyoto Protocol, carbon rationing, taxation on greenhouse gas production, etc. But studies also show that there is a "greenwashing of corporate culture." See Greer and Bruno, *Greenwash*, 30–32, and Vitug, "Forest Policy and National Politics," 11–39.

everyday life" as well as in local cultures and traditions that would make the big initiatives more sustainable and effective. Virtue and character formation of the moral agents who can relate more harmoniously with and stand for the environment should be part of any meaningful attempt to address the environmental crisis. Pope Francis articulates this in his encyclical letter, *Laudato Si'*: "It is not enough to speak only of the integrity of ecosystems. We have to dare to speak of the integrity of human life, of the need to promote and unify all the great values."[3]

Coming from the philosophical and theological traditions of virtue ethics and from the more recent discourses on the theology and spirituality of stewardship viewed from the perspective of the philosophy of alterity and otherness, this chapter investigates how the molding of virtuous character becomes crucial in the responsible stewardship and protection of the environment. Using purposive sampling in qualitative research with the narrative method, I interviewed environmentalists who have different engagements with and advocacy for the environment (in terms of its protection and preservation, or in dealing with its disastrous impacts). The focus is on how they turned out to be involved; what their deepest philosophical, ethical and religious convictions are; what they habitually do for the care of the environment; and how they assess their impact in addressing the environmental crisis. The analysis of their narratives from the said perspective could hopefully contribute to the on-going construction of ecological virtue ethics.

Virtue Ethics and its Genealogy

Contemporary interest in virtue theory started with G. E. M. Anscombe's 1958 essay, "Modern Moral Philosophy," which reintroduced and argued for the viability of virtue theory based on Aristotle.[4] Yet, it was the influential and widely discussed work of Alasdair MacIntyre, *After Virtue,* that brought virtue ethics to the mainstream. With the growing concern for the environment in the last few decades, a fresh articulation of virtue ethics can be traced in works that focused on the character development of paradigmatic figures like Aldo Leopold, Rachel Carson, and Henry David Thoreau, who demonstrated in their lives and works profound concern for

---

3. Francis, *Laudato Si'*, 224.

4. Seth A. Bible writes a concise history of the environmental virtue ethics (EVE) movement. See Bible, *Pursuing Ecological Virtue*, 33–45.

the environment.[5] One can appreciate an increasing amount of literature which has dwelled on a similar subject referred to now as environmental virtue ethics.[6]

The main idea being put forward in environmental virtue ethics is that the way to go about addressing environmental crisis is to mold moral characters that could develop ecological virtues which would help maintain harmony with the whole of the created world. "Rather than ask, as deontologists and utilitarians might, 'What should I do?' virtue ethicists ask, 'What should I be?'"[7] This brings us to another central concept in the Judeo-Christian tradition that may specifically offer a rich resource in addressing environmental concerns, i.e., stewardship of creation.

The Christian Stewardship Ethic

As people awaken to the extent and impact of environmental crisis, stewardship has become one of the prominent concepts around which Christian environmentalists navigate. Laurel Kearns describes Christian environmentalism in the United States as taking three ecotheological ethical paths: the Christian stewardship ethic, the eco-justice ethic, and the creation spirituality ethic.[8] She speaks about the Christian stewardship ethic as starting with the biblical mandate and evangelical theological appeal which projects an image of God that is transcendent and authoritative and identifies human sinfulness and disobedience as the root cause of the environmental crisis. Willis Jenkins, referring to Kearns's models as strategies of Christianity which are situated within one of "three ecologies of grace: redemption, sanctification, or deification," claims that "[s]tewardship theologies rely on tropes of redemption, where encounter with God creates vocational responsibilities to care for creation."[9] The focus is on "faithful practices, describing how to inhabit the providential landscape created by God's special relationship to humans."[10] That relationship defines human identity, dignity, and

5. Moore, "The Truth of the Barnacles" 265–77; Shaw, "A Virtue Ethics Approach," 53–67; Cafaro, "Thoreau, Leopold, and Carson," 3–17.

6. Frasz, "Environmental Virtue Ethics," 259–74; Hull, "All About EVE," 89–111; Sandler, *Character and Environment*; van Wensveen, *Dirty Virtues*; Bible, *Pursuing Ecological Virtue*.

7. Freiman, Review of *Environmental Virtue Ethics*, 133.

8. Kearns, "Saving the Creation, 55–70.

9. Jenkins, *Ecologies of Grace*, 19. Jenkins considers "eco-justice theologies" as relying on a "view of sanctification in which grace illuminates creation's integrity," while "ecological spiritualties" as relying on "appropriate themes of deification."

10. Jenkins, *Ecologies of Grace*, 77.

responsibility as having been "created according to the image and likeness of God." Commenting on this biblical concept, Claus Westermann holds, "By virtue of being created, it bears a responsibility; human dignity and responsibility are inseparable."[11] Ken Gnanakan expounds on this concept and claims,

> The image of God in humanity needs to be seen in terms of re-
> sponsibility as well as privilege. Humans are given the privilege
> of possessing a rational, moral, and spiritual dimension that en-
> ables them to act creatively and responsibly towards the whole
> of creation. Being made in God's image, we are to protect the
> environment in accountability towards our fellow creatures and
> the rest of creation.[12]

That privileged position of humans as the most important creatures who have been given the task to have dominion over creation was criticized for its anthropocentrism and for being the cause of the environmental crisis. Lynn White, Jr., attributes to the Judeo-Christian tradition the domination paradigm that is rooted in the Genesis narrative, which has been interpreted as the basis for rejecting pagan animism and for legitimizing the exploita-tion of the environment.[13] This critique against Christianity has generated a lot of responses both positive and negative. In defense of Christianity, at-tempts have been made to reinterpret the meaning of the resources of tradi-tion that White attacked. Gnanakan, for example, taking a historico-critical hermeneutical approach, presents the wider context within which the word "dominion" could be better understood, not as "heartless domination" but as loving and caring responsibility for others.[14] We see an elaboration of this in Sean McDonagh, who claims that the second, yet older, account of creation describes Yahweh as planting "a garden for humans and '[He] took man and put him in the garden of Eden to till it and keep it' (Gen 2:15)." "Till" in Hebrew—*abad*—has overtones of service, while "keep"—*shamar*—has overtones of preserving and defending from harm.[15] The divine mandate

11. Westermann, *Genesis*, 10ff.

12. Gnanakan, "Creation," 110–20.

13. White, "Historical Roots," 1205.

14. Gnanakan, "Creation, Christians," 110–20.

15. McDonagh, *Passion for the Earth*, 129. He notes the criticisms against the stewardship model: (1) it connotes an absentee God contrary to the biblical concept of God's presence in His creation; (2) "the stewardship metaphor is unable to carry any overtones of the earth as the body of God"; (3) it may give humans propriety rights over the rest of creation; (4) "[s]tewardship also implies that nature is somehow in-complete unless it is improved upon by human hands"; (5) anthropocentrism is "the most dangerous assumption contained in the idea of stewardship" (130–33). He argues

therefore does not give humans the right to exploit and subdue (*radhah* and *habhah*)[16] but the responsibility to take care of nature. George Rupp argues that it is "only when the transcendent God of biblical religion is no longer thought to intervene in the world as either creator or as redeemer that the full force of claims for human dominion over nature becomes evident."[17] Theologically reflecting on this reality and the need to recapture our stewardship of creation from the perspective of redemption, Willis Jenkins holds, "By redeeming and restoring humanity, God redeems and restores creation."[18] Being the model of stewardship, Jesus's lordship and dominion are characterized, not by willful hegemony, but by self-giving and humble service unto death for the other.

Considering White's generative thesis as a challenge to Christianity, Jenkins notes that "if problems arise from a religious anthropocentric worldview with little intrinsic value, then Christian thinkers need to vindicate their cosmology on those terms, recuperate minority resources from forgotten cosmologies, or propose a new cosmology."[19] Gibson Winter has also noted the importance of how worldviews condition our way of life and patterns of behavior. Speaking of root metaphors, he claims that premodern rationality had an organic root metaphor which eventually gave way to a mechanistic root metaphor during modernity.[20] The organic root metaphor had the *body* as the fundamental image in understanding the life and dynamics of social organization.[21] Unity, order, cohesion, stability, and respect for authority formed part of the fundamental values of the hierarchically structured communities. Conditioned especially by their simple

---

for a more ecocentric perspective that speaks of God's immanence in creation and the intrinsic value of the whole natural world.

16. The terms "exploiting" and "subduing" (*radhah* and *habhah*) could be privileged if we "situate the Genesis mandates within God's call to conversion, thus emphasizing repentant obedience rather than free license." Jenkins, *Ecologies of Grace*, 80.

17. Rupp, "Religion," 24–25, cited in Jenkins, *Ecologies of Grace*, 11.

18. Jenkins, *Ecologies of Grace*, 85.

19. Jenkins, *Ecologies of Grace*, 11. There are three assumptions about religious worldviews in White's critique of Christianity: "that they generate social practices, that they should be measured by the criteria of intrinsic value and anthropocentrism, and that salvation stories threaten environmentally benign worldviews" (ibid.).

20. Winter, *Liberating Creation*. For a good synthesis of Gibson's theory about the development of root metaphors and its application to green biotechnology, see Birkenfeld, "Deciphering Moral Landscapes, 233–50.

21. Nisbet traces, in Western thought, the beginnings and the evolution of the organic metaphor to which Winter is indebted. But contrary to Nisbet's thesis, he argues that the mechanical metaphor has replaced the organic metaphor in the later development of Western thought. See Nisbet, *Social Change and History*.

agricultural context, people engaged in productive and economic activities respecting an ordered rhythm of life defined by a seasonal and cyclical perspective of time. The Aristotelian-Thomistic ethics of virtue stood prominent in the moral landscape of the period. What was good and ethical was based on long-standing community practices, which defined the moral standards of a virtuous life. Moreover, such standards were ontologically claimed as corresponding to objective metaphysical reality, which could serve as a *telos* of a well-ordered social network. The metaphysical presupposition of the stewardship model could be well appreciated within such a root metaphor.

With the onset of urban mercantilism and industrial capitalism which flourished in modernity as a result of technological and scientific inventions, the organic root metaphor began to fade into the background. The mechanistic root metaphor gradually became the basis for the emerging modern collective consciousness, giving way to scientific rationality (scientism), radicalization of the autonomy of the subject (individualism), and rejection of the role of religion in society (secularism).[22] "Within the new bureaucratic social system that was based on the mechanistic root metaphor, competition, production, domination, development efficiency, and profitability ranked as the most important values."[23] In a "technological society"[24] driven by the ideology of progress with sophisticated machines and tools dominating all processes of life, technological control of nature legitimizes further explorations and exploitation of the earth's resources as well as the continuous subjugation of its peoples. Especially when technology and science are put under the control of those whose principal value is economic ends, O'Neill observes, "the goals of research and development are set not by the internal goals of scientific disciplines themselves, but by the goals of commerce."[25] Within this mechanistic root metaphor, even life, along with the human body, is understood merely as a machine that can be manipulated and whose parts can be replaced and commoditized.[26] The stewardship concept could hardly function within this model as evident in the more destructive pursuit of individualist, materialistic, and economic ends. Many Christian environmentalists blame the environmental crisis

22. Winner describes how "technology" shapes or misshapes the human spirit. See Winner, *The Whale and the Reactor.*

23. Tuazon, "Biotech Food," 133.

24. See Ellul, *The Technological Society.*

25. O'Neill, *Ecology, Policy, and Politics,* 157.

26. See Nelkin and Andrews, "*Homo Economicus,*" 30–39.

on such unreflective modern rationality.[27] Pope Francis himself traces the "human roots of the ecological crisis" to the globalizing "technocratic paradigm" that is based on "modern anthropocentrism," disregarding the overall design of God for the whole of the created world.[28]

From the Perspective of Otherness

The theological and philosophical discourses on virtue ethics and stewardship ethics that we have examined above seem to belong to a particular tradition that flourished in the past but which was debunked or abandoned by modern rationality, for better or worse. Within a postmodern milieu, contemporary men and women have become aware of the limits of modernity and the dangers of its metanarratives of freedom and reason coupled with its ideology of progress, especially regarding its impact on the environment. Confronted with this reality, one can either journey back into the past with a sense of nostalgia and reject all of the "developments" and "evolution" of the historical human consciousness, or move forward and continue with the trajectory of modern rationality leading to the postmodern ethos. On the one hand, we see the appeal of tradition, which comes along with religion, myths, customary practices, and authoritative claims, finding its way back to our contemporary socioeconomic, political, cultural, and moral landscape. On the other hand, we also see the postmodern celebration of alterity—difference or *différance* (difference with a vengeance, a la Derrida)—giving way to the recognition of small narratives and subjugated voices in what has become now a multicultural, pluralistic, and intercultural social landscape where ethical subjectivism, relativism, and emotivism thrive.

The option we have chosen is a transmodern critical appropriation of the tradition of virtue ethics and stewardship ethics. We shall employ, on the one hand, Winter's third root metaphor, i.e., the artistic root metaphor, in defining how the said resources of tradition could meaningfully and relevantly function within our postmodern landscape. Enrique Dussel's ana-dialectics will serve as a perspective in such critical appropriation, on the other hand. After a short anadialectical elaboration of Winter's artistic worldview, we shall examine the narratives and worldviews of environmental activists and advocates who navigate meaningfully in our contemporary social milieu.

27. De Tavernier speaks of the loss of a theocentric worldview as the most probable reason for the environmental crisis. De Tavernier, "Ecology and Ethics," 249.

28. Francis, *Laudato Si'*, 101–36.

Winter considers that the organic and the mechanistic root metaphors have experienced ideological resistance during the twentieth century. Such dialectical tension, he claims, has paved the way for the emergence of a new root metaphor which he describes as a creative and critical synthesis of the two worldviews, emanating from the strengths of both while overcoming their destructive potentials. Winter has this to say:

> The aim here is not to dispel all other imagery but to relocate these other images in more appropriate places within the authentic processes of human dwelling. Thus, the creativity and self-transcending power of human species life in history and language can be liberated from the oppressive forces of mechanism and from the nostalgic yearning for traditional, organic bonds of blood and soil.[29]

In the artistic root metaphor, the creativity of the mechanistic approach is combined with the value of community, emphasized in the organic perspective. There is recognition of the importance of people's participation in the creative endeavors of solving problems like the environmental crisis and in improving our ecological landscape. The most important values within this metaphor include creativity, empowerment, social justice, integrity, and care of creation, as well as collaboration and networking in the global community. The metaphor rests on the fundamental assumption of interdependence among peoples and the interconnectedness of humanity and nature. It is through an open and critical process of dialogue in these relationships that truth is achieved. Dogmatic, ideological, and totalizing claims are replaced by a deep sensitivity to a revelatory event that opens new horizons and possibilities for creative transformation and participative empowerment. "No longer is order preordained (organic), nor is progress unquestioned and limitless (mechanistic)."[30] The fixed teleology of traditional ethical rationalities, as well as utilitarian and deontological considerations, is allowed to be constantly challenged by new ethical perspectives and a wider moral vision.[31] The reality and perspective of the other, those who have been initially excluded and marginalized by the system, could be allowed to contest the assumption on which the system stands in order to constantly break open its totalizing discourses.[32] Hermeneutical enclo-

29. Winter, *Liberation Creation*, 27.

30. Binkenfeld, "Deciphering Moral Landscapes," 244.

31. Burke's comparative analysis of the agrarian mindset, modern Enlightenment mindset (1750s onward), and emerging (transmodern) mindset (1990s into this millennium). Burke, "Globalization and Ecology," 30–32.

32. In his liberation ethics, Enrique Dussel develops the ana-dialectical scheme,

sures undergo ruptures through new narratives and experiences that sub-
vert long-held presuppositions and give way to the emergence of liberating
metaphors.[33]

Narratives of Environmental Advocates[34]

What follows now are three life stories of people who are deeply engaged in
environmental advocacy. In our research, we have interviewed six people,
but we have decided to limit this discussion to three narratives from which
we can draw new insights toward the development of ecological virtue
ethics.

The first narrative is that of Pya Macliing Malayao, an Igorot from
Bontoc in the Mountain Province of the Philippines. She is the spokes-
person and national coordinator of the National Alliance of Indigenous
Peoples' Organizations in the Philippines (in Tagalog, *Kalipunan ng Katu-
tubong Mamamayan ng Pilipinas*, or KAMP). It was in 2010 that she joined
the national network which was founded in 2007 to consolidate advocacy
efforts of the different local organizations of indigenous communities. Most
of these organizations started in the 1970s and 1980s as a reaction to the
development aggression of companies driven by economic greed and interest in mining, logging, and the building of dams and thermal energy power
plants.

Pya's engagement with the issues of her community started with her
interest in their cultural indigenous heritage. Having been exposed to the
very colorful and contextual celebrations of their community rituals and
sociocultural festivities during summer visits and vacations in her home
village, Pya discovered the issues that confronted the community through
their songs, dance, and theater arts. The conscientization process that she
underwent during those occasions, as well as during her studies at the
University of the Philippines, gradually firmed up her social commitment.
She first joined the Cordillera youth organization and eventually decided
to work full-time in addressing the issues that indigenous peoples are
constantly subjected to. Protection of the indigenous communities means

---

which was influenced by Emmanuel Levinas's ethical concept of the "other." Dussel
speaks of the other as historically and socially embodied in the poor who are marginalized, excluded, and oppressed by the dominant system. See Dussel, *Ética de la
Liberación*.

33. This whole section has largely been argued in Tuazon, "Biotech Food," 135–36.

34. See Ryan, "Narrative Environmental Ethics," 822–34.

ensuring their rights to their ancestral lands which equally means preserving their habitat and environment.

"Our ancestral land along with the whole environment," Pya explained, "is integrally intertwined with our life as indigenous peoples." Elaborating further, she said: "It is in our ancestral land that our system of beliefs and practices in the economic, political, and cultural aspects of our life is deeply rooted. Since the core of our identity and spirituality is intrinsically connected with the land, we therefore consider the land as sacred and alive." In addition, Pya noted that "our natural environment is imbued with the presence of the creator and of the spirits of our ancestors. Therefore, to remove our people from it would be tantamount to destroying our very life and identity." This conviction, according to Pya, comes along with the ethical commitment to protect the environment as stewards especially for the sake of "the future generations who are considered as the true and legitimate owners of the land and its resources."

Pya's advocacy work in the national alliance includes struggle against foreign-driven development aggression which is characterized by exploitation of the environment within a highly monetized, liberal market economy. Through conscientization programs, public information dissemination, petition signing, street parliamentary action, and policy change intervention in Congress, the indigenous network aims to achieve the following: integrity of ancestral lands; quality of life of the community defined in terms of the right to dignity of life, health, and education; and self-determination in the indigenous economic, political, and cultural systems. Though gains through such mobilizations have not really been abundant, the network had reasons to celebrate several victories: a congressional inquiry on some human rights violations associated with people who fought in defense of land and the environment and policy reforms such as the 1997 Indigenous Peoples' Rights Act.

Asked whether her involvement as an environmental activist affects her character as a person in terms of values and virtues, Pya nodded and made the following assertions: "The values and virtues in our community, like simplicity of life (*"mabuhay nang tama at sapat,"* to live with just enough); generosity with others (*"huwag sarilihin ang biyaya,"* not being selfish with blessings); wisdom (*"mayaman sa karunungan at di sa salapi,"* to be rich in wisdom and not just in wealth); courage (*"paninindigan para sa tama at katotohanan,"* standing for what is right and true); integrity in one's life and in creation (*"di ibenta ang dangal at ang kalikasan,"* not selling out one's dignity or the environment); and a sense of unity with the community (*"magka-isa sa laban sa mga panlilinlang,"* being united in the fight against deception) are of outmost importance in being advocates and stewards of the environment and of the Indigenous peoples." She claims that the level to which these values are upheld and lived out in their communities, especially among the leaders, defines to a large extent their success in protecting their land, environment, and life.

The next interviewee was Henry C. Yunez who is the deputy chief executive officer of the Buddhist Tzu Chi Foundation, Philippines. His journey as a volunteer in the foundation started in 1997. The other members of his family, individually and separately attracted to what the foundation does, have likewise joined as volunteers. It was not so much the area of worship and prayers, emphasized in other Buddhist traditions, that convinced them but the concrete works of compassion that Dharma Master Cheng Yen teaches. The massive relief operations and the rehabilitation and reconstruction of the city of Tacloban in the wake of the Typhoon Yolanda (Haiyan) could be counted as one of the many ways the Tzu Chi Foundation has brought hope and life back to people who were devastated by both natural and man-made calamities. In fact, Henry, along with his family, welcomed us for our requested interview in their residence only five minutes after they arrived from Tacloban where they had just finished a ceremony turning over a large number of houses to Yolanda victims. The initial plan to interview Henry gave way to a more communal process with the whole family sharing experiences, reflections, values, and convictions. It turned out to be a "focused group discussion."

The conversation started over a strictly vegetarian dinner that the family prepared for us in their residence. After they became members of the Tzu Chi Foundation, the family, while remaining Christians, started to live out the foundation's Buddhist philosophy, beginning with basic respect for the whole cosmic order. They believe that all sentient beings should be allowed to exist in peace, enjoying their intrinsic value apart from human beings' instrumental and anthropocentric use of them. Sharing their convictions and values, especially about how they relate with the environment, Henry and his family said that "what we have in the world should really be sufficient for all if everyone should have only what is enough for his or her authentic needs." Against the ideology of progress which lies at the heart of the modern project, they also recognize the limits of the earth's resources and the irreparable depletion of its minerals, reasons why there should be no waste in people's use of them. "It starts with the simple practice of not having leftover food on our plates." They spoke about the four strategies in the proper management of what we have: reduce, reclassify, reuse, and recycle. Against the background of contemporary consumerism and materialism, reducing our wants and needs calls for a simpler lifestyle, overcoming desire which in Buddhism is considered the root cause of our human suffering.

Reclassifying facilitates the identification of items that could be used for different purposes. Reusing reduces the need for product manufacturing which imposes a toll on the environment. If the first two are not avoided, one should resort to recycling, which prevents the buildup of waste that has a destructive impact on the environment.

Henry is convinced that everything in nature has a unique, intrinsic value and fundamental equality. He believes that "there is a certain spirit that is present in all of creation." He asserted that "whatever one does in his/her life either sows seeds of goodness or cultivates bad seeds which eventually grow and get back on us." Speaking about "karma," a Hindu concept that seems to persist in Buddhism, Henry spoke of a conviction that "from the good seed one has sown comes rewarding life conditions and from a bad seed comes havoc in our life." Patterns of behavior destructive to the environment will eventually merit the wrath of nature through flooding, strong typhoons, climate change, etc. But responsible virtuous living—especially simplicity, humility, generosity, etc.—will help bring about harmony in creation. Such stewardship of nature is also applicable in the way one deals with people through acts of kindness, concern, love, and compassion. "The seeds of goodness are what we continue to sow in our lives and in our mission, that give people reason to hope again and believe in their capacity to do good and live meaningful lives."

The third narrative is that of Patricia Gwen Borcena, a developmental and environmental sociologist who founded Green Research in 2005. She describes her organization as "a development think tank which prioritizes sociological research and policy analyses on the Philippine environment." Gwen's impressive curriculum vitae demonstrates her high level of commitment and engagement in advocacy work for the environment. She has conducted a lot of research, networking, and consensus-building in order to firm up proposals in Congress for legislative policies in favor of environmental preservation and protection and of sustainable development. The impact of her network's contribution can likewise be seen in the suspension of certain projects or agreements harmful to the interest of the people and to the environment (e.g., the Japan-Philippines Economic Partnership Agreement, or JPEPA); the insertion of environmental perspectives into the Philippine Development Plan; the issuing of executive orders against particular mining ventures; and even political mobilization against politicians who allow programs destructive to the environment).

Gwen's journey on this road less traveled started during her student days, particularly with her involvement in the Ateneo Student Catholic Action. During the dictatorial Marcos regime, the political climate in the Philippines was ripe for social activism which characterized the First Quarter

Storm. The youth's idealism made them work for a new world or social order. Gwen's exposure to the difficult realities of the urban poor, whose areas she regularly visited for her apostolate, made her aspire more to work for justice and social transformation, and it eventually led her to pursue a course in social science and development. She joined the Jesuit Volunteer Program in order to work in areas outside of Manila but ended up working in the metropolis doing community organizing among the urban poor. Some time later, because of her work with non-government organizations (NGOs), government organizations (GOs), and other research institutions—as well as her MA studies in sociology and PhD specialization in environmental sociology—she found herself involved with many other vulnerable sectors of the population: with the fishermen along Laguna Lake, the street children in Manila, the indigenous peoples of Mindoro and Palawan, and farmers in different provinces. All these experiences and exposures solidified her commitment to environmental advocacy, especially concerning biodiversity, illegal quarries, mining, toxic waste, safe food, waste management, and sustainable economy.

Expressing her convictions and beliefs that stem from her experiences, studies, and analyses of the social realities, Gwen identified "the neoliberal market economy and its ideology of progress which rests on consumerism and materialism as a major culprit that gives way to social inequality as well as to environmental crisis." She asserted that "the work for social justice, for the environment, and service of the poor are deeply interconnected aspects of our advocacy." Furthermore, she also said that "the many aspects of our life are, in fact, interconnected as they are permeated with a kind of divine presence." Considering that one could recognize the intrinsic value of life in nature, it therefore follows that "the integrity of creation should be respected." She noted that "as stewards of creation, we are called to take good care of the environment and promote its genuine growth that should be characteristically inclusive, sustainable, climate-resilient, and participatory."

"All of these tasks," Gwen argued, "would require a form of life ruled by particular values and virtues like climate justice, simplicity of life, integrity and consistency, respect for nature, critical rationality, and a certain kind of passion and vigilance for the truth." For her part, Gwen remarked that some of her friends in the corporate world have asked her why she has chosen to work in a field where financial reward is wanting. She would always retort that the happiness and fulfillment she finds in what she does for people and for the environment is something that cannot be bought with money. Such wisdom can come only from somebody who has sought to work for the environment and for others' interests rather than her own.

Analysis and Reflection

The narratives of these three environmental activists and advocates are intertwined with the narratives of the organizations or groups to which they belong. In fact, in some instances, the interviews were done not alone but with others, in pairs or in a group. Each of these activists has different experiences and commitments in relation to their environmental advocacy, yet one can discern certain points of convergence in their narratives.

First, the interviewees share a common critique of the modern rationality and lifestyle that is wasteful, environmentally unfriendly, and socially unjust. Greed and selfishness characterize certain behaviors prevalent within the ethos of economism, materialism, and consumerism. The comfort and ease modern technology provides to contemporary men and women in their activities makes it very difficult for people to make sacrifices. As a result, their desire for convenience consequently exacts more from the environment than necessary. Henry affirms this saying that "what we have in the world should really be sufficient for all if everyone should have only what is enough for his or her authentic needs." The modern lifestyle's excess and waste, along with our ideology of progress, test the limit of the earth's resources.[35] From the more structural side, Pya criticizes the foreign-driven development aggression of companies involved in mining, logging, and other destructive activities motivated by "economic greed and interest" and depriving the weak, the poor, and future generations of their right to live with dignity. She noted that such criticism has been expressed in her community through its songs, dance, and theater arts. Gwen, for her part, blames "the neoliberal market economy and its ideology of progress which rests on consumerism and materialism as a major culprit that gives way to social inequality as well as to environmental crisis." In the defense and protection of the rights of both the poor and the environment—central also to Pope Francis's pastoral agenda—we see that a vigilant and critical posture becomes necessary in the struggle for a just and humane society.

Second, these three advocates also share an understanding of the meaning of a good life which they commonly associate, not with material wealth, but with service to the environment and to humanity, especially those on the margins of society. Gwen has always been encouraged by friends and former classmates to consider high-paying jobs but has always resisted the offer, claiming that she finds greater fulfillment and happiness in what

---

35. The truth about the limits of earth's resources has been likewise argued by scholars. See Nash, "Dimensions and Dilemmas," 40–63. Among the causes of the crisis, he identifies resources exhaustion, population progress, maldistribution, radical reductions and extinctions of species, and genetic engineering.

she does for the environment and for society. Identifying herself with the indigenous community, Pya claims that a good life is associated with the land where her culture can flourish, and this is the reason they need to fight for their ancestral lands and environment. It becomes clear here that what matters most is not what one possesses but how one realizes oneself and achieves *eudaimonia* or happiness. This, in fact, is the goal of virtue ethics.

Third, running deep in their advocacy work is a fundamental understanding of their identity as stewards of creation. Pya is convinced that her people's identity is tied up with the land and environment. She speaks of her people as "stewards" of the land and of the natural environments which truly belong to the future generations. Henry argues that our responsibility is to ensure harmony and balance in nature. Gwen speaks of our identity as "stewards of creation . . . called to take good care of the environment and promote its genuine growth that should be characteristically inclusive, sustainable, climate-resilient, and participatory." Basic human dignity resides in the basic identity created according to God's image and likeness, understood in biblical terms as being an ambassador or steward of God in His creation.

Fourth, their worldviews are somehow influenced by their religious traditions or affiliations but also go beyond them. Their commitment is rooted in their worldview and overall understanding of life. Coming from his Buddhist tradition, Henry notes that "there is a certain spirit present in all of creation." This makes him and others in the Tzu Chi Foundation appreciate the unique and intrinsic value and fundamental equality of all in nature. Pya shares a similar belief from her indigenous tradition, that their ancestral land is sacred and alive: "our natural environment is imbued with the presence of the creator and of the spirits of our ancestors." Rooted in her Christian faith, Gwen also expressed that "the many aspects of our life are in fact interconnected as they are permeated with a kind of divine presence." It becomes clear here that one's vision and the self-understanding of one's identity as a virtuous person are appreciated within the rich cultural ecology of one's tradition of beliefs.

There is a strong sense of openness in the consciousness of these three individuals. While their commitment to the work of environmental advocacy is initially and ultimately oriented to their desire for humanity's well-being (both now and in future generations), they see that in our basic respect, care, and responsibility for the environment, we should also be able to appreciate the intrinsic (and not only instrumental) value of other creatures. Henry, in particular, expresses his sensitivity especially to sentient beings which should not be harmed or hurt by the human need for consumption. It becomes clear, through their concern for other human beings (still within anthropocentrism) and especially those who suffer the wrath of the Mother Earth, that they believe humanity should also be at the service of the environment. The hermeneutic enclosures and limited vision, therefore, of one tradition are evidently opened up with new emerging realities and experiences.

Fifth, our three respondents also give great importance to the community and the need to be in solidarity through partnership and networking with other groups who share a similar vision and advocacy. Each one of our respondents is deeply connected with a wide network of social organizations, belonging to national, regional, and even international coalitions. Pya is a national coordinator of the National Alliance of Indigenous Peoples' Organization in the Philippines which is linked with regional and international networks. Henry claims that Tzu Chi Foundation has a large network and is present in different parts of the globe. Gwen's Green Research is part of a national coalition for environmental protection called Green Convergence. We could therefore say that, beyond individual character excellence, there is "the excellence of human individuals who also share a collective life as members of a society, of common humanity, and of the broader community of life on earth."[36] This becomes the basis for dialogue on different levels in order to respond to the common problems or crises that humanity faces today, especially with regard to the environment.

Sixth, in the effort to contribute to the protection of the environment and vulnerable communities, there is a need to uphold important values and develop particular virtues.[37] Asked what particular virtues they have developed or feel to be very important to inculcate among the people they organize in their advocacy work, the interviewees identify the following: (1) simplicity of lifestyle is the most common virtue that the respondents present as an antidote to the greed that gives way to exploitation of the weak and of the environment; (2) love and generosity, expressed in their commitment to service for the other as definitive of their own sense of meaning in life and their greater self and fulfillment; (3) integrity and consistency, which touches the core of the steward's identity and without which, individuals would not be able to stand on their convictions and principles and could be easily bought; (4) wisdom and justice, two virtues which are necessary to have a more profound perspective in life, one that respects balance in nature and equality among people; (5) courage, which is very important to face

36. Thompson and Bendik-Keymer, *Ethical Adaptation*, 13.

37. Environmental virtue ethicists come up with a different set of ecological virtues. Nash identifies ecological virtues (sustainability, adaptability, relationality, frugality, equity, biodiversity, sufficiency, and humility) as necessary to address the environmental crisis he has analyzed. Nash, *Loving Nature*, 64–67.

the challenges and threats that may come from those whose interests are at stake in their advocacy work; and (6) humility, which has been identified as necessary to recognize the voice of, and be capable of listening to, the other. It is noteworthy that the virtues identified by the interviewees are those that are necessary to sustain them in their struggle for a much better society. The virtues are transformative and are at the service of leading society to change and transformation.

Seventh, it is important to note that the respondents' ecological awakening was occasioned by their experience of the poor, the victims of environmental devastation. Pya's concern and advocacy for the environment was a result of her realization of the oppression that her indigenous community, and others, suffered especially through displacement from their ancestral lands. Henry was awakened by his work with the victims of natural and man-made calamities. Gwen's long exposure, as a social activist, to the conditions of the poor in informal urban settlements led her to take an interest in sociology which eventually ushered her into environmental issues. These individuals' interest and engagement in environmental advocacy started with a consciousness awakening that was triggered by the experience of the "other"—the poor, the victims, the marginalized in society. In some cases, the poor are not seen only as victims but also as agents of transformation in their own lives. A study done on the communities at the margins confirms this observation.[38] Such capacity may have led the interviewees also to be open to the demands of the environment, an "other" beyond the human other.

Conclusion

Based on the analysis of the data of the respondents' narratives, we can see that those who do environmental advocacy work demonstrate a profound sense of commitment that touches the core of their identity as stewards of creation. This identity is derived from a worldview that is much bigger than oneself and recognizes a sense of transcendence. There is something in the environment that inspires in one a sense of awe and wonder. There is a kind of spirit that manifests itself in the abundance that Providence has entrusted to us. What comes along with that is a corollary responsibility. This responsibility comes from the "other" and demands of us a certain form of life characterized by simplicity, generosity, integrity, wisdom, justice, courage, and humility—virtues that are necessary to make us servants of the "other." The "other" here is understood in terms of the vulnerable, whether "other

38. See Umehara and Bautista, *Communities at the Margins*.

human beings" or "other creatures," whose existence should be respected and protected in order to achieve a more balanced and harmonious cosmic order.

From the above assumption, one could speak of the environmental crisis as a consequence of irresponsibility. This is evident on the personal level, where greed and the excessive accumulation of goods too often stem from the fear of want or inconvenience. When greed becomes a manifestation of the basic insecurity of not being authentically and unconditionally cared for and loved, one seeks to fill that void through an obsessive compulsion for wealth and power, sometimes identifying one's dignity with material success. One needs to realize that he or she has reason to trust in the abundant and sufficient blessings of life for everyone. Greed may also find its expression on the structural level in the form of economisn, consumerism, and materialism that is based on our modern and highly technological society's ideology of progress. Large-scale companies' economic development aggression, too often driven by profit, not only negatively impacts the environment per se but also the life of those communities whose existence depends on their environment.

We therefore see the need for social reform on the structural level through policy change and legislation, which are not purely based on a cost-benefit or risk-benefit analysis of the consequentialist logic of utilitarian ethics, nor on universalist claims of deontological ethics, but on an analectic or ana-dialectic sensitivity to the clamor of the most vulnerable victims: the poor and the environment. To ensure that such a social reform agenda becomes more fruitful and just for all, it becomes equally important to address the need for personal transformation of individual and collective consciousnesses through the formation of moral character into virtuous living. This gargantuan task of virtue formation does not lead us to a nostalgic return to the past which would discount modern creativity; rather, it critically engages contemporary development and is vigilant of its excesses and its dangerous propositions that do not lead humanity toward developing a quality of life that is authentically integral and sustainable. The virtuous persons that we envision for our contemporary society should not conform to the social order but firmly and consistently stand their ground in order to become authentic stewards of creation.

13

Christian Christmas Consumption: Ethical Considerations of the Environmental and Social Impacts of Holiday Spending

CHRISTIE KLIMAS

Ever since Joel Waldfogel's 1993 paper titled "The Deadweight Loss of Christmas," there has been a back-and-forth in the economics literature, debating how much money is "wasted" at Christmas. Deadweight loss occurs around Christmas whenever someone purchases a gift that is worth less to the recipient than the giver paid for it. So, if my husband planned to purchase a $25 gift for me, he might choose between a $25 box of chocolates (for which I would easily pay $30) and a $25 sweater (which I would never purchase at any price). If he chose the sweater, this would be the equivalent of throwing money away. The deadweight economic loss would actually be $30: the difference between what I would pay for the chocolates, or the best comparable gift, and what I would pay for the sweater.

My husband is actually quite good at minimizing deadweight loss, but that's not universally true, and deadweight loss tends to be higher when we purchase gifts for those we don't know as well. Joel Waldfogel conservatively estimates that, in 2007, there was an annual deadweight loss of $12 billion in the U.S. This is approximately 18 percent of the $66 billion in U.S. holiday spending that year.[1] Much of the research on deadweight loss has explored the welfare loss or gain associated with gift-giving[2], though other lines of

1. Waldfogel, *Scroogenomics*, 32–6.
2. Waldfogel, "The Deadweight Loss of Christmas, 1328–36; Waldfogel, "The Deadweight Loss of Christmas: Reply," 1306–08 and 1358–59; Solnick and Hemenway, "The Deadweight Loss of Christmas: Comment," 1299–1305; Solnick and Hemenway,

research explore the environmental impacts of Christmas consumption[3] and how environmental considerations are expressed in the gift economy.[4]

The goal of this essay is not to discuss the "true" value of deadweight loss associated with Christmas, but rather the environmental, social, and ethical implications of this wasted spending from a Christian perspective. Extraction of resources for production involves environmental impacts of varying types and scales, depending on the resource used for production. For example, jewelry is a popular gift: 23 percent of spending at U.S. jewelry stores occurs in December.[5] Life-cycle assessments have shown that, compared on a per kilogram basis, the platinum group metals and gold have the highest environmental burdens (as compared with other metals), as measured by cumulative energy use, global warming potential, human health implications, and ecosystem damage.[6] While this only compares metals and metals, not metals with other gift categories, the high impact of platinum and gold groups—those metals most commonly used in jewelry—is concerning for the environmentally conscious consumer. Consumers are increasingly interested in the impacts of their consumption, as is evident by the rise in goods with eco-labels that tout their environmental benefits.[7] Pope Francis suggests that we should attend to environmental impacts all the more if we are Christians, citing John Paul II in his support: "If the simple fact of being human moves people to care for the environment of which they are a part, Christians in their turn 'realize that their responsibility within creation, and their duty toward nature and the Creator, are an essential part of their faith.' It is good for humanity and the world at large when we believers better recognize the ecological commitments which stem from our convictions."[8] These faith-based ecological commitments extend to

"The Deadweight Loss of Christmas: Reply," 1356–57 and 325; List and Shogren, "The Deadweight Loss of Christmas: Comment," 1350–55; Ruffle and Tykocinski, "The Deadweight Loss of Christmas: Comment," 1299–1305; and Principe and Eisenhauer, "Gift-Giving and Deadweight Loss," 215–20.

3. Hancock and Rehn, "Organizing Christmas," 737–45; Stichnothe et al., "Carbon Footprint Estimation of Food Production Systems," 65–71; and Haq et al., The Carbon Cost of Christmas, 1–11.

4. Farbotko and Head, "Gifts, Sustainable Consumption, and Giving Up Green Anxieties at Christmas," 88–96.

5. Waldfogel, Scroogenomics, 27.

6. Nuss and Eckelman, "Life Cycle Assessment of Metals: A Scientific Synthesis," 1–12.

7. Carlsson et al., "Consumer Benefits of Labels and Bans on GM Foods," 152–61; Bjorner et al., "Environmental Labeling and Consumers' Choice," 411–24; Nichols, Strategic Options in Fair Trade Retailing, 6–17; Teisl et al., "Can Eco-Labels Tune a Market?" 339–59; Mahé, "Are Stated Preferences Confirmed by Purchasing Behaviours?" 301–15.

8. Francis, Laudato Si', 31.

multiple aspects of Christmas celebrations. A study in the United Kingdom looked at household carbon emissions from food, travel, lighting, and gifts during the Christmas season. The authors concluded that carbon emissions from just these four categories during the Christmas period (which encompasses less than one percent of the year) accounts for 5.5 percent of annual household carbon emissions.[9] All consumption comes at an environmental cost, depleting scarce resources. This does not mean that all consumption is contrary to our Christian call to care for creation. All individuals have a basic and obvious need for resources to live. As Pope Francis states: "Each community can take from the bounty of the earth whatever it needs for subsistence." However, he wants us to acknowledge that our consumption has limits and entails responsibilities, continuing "but [each community] also has the duty to protect the earth and to ensure its fruitfulness for coming generations."[10]

The true cost of deadweight loss at Christmas does not end with the inappropriate use of resources. We are stealing from the future and future generations when we use more than what we need. Pope Francis summarizes some of these losses: "The loss of forest and woodlands entails the loss of species which may constitute extremely important resources in the future, not only for food but also for curing disease and other uses. Different species contain genes which could be key resources in years ahead for meeting human needs and regulating environmental problems."[11] Yet, the impacts of environmental degradation are occurring now. Pope Francis continues: "Every year sees the disappearance of thousands of plant and animal species which we will never know, which our children will never see, because they have been lost forever. The great majority become extinct for reasons related to human activity. Because of us, thousands of species will no longer give glory to God by their very existence, nor convey their message to us. We have no such right."[12]

The large-scale loss of biodiversity associated with our consumption patterns indicates, at best, a global indifference or, at worst, enmity toward other species. When dire necessity of those in poverty forces choices that cause environmental degradation, this is understandable. However, when we are using resources to buy things that the recipient doesn't actually want, or would not purchase for themselves, we're mortgaging the future for no reason (and throwing away money at the same time). I don't pretend to

9. Haq et al., *Carbon Cost of Christmas*, 1–11.

10. Francis, *Laudato Si'*, 33.

11. Ibid., 16.

12. Ibid.

ignore the positive social bonds associated with gift-giving,[13] nor the endowment effect where people tend to ascribe more value to what they own: people will pay more to keep something they own than to buy something owned by someone else.[14] From a Christian standpoint, however, these reasons are not sufficient to justify the environmental cost, nor the opportunity cost associated with the way we spend our money. In other words, spending money on gifts means that we did not spend that money elsewhere. This is concerning since, on a societal level, there are many pressing global needs. Recent press has focused on the refugee crisis in Europe,[15] but there are issues that get less attention, like agricultural development,[16] providing safe drinking water, access to high-quality health services in rural areas, educating the impoverished (especially girls),[17] and improving maternal health and childbirth outcomes, to name a few. Therefore, "throwing money away" when there are so many uses for that money is gravely concerning. And yet, much like in our calculation of deadweight loss, the money we throw away should not be calculated as the $30 difference between what I would have spent my money on and the gift that my husband actually purchased. If we look at this more holistically (on a societal level), we want to calculate the difference between the highest and best use of the money[18] and the value of the gift to the recipient. A $25 gift to provide clean drinking water near a school might provide $50 in value—$25 for the gift recipient and $25 for those individuals living near the new well. Therefore, our calculation of deadweight loss (which includes only the difference between the price paid and the value to the recipient) ignores the potential benefit of alternative uses of that money. This is particularly concerning given our Christian call to universal communion. Indeed, Pope Francis states that

> we should be particularly indignant at the enormous inequalities in our midst, whereby we continue to tolerate some considering themselves more worthy than others. We fail to see that some are mired in desperate and degrading poverty, with no way out, while others have not the faintest idea of what to do with their possessions, vainly showing off their supposed superiority and

13. McKechnie and Tynan, "Social Meanings in Christmas Consumption," 130–44; Yan, "The Gift and Gift Economy," 205; and Mauss, *The Gift*.

14. Carmon and Ariely, "Focusing on the Foregone," 360–70.

15. Weaver, "Refugee Crisis."

16. Thurow and Kilman, *Enough*, 17–34; Thurow, *The Last Hunger Season*.

17. Yousafzai, *I Am Malala*.

18. The highest and best use is easily subject to debate, but framing "highest and best" using Catholic social teaching would likely lead us to investments in improving the lives of the poor.

leaving behind them so much waste which, if it were the case everywhere, would destroy the planet.[19]

The fact that our celebration of the birth of Christ, born poor to serve the poor, is commemorated by throwing money away in the context of overwhelming global need is further exacerbated by the fact that some of the goods that we purchase are made using unjust labor practices[20] or otherwise further marginalizing the poor. Indeed, the gains of development tend to disproportionately benefit the well-off, while environmental degradation disproportionately harms the poor, who use natural resources as a safety net for lean times. Using deforestation as an example, evidence shows that relative standards of living, literacy, and life expectancy increase as deforestation begins, but as the deforestation frontier evolves, levels of human development return to the low standards prior to deforestation.[21] However, for the poor, life following deforestation is worse. Where impoverished local communities could turn to the forest for fish, game, and food prior to deforestation, this important safety net has literally gone up in flames.

An Opportunity for Change

Eliminating deadweight loss during the Christmas season will not solve all the world's environmental, social, and ethical problems. However, I think the "wasted spending" at Christmas is an opportunity for hope, and potentially, a low-hanging fruit in a world where we work together to, in the words of Pope Francis, "integrate questions of justice in debates on the environment so as to hear *both the cry of the earth and the cry of the poor*."[22] There are many suggestions to improve upon the current system. Gifts from those with plenty to those with little "can increase society's net satisfaction."[23] This is due to the economic concept of diminishing marginal utility. Imagine that you wake hungry and come into a room with a box of doughnuts. Eating the first doughnut, or first bite of doughnut, would give you relatively high satisfaction (assuming you like doughnuts), but after a point, you would not want to eat any more doughnuts. If you had to eat the whole box, you might even reach a point where you would be willing to pay someone else to

19. Francis, *Laudato Si'*, 44.

20. Barrientos and Dolan, *Ethical Sourcing in the Global Food System*, 79–127.

21. Rodrigues et al., "Booom-and-Bust Development Patterns across the Amazon Deforestation Frontier."

22. Ibid., 23.

23. Waldfogel, *Scroogenomics*, 120.

eat the doughnuts for you (where not eating the doughnuts would give you more satisfaction than continuing to eat doughnuts). Societally, happiness would be greater if, instead of one person eating a box of doughnuts, those doughnuts were distributed so that no one individual had too much. This effect is evident with money as well. Using billionaires as an example, we can see that charitable giving is one way to improve societal happiness after individuals have reached declining marginal utility from their money.[24] In both of these examples, these donations are voluntary. And voluntary donations are not limited to billionaires: according to the National Center for Charitable Statistics, Americans who itemized charitable contributions on their tax returns gave over $174 billion to charity in 2011.[25] This was a 2.8 percent increase over 2010, which in turn, was an 8 percent increase over 2009 (2008 and 2009 saw decreases in charitable giving). Some of this giving occurs during the Christmas season. Organizations like Heifer International, known for their work in increasing family assets of the poor through gifts of livestock,[26] send out catalogs for Christmas encouraging socially responsible gifts. Catholic Relief Services (CRS) and other organizations promote fair trade gifts,[27] where gift purchases can help support jobs for impoverished individuals that give them a hand up [out of poverty] instead of a handout. Indeed, our Christmas giving allows us an opportunity not only to solidify relationships with friends and family through exchange of gifts but to improve our relationships with those who create our gift (even if we never meet them). Christmas is an opportunity to explore our universal communion with others by exploring the environmental and social effects of the gifts we purchase and making sure that our gifts are compatible with our faith. There is good news on this front: some evidence points to an increase in charitable giving for Christmas. Charitable donations in Ireland increased over the 2012–2013 Christmas period: total annual fundraising was 7 percent greater at Christmas 2013 than the previous year.[28]

Charitable donations are not a panacea, however, as replacing physical gifts with good elsewhere may not create the same type of bond between giver and recipient when a third party receives the benefits.[29] Conscious gift-giving, which includes consideration of the "hidden" environmental

24. Ibid., 123.

25. National Center for Charitable Statistics, "Profiles of Individual Charitable Contributions by State, 2011," 1–6.

26. See the Heifer International website: http://www.heifer.org.

27. See the CRS website page on fair trade: http://www.crsfairtrade.org.

28. Ryan and McCarthy, "An Analysis of Donation Rates at Christmas."

29. Farboko and Head, "Gifts, Sustainable Consumption, and Giving Up Green Anxieties at Christmas, " 88–96.

and social impacts of a gift, is also an essential part of making Christmas consistent with its associated theology. But giving may be obscuring the true meaning of Christmas. Josef Pieper states, "As everyone has observed, the real festival is almost disappearing behind the commercialized folderol that has come to the fore."[30] Patriarch Bartholomew, cited by Pope Francis, asks us to replace consumption with sacrifice, greed with generosity, wasteful- ness with a spirit of sharing, an asceticism which "entails learning to give and not simply give up. It is a way of loving, of moving gradually away from what I want to what God's world needs. It is liberation from fear, greed and compulsion."[31] This type of generosity is difficult, especially as it is truly countercultural in today's world, yet this is the exact type of generosity that we celebrate on Christmas. Indeed,

> the biblical sentence remains inviolate: that the festival is a day "the Lord has made" (Ps 117:24). It remains true because while man can make the celebration, he cannot make what is to be cel- ebrated, cannot make the festive occasion and the cause for cele- brating. The happiness of being created, the existential goodness of things, the participation in the life of God, the overcoming of death—all these occasions of the great traditional festivals are pure gift.[32]

While it is possible that removing gifts and celebrating the true gift of Christmas is necessary for a more true celebration, a first step on the path toward more God-like generosity could be considering our moral obliga- tions to others during Christmas, not just those for whom we purchase gifts, but also for those who made those gifts and those who were affected by gift production (including other species). Starting with the estimated 12 billion dollars we destroy during the Christmas provides a unique opportunity to do so.

---

30. Pieper, *In Tune with the World*, 61.

31. Francis, *Laudato Si'*, 4.

32. Pieper, *In Tune with the World*, 62.

PART FIVE

Pastoral Resources

14

Rooting the Church in African Soil and the Bethany Land Institute: A Theological Experiment

EMMANUEL KATONGOLE

The goal of African theology and Christianity must be to transform Africa rather than just explain it; to change it positively rather than just study it; to create history rather than just to interpret it.

—KÄ MANA[1]

We have not yet managed to adopt a circular model of production capable of preserving resources for present and future generations, while limiting as much as possible the use of non-renewable resources, moderating their consumption, maximizing their efficient use, reusing and recycling them.

—POPE FRANCIS[2]

In the recent encyclical letter, *Laudato Si'*, Pope Francis draws attention to the immensity and urgency of the ecological crisis. Drawing on the best scientific research available, Francis reviews several aspects of the ecological crisis—the irrational belief in progress, modern modes of production and

1. See Mwambazambi, "Kä Mana," 154.
2. Francis, *Laudato Si'*, 22.

219

consumerism, a throw-away culture, etc.—that have all been contributing factors. The world—"our sister," Francis notes—is "crying" under the weight of various burdens: global pollution, water poverty, loss of biodiversity, global inequality, and, overall, the decline in quality of human life.[3] Francis is not the only one to make this observation. A number of others before him—Bill McKibben, Norman Wurzba, Fred Bahnson, Wendell Berry, and Wes Jackson,[4] for example—have been pointing to the cry of the earth, drawing our attention to the unsustainable patterns of production and consumerism, and like Francis, noting the adverse effect of the ecological crisis especially on the poor around the world. What perhaps is often not fully attended to—and this is where Francis's *Laudato Si'* significantly advances the discussion—are the spiritual and theological roots of the ecological crisis. For even as Francis highlights the complex economic, social, cultural, and political factors that contribute to the ecological crisis, at the basis of these factors, he notes, lies a "wound" that he also calls a "sin." This sin has to do with our inability to see and acknowledge our deep connection with the land: "We have forgotten that we ourselves are dust of the earth (Gen 2:7), our very bodies are made of her elements, we breathe her air and we receive life and refreshment from her waters."[5]

In this essay, I would like to advance Pope Francis's conclusion by making explicit the connection between our inability to see and acknowledge our deep connection with the land, and our attempt to escape from the vocation to "till it and keep [take care of] it" (Gen 2:15 NRSV). Beginning with the story of my village, I will trace the attempt to escape to the illusory promises of modernization and civilization in Africa. The result of this effort has been a vision of progress and an economic system that not only excludes the majority of Africans but has contributed to the emptying out of villages, the destruction of the natural resources, the deepening of the food crisis, and overall, to the entrenchment of poverty, especially in rural Africa. The goal of my analysis is not simply to lament the fact that dominant missiological models have not questioned or offered an alternative to this myth of progress but also to highlight the unique pastoral and theological opportunity that the ecological crisis presents to the church. The ecological crisis is, in other words, a kairos moment for the church in general and the church in Africa in particular. And as the South African theologians noted in their famous 1985 Kairos Document, a kairos moment is a time

---

3. Ibid., 15.

4. See, for example, McKibben, *Deep Economy*; Bahnson and Wirzba, *Making Peace with the Land*; Jackson, *Consulting the Genius of the Place*.

5. Francis, *Laudato Si'*, 2.

of judgment but also a time of rare opportunity.[6] Accordingly, the "call to action" that Francis issues in *Laudato Si'*, requires innovative practical and theological experiments that reflect man's deep connection with the land and will develop attitudes and practical skills necessary to live out the vocation to "till the land and take care of it" in Africa. I will describe the Bethany Land Institute as one such experiment.

What is Going On? Two Images of Malube

The village of Malube is sixteen miles west of Kampala, off the Kampala-Fort Portal Highway. When I was growing up in the 1960s, our lives and daily routines were shaped by and around the three-acre plot of land that my parents bought when they migrated from Rwanda in the late 1940s. That is where my six siblings and I were born and grew up. My father would wake us up at five in the morning and send us to the garden, where we grew coffee, beans, maize, bananas, and other food crops. A couple of hours later, our morning work in the garden over, we would trek down into the forest to draw water from a spring. We would then wash up quickly and run two miles to school in order to be there before the opening bell at eight. When school got out at four in the afternoon, we ran home and ate quickly before joining our parents in the garden. Ours was a small piece of land, but it produced enough food to feed our family and occasionally provide a surplus, which we would sell, together with the coffee, to earn money to pay for our school fees and buy other essential commodities in the home. To be sure, there was nothing romantic about growing up in Malube. Life was tough. But if ours was a simple and "primitive" lifestyle, it was marked by a deep sense of belonging: to family, community, land (that supplied our food), and forest (where we collected firewood, drew water, and on whose outskirts we played).

That was then. Now, when I visit my mother, who still lives in the same village, I cannot but notice that a number of things have changed: that there are more people living in it; that the forest that surrounded it has all been

---

6. Thus, the South African theologians wrote in relation to apartheid: "The time has come. . . . It is the KAIROS or moment of truth not only for apartheid but also for the Church. . . . We as a group of theologians have been trying to understand the theological significance of this moment in our history. It is serious, very serious. For very many Christians in South Africa this is the KAIROS, the moment of grace and opportunity, the favorable time in which God issues a challenge to decisive action. It is a dangerous time because, if this opportunity is missed, and allowed to pass by, the loss for the Church, for the gospel, and for all the people of South Africa will be immeasurable" (Kairos Southern Africa, "The South Africa Kairos Document of 1985").

cut down for firewood and to make room for cultivation; that the spring has dried up, and around where it used to run are young men burning bricks. There is, therefore, acute "water poverty" in the village.[7] Also, a number of village plots, as well as what used to be a virgin forest, have been planted with eucalyptus and pine trees—monoculture forests which, while good for revenue, are an ecological hazard.[8] On the whole, therefore, the land looks dry, and banana trees that dot the village, as well as the other crops, all look miserable. It is not surprising that there is not much food produced on the land. Where in the past we had to carry food for relatives living in the city, now whenever I visit home, I have to buy food and groceries in the city to bring to the village.

Malube is not unique but in countless ways is a microcosm of what is happening in many parts of Africa where a combination of factors—prolonged civil wars, poor or nonexisting food policies, mass deforestation, lack of energy policy, plus a growing population[9]—have all contributed to bring Africa to a looming food, water, and ecological crisis. The effects of this crisis are becoming increasingly obvious in growing cases of starvation and food insecurity, land and water disputes, and overall, more conflicts and civil wars.[10]

But even while not denying the complex political, economic, cultural, and policy factors contributing to this ecological crisis both at the local and global level, the obvious neglect and exploitation of the land reflects an underlying theological problem. This is the "wound" that Pope Francis refers to and which has to do with our failure to appreciate our deep connection—in fact, intimacy—with the land and our desperate attempt to escape from our human vocation to "till the land and care for it." This conclusion is even more surprising in Africa where, from an African traditional point of view, the African sense of "belonging"—and thus, the sense of who

7. Ten years ago, through a nonprofit organization called Share the Blessings (http://www.share-the-blessings.org), I helped raise funds for a borehole for the village.

8. See, for example, Lyons et al., "The Darker Side of Green."

9. In 1969, Uganda's population was 9.5 million; in 2002, 24.5 million; in 2011, 34 million; and by 2014, it was 37.5 million. According to a January 2013 news report in "Uganda Population at Record 37 Million," with an average pop growth rate of 3.1 percent, the population is expected to increase fivefold by 2100, pushing Uganda to the top ten most populated nations in the world, according to the latest world population prospects by the United Nations Social and Economic Affairs Division in New York. The report also points out that the fertility rate of Ugandan women is at 5.9 children per woman and notes that Uganda has the world's second youngest population after Niger, with the current median age registering at 15.8.

10. See, for example, Hendrix and Glaser, "Trends and Triggers," 695–71, and Muhamed, *Ecology, Politics, and Violent Conflict.*

one is—is always mediated through an intimate connection with the land. This is to say that, from a traditional point of view, the African is always "grounded"—a son and daughter of the soil—thus, the saying that "you can take an African out of the village but cannot take the village out of him or her." Unfortunately, this traditional sense of belonging to the land—and with it, the love and care for it—has been undermined through a modern vision of "progress" and pressure for "modernization." The latter not only involves a disdain for "manual" labor, but it has also resulted in producing masses of uprooted Africans who have lost any sense of what it means to love the land, till it, and take care of it.

Running Away from the Land:
On the Civilizing and Evangelizing Mission of Africa

A full discussion of Africa's modernity, and how the vision of "progress" and "civilization" that drives it has had disastrous effect on the African's view and relation to the land, is not possible here, but hopefully a brief sketch will convey the picture. Riding the coattails of the Enlightenment in Europe and the Industrial Revolution, the colonization of Africa had as one of its stated objectives, the transformation of "primitive" African societies into "developed" nation-states after the model of Europe. The African "village"— in particular, the deep attachment of the natives to their land—represented all that was primitive and evil (customs, animism, superstition, etc.) that had to be left behind if African communities and individuals were to be brought into the sunny future of civilized modernity. Nowhere was this attempt to free Africans from such backwardness so obvious as in the forms of colonial education that aimed to transform its subjects into learned and civilized individuals. Unfortunately, the underlying philosophy and major building blocks of this education system have remained in place in independent Africa. Let me provide an illustration. By the time my friends and I had graduated from high school, we had mastered the parts and mechanics of the four-stroke engine, even though we could count the number of times we had traveled by car. But I do not remember a single lesson about the goats, millet, bananas, and beans on which we lived! The effect of this education system has been to produce individuals who are alienated from the land (its care, tilling, and love), but a vision of progress that excludes the majority of Africans. This is what partly explains the "disproportionate and unruly growth" of slums in Africa—slums often occupied by young, semi-educated, half-starving Africans, totally alienated from their village environments, loitering in the cities in an attempt to find "modern" employment that is not available.[11]

The unfortunate part of the story is that the civilizing mission of colonial education and the evangelizing mission of the church reinforced each other in a number of ways. The enlightenment dualism between matter and mind found its theological nemesis in the body-soul dualism, where the soul was viewed as the spiritual center and the focus of the church's mission (to save souls). Thus, mission efforts encouraged and preached their own version of "evacuation." While the education provided was meant to free us from "primitive" ways of thinking, which just happened to include a belief in the sacredness of land, the evangelizing mission was meant to free us from interest in the material world to focus on the other worldly existence, whose ultimate goal was the eternal life of the soul in heaven. The attachment to the land—in as much as it evoked practices such as animism, witchcraft, and ancestral veneration—remained a constant point of attack in the church's preaching.

Those of us training for church ministry received a double portion of the determined efforts to detach from anything associated with land, including the patterns of growing food. At the seminary, people were employed to cultivate the land and grow food, but not the seminarians. I do remember an incident, however, in the 1980s when some professors who had trained in the U.S. attempted to change this. We regarded these professors, including our then rector, as dangerous Marxists or communists. They introduced a communal day of work, on which we the seminarians would work on the farm and also prepare our food. We resisted the policy and organized a sit-down strike, deciding to boycott not only the work on the farm but classes

11. Mike Davis in *Planet of Slums* offers one of the most accessible but penetrating studies in the scale and velocity of third world urbanization, a factor that has contributed to the fact that, for the first time in the world's history, the urban population of the world outnumbers its rural population. The remarkable aspect of this trend is that, especially in Africa, slums are growing at twice the speed of the continent's exploding cities. Writing in 2007, Davis had projected that, by 2015, black Africa will have 332 million slum dwellers, a number that will continue to double every fifteen years (19). Thus, "instead of cities soaring toward heaven, much of the twenty-first century urban world squats in squalor, surrounded by pollution, excrement, and decay" (19). While the factors behind the *slumization* (my terminology) of Africa are many, Davis points to the economic dreams and policies of late capitalism: "as a result of urban growth in the context of structural adjustment, currency devaluation and state retrenchment has been an inevitable recipe for the mass production of slums" (17). The irony is that, while many rural poor move to the cities in order to "escape" poverty, "overurbanization is driven by the reproduction of poverty, not by the supply of jobs" (16). Davis's description of the life in the slums is at once chilling and true, describing the slum dwellers as "surplus humanity" (201), living within what can only be described as "marginality within marginality," as a "zone of exile" and a "semi-death" (201).

for a week. Our logic was sound, so at least we thought. We were not only college/university students, but we had come to study philosophy and theology, to grasp the eternal mysteries of being and salvation, to attune our minds to the great thinkers such as Hegel, Descartes, and Hume, and our souls to inner spiritual disciplines after masters like Meister Eckhart and Teresa of Avila. And here was a "misguided" faculty wanting us to go work in the fields! Come on! That was way below us. We had already attained a certain level of civilization that gave us the privilege of not doing manual labor. That was the work of people who had not gone to school, the work of peasants, like my parents. We were university students.

I tell the story because it nicely captures the unfortunate existential and theological challenge related to land in Africa. The issue is not simply one of seeing the connection that exists between the education system, the idea of "progress," the emptying out of villages, the neglect for the land, the rapid deforestation, exploitation of natural resources, mass poverty, and unemployment in Africa. Everything, as Pope Francis reminds us in *Laudato Si'*, is connected.[12] The issue is to see how the church in Africa, by remaining beholden to a modern vision of "progress," has missed a great opportunity to affirm our intimacy with God, which is related to our intimacy with the land. This is to say that, whereas the church has often cited the mandate of Genesis 1:28 to "fill the earth and subdue it," it has very rarely drawn attention to the story of Genesis 2, which not only establishes both God's and man's intimacy with the "soil" but highlights man's vocation to "till it [the land] and keep it" (Gen 2:15). A closer look at that story of "in the beginning" offers a good starting point for re-grounding the church's mission in African soil.

A Love Affair with Soil: God, Human Beings, and Creation

Given the attempt outlined above to deny our intimate connection with land, it is perhaps not surprising that the story of Genesis chapter 2 has not exercised much influence in shaping the theological imagination of the church in Africa. Yet, it is such a beautiful story that underscores both God's relationship with the land, man's identity as made from the earth, and man's vocation in relation to the land. A reading of Genesis 2:4–15 reveals a number of key observations. Five stand out:

12. See, for example, 10, 46, 48, 56, 91, 117.

1. God's love for the soil

In Genesis 2, we see God working with the soil: He fashions everything (creates) out of the soil he molded; like a potter (an image the prophets, especially Ezekiel, play with a lot), he creates man out of the soil (2:7), and he plants a garden (2:80). As Norman Wirzba notes, God not only loves the soil; the soil is God's first love—so before God's love for man is God's love for the earth![13] Thus, the image of God that emerges from this story is of God kneeling on the ground, hands in the soil, getting dirty in the earth.

2. God as farmer

Genesis 2:8–9 states (NIV, emphasis mine): "Now the Lord God had *planted* a garden in the east, in Eden; and there he put the man he had formed. The Lord God *made* all kinds of trees grow out of the ground—trees that were pleasing to the eye and good for food." Eden. God's work as a farmer produces two effects—beauty and abundance: The Lord God made all kinds of trees and fruits that were "pleasing" to the eye. So we see, first, by working the soil, in fashioning things out of the ground, God's finds delight, and the Garden is Eden, which simply means delightful, "pleasing to the eye." Secondly, the verse says there were all sorts of trees and fruits good for food. God thus is depicted as a master farmer—an image that also appears in Psalm 65 (without a doubt one of my favorite psalms):

> You care for the land and water it;
> you enrich it abundantly.
> The streams of God are filled with water
> to provide the people with grain,
> for so you have ordained it.
> You *drench* its furrows and *level* its ridges;
> you soften it with showers and *bless* its crops.
> You crown the year with your bounty,
> and your *carts overflow* with abundance.
> The grasslands of the wilderness overflow;
> the hills are clothed with gladness.
> The meadows are covered with flocks
> and the valleys are mantled with grain;
> they shout for joy; they break into song.

3. Man (finally, we come to man): Fashioned out of the soil

---

13. Wirzba and Bahnson, *Making Peace with the Land*, 16.

God fashioned man (Adam) out of soil (adamah) (Gen 2:7). Here, we see the Hebrew play on words: the intimate (organic) connection between man (adam) and the soil (adamah).

4. Man's vocation: To till and take care of the land

"The Lord God took the man and put him in the garden of Eden to *till it and keep it*" (Gen 2:15 NRSV, emphasis mine). The American Standard Version translates "to till it" as to "cultivate," which has the same connotation as "nurture" (when you cultivate something, you grow, you nurture; but nurture also has a sense of "feeding"). Here lies the crucial image of the earth as mother. Given the play on words (*adam, adamah*), man's relationship to the land is one of "mothering." So we can say that man's vocation is to mother the earth and take care of it. And he is to do so just in the same way that God does. This is the equivalent of what Genesis 1 refers to as being created "in the image of God" (Gen 1:27). What this means is that when we come to love the earth, to live in the garden, we share God's feeding, healing, reconciling, and sustaining ways with the world.[14] But also that when we mother the earth—in the same way that God does—the earth truly becomes "mother" earth. A mutual mothering exists, a symbiotic love between "adam" and "adamah," or as Pope Francis notes, an implied "relationship of mutual responsibility between human beings and nature."[15] We must, therefore, "forcefully reject the notion that our being created in God's image and given dominion over the earth justifies absolute domination of other creatures."[16]

5. Creaturely existence and limits

What is underscored in the story of Genesis 2 is that "human life is grounded in three fundamental and closely intertwined relationships: with God, with our neighbor, and with the earth itself."[17] These relationships of mutuality are what define our status as "creatures" but also "our creaturely limitations." When man seeks to deny or overcome man's status and limits as a creature made from the soil (a story that is anticipated in the third chapter of Genesis by man's desire to "be like God"), the harmonious relationships between human beings and God, with other human beings, and with nature are disrupted. Accordingly, one can say that the environmental crisis of our time is prefigured and anticipated by the story of Genesis 3 where, because of man's

14. Ibid., 18.
15. Ibid., 67.
16. Ibid.
17. Ibid., 66.

sin, the earth is "cursed," filled with "thistles and thorns," and its tilling has become a burden for man.

As my brief analysis shows, a model of development in Africa has brought us to this stage where rapid deforestation, the depletion of natural resources, and a vision of progress that excludes the majority of Africans— who are left without access to basic needs and who constantly wonder about their worth and dignity—are the order of the day. However, while it is important to understand how we arrived at our current situation and the "wound" at the basis of our ecological crisis in Africa, it is even more important to consider whether and how the African church can recover something of the beautiful and integral vision of Genesis 2. Can a vision such as this become a narrative template for a new theological praxis in Africa? And if so, what role can the church play in such an integrated ecological and economic vision for Africa? Thus we also need to think about what role theology needs to play within that revolutionary agenda. For, as the Congolese theologian Kä Mana rightly notes, "The goal of African theology and Christianity must be to transform Africa rather than just explain it; to change it positively rather than just study it; to create history rather than just to interpret it."[18]

It is this same impetus for conversion of our current patterns of production and consumerism that lies behind Francis's repeated call to action in *Laudato Si'*, and his often repeated mantra: "realities are more important than ideas."[19] In this connection, Francis offers a number of very concrete suggestions for the realization of a new ecological culture, suggestions that range from everyday actions such as avoiding the use of plastic and paper, reducing water consumption, separating refuse, cooking only what can reasonably be consumed, showing care for other living beings, and planting trees[20] to education, economic, and political and social policies for an integrated ecology. However, over and beyond these concrete measures, the pope calls for a comprehensive and revolutionary revision of our essential membership in creation, which affects all our spirituality, policies, and modes of production and consumerism. As he states:

> Ecological culture cannot be reduced to a series of urgent and partial responses to the immediate problems of pollution, environmental decay and the depletion of natural resources. There needs to be a distinctive way of looking at things, a way of thinking, an educational programme, a lifestyle and spirituality

18. See Mwambazambi, "Kä Mana," 154.

19. Francis, *Laudato Si'*, 110, 201.

20. Ibid., 212.

which together generate resistance to the assault of the technocratic paradigm.[21]

Thus, Francis's call points to the need to recover man's essential connection with the land and the vocation to till and care for it as the basis of
a new economic and social vision for the world. It still remains to be seen
how this revolutionary "way of thinking" would look in the West, and what
forms of "educational programme[s]" might sustain it today.[22] However, in
Africa, where the majority of people live in rural communities and villages,
the cultivation of a new way of thinking about the land and their vocation to
till and care for it becomes an urgent pastoral theological task. This is a task
that calls for fresh experiments and education initiatives connected to land;
a task that brings together theology, food production, economics, and ecological consciousness. The Bethany Land Institute is such an experiment.

The Bethany Land Institute: Rooting Missio Dei in African Soil

The vision of the Bethany Land Institute was inspired by a visit to St. Jude's
Farm near Masaka in southern Uganda. When I first visited the farm in
the summer of 2007,[23] I was struck by a number of things. First, I did not
know that something like this existed: a beautiful, integrated farm, sitting
on three and a half acres of land with a variety of crops, animals, a fish pond,
bee hives, and all kinds of shade and fruit trees. As the instructors took
us around the farm, they emphasized again and again how "everything is
connected to everything else": the crops feed the animals, and the animals
produce manure to fertilize the land and also produce biogas for cooking.
The instructors also stressed how they tried to do everything in a "natural"
way. Accordingly, they do not use chemical agents, and they produce their
own pesticides from herbs that grow on the farm. Indeed, the high yields
from St. Jude's Farm reminded me of something I had read that pointed out
that natural methods of farming are far more productive than conventional

21. Ibid., 111.

22. However, the story of the National Catholic Rural Life Conference (NCRLC) offers a good historical case. Their efforts, especially in the 1930s and '40s to spearhead
a "green revolution" by empowering rural communities, supporting small farms and
local businesses, promoting responsible land stewardship, and creating a platform to
connect rural farmers and enhance their advocacy provide the kind of ecclesially-based
ecological effort that is needed. For a good introduction and account of the efforts of
the NCRLC during this period, see especially Hamlin and McGreevy, "Greening of
America," 464–99.

23. For the story of the visit and its implications for world Christianity, see Katongole, "Mission and the Ephesian Moment," 183–200.

mechanized agriculture.[24] The farm offered a completely different (delightful) picture from that of my native village of Malube.

Second, listening to the story of Josephine Kizza and her late husband (the farm's founders), I learned that they started out only with two piglets. But over the years, the farm has grown into such a flourishing model farm (the president of Uganda has visited three times and called it *Muzukusa*—one who awakens) that it has paid off and is truly a testament to the spirit of determination and hard work. Josephine now earns over $3,000 a month.

Third, the farm demonstrates the simple but profound practical theology that points to the land as mother who feeds us: "God has given us everything we need," Josephine explained. But He has asked us one thing: "Feed the land so that the land can feed you."

Fourth, because St. Jude's Farm serves as a "Rural Training Centre for Integrated and Sustainable Agriculture," it has trained over 250 rural farmers, mostly women from neighboring villages.

My first visit was short, but it offered me a glimpse of what each and every African village can and should look like. With its beauty, bounty, and variety, St. Jude's evoked my scriptural imagination of the Garden of Eden. That I could see its reality, right in the middle of Africa, inspired a vision for a land-based initiative that would bring together theology, food production, economics, and ecological awareness. Such an initiative would build on and expand the ecological and economic possibilities of St. Jude's Farm, while serving as a catalyst for rural transformation, youth employment, and reforestation efforts throughout the country. At its heart would have to be an explicit theological narrative—a narrative that would itself become the argument and evidence of the church as a sign and sacrament of God's new creation in Africa.

I shared my experience at St. Jude's Farm and the outline of an emerging vision with two of my priest friends, and in 2013, we bought fifty-seven acres of land in rural Luweero and began work to set up a foundation, the Bethany Land Institute, as an education program for a practical theology of land, peace, and creation care. The choice of the name "Bethany" was intentional. It was based on an earlier reflection in which I pointed to the biblical village of Bethany (*beit-aniae*: house of the poor) as an image for

---

24. Questioning the "mirage of abundance" of modern industrialized farming, Fred Bahnson notes, "Using conventional agricultural practices, it takes just over an acre of land to feed one person in the United States for a year, and far more energy and topsoil are wasted than are produced in food calories. Using biointensive methods, you can feed ten people for a whole year on that one acre, and you can build soil fertility while doing it. That same acre, by the way, would feed one cow for a whole year, or it would fill up the gas tank of your car with ethanol exactly twice" (Wirzba and Bahnson, *Making Peace with the Land*, 97).

Africa.[25] But as the biblical Bethany—the home of Jesus's friends (Mary, Martha, Lazarus, Simon the leper . . .)—was both the place of "resurrection" and of mission, so too the hope has been that the Bethany Land institute will be a catalyst for a revolutionary ecological and economic resurrection of rural Africa.

Even though plans for the Bethany Land Institute predated Pope Francis's *Laudato Si'*, it answers Francis's call for an "educational program" to form and nurture a fresh "way of thinking," and a "new lifestyle and spirituality" in relation to land in Africa. Inspired by the story of Genesis chapter 2, the Bethany Land Institute seeks to cultivate love for the land and form habits and skills that advance man's vocation to "till and take care of the land" in Africa. In doing so, it addresses three immediate and major problems of the ecological crisis in Africa: food shortage, deforestation, and youth unemployment. It will do so under three major programs:

1. An integrated farm (similar to St. Jude's Farm) that will run both an outreach and residential program to train local farms in methods of sustainable (natural) land care and food production. Upon gradua-tion, interns of the residential program will set up their own model farms in villages, where they will mentor at least two farmers every year, thus becoming catalysts for rural transformation.

2. A natural forest that will serve as a demonstration and catalyst for a major re-greening effort throughout the country. The vision is that, through the forest and the outreach program, one million trees will be planted by 2050.

3. A roadside market where interns will sell the produce from the land, but which will also serve as a rest stop on the highway and operate a micro credit scheme for rural farmers.

Conclusion

In *Laudato Si'*, Pope Francis notes that "We have not yet managed to adopt a circular model of production capable of preserving resources for pres-ent and future generations, while limiting as much as possible the use of nonrenewable resources, moderating their consumption, maximizing their efficient use, reusing and recycling them."[26] It is this circular mode of pro-duction that the Bethany Land Institute seeks to catalyze in Africa in a way

25. See Katongole, *Stories from Bethany.*
26. Francis, *Laudato Si'*, 22.

that reconnects the ecological and social questions; for, as Francis states, "a true ecological approach *always* becomes a social approach; it must integrate questions of justice . . . so as to hear *both the cry of the earth and the cry of the poor.*"[27]

More specifically, the Bethany Land Institute will seek to reconnect issues of ecology and economics in Africa to the story of God in Genesis 2. For as Peter Maurin, cofounder of the Catholic Worker movement, once noted, the main problem with society is that that "sociology, economics, and politics had all been separated from the gospel. In the process, society had lost any sense of the ultimate, transcendent purpose of human activity."[28] The assumption is that reconnecting in a concrete and visible way the love and care for the land with the story of God in Genesis, the Bethany Land Institute will contribute towards reinvesting what modernity has tended to see as menial and primitive occupations reserved for failures and school dropouts, with a sense of the ultimate. This will not only contribute to a new appreciation of the noble vocation to till and care for the earth in Africa, but it will also offer millions of Africans (especially the youth) a livelihood and a new sense of their worth and dignity, even while recreating beauty and abundance in Africa's villages.

No doubt, in the face of immense ecological problems, such efforts cannot but appear small and insignificant. But as Dorothy Day used to say, "it is little by little that we are saved." Moreover, it is through such little efforts that we can hope, as Peter Maurin and Dorothy Day hoped, to build "a new world within the shell of the old."[29] Or as Pope Francis puts it, even such small efforts, "can restore our sense of self-esteem," and enable us "to live more fully and to feel that life on earth is worthwhile."[30]

27. Ibid., 49.
28. See Ellsberg, "Introduction," xxvi.
29. Ibid., xxvii.
30. Francis, *Laudato Si'*, 212.

15

Religious and Cultural Beliefs Related to Disaster Risk Reduction: The Case of Super Typhoon Haiyan

AGNES M. BRAZAL

The World Health Organization noted that there has been an increasing number of disasters both nature-related[1] and human-made since the mid-1990s, with Asia as the most frequently hit. In the 1990s, two out of three deaths from disasters were in Asia.[2] There has been a void, however, in scientific disaster research on the relation between cultural and religious beliefs of the people affected by nature-related disasters and disaster mitigation. The model of research on religion and nature-related disasters in the past has been plagued by (1) a lopsided focus on the Judeo-Christian tradition, (2) a secularized view of religious views as backward or due to ignorance, and (3) a Western model of effective risk reduction based solely on efficiency and sustainability.[3] The anthropologist Greg Bankoff was among the first to point out the importance of traditional knowledges in disaster risk reduction.[4]

1. The United Nations Office for Disaster Risk Reduction (UNISDR) underlines, "There is no such thing as a 'natural' disaster, only natural hazards." The impact of these hazards depends on the social structures, beliefs, decisions, and actions of people. UNISDR, "What Is Disaster Risk Reduction?"

2. World Health Organization, "Gender and Health in Disasters."

3. Harris, "The Impact of Cultural and Religious Influences during Natural Disasters (Volcano Eruptions)."

4. Bankoff, "Rendering the World Unsafe." Disaster risk reduction aims to lessen the damaging impact of natural disasters by systematically analyzing and reducing the factors that make people vulnerable, including cultural and religious beliefs. UNISDR,

233

This research focuses in particular on the cultural and religious discourses in the Super Typhoon Haiyan mega-disaster and their potential to
mitigate or block disaster risk reduction. This essay further contends that
the church can contribute toward risk reduction in its ministry to disaster
victim-survivors as well as in mediating between folk, religious, and scientific viewpoints.

By religious belief, we mean "belief in supernatural forces or beings
that influences a person's behavior and/or understanding of the world
around them through certain teachings or tomes."[5] Cultural belief is the
more encompassing term that includes religious beliefs as well as other
philosophical views, meanings, ideas that underpin cultural practices or
recurrent ways of interacting or behaving.

The Natural Hazard/Disaster and the Primary Respondents

The strongest tropical cyclone ever recorded to hit land rampaged the central
Philippines on November 8, 2013. Based on the reading of the Joint Typhoon
Warning Center, the super typhoon Haiyan (locally named "Yolanda") had,
at landfall, estimated one-minute sustained winds of 190–195 mph[6] (315
km/hr).[7] This wind created a 2.3- to 5-meter (between eight and sixteen
feet) storm surge that swept almost everything in its path.[8] The scope of this
super typhoon covered the distance between Berlin and London, plowing
through fourteen provinces in the Philippines. Estimated to be much more,
the number of recorded deaths had been pegged at 6,300 (the government
stopped counting at this number), still making it the deadliest natural disaster in the history of the Philippines; the number of missing totals 1,061;
typhoon-related reported injuries number 28,689;[9] households damaged
are estimated at 1.1 million; and people displaced surpassed four million.[10]

"What Is Disaster Risk Reduction?"

5. Harris, "The Impact of Cultural and Religious Influences during Natural Disasters (Volcano Eruptions)."

6. At 170 kt (87.5 m sl) at landfall, Haiyan exceeded the strength of Hurricane Patricia (2015), Hurricanes Camille (1969) and Allen (1980) in the North Atlantic Basin,
and Super Typhoon Tip (1979) in the Western North Pacific. The next second strongest
at landfall was Hurricane Camille which hit Mississippi with 190-mph sustained winds.
Fischetti, "Was Typhoon Haiyan a Record Storm?"

7. Neussner, "Assessment of Early Warning Efforts in Leyte for Typhoon Haiyan/
Yolanda."

8. Ibid.

9. Locsin, "NDRRMC."

10. Sherwood et al., "Resolving Post-Disaster Displacement," 1.

Haiyan's one-minute sustained winds of 195 mph were twenty-one mph stronger than Katrina's 174-mph winds. Hurricane Patricia, which is the strongest tropical cyclone recorded at 200 mph, weakened to 165 mph at landfall.[11]

Super Typhoons and Climate Change

While it is difficult for climatologists to show a direct correlation between climate change and specific extreme weather disturbances such as Typhoon Haiyan[12] or Hurricane Katrina, these experiences show what can happen when extreme weather events occur in the future with greater frequency, due to global warming.[13]

In 2007, the Intergovernmental Panel on Climate Change had established that, indeed, anthropogenic climate change was already producing severe effects on our environment including more natural hazards.[14] Its 2013 report confirms the following about climate change:

---

11. Dube Dwilson, "The Strongest and Deadliest Hurricanes in History."

12. NASA climatologist Bill Patzert noted that the contribution of climate change to strengthening Haiyan was minimal (as in adding 5 mph to create a 200-mph wind strength). The rise in the Philippine Sea, which is the fastest in the world, could have worsened the flooding which caused massive destruction but again, this is minimal considering that the wind strength caused a sixteen-foot surge. So it seems that with or without climate change, Haiyan could have occurred. Walsh, "Climate Change Didn't Cause Super Typhoon Haiyan."

In fact, two similar disastrous typhoons happened a century ago in Tacloban. One was in October 1897, when an intense typhoon following the same path that Haiyan struck created a storm surge of 4–7.3 meters. Hundreds died, and communities and churches in Samar and Leyte were destroyed. In 1912, there was another typhoon which killed 15,000 people and practically obliterated Tacloban. Diola, "1912 Reports on Tacloban Storm 'Killing'"; Lotilla, "Flashback."

Patzert recognizes, though, that climate change can result in more extreme weather conditions. Totten, "How Typhoon Haiyan Became So Powerful."

13. Nicholls et al. "Coastal Systems and Low-Lying Areas." There is debate on the correlation between climate change and tropical-cyclone intensity, partly due to "poor historical data around tropical cyclones." The Intergovernmental Panel on Climate Change (IPCC) stated in September 2013 that there is "low confidence in the attribution of changes in tropical-cyclone activity to human influence." It likewise has "low confidence" in stronger tropical cyclones in the coming decades; rather, this is "more likely than not" (meaning 50 percent probability or higher) to occur at the end of the twenty-first century. This contrasts with IPCC's 2007 claim that it is "likely" (66 percent probability or above) that there would be heightened tropical cyclone activity due to global warming. IPCC, *Climate Change 2013* and Pachauri et al., *Climate Change 2007*; "Climate Change Didn't Cause Super Typhoon Haiyan?"

14. Pachauri et al., *Climate Change 2007*. See also Francis, *Laudato Si'*, 23.

- Warming of the climate system is unequivocal, and since the 1950s, many of the observed changes are unprecedented over decades to millennia. The atmosphere and ocean have warmed, the amounts of snow and ice have diminished, the sea level has risen, and the concentrations of greenhouse gases have increased.[15]

- Human influence on the climate system is clear.[16]

- Cumulative emissions of CO_2 largely determine global mean surface warming by the late twenty-first century and beyond. Most aspects of climate change will persist for many centuries even if emissions of CO_2 are stopped.[17]

Being better at long-term predictions, climatologists confirm that models point to more intense, if not more frequent, tropical cyclones that will happen with global warming, especially toward the late twenty-first century and which will be more prominent in the western North Pacific hit by Haiyan.[18]

People in the Philippines are among those already experiencing such unpredictable or more frequent extreme weather events. Within less than a year, Haiyan was the second super typhoon to hit the country after Super Typhoon Bopha which rampaged through the southern regions in December 2012. A little more than a year later, in the first week of December 2014, Super Typhoon Hagupit (which thankfully decreased in strength when it made landfall) threatened again the eastern coast of the Philippines. The year 2015 was an unusual year with twenty-five storms forming in the Pacific by August, six of them reaching the maximum Category Five status.[19]

---

15. Intergovernmental Panel on Climate Change, *Climate Change 2013*.

16. Ibid.

17. Ibid.

18. See, for instance, Emanuel, "Downscaling CMIP5 Climate Models." And see Philippine Atmospheric, Geophysical, and Astronomical Services Administration (PAGASA), "Impacts of Climate Change," 9: "All areas of the Philippines will get warmer, more so in the relatively warmer summer months. Annual mean temperatures in all areas in the country are expected to rise by 0.9 C to 1.1 C in 2020 and by 1.8 C to 2.2 C in 2050.... Projections for extreme events in 2020 and 2050 show that hot temperatures (indicated by the number of days with maximum temperature exceeding 35°C) will continue to become more frequent, number of dry days (days with less than 2.5mm of rain) will increase in all parts of the country and heavy daily rainfall (exceeding 300mm) events will also continue to increase in number in Luzon and Visayas."

19. Hannam, "Twin Typhoons Spin in the Pacific."

Respondents

The primary data for this research was based on eyewitness accounts and formal semi-structured interviews, conducted in January 2015 with thirty survivors (fifteen women and fifteen men) from three coastal barangays/villages in Tacloban.[20] I employed content analysis to categorize the responses of the respondents. Secondary data was drawn from published news articles and other literature on Haiyan. All of the respondents' houses and communities were wiped out by Typhoon Haiyan. Among these survivors, four have immediate family members who died (husband, child); two had immediate relatives who were seriously wounded. All of them have neighbors and friends who perished. All of them have seen dead bodies in the streets, many of which were swept to their shore from the areas that were wiped out across the bay. Their communities have since been declared a "no build zone." However, because of the government's slow rehabilitation process, most of them have gone back to rebuild their houses in the same area along the coast of Cancabato Bay. Though not intended, the interviews ended up being group interviews, as they were held in people's houses. The respondents have completed either some years of high school or college level education, and all of them are Catholic.

Cultural and Religious Beliefs Around Typhoon Haiyan

Anthropologists have largely affirmed the existence of syncretism of Catholic rituals and pre-Hispanic animistic practices in the lowland Philippines.[21] Tacloban City, which had the most deaths due to Typhoon Haiyan, is part of the Eastern Visayas region, or the Waray society. The Waray worldview consists of a high God who is approachable through the mediation of the Virgin Mary and the Catholic patron saints, as well as a host of spirits. When a person dies, he or she becomes an *anito*, or an ancestral spirit. There is also an array of environmental spirits whose names vary depending on the region. The saints and spirits function as mediators between humans and the high

20. Barangay is the smallest administrative unit in Philippine society.

21. Schumacher, "Syncretism in Philippine Catholicism." Syncretism here is differentiated from "legitimate folk Catholicism" which integrates or tolerates folk beliefs or practices within a basically Catholic belief system. Schumacher identified various factors that left the Visayan provinces including Leyte and Samar without a priest, and thus, the incomplete evangelization especially of the peoples in the uplands: the Jesuits expulsion in the eighteenth century; the refusal of friars to submit to the archbishop; the wars of Spain in Europe; and the Moro raids. Ibid., 261–62, 265.

God.[22] Animals, plants, forests, rivers, and mountains are believed to be animated by both environmental and ancestral spirits. The spirits own the land and the resources, and the users consult and negotiate with the spirits by means of rituals. The Catechism for Filipino Catholics has affirmed this: "Filipinos are spirit-oriented as seen in our popular beliefs about spirits dwelling in homes, trees, persons."[23]

These religious beliefs, together with other cultural beliefs, figured in the discourse on what or who caused typhoon Haiyan, in the survivors' coping with deaths in their family, and in their healing or rising up from the disaster.

What/Who Caused Typhoon Haiyan?

Unlike in the 2004 earthquake-triggered tsunami in Aceh, Indonesia,[24] the image of a punishing God was not dominant among the victim-survivors. Some attributed Haiyan to human actions (27 percent: 24 percent men and only 3 percent women). These actions vary from human-induced actions that impact the climate,[25] which range from the thinning of the ozone layer to the cutting of trees, to theories that Haiyan itself was human-made. Even before Haiyan hit land, there was a posting on the Web about how two tropical storms in Asia were caused by large microwave pulses from a U.S. Air Force base.[26] This news, filtered and passed on through word of mouth, has been received differently. Some respondents speak of nuclear testing in the Pacific (either initiated by North Koreans or by Americans).

Others view Haiyan as an act of nature itself beyond human control. A small minority believe, however, that Haiyan was caused by God, that it was a trial, a reminder, a call to conversion, or even a punishment to those who do not believe (13 percent: 10 percent women and 3 percent men). It was not necessarily the evil ones who died, for some were just casualties of society's collective sins. The majority do not believe, though, that God willed

22. See Johnson, "A Study of the Animistic Practices of the Waray People"; Recepcion, "Filipino Transpersonal Worldview," 67–75.

23. Catholic Bishops' Conference of the Philippines, *Catechism for Filipino Catholic*, 34–44.

24. Pearlman, "Tsunami-Ravaged Aceh in Indonesia Now Faces Rising Islamic Fundamentalism."

25. Only very few, however, know about climate change; the community leaders are just beginning to be conscientized about this.

26. Helton, "Philippines Typhoon linked to 'Man-Made' Microwave Pulses"; Janitch, "Large Microwave Pulse."

Haiyan to happen because God is good. Didith[27] who lost her husband and eldest daughter is convinced that Haiyan was the devil's doing.

Reflecting indigenous beliefs, Norma explicitly expressed that "other beings in the sea got mad," because of the garbage that was being thrown into their dwelling place. Similarly, there are those who said, "What we have thrown into the sea, the sea has thrown back at us." They described the water that engulfed their communities as black and murky,[28] carrying with it all the garbage that they have dumped into the sea. Now, the sea is clear ("*Wala ng burak; dati hanggang tuhod ang burak!*"). A familiar folk story among the survivors that similarly reflects the lack of reciprocity and propriety as a possible cause of Haiyan was related by another respondent. This is the story of the old woman who was going from house to house begging for water to drink. As nobody had mercy on her to give her water, she punished their communities with what the witnesses described as three successive huge waves of water.

Beliefs/Practices and the Evacuation

What would account for the large number of deaths? According to a scientific study of early warning efforts for the super typhoon, 94 percent of the deaths in the three cities with the most deaths (Tacloban among them) could have been prevented if people had evacuated. The government and media called coastal residents to evacuate days before the typhoon, resulting in the evacuation of around 800,000 residents, but many others remained in their houses. The warnings given by the Office of Civil Defense and local government units failed to make the residents understand that they could die if they did not evacuate.[29]

When there are evacuation warnings in these coastal communities, it has also been a common practice that the men stay behind to guard their domestic belongings and animals like pigs from looters. This gender division of labor is premised on the belief that the men are physically stronger

27. The names here are not the respondents' real names in order to protect their identity.

28. A testimony from a news article also described the water that had slowly engulfed their house as "dark seawater mixed with foul-smelling water from canals." Lichauco de Leon and MacLeod, "Philippines Sifting through Horror in Typhoon Haiyan."

29. Tacloban has a tropical rainforest climate which is hot and wet the whole year round and characterized by heavy and frequent rainfall. An average of twenty typhoons hit the country every year, mostly passing by Northern Luzon or Eastern Visayas (where Tacloban is located). The people of Tacloban are therefore used to typhoons.

and will be able to weather the typhoon better in case it really becomes dangerous. Thus, despite the orders to evacuate ahead of Haiyan, many of the men stayed behind. When some saw the seawater recede (and dry land appear), or later, when the waters started to come in, the men rushed to the barangay halls and went up to their roofs as the swirling waters rose. Some were not able to climb up and were drowned, like Didith's husband who refused to let go of the pig they were hoping to sell for their daughter's college tuition. Many others fell from the roof and were swept away by the raging waters.

Others also thought, as in previous warnings of storm surge, that the water would reach only the shores. Whole families living in concrete houses on the side of the road and not directly in front of the coast did not evacuate, believing that their homes could withstand the strong wind and the waters would not reach them. While most people knew what a tsunami was, they did not understand what a storm surge was.

Furthermore, as traditionally practiced, the people observed the weather the day before the typhoon hit, and it was sunny and the sea was calm. Jose, who had a few years of college education, combined his scientific knowledge about the typhoon from the weather forecasts with his folk knowledge about the behavior of animals before a disaster; he noted that, though the sky was clear with no clouds at all, there were no birds, the rats were in a frenzy, and the dogs were restless. He deduced that this was something different from all other typhoons they have had. Nevertheless, though he was in the evacuation center with his four siblings and a niece; his stepfather, mother, and other siblings remained to guard their house and belongings.

The Restless Spirits

After the wrath of Typhoon Haiyan subsided, the streets were littered with bodies. Many remained for months under mountains of debris, or deep in the ponds and other bodies of water. The trauma of witnessing widespread death brought about by a natural hazard has manifested itself in terms of ghost sightings and wails and moans in the dark of the night.[30] In Tacloban, drivers of public vehicles traversing the Tacloban-San Jose route to the airport, where thousands died during the super typhoon, report wet passengers

---

30. In the aftermath of the 2011 earthquake-triggered tsunami, a similar phenomenon was observed in technologically-advanced Japan which continues to maintain strong animist beliefs. See Villar and Knight, "Haunted by Trauma."

boarding and alighting at San Jose.[31] Others hear sounds of crying, wailing, or moaning in so-called "dead spots" where many corpses were found, or where dead bodies were temporarily placed as they awaited identification and burial. Voices of lamentation were also said to be heard in deep ponds where, the people believe, human remains were left unretrieved.

The lack of proper handling of human remains and a decent burial may have added to the guilt of the bereaved. With thousands of human remains around, and the fear of an epidemic breaking out, the soldiers instructed the people not to touch the dead bodies of their relatives. The bereaved could only look helplessly at their loved ones, who were left decaying on the streets before being buried. It took weeks before the bodies from these barangays were picked up, as priority was given to the thousands of dead in San Jose. The manual for the management of dead bodies clearly indicated that: "Careful and ethical management of dead bodies, including disposal, should be ensured, including respect for religious and cultural sensibilities."[32] But pressed for time and with the massive number of bodies, the soldiers unceremoniously put the human remains in body bags, loaded them into trucks and, after they were processed for identification, threw them into mass graves, which initially had no crosses at all. At the time of her interview, Gloria did not even know in which mass grave they had buried her husband. Aside from being left with no resources to bury her husband in a private lot, she had to take care of her son who has a disability and requires medical treatment.

Ancient Visayans had elaborate rituals which showed how they revered their dead. The body would be washed very well and, if the person was of high status, anointed with oil, adorned with gold and other precious items, shrouded, and placed on a high platform for the viewing of the deceased. After three to seven days, the body was later placed in a casket made from the hardest incorruptible wood (if wealthy) or soft wood (if poor). At the end of one year, they opened the casket to wash the bones and anoint them with oil. They placed the bones in a smaller container made from incorruptible wood, or in large jars, and stored this in the house ceiling or under the house (at ground level).[33] The *babaylan* (native priestess) led a ritual in which the dead person's soul receives the offering to it. With this rite, it was believed that the dead, now satisfied, would not come back to take

31. See also Basilio, "The Ghosts of Yolanda"; Petilla, "True Ghost Story from Leyte's Saintly Priest."

32. Cited by Gaspar, *Desperately Seeking God's Saving Action*, 137.

33. To know more about the ancient Visayan burial practices, see Alcina, *History of the Bisayan People in the Philippine Islands*, 305–33.

with him/her the family members left behind.[34] Then, a feast followed the funeral rites.

With the influx of Christianity, this ritual had been replaced, especially among Catholics, with a rite which accommodated the practice of a wake to view the deceased for days or a few weeks. If proper funeral rites were followed, there was the possibility as well of being forgiven by God of one's sins.[35] This means the body had been blessed with holy water by a priest—who has replaced the traditional *babaylan*—usually after Mass had been celebrated, and before the dead was finally laid into the ground for burial. It was, however, impossible for many of the survivors—who either could not find the remains of their loved ones, who still needed to attend to the living, or who had been left with no resources at all—to be able to provide such a proper burial for their dead, thus adding to their sorrow and guilt.

Searching for God in the Mega-Disaster

Where was God at the height of Typhoon Haiyan? For the majority, God (interchangeable with Mary and the saints) was the one who saved them as they clung to the roof beams, or swam in the murky waters, or watched the water rise, or braved the winds to move to safer structures. At the intensity of the super typhoon, they were praying for the wind to subside and believed that God caused the strong wind and the storm to cease. Some attributed the fact that no one died in their place to the procession of the statues of Mary, the Trinity, and the saints, which they held the day before the storm. Jose, who was also among those who led the procession, asked God to grant him courage and presence of mind. This helped him save himself and his siblings as he led them to a safer place than the school evacuation center where some classrooms collapsed due to trees crashing and the sea wall breaking down, killing at least thirty people.[36] After the typhoon, for the respondents, God continued to be present in the people and groups who helped them rise up.

Some cited biblical stories that capture the people's struggle to survive, such as the story of the Great Flood. Like their experience of clinging to their roofs, Noah's ark is a story of survival against the waters. One of them believes that this will never happen again, just as God promised Noah that he will never punish his people again. Another recalls the story of Jesus calming the waves and the strong winds (Mark 4:35–41) and still another, the crossing of the Red Sea between huge waves on the left and the right.

34. Ibid.
35. Gaspar, *Desperately Seeking God's Saving Action*, 130.
36. McClean, "Disaster Zone Schools."

For two men, however, this is just the beginning of the "end of the world." "The day was like night; there was zero visibility. The rain was not stopping." Ernesto said: "According to the old people, at the end of times there will be calamities." For Jose, though, the end of times is a process, and it has already started and will continue if people do not repent of their collective sins.

The Beliefs and Disaster Risk Reduction

Cultural and religious beliefs can be helpful when they "help people cope" and "provide a reserve of social capital" and "a platform for education about risk reduction." They can be less helpful if they "hamper building back differently or relocating," "contribute to vulnerability," or "make it difficult to educate about risk reduction."[37]

Reciprocity and Propriety in Relation to Nature

As was earlier noted, in the people's folk beliefs, reciprocity and propriety are morally expected in the relationship of humans with "supernatural" beings.[38] Reciprocity and propriety here are actually related because mutual consideration requires propriety. Propriety means that each one's "home" and "place" has to be respected. "[A]n attitude of respect is called for as proper and necessary in maintaining that each individual or social group (family, community) and, likewise, the symbolically identified spirits can enjoy the privacy of their own place."[39] Environmental spirits are believed to take revenge if one damages or trespasses on their dwelling. Behind this is the worldview that humans have only borrowed the earth's resources from the environmental spirits and must therefore acknowledge their indebtedness to the spirits.[40]

One of the women respondents put it this way: "Nature is a blessing, a gift, if humans know their proper place." Having learned from the sea spirits' wrath, another vowed to no longer throw her garbage into the sea and to employ proper garbage disposal. From a Christian standpoint, reciprocity and propriety can be linked to how Sallie McFague redefines sin in an ecological perspective, that is as "refusal to accept our place" in the scheme of

37. Cannon et al., "How Religion and Belief Influence Attitudes to Risk."

38. Pertierra, *Religion, Politics and Rationality in a Philippine Community*, 131–32.

39. Guzman, "Creation as God's *Kaloob*," 337.

40. Love, "Samahan of Papa God," 131.

creation, where humans live together with other creatures and are the most dependent on the rest of creation for survival.[41]

Christian Beliefs and Stories

While among Catholics, faith beliefs were not a significant factor in influencing evacuation,[42] faith did matter during the height of the super typhoon Haiyan itself, when the victims drew strength from their faith in order to survive. The majority believe that is it is God (interchangeable with Mary and the saints) who saved them, who gifted them with a second life, caused the wind to subside, and has given them the strength to persevere. And after the typhoon, God continued to be present in the people and groups who helped them.

Religious narratives can also have a powerful effect on ethical behavior. In an era of climate change, some religious stories may or may not help in disaster risk reduction, depending on how they are interpreted. On the one hand, the interpretation of the story of Noah's Ark—that, as God promised, this disaster will not happen again—may result in people becoming complacent and returning to their old ways.[43] On the other hand, the image of Noah's Ark has also been employed by activists to stress the importance of human agency, conservation, and repentance in the face of climate change.[44] In the historic climate march in New York City involving 300,000 protesters, peoples from various faiths walked beside a Noah's Ark replica which bore the words: "We are all Noah now."[45] Noah's Ark remains a powerful image that can be interpreted/reinterpreted to prevent disaster.

To Be Alert as the Animals

As earthquakes and super typhoons are difficult to simulate, it is hard to study and replicate animal reactions to these natural hazards. If ever there

41. McFague, *The Body of God.*

42. More important factors are their individual or collective attachment to the land, farm, their livestock, or the local government's lack of support for the evacuation. Chester, "Natural Disasters and Christian Theology," 17.

43. This story of Noah's Ark has been used, too, by a Texas Congressman to argue that climate change is not anthropogenic since there was a Great Flood even before there was overdeveloped hydrocarbon energy. Goldenberg, "U.S. Congressman Cites Biblical Flood."

44. Schaper, "Noah's Ark."

45. Fiedler, "Faith Leaders March for Climate."

is something to be learned from these, it is the need to know one's surrounding and to be alert as the animals. According to Ravi Corea, president and founder of the Sri Lanka Wildlife Conservation Society, "Wild animals survive by being always alert. That's what keeps them alive. Nature is very resilient. We shouldn't forget the fact that we are also part of nature."[46]

Many of the respondents expressed that they are now more alert . . . more attentive to the weather condition. Thirty percent expressed explicitly that they now immediately evacuate when there is a strong typhoon warning. They listen to the weather forecast instead of simply watching the waves to know what the weather will be. Today, each barangay has a designated relocation area, and there is an evacuation committee in the communities. One of the male interviewees in charge of looking for vehicles to transport people to the evacuation centers says that this is his newfound "mission" in life.

Thus, in 2014, even before the government ordered them to evacuate for the impending Typhoon Hagupit/Ruby—initially a super typhoon—some had already evacuated after hearing warnings from the newscast. The threat of Typhoon Hagupit led to the evacuation of more than a million people.[47]

Relative Gender Equality[48]

The relative gender equality in the Philippines helps in disaster risk reduction. In the 2004 Asian tsunami, 77 percent of those who died in Aceh, Indonesia, were women; in Tamil Nadu, India, 73 percent; and based on anecdotes, around two thirds in Sri Lanka.[49] In Sri Lanka, for instance, one of the various reasons for the large number of women who died (including the fact that there was no warning and thus no time to evacuate) was that the rural women neither knew how to climb trees nor swim; they wore the long, traditional saris which prevented them from running and weighed them down in the water; and with their extreme sense of modesty, they did not take off these clothes.[50] I was not able to find a gender-based statistic of the Haiyan casualties. My own data from seven coastal villages in the Redemptorist parish reveal that 57 percent of those who died, and 54 percent

46. Donaldson-Evans, "Tsunami Animals?"

47. Australian Red Cross, "Largest Peacetime Evacuation as Typhoon Hagupit Hits Philippines."

48. Ross, "Why Gender Disaster Data Matters."

49. Aglionby, "Four Times as Many Women Died in Tsunami."

50. Kakuchi, "Women Put Modesty Above Survival."

of those missing, were women.[51] In fact, in Barangay 54A, there were more men who perished (66 percent) because, as mentioned, it is commonly their task to stay behind to watch over the livestock when there are strong typhoons. Unlike their south Asian rural counterparts, Filipinas who grew up along the coast typically know how to climb trees, and they learn how to swim as children.[52] Compared to other post-disaster contexts, incidents of gender-based violence outside the household seem to be fewer, but within the household, 11 percent of women interviewed in a study by the Philippine Statistics Authority expressed that they have been physically abused by their intimate partners since Typhoon Haiyan.[53] Fewer victims of violence are found among those who live with relatives, pray daily, and whose male partners are actively looking for a job. The many widows after the typhoon, however, complain that a number of organizations interviewed only the men with regard to the need for permanent housing. This even prompted one focus group discussion of women participants in one barangay to complain, but the officials did not respond to them.[54]

The Church as Mediating God's Presence in Disaster

Theodicy aims to reconcile the belief in a loving, just, and all-powerful God with the experience of human suffering. David Chester outlined various models of theodicy and focused in particular on those that are most prominent in nature-related disasters.[55]

Models of Theodicy

Retributive theodicy sees disaster as God's punishment for people's sins. The Old Testament is replete with this view that God causes disasters to happen. This model is paramount in Christian explanations of earthquakes

51. This data was culled in January 2014 from the parish's list of deaths/missing for Barangays 51, 52, 61, 54A, 54, 58, and 60A. I added to the numbers those which have not been recorded, as corroborated by my interviewees.

52. The Philippines ranks ninth in the Global Gender Gap 2014 Report and has been in the top ten countries with less disparity in gender treatment for nine years since the study sponsored by the World Economic Forum began. Delavin, "PHL Slips in Gender Index Rank."

53. Castro, "Assessing Vulnerabilities of Women and Children Exposed to Disaster."

54. Sherwood et al., "Resolving Post-Disaster Displacement."

55. Chester, "Natural Disasters and Christian Theology."

and volcanic eruptions. With industrialization and development of scientific rationality from the late eighteenth century, this view now has less of a following especially in the more economically developed countries, though it has not been completely eradicated.

The seventeenth-century philosopher Gottfried Wilhelm Leibniz offered a more scientifically based explanation, referred to as the "best of all possible worlds" theodicy. This is described by Chester as follows:

> The universe is controlled by the laws of physics and not by special laws (i.e., providences). Despite the suffering caused by disasters, the earth is the *Best Possible World* (Leibniz) that could be created. Suffering occurs to achieve a *greater good* (e.g., without earthquakes, tectonic activity would not be possible and without volcanic activity, no atmosphere would have formed). The occurrence and magnitude of earthquakes and volcanic eruptions obey the laws of probability. Our "law controlled" world facilitates spiritual growth, through dealing with suffering.[56]

Here the image of God is one who continues creative work in creation, but God's providence remains especially for the most tragically affected. In both the retributive and best-of- all-possible worlds theodicy, Christian response, which is normally a combination of prayers of intercessions for victims and Christian charity, is based on the command to love one's neighbor and to see in the disaster victims the suffering Christ.[57] The Leibnizian model has been criticized for reducing human responsibility in disasters[58] and can be used by capitalists and government as an excuse for ecological irresponsibility.

Beginning in the 1980s and continuing into the 1990s, concurrent with the United Nations' International Decade for Natural Disaster Reduction, there was a shift in looking at disasters from the perspective of vulnerability. Poverty and marginalization, inadequate building codes, and lack of preparations for disaster have been recognized as important factors in the greater number of deaths and destruction during disasters in developing countries.[59] A strand of post-Leibnizian approach—-liberationist theodicy—brings societal responsibility to the center. "'[S]tructural sinfulness,' so we have argued, lies behind global differences in wealth and power, as well

56. Ibid., 2.
57. Ibid., 12.
58. See Tilley, *The Evils of Theodicy*.
59. Ibid., 13.

as dissimilar and unequal disaster outcomes."[60] The same was stressed by
Pope Francis in *Laudato Sí*: "the deterioration of the environment and of
society affect the most vulnerable people on the planet."[61] Following Jürgen
Moltmann, this liberationist theodicy stresses the immanence of God so
that even as disasters occur because of natural processes and structural sinfulness, God continues to be in solidarity with the suffering of humanity.[62]

All of the above three models of theodicy are represented in the
people's responses as to why Typhoon Haiyan happened: it is God's punishment for people's collective sins; it is an act of nature; and for others, it is
caused by humans themselves through their ecological irresponsibility or
experimentation.

Based on studies in the past century, Chester argues that, specifically
for Catholics, the model of theodicy they espouse (e.g., retributive theodicy) does not prevent them from evacuating. Furthermore, regardless of the
model of theodicy a particular church holds, churches have often helped
in victim identification and engaged in relief distribution and counseling.
I would wager, however, that if a church holds a liberationist theodicy, it
would more actively engage further in a campaign against environmental
degradation and corruption that renders people poor and vulnerable to
disasters.

The Redemptorist Church in Tacloban

The Redemptorists in the Philippines have been known for their liberationist approach to mission and seem to operate from a post-Liebnizian
liberationist theodicy that is at the same time sensitive to the traditional
beliefs of the people. Their church in Tacloban served as an evacuation
center for around three thousand evacuees during, and for a month after, ·
the super typhoon. Following an Extraordinary Provincial Council Meeting
held in November 2013, the Redemptorists in the Philippines decided to
conduct a General Mission in a post-Haiyan context, starting in Tacloban
and expanding to other nearby parishes depending on the willingness of
the archbishop.[63] In the conduct of the General Mission, the church helped

---

60. Chester, "Natural Disasters and Christian Theology," 16.

61. Francis, *Laudato Si'*, 48.

62. This theodicy, however, only partially explains disaster, as there are those in
economically developed countries, who, employing their free will, choose to continue
to live in disaster prone places. Ibid., 16–17.

63. Gaspar, *Desperately Seeking God's Saving Action*, 166. For the tentative concept
paper of the General Mission, see ibid., 170–72. The theme of the General Mission was
"Re-nurturing Faith, Re-kindling Hope, Re-building the People of God."

people cope, through their faith, with their bereavement. Being sensitive to the traditional beliefs of the people, the Redemptorists found themselves mediating between people's folk beliefs, scientific, and contemporary faith perspectives.

Folk Beliefs and Healing

The General Mission responded to people's requests for blessings not only for the dead but for the dead spots where the people heard cries of lamentations. In the blessing of the dead spots, the people in the neighborhood were invited to gather and remember their departed loved ones and to pray for the repose of their souls.[64] Together with these, they also conducted psychosocial spiritual integration, employing art therapy. Hundreds of liturgical celebrations that allowed participants to talk about their departed loved ones and express what they wanted to say were also held. There were occasions when they invited the participants to construct miniature coffins, with the names of their departed inside, which they buried with a small cross over the grave. The priest then blessed these mini graves. And as in traditional practice, food and drinks were shared afterwards.[65] This helped relieve the bereaved who were not able to provide their dead with the proper wake and burial ritual.

In commemorating the super-typhoon disaster a year after, the Redemptorist parish did not join the common memorial in Tacloban; instead, it had its own. At 7:00 in the evening, on November 7, 2014, a play was staged meant to trigger collective grieving. This was followed by a vigil, according to age groups, which lasted until 6:00 a.m. when an "aurora" (dawn) procession was held. At 8:00 the next morning, a noise barrage was conducted in the "dead spots." Jose interpreted the noise barrage as a way to "send away the bad spirits." In indigenous belief, one can exorcise evil spirits through strong smell (e.g., manure) or loud explosions like those produced by firecrackers.

As to how they dealt with the people's folk beliefs, Karl Gaspar, CSsR, wrote:

> Indeed, on one hand, we could be critiqued as reinforcing superstitious popular beliefs of the poor who cling on to these given the deep insecurities they have by way of dealing with the spirit world and the whole mystery of the unfolding of calamities. . . . But . . . we should still do our best to not just go through the

64. Ibid., 123.
65. Ibid., 124–25.

act of blessing but provide a discursive space where the people could realize themselves that the blessing is not there to drive evil spirits away but to strengthen the spirit within them so that individually and communally they would act to transform their oppressive situation which is the root cause of their deep insecurities and anxieties of both natural and supernatural realms of existence.[66]

Transforming the Image of God

Fr. Edwin Bacaltos, the Redemptorist parish priest, was also intent on correcting false impressions of God. In his homilies, he stressed that Haiyan was not a punishment by God. While the majority of the people do not hold the view of a punishing God, it is important to affirm and reinforce this with positive teaching, as well as by reinterpreting biblical stories such as that of Noah's Ark, and more importantly, to witness to God's compassion and healing presence.

One barangay, during the anniversary, wanted to hold a separate thanksgiving mass because nobody died there. The priest advised them instead to be in solidarity with the other villages that had suffered deaths, by joining just one commemoration in the whole parish. This was to prevent one group from thinking that they had the special protection of God over other communities.

Fr. Bacaltos also clarified to the people that the Redemptorist parish was spared from destruction, not because of a miracle that defies nature under God's special protection, but because the hospital in front of it served to protect it from the waves. This more scientific rationale can help the people toward thinking of more scientific ways to reduce disaster risk.

Community Organizing and Conscientization

In collaboration with the Urban Poor Associates (UPA), the parish is helping provide permanent homes for those in the no-build zones. The UPA is an NGO that educates, advocates, and organizes around housing rights for the poor. They work closely with religious leaders, especially Catholics as 90 percent of the urban poor are Catholics. Through the UPA, a two-hectare lot was bought where those in the no build-zone areas can have a housing unit. This is the parish's entry point for organizing the communities and

---

66. Ibid., 256–57.

integrating faith formation, as well as educating them on climate change and environmental protection.

Conclusion

This essay has elaborated on the religious and cultural beliefs related to Super Typhoon Haiyan that facilitated evacuation, helped people cope, provided them with the social capital to survive, and enabled education in risk reduction, as well as those that blocked or can hinder disaster risk reduction.

Certain indigenous beliefs have proved helpful as evacuation warnings, such as the sight of the sea water receding (a traditional sign of an impending sea hazard) or the strange behavior of animals the day before the super typhoon. Indeed, indigenous beliefs can be tapped for disaster risk reduction. The need for reciprocity and propriety in relation to the spirits that inhabit the environment can be a starting point for fostering care for creation, including the poor. The restlessness of animals before a disaster shows their alertness and sensitivity to what is happening to the environment, which people, who are also part of nature, should emulate. Relative gender equality seems to have been a factor as well in the greater survival rate of women and of lesser violence outside the household.

For coping with the disaster, the Redemptorists found it necessary to consider the people's animist worldview. They helped relieve people's guilt about the lack of proper burials for the dead by holding Masses and blessings not only for their loved ones, but also in the dead spots where lamentations of restless spirits had been heard. At the same time, they provided opportunities for collective grieving, therapy, and psycho-social-spiritual integration. In these ways, the church has mediated between folk beliefs and scientific processes, helping the victim-survivors rise up from the disaster.

The church mediated God's presence by providing a sanctuary for the evacuees; aiding in relief distribution; offering intercessory prayers, healing, and therapy; and even helping provide a relocation site for those in the no-build zones area. The model of theodicy a church holds can be crucial to how it responds to a nature-related disaster. Going beyond a retributive theodicy, the Redemptorist parish corrected mistaken concepts of God and educated the people toward understanding the scientific causes of certain phenomena. Understanding better the structural causes of vulnerability and disaster, as in a post-Liebnizian liberationist theodicy, it aims to conscientize the communities about climate change and organize them toward greater sustainability and resilience.

16

Nurturing Communities, Sustaining Fragile Ecologies

RANDY J. C. ODCHIGUE

The premise of this paper is that the fragility of ecosystems reflects the fragility of human communities. The experience this paper hopes to narrate will hopefully reinforce our belief that in a globalized context, the issue of caring for our fragile ecology begins with the task of birthing and caring for just communities.

Context

In 2012, *Guinness World Records* announced that a large crocodile measuring 20.24 feet (6.17 meters) was captured in the southern Philippines in a town called Bunawan. The crocodile's name was Lolong, and he has broken world records in terms of size. The town is part of what is known as the Agusan Marsh. The marsh, which is the hunting ground of Lolong, is an extensive floodplain in the middle of Agusan River Basin in eastern Mindanao of the southern Philippines where rivers, creeks, and tributaries from the nearby provinces converge and drain toward Butuan City where this author works and resides.

The marsh encompasses some 111,540 hectares covering fifty-five barangays and eight municipalities. The catchment area of the marsh is roughly about 661,200 hectares, an impressive expanse. The name "Agusan" comes from "Agasan," which means "where water flows" and "where food was in abundance."[1] Its habitat is basically composed of open water eco-

1. Primavera and Tumanda, "Agusan Marsh," 5, 7.

systems, swamp forests, herbaceous swamps, and inundated forest types. Known to be one of the most important biodiversity areas in the Philippines, the marsh is home to over two hundred bird species some of which are migratory birds from northern Asia and Siberia.[2]

Living within the marsh area are communities of indigenous peoples called the Manobo.[3] They live in houses made of stilts, and they depend on the marsh for their day-to-day sustenance. Key informants narrate that, in relation to the conservation of environmental resources, the indigenous knowledge systems of the Manobo have enabled their communities to survive for many decades. These knowledge systems involve their familiarity with the cycling of rainfall and flooding; their observance of a fallow period before re-cultivating land for it to regain its fertility; and their highly spiritual relationship with the land shown in their many rituals for hunting, fishing, and farming in which they negotiate with the deities so that they may be allowed to utilize the resources of the marsh.[4]

Recently, threats to the fragile ecology and community in the marsh have become all too real. They come in three forms. The first are invasive species like the golden snail and janitor fish, and the economically-driven introduction of non-native fish (tilapia) and plants (rice and palm oil) for food security and corporate profit.[5]

The second threat is to water quality and hydrology and comes in the form of mining, particularly widespread mining on Mt. Diwata whose waterways are tributaries that feed into the Agusan Marsh. Not following sound environmental management, the mining activities on Mt. Diwata result in an estimated three hundred thousand tons of mine tailings going into the Agusan River every year.[6] These mine tailings contain lethal amounts of mercury used in the processing of gold on Mt. Diwata. Scientific studies have proven that large amounts of mercury are found in the aquatic life in the marsh and have contaminated rice paddies within and around the

2. Sucaldito and Nuñeza, "Distribution of the Avifauna of Agusan March," 51–68.

3. Data from the Philippine National Statistics Office in the year 2000 show that the total population in the key biodiversity area of the marsh is 231,693 distributed among 43,458 households. One study shows that the percentage of the Manobo and other indigenous groups inhabiting the marsh and its fringes is between 60 and 70 percent of the area's total population; see Bracamonte et al., "Social and Economic Aspects of the Agusan Marsh Key Biodiversity Area," 85–87.For studies on the Manobo, see Garvan, *The Manóbos of Mindanao*; Gatmaytan, " Traditional Manobo Agriculture," 1–52, and Gatmaytan, "The Hakyadan of Froilan Havana," 383–426.

4. Bracamonte et al., "Agusan Marsh Key Biodiversity Area," 87.

5. Primavera and Tumanda, "Agusan Marsh," 11.

6. Ibid.

vicinity of the Agusan Marsh.[7] High mercury levels are also found in fish and mussels harvested from the tributary rivers and consumed by the area's inhabitants.[8] Another peril to the hydrology of the marsh is the "development" initiatives funded by agencies like World Bank and Asian Development Bank. Without proper assessment of the field and the heterogeneous practices of communities within the Agusan Marsh's ecosystems, these funding agencies are unwitting funders of the exploitation of the Agusan Marsh through dam and irrigation construction that does not take into account the precarious balance of the marsh ecosystem.

The third form of threat is illegal logging of the forest and watershed reserves. It is well-documented that there is both small-scale and large-scale illegal logging by companies that cut down trees outside their legally approved areas. At present, for example, there is a company from New Zealand operating under the legal instrument of the Integrated Forest Management Agreement which is sanctioned by the government.[9]

Taken together, these risks present a clear and present danger to the fragile ecosystem and the human community of the Agusan Marsh. The wanton destruction and disrespect of the Agusan Marsh ecosystem destroy the balance that regulates the water supply of and provides vital ecosystem services to the eastern side of Mindanao. Any development must be in harmony with the ecological, hydrological, and sociocultural, human dynamics within the Agusan Marsh and the Agusan River Basin.

Even after a cursory glance at the situation in the Agusan River Basin and the Agusan Marsh, there are several issues that surface. While these can be framed in many ways, I choose to see these local issues from the broader two-fold perspective of sustainability discourse: the question of intragenerational justice on the one hand and of intergenerational responsibility on the other.[10]

Intragenerational Justice

Perhaps we can begin our discussion here with the definition of sustainability, seen from the perspective of intragenerational justice as "meeting human needs in a socially just manner without depriving ecosystems of their

7. Roa, "Mercury Pollution," 35.

8. Primavera and Tumanda, "Agusan Marsh," 11.

9. Ibid., 11–12.

10. Among the known proponents of this double perspective in the question of sustainability are Agyeman and Evans. See, for example, Agyeman and Evans, "Justice, Governance and Sustainability," 185–206.

health."[11] This perspective already hints at a multidisciplinary approach to sustainability. It has five intertwining components: (1) developing efficient technologies and markets for meeting human needs; (2) understanding the state and nature of ecosystems; (3) understanding how exploitation affects ecosystems; (4) understanding how exploitation affects human culture; and (5) understanding the meaning of normative concepts such as human needs, social justice, deprivation, and ecosystem health.[12]

I believe this perspective to be generally anthropocentric—for example, it does not encompass understanding how certain cultures' normative beliefs, which influence their actions of exploiting or nurturing the environment and its human communities, fall under the purview of religion, established or indigenous. This can serve as our initial lens for sharpening the problem. We will come back to this point later but already, at this point, we can say that the framework does not seem radical enough, because it does not also take into account the non-anthropocentric approaches to ecology. Do we care for the environment because ecosystems are intrinsically valuable independent of human persons? Do we care for the environment because we are part of the intertwining ecosystem defined as intrinsic relationalities between humanity and the rest of the environment? I believe it is necessary to ask these questions, because "if the goodness of an action rises primarily from the motivation and values that motivate an action,"[13] then motivations springing from different perspectives, or coming from an integration of these aspects, will lead to profoundly different outcomes.

Despite the foregoing critique, we can say a few things regarding the Agusan Marsh from the lens of intragenerational justice framework. The threats besetting the Marsh appear to be classifiable under dynamics between exploitation and development—and they are not mutually exclusive. The mercury contamination resulting from the mining activities in the mountain ranges surrounding the Marsh is the result of several layers of neglect. On one level, there appears to be a failure of government agencies to implement regulatory policies for small- and large-scale mining. The situation in the Agusan Marsh might be considered a microcosm of what is happening throughout the whole country. This can also be said in relation to illegal logging. It is widely known that, in the hinterlands of Agusan, loggers routinely harvest endemic tree species while government agencies appear to do a dismal job of curbing the practice despite protests from civil society

11. Vucetich and Nelson, "Sustainability," 539.

12. Ibid., 539–40.

13. Ibid., 543.

groups. Land-use conversion into plantations owned by foreign companies also continues to be a threat to the sustainability of the marsh.[14]

On another level, there appears to be no regard for the consequences that resource extraction activities have on the ecosystem. There seems to be wanton disregard and a failure of awareness of the ridge-to-reef connection—the mercury contamination will not only be lethal to those who consume the aquatic resources, but it will also cause coral bleaching, eventually destroying the aquatic habitat, and this has long-term effects on the food security of northeastern Mindanao. Logging will have consequences on the forests' water-holding capacity—the fewer the trees, the higher the risk of increased water levels and frequency of flooding. With annual flood levels rising, the Agusan Valley and Butuan City have already been identified as flashpoints among the disaster-prone areas in the Philippines. Still on another level, the irresponsible mining and logging activities betray not only an ecologically exploitative mindset but also a blatant disregard for the question of justice in relation to the effects these extraction activities have on area communities. The fact that mercury contamination and flooding endanger these communities' health and well-being, and threaten their very existence, is more than enough proof of unjust social and economic dynamics in Agusan.

Ecological degradation has dire effects on the poorer sectors of the society—those sectors which do not have access to health care or professional help to seek justice for and financial freedom from the exploitative dynamics at play. An economic paradigm that creates the conditions of possibility for a sustainable and equitable future should problematize concentrations of economic, state, and transnational corporate power in order to expose the effects of marginalizing economic growth on the welfare of less powerful individuals and communities.[15] Boff was right when he concluded that the cry of the earth is also the cry of the poor.[16] Benedict XVI problematizes this in his encyclical *Caritas in Veritate*: "The world's wealth is growing in absolute terms, but inequalities are on the increase."[17] Benedict XVI stresses the responsibility towards the poor, and he argues that "the development of peoples depends, above all, on a recognition that the human race is a single family working together in true communion."[18] In his encyclical *Laudato*

14. Bracamonte et al., "Agusan Marsh Key Biodiversity Area," 91–93.

15. Moe-Lobeda and Spencer, "Free Trade Agreements and the Neo-Liberal Economic Paradigm," 714.

16. See Boff, *Cry of the Earth, Cry of the Poor*.

17. Benedict XVI, *Caritas in Veritate*, 22.

18. Ibid., 53.

Si', Pope Francis pushed this critique further, connecting the deterioration of the environment to cultural and ethical decline. Francis argues that "our inability to think seriously about future generations is linked to our inability to broaden the scope of our present interests and to give consideration to those who remain excluded from development. Let us not only keep the poor of the future in mind, but also today's poor, whose life on this earth is brief and who cannot keep on waiting. Hence, 'in addition to a fairer sense of intergenerational solidarity there is also an urgent moral need for a renewed sense of intragenerational solidarity.'"[19] This brings us to the next point.

Intergenerational Responsibility

Intragenerational justice must be coupled with intergenerational responsibility, which refers to the acute awareness that an essential criterion in the ethics of our behavior today is whether we have ensured that we will leave behind a habitable world that is able to support life for many future generations. Some authors subsume this responsibility under the virtue of solidarity as an obligation to future generations arising from the acute awareness of one's belonging to the past, present, and future community of persons.[20] Thomas Berry also adds to this;[21] in his book, *The Christian Future and the Fate of the Earth*,[22] he expounds his perspective of cosmic evolution which is highly influenced by the pioneering work of Teilhard de Chardin.[23] An advocate of deep ecology, Berry seemed to believe that there needs to be a continual widening of the circle of solidarity and compassion. This project of widening the circle of compassion makes a serious ethical argument that we must take into account the interests of those who will come after

19. Francis, *Laudato Si'*, 162.

20. Moody and Achenbaum, "Solidarity Sustainability and Stewardship," 152.

21. See Laszlo and Combs, *Thomas Berry, Dreamer of the Earth*.

22. Berry, *The Christian Future and the Fate of the Earth*.

23. Teilhard de Chardin is a Jesuit paleontologist who took part in the discovery of Peking Man. He has influenced Thomas Berry in his views on evolution. His oeuvre includes *The Phenomenon of Man* (New York: Harper, 1959), which is a sweeping account of the evolution of humanity that ultimately culminates in its union with Christ, the Omega point which de Chardin defines as the summit point of all complexity and consciousness. De Chardin was also referred to by Pope Francis in *Laudato Si'*—section 83, footnote 53—as the backdrop of the statement: "all creatures are moving forward with us and through us towards a common point of arrival, which is God, in that transcendent fullness where the risen Christ embraces and illumines all things. Human beings, endowed with intelligence and love, and drawn by the fullness of Christ, are called to lead all creatures back to their Creator."

us in the future. The boundaries of compassion are not just extended in time, into the future, but are also extended to include—in a wider sense of solidarity—those of nonhuman species. The medieval figures of Hildegard of Bingen and St. Francis of Assisi pleaded for compassion for all of God's creatures and all of God's creation.[24] Intergenerational responsibility, therefore, proposes an ethics across generations in which we feel and become acutely aware that we are connected to future generations of the unborn human—and nonhuman—species.

In *Laudato Si'*, Pope Francis devotes an entire section to justice between generations. He argues that we cannot "speak about sustainable development apart from intergenerational solidarity."[25] He argues that, once we take on solidarity with those who come after us, we realize that the gift of the world we freely received must be shared with others. This paves the way for an awareness that "we can no longer view reality in a purely utilitarian way, in which efficiency and productivity are entirely geared to our individual benefit. Intergenerational solidarity is not optional, but rather a basic question of justice, since the world we received also belongs to those who will follow us."[26] Francis quotes the reflections of the Portuguese bishops: "The environment is part of a logic of receptivity. It is on loan to each generation, which must then hand it on to the next."[27]

In the experience of the Agusan Marsh, it is quite evident that the perpetrators of actions leading to its destruction have not taken into account—and do not lose sleep over—how precarious the balance is between the Marsh and the people whose sustenance depends on it, as well as those farther away who will be affected should the natural barriers of the inundated and swamp forests give way and result in tragic flooding. They appear to have lost awareness of what might happen, if the marsh is destroyed, to the future generations of people whose livelihood depends on it.

Looking at the "cracks in the planet we inhabit," Francis outlines broad, actionable approaches to respond to the many challenges presented by intragenerational justice and intergenerational solidarity. To address climate change and sustainable efforts, for example, he proposes dialogues between nations;[28] between local and national policies;[29] between politics and economy, taking into account human fulfillment;[30]and between science

24. Moody and Achenbaum, "Solidarity Sustainability and Stewardship," 154.

25. Francis, *Laudato Si'*, 159.

26. Ibid.

27. Conferência Episcopal Portuguesa, Carta Pastoral, 20.

28. Francis, *Laudato Si'*, 164–75.

29. Ibid., 176–81.

30. Ibid., 189–98.

and religion.[31] The next section outlines the frameworks upon which such dialogue for actionable approaches may be formulated.

Frameworks for Strategic Responses

The frameworks are discussed from the perspective of the relationship between theological reflection and environmental ethics. There appear to be three broad lines of relationships, each demonstrating a unique way the environment comes to matter for human experience, practical reason, and theological ethics.[32] The first is organized around nature's standing, the second around human agency, and the third around ecological subjectivity. In the first framework, practical reason illuminates the claim that nature's moral standing exerts on human experience. In ethical discourses, this is known as the framework of ecojustice that emphasizes the intrinsic value of nature. From this perspective, integrity of creation denotes "the value of all creatures in themselves, for one another, and for God, and their interconnectedness in a diverse whole that has unique value for God."[33] In this framework, injustice is embodied in policies and actions that impinge on the integrity of creation. However, ethicists of this persuasion need to grapple with the issue of how nature's intrinsic value and justice are to be understood in the face of natural calamities: are tsunamis, earthquakes, etc., and natural predation properly "justice" issues?[34]

The second framework shows how human experience and agency responsibly care for, develop, and utilize nature. In theological circles, this is commonly referred to as Christian stewardship. This framework emphasizes the human's task to be the steward "entrusted by God with the goods of the earth."[35] This framework has been criticized for not having fully rid itself of the vestiges of anthropocentrism,[36] with the idea that creation is a reified property that is manipulable, manageable, and tradable.[37] For McDonagh, this seems to stem from the pretension that the *anthropos* has a compre-

31. Ibid., 199–201.

32. In this section, we follow closely the sketch drawn by Jenkins, *Ecologies of Grace.*

33. McDaniel, "'Where is the Holy Spirit Anyway?'" 165.

34. See Odchigue, "Ecclesial Contribution to Sustainable Communities," 172.

35. Ibid., 173.

36. See, for example, Gaspar, "To Speak with Boldness," 19–38. Gaspar problematizes what appeared to be an ambivalence in Benedict XVI's "Message for the 2010 World Day of Peace"; see section 13 as an example.

37. Odchigue, "Recasting Christian and Cultural Resources for Environment and Sustainability," 274–77.

hensive knowledge of nature such that he is able to administer it fully and responsibly in all its complexities.[38] The issue that seems to concern stewardship theologians is the key difference between God and creation on the one hand, and between nature and humankind, on the other. Benedict XVI, for example, problematizes the position of biocentrism, in that it appears to erase the identity and worth of human beings in comparison with other living things and it seems to lead one towards pantheistic positions.[39]

The third framework follows the intimate connection of ecological conditions and human subjectivity.[40] Commonly called eco-spirituality, this strategy "addresses the embodied, earthly, and intimate relationships among self, social, community, ecosystems, and God."[41] In *Laudato Si'*, Francis develops a whole chapter on ecological education and spirituality,[42] whereby he calls for a comprehensive conversion of mindset and lifestyle, attuned to the interrelatedness of everything and founded upon communion in the Trinity.

Our position seems to be nearer to the third, which is a combination of the intrinsic value of nature, human agency, and the interrelatedness of these with God. This position may be summarized in the following terms: (1) the intrinsic or inherent value (good in itself, purpose, significance, order, freedom, etc.) that exists in each entity and the whole natural world; (2) the well-being of humanity (human welfare, future generations) and thus, the importance of human stewardship; (3) the sacred nature of each entity and the whole natural world as the handiwork of God (faith and moral living).[43]

Is assigning intrinsic value to creation a move towards obliteration of ontological and axiological difference among creatures? The Catholic Church's magisterium is opposed to such obliteration; however, it appears that what it opposes is only the idea of ontological and axiological equality

38. McDonagh, *Passion for the Earth*, 133.

39. Benedict XVI, "If You Want to Cultivate Peace, Protect Creation," 13.

40. Jenkins, *Ecologies of Grace*, 41.

41. This approach is often criticized for failing to distinguish between humanity and God. I have argued that this criticism "can be deflected by articulating the cosmic scope of God's communion with creation. In other words, it is precisely through the capacity for creativity—a trait that is, in significant ways, unique to humans—that humans participate in God's grace." Odchigue, "Ecclesial Contribution to Sustainable Communities," 173.

42. Francis, *Laudato Si'*, 202ff.

43. Hans Jonas, a German philosopher, has seminal ideas of this effect found in his works, *The Imperative of Responsibility* and *The Phenomenon of Life*. In relation to a discussion on Jonas's ideas, see Macauley, *Minding Nature*, 167–85. See also Hayward, *Ecological Thought*, 162–72.

among all species and beings.[44] Certainly, the human person occupies a special place among God's creatures as he/she is believed to be imbued with the
Imago Dei. But it is important that the subjectivity of the human person be
defined always as part of the interrelated web of all of God's creation. Pope
Francis repeatedly asserts the interrelationship and interconnectedness of
everything.[45] And it seems that, for Francis, subjectivity is at the very essence of this interconnectedness.[46]

Ecology and *Oikos*[47]

The intimate relationality and the attendant responsibility that the connectedness of everything entails is understood by Pope Francis from the
perspective of the earth as our common home, "like a sister with whom we
share our life and a beautiful mother who opens her arms to embrace us."[48]
In *Laudato Si'*, Francis calls our attention to the root metaphor through
which we can commonly view our ecological problems with the proper
perspective. *Oikos*, the root word of ecology, means "home." The idea that
is clearly stressed here is that the earth is a place of "intimate relationships,"
where each component constitutes part of the integrated whole. From
Francis of Assisi, Pope Francis borrows the nurturing and caring images
of the "sister" and "mother" in order to buttress this relational intimacy.[49]
The focus, therefore, goes beyond giving importance to individual parts in
order to stress nature's mutualities and interdependencies. While in contemporary environmental discourse there seems to be a forgetfulness of the

44. Pontifical Council for Justice and Peace, *Compendium*, 287; John Paul II, "Address to Conference on Environment and Health," 5.

45. Francis, *Laudato Si'*, 42, 70, 91, 92, 117, 119, 120, 137, 138, 142, 220, 240.

46. Ibid., 119: "Christian thought sees human beings as possessing a particular
dignity above other creatures; it thus inculcates esteem for each person and respect for
others. Our openness to others, each of whom is a 'thou' capable of knowing, loving,
and entering into dialogue, remains the source of our nobility as human persons. A
correct relationship with the created world demands that we not weaken this social
dimension of openness to others, much less the transcendent dimension of our openness to the 'Thou' of God. Our relationship with the environment can never be isolated
from our relationship with others and with God. Otherwise, it would be nothing more
than romantic individualism dressed up in ecological garb, locking us into a stifling
immanence."

47. In this section, I rely on the reflections of Pope Francis in *Laudato Si'* and of
Paul Wapner in "Toward a Meaningful Ecological Politics."

48. Francis, *Laudato Si'*, 1.

49. See St. Francis's *"Canticle of the Creatures"* in Armstrong and Hellman et al.,
Francis of Assisi, 113–14.

262 FRAGILE WORLD   PART FIVE

connection between the earth and the familial notion of home,[50] *Laudato Si'* seems to appeal to our common humanity and common responsibility to care for mother earth.

Francis's encyclical on the environment seems to be a mild rebuke even to the liberal environmentalist of the greenest sort or to those employing pragmatic strategic solutions who sometimes fall into the mindset of wanting to focus on protecting the environment as a physical object but not as a set of intricate relationships. We encounter many ecological advocates and activists who simply accept the mindset that the earth is a storehouse of natural resources, and the question of our common home's fragility becomes more often than not a question of judicious balance, of how to utilize the earth's resources without overstretching its carrying capacity. In the area of environmental politics, this mindset seems to be one of the most reasonable approaches in the face of the arguments by mining and energy companies about fiscal responsibility that continue to actively emasculate the formulation and implementation of environmental policy.[51] Some simply view ecological problems from the perspective of the corporate adage that says, "economy is a wholly owned subsidiary of the environment."[52]

It seems that, from the perspective of Francis's encyclical, this has not gone far enough. It seems to me that liberal environmentalism is unable to go beyond the perspective of regarding nature as *res extensa*. Its technocratic, scientistic, and economistic character seems to reaffirm the very attitudes that created the ecological crisis in the first place. It seems to endeavor to show that environmental protection need not change the attitudes of growthism[53] as long as we pursue the balance between justice and sustainability with efficiency. But this has not gone far enough in the sense that it does not really ask the question of "being": "Liberal environmentalism is unconcerned with reflecting upon who we are, our place in the global ecosystem, and our relationship with the other species who also inhabit the earth—issues that strike at the heart of a genuinely ecological politics."[54]

On the other hand, the politics and ethics of the home stress connections. They also call forth the responsibility that accompanies the awareness of collective ownership. When Francis observes that "the earth, our home, is

50. Wapner, "Toward a Meaningful Ecological Politics," 21.

51. Examples of this abound in the Philippine setting: for example, spillage in Benguet and "exploratory" mining in the Caraga region. See also Wapner, "Toward a Meaningful Ecological Politics," 21.

52. Timothy Wirth, Undersecretary of State for Global Affairs, as quoted in Maguire and Rasmussen, *Ethics for a Small Planet*, 2.

53. Christian Aid, "A Rich Seam?" 28–29.

54. Wapner, "Toward a Meaningful Ecological Politics," 21.

beginning to look more and more like an immense pile of filth"[55] and "our common home is falling into serious disrepair,"[56] he wants to locate ecological problems within the sphere of self-reflexive critique. For Francis, the root metaphor of "home" that increases our sense of belonging and rootedness[57] has something to do with how we look at our place in the universe and how we forge relationships with those around us. This ecological connection "sees our lives as webs of relations constituted by mutual support, respect, and care. Connection places us in the world and allows us to experience and concomitantly invigorate the networks of interdependence of which we are a part."[58] This means that the earth as our home calls for positive consciousness and awareness that we are braided into the complex fabric of the life processes around us. This perspective goes beyond the realization that we need and depend on a healthy world to sustain us. It also recognizes "that we are literally of the earth and intertwined with its life. Ecological connection is about the warmth of intimacy that develops as we no longer simply use the earth for our own gain but attempt to live with it with a sense of care and respect."[59] Calling Earth our home summons our reflexivity by asking questions about the hierarchy of our values as human persons. Herman Daly formulates such questions in this manner: "The material and the spiritual interpenetrate: the spiritual is incarnated, the material is hallowed. Economics is really about that interpenetration. Are our highest values being incarnated first, or is their place usurped by lower values? Are all materials equally capable of serving as vessels of spiritual values? Are we squandering potentially hallowable material for trivial uses? Are all values expressible as individual wants, or does the community give rise to an order of values not reducible to individual wants?"[60] The root metaphor of a common home makes us realize we are part of an interdependent world that in turn compels us to face the reality of the "negative effects of certain lifestyles and models of production and consumption."[61] Positively, it empowers us to look for common solutions from a global perspective: "interdependence obliges us to think of one world with a common plan."[62]

55. Francis, *Laudato Si'*, 21.

56. Ibid., 61.

57. Ibid., 152.

58. Wapner, "Toward a Meaningful Ecological Politics," 21.

59. Ibid.

60. Daly, "Steady-State Economy," 108.

61. Francis, *Laudato Si'*, 164.

62. Ibid.

Hence, the importance of the metaphor of connectedness in the home—that goes beyond the framework of understanding ecology as *res extensa* into the realm of being in the human—reconfigures the politics of participation beyond the idea of ecological citizenship. Citizenship as a political category remains in the realm of participation external to the realm of personhood and being. This means that the mode of being goes even beyond the questions of intragenerational justice and intergenerational sustainability. The question of connectivity is related to what might be called ecological personhood. This idea goes well beyond the plea of Wapner when he says, "we must insert ourselves, practically as well as emotionally, intellectually, and spiritually into the ecological fabric of the planet and play our roles as biotic citizens."[63] The realization of our ecological personhood brings an awareness that we are not asked to "insert into" the web of interrelationality. This means that, as ecological citizens, we are being-in-relation and interrelation. There is much to be said about the ontological anthropology of this, but suffice it to say that John Zizioulas develops an ontology of personhood that can serve as a metaphysical structure to argue for the importance of being as communion.[64] In a slightly different formulation, Francis reflects that the foundation of interrelatedness is found in the understanding of the divine Persons as "subsistent relations, and the world, created according to the divine model, is a web of relationships. Creatures tend towards God, and in turn it is proper to every living being to tend towards other things, so that throughout the universe we can find any number of constant and secretly interwoven relationships."[65]

Oikos and Oikumene

The platform upon which this ecological subjectivity may be realized begins with the bio-regional awareness of our local ecosystems and campaigning for a broad movement of ecological consciousness in the global *oikumene*. This means that there is a continuing challenge to create an ecological consciousness that transcends nation-state political boundaries. As an example, there are over one hundred species of birds migrating from Siberia and Northern Asia to the Agusan Marsh during the winter. These migratory birds are without political borders. The Marsh is as much a home to the Siberian species as it is to the endemic birds of the Philippines. The same

63. Wapner, "Toward a Meaningful Ecological Politics," 21.

64. Zizioulas, *Being as Communion*.

65. Francis, *Laudato Si'*, 240. Francis refers to Thomas Aquinas on this point: Aquinas, *Summa Theologica* 1.11.3, 21.1.3, and 47.3.

can be said of the elemental components of humanity's survival: air, sun-light, water, etc. This means that "the divide between political and ecological spheres must be softened at least to the extent that one can extend one's sense of caring beyond the nation-state."[66]

This broad ecumenical awareness must also be complemented with participatory localism. This means that, while there are differences in the extent of ecological damage and responsibility (the island nation of Nauro is, of course, in worse shape than the Agusan Marsh), we are all responsible for ecological well-being. This participatory localism needs to recognize the indigenous Manobo's experience and knowledge systems related to the en-vironment. Pope Francis recognizes the dignity of the indigenous and their own capacity to care for their land in the following statement: "They are not merely one minority among others, but should be the principal dialogue partners, especially when large projects affecting their land are proposed. For them, land is not a commodity but rather a gift from God and from their ancestors who rest there, a sacred space with which they need to interact if they are to maintain their identity and values. When they remain on their land, they themselves care for it best."[67]

In relation to Francis's point, Alasdair MacIntyre observes that the philosophical literature on ethics across generations, however, is for the most part curiously lacking in recognition of actually-existing communities which experience intergenerational sustainability in the very form of life as especially demonstrated in the primacy of virtue in sustainability dis-course.[68] While there needs to be nuance on the question of the relationship and degree of resonance between virtue ethics and ecological personhood, I agree with MacIntyre's proposal to look at practices of local communities and how they might become prophetic witnesses to communities "building arks."[69]

Indigenous Knowledge on Environment and Sustainability

The points asserted by Francis and MacIntyre resonate with some of the research findings by Filipino anthropologists who are interested in indig-enous knowledge. In research by Fr. Saturnino Urios University (FSUU),[70]

66. Wapner, "Toward a Meaningful Ecological Politics," 21.

67. Francis, *Laudato Si'*, 146.

68. MacIntyre, *After Virtue*.

69. Gorringe, "On Building an Ark," 31.

70. The study, with 110 participants, covered the two municipalities of Esperanza and San Luis in Agusan del Sur within the fringes of the Marsh. See Eleazar et al.,

it was validated that the value of the land, of nature, for the Manobos is sacred. It has an integral connection to their survival and identity. Some attach economic value to it as it provides everything they need for survival. Some attach spiritual significance to nature because it is created and consequently connected to the sacredness of *Magbabaya* (God) the creator.[71] Moreover, the highly spiritual culture of the Manobo regards nature as a womb of memories as it is the place where ancestors are buried: "The very ground is hallowed by spirits of the ancestors after their death. Life and death makes the land sacred."[72]

Moreover, in an ethno-ecological study of the knowledge systems and practices of the Agusan Marsh indigenous, it was found that biodiversity conservation for indigenous peoples (IP) is not simply a program or a project—it is a way of life.[73] However, because of its very nature as a way of life, there is a dearth of studies on the dynamic relationship between human beings and the natural world seen from the eyes of the Manobo (IP) and their interrelationship with biodiversity and conservation.[74]

In answer to this research gap and in relation to the framework we have been trying to propose, future research engagements might need to focus on two things. First, to do research and to craft policies taking into account what Bennagen calls the life cycle approach in relation to indigenous belief systems and practices. "This uses the life cycle from birth to death. It documents the beliefs, practices, in effect IKSPs [indigenous knowledge systems and practices], of households and communities related to various stages of the life of an individual. For purposes of biodiversity conservation, the life cycle study shall focus on the connection between the life cycle IKSPs and biodiversity and biodiversity conservation. It documents how the Manobo perceive the Agusan Marsh, the elements of the natural environment, and how the IKSPs emanating from this human-nature relationship are learned, practiced, changed, and transmitted from generation to generation."

A second focus would be the community annual cycle approach. This approach documents IKSPs within an annual time frame. The term "annual"

"Cultural Practices and the Realm of Meanings of the Lumad in Agusan on Gender, Reproductive Health, and Sexuality."

71. Eleazar et al., "Cultural Practices," 2.

72. Ibid., 20.

73. Bennagen, "Study on Indigenous Knowledge-Systems," 34.

74. The need to document this interrelationship is very urgent now with the increasing threats to sustainability and biodiversity. Bennagen confirms the findings of Primavera that those come from heightened activities of the natural resource extractive industries, population growth, and climate change possibly resulting in high weather variability.

may refer to an indigenous calendar or, for some, simply the Gregorian calendar. In shifting cultivation, the annual cycle usually begins with the site selection and ends with harvest. From an ethno-ecological approach, however, the way time and the seasons are perceived—and how the Manobo act according to their perception and knowledge about time and the seasons as these relate to biodiversity—should be investigated.

> In any case, the annual cycle approach allows observations and documentation of biophysical, hydrologic, meteorological, ecological, socio-economic, political and IKSPs for a longer period of time than the short-term visits of external observers. With focus on how the Manobo themselves perceive, know, and act on the natural world, it allows the actual and active participation of the villagers themselves in knowledge production for their own use.[75]

Not a Conclusion but a Challenge

When we place the question of justice and sustainability within the ambit of ecological personhood, we cease to think of ourselves as trying to apprehend—control or manipulate or exploit—the earth and the environment as *res extensa*. When we recognize our ecological subjectivity, we no longer fight for just sustainability of our virtue or the goodness of our hearts. We pursue ecological well-being because the earth is us. We are ecology.

The root words of ecumenism are *oikoumenē* ("the inhabited world") and *oikos*. The latter (*oikos*) is also the root term for ecology which means household, home, or family. The task of sustaining ecology is to make sure that our collective home continues to be able to support our collective human community. To sustain ecology is to nurture the human family and vice versa. Nurturing communities—the microcosmic mission of the "local" to mold communities that are just and caring—mirrors sustaining ecologies, the global vision of nourishing the earth, the collective household of humanity.

75. Bennagen, "Study on Indigenous Knowledge-Systems," 36.

PART SIX

Eschatology

17

Ecology and the Apocalypse

DANIEL F. PILARIO, CM

Our historical location is defined by the fact that environmental catastrophe does not lie before us; rather, we are in the midst of it.

—GERNOT BÖHME[1]

Apocalypse is "the single most powerful master metaphor that the contemporary environmental imagination has at its disposal."[2] The present environmental crisis—announcing itself as apocalypse—engenders a whole range of responses. It has been "debunked, resisted debunking, has been reworked, and has been dramatically diversified and expanded, resurfacing in unusual forms."[3] On the one hand, its cataclysmic language provokes anxiety and polarization, fear and paranoia, apathy and inaction sometimes turning itself into a self-fulfilling prophecy.

Environmental apocalypticism, it is argued, "tends to create feelings of helplessness and isolation among would-be supporters."[4] And since it is

1. Böhme, *Die Natur von uns. Naturphilosophie,* cited in Rigby, "Noah's Ark Revisited," 163. Gernot Böhme is a German philosopher and the director of the Institute of Practical Philosophy in the Technological University of Darmstadt, Germany.

2. Buell, *From Apocalypse to Way of Life,* 285.

3. Ibid., xii.

4. Shellenberger and Nordhaus, *Death of Environmentalism,* 30. See also Feinberg and Willer, "Apocalypse Soon?" 4–38; Lewis, "Science, Progress, and the End of the Modern World," 307–32; Barrett Gross and Gilles, "How Apocalyptic Thinking Prevents Us from Taking Political Action."

mostly articulated in religious paradigms, it tends to be disregarded as insignificant in the scientific field. On the other hand, other thinkers argue that it is precisely this emotionally charged language that seizes people's attention and imagination; it is this kind of rhetoric that can really motivate people toward some responsible social engagement. This assertion is not only anecdotal but empirical. In a national survey that investigated the American perception of climate change, it was found that alarmists "were significantly more likely to have taken personal action to reduce greenhouse emissions" than those that consider climate change a non-issue or less threatening than it is projected.[5]

Beyond this impasse in scientific discourses, this article aims to propose some viable frames within which to read contemporary environmental apocalypticism in order to guide us toward an engaged Christian spirituality in the world. I will proceed in three steps. First, I will present a cursory map of present responses to the ecological crisis. Second, I will present contemporary religious and secular apocalyptic discourses on the environment. Third, through some chosen philosophical and theological frameworks, I will try to outline a Christian apocalyptic spirituality in the context of what I call the "apocalyptic experiences" at "Ground Zero."

Eco-Criticism: A Cursory Map

There are many ways in which to view contemporary responses to the present ecological crisis. In this article, let me only present three basic positions: the cornucopian, the pastoral, and the apocalyptic.

The cornucopian position believes that the world affords a life of abundance and endless provision for all humanity. Derived from the Latin *cornu copiae* ("the horn of plenty"—in Greek mythology, the horn-shaped basket overflowing with fruits of the earth), the cornucopian believes that the earth contains enough matter and energy for all. And if ever population increases in leaps and bounds, so does technology, to provide for all our needs. If the Malthusians are called "doomsters," the cornucopians are dubbed "boomsters." From this perspective, the problem of climate change is mere scaremongering and hysteria which are not really backed up by hard empirical evidence. In short, these cornucopian optimistic futurists believe that the world evolves in progress toward its perfect end. If challenges—ecological or political—appear on the present horizon, they are but

---

5. Cf. Leiserowitz, "American Risk Perceptions," 1433–42; Veldman, "Narrating the Environmental Apocalypse," 1–23. For parallel arguments, see Leiserowitz et al., *Global Warming's Six Americas 2009.*

part of the whole evolutionary process. Some theorists of this position are the American political scientist Aaron Wildavsky, the economist Julian Simon, and the Danish writer Bjørn Lomborg.[6] Coming from different fields, these thinkers agree that, first, there is no link between global warming and greenhouse gas emissions (or at least, it is not sufficiently supported by evidence); second, if there is a scarcity of resources, it is only temporary (the earth is resilient and can recuperate); third, we are technologically capable of providing food, clothes, energy, and other resources (we only need to develop it); and fourth, it is a big waste to divert our present resources in order to avert climate change (it should be used productively somewhere else). Often supported by First World capitalists, the problem with this optimistic position is its selective assessment of scientific evidence. Lindsey Grant has already identified the fallacies of the cornucopian view: it makes assumptions and chooses methodologies that dismiss critical issues—climate change, the situation of the poor, non-sustainable technological growth, etc.[7] Moreover, the cornucopian view of nature is downright instrumentalist, as the environment is only valued insofar as it is useful to the human species—a position which is condemned as unabashedly anthropocentric in our ecological age.

The second response to the ecological crisis is that of the pastorals. Pastorals have had a long history before the age of eco-criticism. From Theocritus's *Idyllis* to Virgil's *Eclogues,* a selected past is valorized and set as an ideal against present exigencies. From then up until our times, the pastorals refer to the idealization of the country and rural life; consequently, they encourage a retreat from the city and its technological progress. This discourse can be explained through five Rs: refuge, reflection, rescue, requiem, and reconstruction. "Refuge" refers to the element of pastoral escape and "reflection" to the backward-looking tendency to seek settled values in the past, requiring a "rescue" in a nostalgic "requiem" that is also a politically conservative "reconstruction" of history."[8] While the cornucopians look to the future with assured optimism, the pastorals go back to the past as a "pristine existence" and lost ideal that need to be recovered to evaluate and prescribe a model for the present and the future. The pastoral response has three recognizable types: the *elegy,* which "looks back to a vanished past

6. Simon, *The Resourceful Earth*; Wildavsky, *Searching for Safety* and *But Is It Really True?*; Lomborg, *The Skeptical Environmentalist*; Lomborg, *Cool It*; Lomborg, *Smart Solutions to Climate Change*; Lomborg, *How Much Have Global Problems Cost the World?*; Bailey, *Eco-Scam.*

7. Grant, *TEF Report*, and "The Cornucopian Fallacies," 16–22; Lane, "The Resolution of the Cornucopian-Ecologist Issue," 87–93.

8. Gifford, "Pastoral, Anti-Pastoral, Post-Pastoral," 20.

with a sense of nostalgia; the *idyll*, which celebrates a bountiful present; and the *utopia*, which looks forward to a redeemed future."[9] It appears in different literary forms and rhetoric—e.g., romantic poetry, a theological re-reading of Genesis 1–3, the "back-to-nature" campaign of green politics, and more. The idea of "pure wilderness"—a state uncontaminated by civilization—as ideal existence becomes sacramental. Acting as a tool for nostalgia, it also doubles as utopia: "the promise of a renewed, authentic relation of humanity and the earth, a post-Christian covenant, found in a space of purity, founded in an attitude of reverence and humility."[10]

The problem, however, is that in the pastoral view, nature can only be genuine when it is untouched by humanity. Its purity is "achieved at the cost of an elimination of human history" and civilization—which includes you and me. "This model not only misrepresents the wild but also exonerates us from taking a responsible approach to our everyday lives: our working and domestic lives are effectively irredeemable alongside this ideal, so the activities we carry out there escape scrutiny."[11] The cultural-literary critic Raymond Williams identified another problem with the pastoral view: its selective retrieval of the past. Even as criticism is necessary in the present ecological crisis, the selected and idealized values of some past (of the "country" as being against the "city") defend a "certain kind of order, certain social hierarchies, and moral sensibilities, which a have a feudal ring but a more relevant and more dangerous contemporary application."[12]

The third response to the ecological crisis is the apocalyptic genre.[13] The classical precursor of environmental apocalypticism is Thomas Malthus's *Essay on the Principle of Population* (1798),[14] which posits that population can increase exponentially but our resources cannot provide for its subsistence, thus leading the whole of humanity into grim competition for survival. Though Malthus did not predict a dramatic endgame, his theory can lend inspiration to contemporary popular dystopian films like *Mad Max* or *The Hunger Games*. But the apocalyptic literary genre also had a long history, and it appears on the scene in times of great crisis.[15] In the Jewish-Christian context, we read the same apocalyptic vision in Isaiah 24–27, Isaiah 56–66 and Zechariah 9–14 as reflective of the chaos and tumult

9. Garrad, *Ecocriticism*, 42.

10. Ibid., 66.

11. Ibid., 78.

12. Williams, *Country and the City*, 36.

13. Mellor, "The Lure of Wilderness"; Rigby, "Confronting Catastrophes," 212–25.

14. Malthus, *Essay on the Principle of Population*.

15. Primavesi, *From Apocalypse to Genesis*, 67–84.

of the sixth and fifth centuries BCE. Mark 13 and the Book of Revelation stem from the Roman persecution of Christians at the time of their writing. We find a common thread running through all apocalyptic literature: the imminent and cataclysmic end. It either engenders hope or despair, a look backward to history or a longing for a totally different future in order to make sense of an impending disaster.

Environmental Apocalypticism: Religious and Secular Discourses

Environmental apocalypticism is a sub-discipline of what authors call the "return of apocalypticism" in the global and postmodern contexts.[16] There are two main apocalyptic trends prevalent in environmental discourses. The first is the religious apocalyptic discourse (mostly present among the Christian "right") which assesses the world to be in moral, political, and economic decline. Thus, the environmental catastrophe is what the Bible has already foreseen, from the Synoptic prediction of the fall of Jerusalem to the planetary disaster in the Book of Revelation. Some more fundamentalist quarters think that this "Rapture" and "Armageddon" are God's vengeance and punishment which we can do nothing to avert.[17] The impending ecological cataclysm also spells our eschatological end, sadly inevitable but necessary for God to ultimately establish his victorious reign. While this ultimate eschatological optimism mainly leads to metaphysical fatalism ("all we have to do is wait"), some evangelicals think that that there is actually no certainty of this positive end and, thus, also challenge their followers to be responsible stewards of creation.[18] The evangelical apocalyptic discourse is thus double-edged: either passive or transformative depending on one's theological interpretation of the eschatological end but also on one's economic-political affiliation.[19]

Beyond evangelical concerns, however, there is also a perceived "return of apocalypticism" in general theological discourse.[20] From its bibli-

16. Haker et al., *The Return of Apocalypticism*.

17. See, for instance, Walvord and Hitchcock, *Armageddon, Oil, and Terror*; Swyngedouw, "Apocalypse Now!," 9–18.

18. Graham, *Approaching Hoofbeats*; Borchardt, *Doomsday Speculation as a Strategy of Persuasion*.

19. Dittmer and Sturm, *Mapping the End Times*; Nagle, "The Evangelical Debate over Climate Change," 53–86.

20. See, for instance, Bunzl and Havrelock, eds., *The Apocalypse Issue*; Haker et al., *The Return of Apocalypticism*; Wilkinson, *Political Spirituality in an Age of Eco-Apocalypse*.

cal moorings, contemporary apocalypticism takes as its background the end of modernity's systemic violence, the inevitable breakdown of global capitalism, the "superflat" apocalypticism of the Internet age or the ecological crisis.[21] From a theological perspective, apocalyptic reason resists and refuses the dictates of systemic evil represented by the empires it is protesting against. These empires are "monsters." They are powerful, but they also have "clay feet," and thus are vulnerable in the face of divine judgment. "This is how the book of Daniel describes the empires of the Babylonians, Persians, and Greeks (Dan 2 and 7). The New Testament apocalypse applies the same images to the Roman Empire, which it represents as an animal rising from the pit and as a new Babylon. These images manipulate mythic fears but also prohibit them and thus break the spell of fate. For the beasts they show are vulnerable, have clay feet, are mutually destructive, and are all subject to divine judgment in the end. Consequently, faith means refusing to worship them as they demand."[22]

The second apocalyptic trend is found in secular discourses which, for the most part, tend to be dystopic in character.[23] Environmental degradation has been described by secular eco-activists in apocalyptic terms such as "ecological disaster," "war on nature," "nuclear fallout," "no man's land," or "environmental hell." Popular forms abound, ranging from the "end-of-the-world" blockbuster movie *2012*, which is based on an obscure Mayan calendar prediction, to Al Gore's science-based documentary film, *An Inconvenient Truth*, which also won two Academy Awards in 2006. In the form of a slideshow, Gore seeks to convince his audience of the increasing "planetary emergency" caused by global warming. Unlike in evangelistic rhetoric, it is not God who is punishing us but we humans who brought this impending disaster upon ourselves through our unrestrained greenhouse gas emission. "Our civilization is destroying our planet," Al Gore proclaims. Commentators call this approach a "scare-them-green" tactic. This apocalyptic direction was already present in Rachel Carson's *Silent Spring* (1962) with her warning about the use of DDT and other pesticides and in Paul Ehrlich's *The Population Bomb* (1968) with his prediction of starvation caused by an impending population explosion. Beyond the genre of literature, the

---

21. Mendoza Alvarez, "Eschatology and Apocalypse in Post-Modern Times," 71–82, "Apocalyptic and Global Crisis," 83–95, and "Superflat Apocalypticism in the Internet Age," 111–20; Bredin, "Ecological Crisis and Plagues (Revelation 11:6)," 26–38.

22. Taxacher, "God in Opposition," 64.

23. For a recent book on this theme, see Rigby, *Dancing with Disasters*. A cursory survey of apocalyptic fiction both in movies and literature can be found in Banks Miller, "Ecology and the Post-Apocalypse."

secular apocalyptic can also be discerned in the advocacies of worldwide movements like Greenpeace or Earth First.[24]

Nothing can surpass this dystopic view in *The Population Bomb's* opening sentence: "The battle to feed all of humanity is over. In the 1970s, hundreds of millions of people will starve to death in spite of any crash programs embarked upon now. At this late date, nothing can prevent a substantial increase in the world death rate."[25] Even as the writers acknowledge that what is predicted does not actually exist since it did not really happen,[26] "this imagined tragedy may easily become a stark reality we all shall know."[27] And since God is not there to save the world, there is no promised ultimate emancipation. The world as we know it will never be restored to its original splendor. The only option left is to change the present course as much as we can, that is, *if* we still can. While religious apocalyptic discourse is aimed at providing its readers the hope of a better world, secular discourse is mainly dystopic and pessimistic, "positing potential means of extinction and predicting the gloomy probabilities of such ends."[28]

Religious and secular apocalyptic rhetoric possesses some common features: the predictions are projected with absolute authority; the material threat and their advocates are "evil"; the failure to listen would be catastrophic; and the disaster is not only imminent but well underway.[29] On the one hand, environmental apocalyptic literature positively contributes to galvanizing otherwise disparate eco-critical positions into some united program of action through its use of imaginative-metaphorical tragic rhetoric. On the other hand, the emotionalism that usually accompanies apocalyptic language tends to polarize and demonize other positions, simplify complex arguments, and blur the real issue—making it easy material for journalistic sentimentalism and consequent passive skepticism. Thus, in the end, dystopic apocalyptic genres can either lead to the embarrassment of failed predictions or self-fulfilling prophecies.[30]

---

24. See http://www.greenpeace.org/international/en and http://www.earthfirst.org.

25. Ehrlich and Ehrlich, *The Population Bomb.*

26. See how the authors revisit their arguments and respond to objections forty years after the publication of *The Population Bomb* in Ehrlich and Ehrlich, "The Population Bomb Revisited."

27. Carson, *Silent Spring*, 3.

28. Rosen, *Apocalyptic Transformation*, xv.

29. Garrard, *Ecocriticism*, 103.

30. Ibid., 113–16.

Toward an Eco-Apocalyptic Spirituality

How do we rescue environmental apocalypticism from producing both despair and inaction? Can present apocalyptic rhetoric help construct Christian hope and responsible political engagement? With the limitations of space, let me just outline a viable apocalyptic spirituality with the help of three disparate sources: James Berger's analysis of the "post-apocalyptic"; Johann-Baptist Metz's reflections on the apocalyptic; and stories that I heard, experienced, and read about at Haiyan's "Ground Zero" more than a month after the "apocalyptic super typhoon" struck the Philippines on November 8, 2013. More than a month after Super Typhoon Haiyan (local name: Yolanda) struck the Philippines, I volunteered to help in the relief operations and pastoral work in one mission parish of Barangay San Antonio, Basey, Samar. This small village with two thousand inhabitants was badly hit by the typhoon with forty-two confirmed dead days after the storm, not to mention the many people who were still missing and hundreds of houses carried away by the fifteen-foot storm surge and strong winds.[31] It is my intention to reflect on these experiences and inquire what these apocalyptic "rough ground" experiences teach us about human responsibility and Christian spirituality in a post-apocalyptic age.

After the End: Hope at the (Post)Apocalypse

In his book, *After the End,* James Berger presents the idea of the "post-apocalypse." He observes that almost every apocalyptic text is a paradox: "The end is never the end. The apocalyptic text announces and describes the end of the world, but then the text does not end, nor does the world represented in the text, and neither does the world itself. In nearly every apocalyptic presentation, something remains after the end. . . . Something is left over, and that world after the end of the world, the post-apocalypse, is usually the true object of the apocalyptic writer's concern."[32] The talk of an *ending* gives way to the vision of what is *after the end.* The Temple of Jerusalem has fallen, and the world continues, and so with the French Revolution, the Holocaust, Hiroshima, the Vietnam War, and so on. These events were seen as decisive breaks from the past, definitive historical ruptures,

31. To see how things appeared right after the storm, see the images in "The Mystery of Faith" at https://www.youtube.com/watch?v=MgL_oVPPGs4. My initial reflection is published as Pilario, "(Post)Apocalyptic Reflections from 'Ground Zero,'" 104–10.

32. Berger, *After the End,* 5–6. See also Heffernan, *Post-Apocalyptic Culture,* and Fiddes, *The Promised End.*

"fulcrums separating what comes before from what comes after." Yet these apocalyptic ends are not the end of the world. "[T]he world, impossibly, continues, and the apocalyptic writer continues to write. It is a common pattern. A disaster occurs of overwhelming, disorienting attitude, and yet the world continues."[33] What is more important is the "new heaven and the new earth," or the post-apocalyptical wasteland where new life can again start to emerge.

Such an interpretation of apocalypse serves two purposes. First, it engenders a sense of hope among the victims. If God's concern is not about the end but its aftermath, hope no matter how modest glimmers at the horizons. This is the reigning feeling at Haiyan's "Ground Zero." On the morning after the storm, though the dead were not yet buried, people raised the nation's tattered flag as act of defiance against defeat. For three to five days after the storm, phone signals were down; there was no electricity to charge remaining gadgets; and family members from outside the island were very worried and eager to hear news about their loved ones. What the survivors did was quite touching. They scribbled on sheets of paper words like "Don't worry about us; we are alive," signed their names on them, and asked TV outfits to project them on their screens for their loved ones to see. Ironically, it is the sense of hope and strength of the human spirit among these already battered and hungry people that made them reach out to their friends and families in much better conditions and assured them not to worry. Anderson Cooper, CNN's famous newscaster, could not believe his eyes: "Can you imagine the strength it takes to be living in shock, to be living, sleeping on the streets next to the body of your dead children? Can you imagine that strength? I can't. And I've seen that strength day in and day out here in the Philippines."[34]

A barber whose shop had been carried away by the waves got an old chair and started to do haircuts for his neighbors. He said that even without food or houses, it is always a good feeling to look handsome.[35] When the small fishing boats were all gone, the fishermen floated old refrigerators, navigating the waters again and going fishing for their daily sustenance. A week after the storm, a small basketball court was set up for the boys to play again. A group of women started to plant vegetables in an empty lot and, weeks later, the green backyard garden became the source of nourishment for the community. On a tree in front of what was left of one little hut was a board which announced to those involved in relief operations: "We need

33. Berger, *After the End*, 6.
34. Cf. Cooper, "New Official Death Toll from Typhoon Aftermath."
35. Evangelista, "After Yolanda."

house and lot, car, swimming pool!" A little joke and fun are signs of a sheer willingness to survive—and resourcefulness, too.

In the post-apocalypse, not everything is perfect. Days after the event, bodies of family members could not be found yet. Weeks after, people still ran after relief goods, and in their silent stares asked God why things happen this way. But this hope, no matter how fragile, can be heard in one mother's reply: "If there is no God, who else is there?" Two years after the typhoon, many still have not built houses. People are still in mourning. The reality of loss has slowly begun to set in. But people are back on their feet again. Life continues. Unlike the bleak apocalyptic predictions in films and novels, the victim-survivors enact a different narrative. The hope and resilience of these people on the ground is a stinging critique of the dystopia and pessimism the ecological "doomsters" preach both in their religious and secular varieties.

The second use of the apocalyptic is its comprehensive critique of any existing order. Exegetes tell us that this is the purpose of John's Book of Revelation: a critique of and nonviolent resistance to the dominant Roman civilization, which the author assesses as oppressive, demonic, and "beastly."[36] Apocalyptic discourse tells people that only a total overhaul of the system can bring about survival and wholeness. The usual state of affairs does not work anymore. Things should change from now on if we want to survive in the post-apocalypse. This brings me to the next point.

Apocalypse as Interruption

Johann-Baptist Metz's theology is a reaction to Nietzsche's central concept of "eternal recurrence," i.e., events will occur again and again infinitely.[37] For Nietzsche, the world is nothing but a timeless repetition of one and the same. For Metz, this view of endless recurrence and omnipresent time has tragic repercussions on human suffering because with it, radical change is never possible. Metz identifies utopian and evolutionary thinking as eternal recurrence's present expressions. In the evolutionary logic, "the category of fulfillment is regarded as an evolutionary process and the kingdom of God is seen as a pure utopia that is achieved by means of human progress."[38] For Metz, such a self-enclosed scheme does not offer any way out for the victims of history. History merely repeats itself, playing out its own inevitability.

36. See, among others, Baucham, *The Theology of the Book of Revelation*, and Witherington, *Revelation*.

37. Cf. Eggemeier, "Christianity or Nihilism?" 7–26.

38. Metz, *Faith in History and Society*, 174.

"Catastrophes are reported on the radio," Metz writes, "in between pieces of music. The music continues to play, like the audible passage of time that moves forward inexorably and can be held back by nothing. As Brecht has said: 'When crime is committed, just as the rain falls, no one cries: Halt!'"[39]

Metz criticizes evolutionary thinking present in both scientific-technological and religious-theological discourses. Instead of the symbolism of discontinuity in the apocalyptic discourse, what dominates people's consciousness is timelessness. "In it, time has been made indifferent and has come systematically to control man's [sic] universal consciousness. Everything is timelessly and continually reconstructed on the basis of this philosophy."[40]

> The modern world, with its scientific and technical civilization, is not simply a rational universe. Its myth is evolution. The silent interest of its rationality is the fiction of time as an empty infinity, which is free of surprises and within which is enclosed without grace. The social signs are easy to discern—on the one hand, widespread apathy and, on the other, unreflecting hatred; on the one hand, fatalism and, on the other, fanaticism.[41]

Long before capitalism became global, Metz had already predicted the contradictory social phenomena that dominate the headlines in our times: apathy and hatred, fatalism and fanaticism. Globalization and its contradictions are the obvious heirs of evolutionary utopianism. Pope Francis calls it the "economy of exclusion," a "throw-away society," a "globalization of indifference" where profit is valued over persons. In this worldview, its human victims—considered collateral damage—could not hope for something different, for some "surprise," for some respite. In its self-enclosure and endless repetition, no one cries "halt" to the victims' pain and suffering. As Metz quotes Nietzsche, "evolution does not aim at happiness; it is only concerned with evolution."[42]

Apocalypse as "interruption" thus becomes salvific and necessary. "The shortest definition of religion," he says, "is *interruption*."[43] While utopian and evolutionary thinking considers time to be a "homogenous continuum without surprises," only through the apocalyptic vision can the Messiah enter and interrupt history. "Christology without an apocalyptic

39. Ibid., 170–71.
40. Ibid.
41. Ibid., 172.
42. Ibid., 171.
43. Ibid. Emphasis mine.

vision becomes no more than an ideology of conquest and triumph."[44] Ernst Käsemann considers the Jewish-Christian apocalyptic vision as the "mother of Christian theology." This catastrophic nature of time, the feeling of discontinuity, the sense of the end "calls the future into question" through which it also becomes an "authentic future."[45] It is this apocalyptic direction that separates Metz from his teacher, Karl Rahner. Founding his theology on the radical experience of evil and suffering of World War II, Metz's mystical-political theology differentiates itself from the Rahnerian transcendental "theology of the everyday" in his own emphasis on *Leiden an Gott* (suffering unto God). Beyond the Lukan last words ("Father, into your hands, I commend my spirit"), Metz's sensitivity to senseless yet redemptive suffering focuses on Mark's disturbing and apocalyptic emphasis: "My God, my God, why have you forsaken me?"[46]

Unlike the assured optimism of utopian thinking, the future and hope afforded by apocalyptic consciousness do not possess a sense of evolutionary inevitability. Unlike the global capitalist mindset, it does not believe in the inevitable triumph of liberal capitalist democracy in what Fukuyama calls "the end of history."[47] Apocalyptic hope is fragile; it can be founded only on faith, not on some predestined, evolutionary utopian logic. Unlike the cornucopians' over-confidence in technological development or the Christian right's omniscient anticipation of eschatological victory, apocalyptic spirituality does not fully know the certainties of what is to come. Its constant companions are the doubts and fears born out of the tragic and painful experience of disaster. Several weeks after the typhoon, hundreds would still run to the hills when it rained hard or someone maliciously shouted "tsunami." But beyond these fears is a deep, fragile hope that "previous hegemonic narratives—of religious, political, scientific kind which had held the world in grip with their monstrous prognoses of a 'glorious end' (but one which turned them into victims)—will not rule them again. No one is actually certain what the future brings, but the apocalyptic interruption opens their lives to a more humane world of other liberating possibilities."[48]

The parish I worked with had its church building all washed away except for the altar wall. The day after the storm, the people collected its headless statues, placed them on the altar, and started to pray amidst the

44. Metz, *Faith in History and Society*, 176.

45. Ibid., 175–76. See also Dickenson, "Are the Only True Atheists Actually Theologians?" 51–59; Taxacher, "God in Opposition," 60–70.

46. Cf. Ashley, *Interruptions*, 171–91.

47. Fukuyama, *The End of History and the Last Man*.

48. Pilario, "(Post)Apocalyptic Reflections from 'Ground Zero,'" 107.

debris and dead bodies. During those early morning Masses which we celebrated in these destroyed chapels, people were just there with their flashlights (since there was no electricity yet) and their umbrellas (since it was always raining and the roofs had been blown off). In the dark and cold, I could sense their fatigue, fears, and insecurity. Some were silent; others were singing as they waited for Mass to start in order to keep the cold and fears away. But they did not leave. As they were courageously standing there, their fragile hope became a stinging indictment of all the world's—and my own heart's—over-confidence, indifference, and apathy.

Apocalypse as Solidarity and Compassion

Apocalyptic discourse is blamed for apathy and inaction. If the world will surely end in catastrophe and dystopia, can our insignificant steps prevent it? If God will ultimately and single-handedly restore creation, what is the value of human action? What is the space of human responsibility in apocalyptic spirituality? It might be helpful to quote Metz in full:

> A passionate expectation of the day of the Lord does not lead to a pseudo-apocryphal dream-dance in which all the claims made by the imitation of Christ are obscured and forgotten, nor does it lead to an unreflecting radicalism, for which prayers of longing and expectation can only be perceived forms of refusal or self-deception. Imminent expectation does not allow the imitation of Christ to be postponed. We are not made apathetic by the apocalyptic feeling for life, but by the evolutionary idea. It is the evolutionary symbol of time that paralyzes the imitation of Christ. Imminent expectation, on the other hand, provides hope, which has been pacified and led astray by the evolutionary idea, with perspectives of time and expectation. It introduces the pressure of time and activity into Christian life. It does not deprive responsibility of its power, but rather provides it with motivation. Our apocalyptical consciousness is not threatened with a paralyzing fear of catastrophe. It is, on the contrary, called upon to display a practical solidarity with the least of the brethren; that is clear from the apocalyptic chapters at the end of the gospel of St. Matthew."[49]

There are three important points that Metz wants to emphasize in the long quote above. First, it is evolutionary logic, not apocalyptic thinking, that leads to apathy and paralysis of action. If reality turns out to be

49. Metz, *Faith in History and Society*, 177.

repeatedly one and the same, what then is the value of our efforts to change it? Second, neither does apocalyptic consciousness lead us to some mis- guided and "unreflecting radicalism." Third, it is the sense of the end that leads us out of ourselves and to be responsible for the marginalized and the excluded. Apocalyptic spirituality is not about a frantic and self-enclosed concern for one's salvation in the face of God's imminent arrival. No, it is about being in "practical solidarity" with the hungry, the thirsty, the mourn- ful, and the lowly—for this is a sign that God's kingdom has come into our midst (Matt 25).

A Navy officer was assigned by his unit on another island of Mind- anao far from the typhoon area. Before Haiyan struck, his children in Samar called him to come home and to bring their favorite delicacy with him. Be- fore long, he heard that the cataclysm had happened. He hurried home and brought with him the food that his children requested. When he arrived, his house was gone and no one was around. His neighbors told him that his wife was in the cemetery for the funeral of his children. He was devastated and, out of despair, wanted to throw away the food that he brought for them. But he thought twice. He was thinking of the hundreds of hungry children around who had, in turn, lost their parents. The food was for them.

In one of those debriefing sessions, I asked a group of farmers whose farms were destroyed by the typhoon, "What is next after Yolanda/Haiyan?" One old farmer stood up and said: "We want to go back to our farms." Sev- eral days after, it was raining hard on Christmas. From afar, I was watch- ing a group of farmers starting to plant rice again. I told myself: "Like the first Christmas, there are no angels who come down from heaven singing 'Alleluia!' But I guess Jesus is born here, too, today." The experience of the "apocalypse" did not paralyze people; it moved them to act in defiant resis- tance of the palpable death on their horizons.

Some studies, in fact, show that there is a close link between apoca- lyptic narrative and responsible, pro-environment moral behavior.[50] First, apocalyptic endings lead to considering everyday decisions as *moral* deci- sions. For example, to recycle or not, to reduce one's carbon footprints or not, in view of impending ecological disaster, become ethical issues, not merely matters of individual preference or personal convenience. Second, dramatic apocalyptic stories bring the point "home," making an other- wise distant social issue a personal issue. Developing this connection is important "because without that felt sense of connection to the world of lived experience, people are much less likely to become convinced that it

50. Veldman, "Narrating the Environmental Apocalypse," 1–23.

is incumbent upon them to act."⁵¹ Third, the magnitude of the impending disaster makes one responsible for acting on one's moral intuition. Only apocalyptic language can bring out its urgency to act.

In theological language, Metz writes a parallel conviction: "The Christian idea of imitation and the apocalyptic idea of the imminent expectation belong together. It is not possible to imitate Jesus radically, that is, at the level of the roots of life, if 'the time is not shortened.' Jesus's call, 'Follow me!' and the call of Christians, 'Come, Lord Jesus!' are inseparable."⁵²

51. Ibid., 12.
52. Metz, *Faith in History and Society*, 176.

18

Political Theology for Earthlings: Christian Messianism and the Ecological Ruins of Global Corporate Capitalism

MICHAEL S. NORTHCOTT

I traveled to Malacca in July 2013 on my way to teach a summer course at Universiti Gadja Mada in Yogyakarta, on the Indonesian island of Java. I stayed in the Anglican rectory near the old Portuguese settlement where I had spent my first Christmas as a mission priest in 1984 leading the Christmas and New Year services in the parish of Christchurch, Malacca. The current rector of the parish was a former student and Anglican bishop in the south of the Diocese of West Malaysia. I woke in the middle of the night because of a smell of burning coming through the air conditioner in my bedroom. My first thought was: "Has my host taken up smoking?!" But I doubted this. Well, I am obviously not very risk averse, because I then turned over and went back to sleep. I awoke again at 6:30 and looked outside, and I could see no more than twenty meters, because the buildings and trees outside were shrouded by smoke. When we walked the short distance to the church for the Sunday eucharist, the air smelled like a fall bonfire. The radio news indicated that the source was a fire in the forests of the large Indonesian island of Sumatra just twenty miles from Malacca across the Malacca Straits.

I preached that morning on the texts from the Revised Common Lectionary and, as so often, they were highly appropriate. The Old Testament reading was the story of Naboth's vineyard from 1 Kings 21. This is a classic biblical story about kingship, the abuse of power, and land theft. Naboth's vineyard land was adjacent to the king's palace in Samaria. And Jezebel,

King Ahab's wife, desired to take over the vineyard of Naboth and turn it into a vegetable garden for the palace. But when she approached Naboth and offered him an alternate vineyard if he would give her his, he refused saying that he had received it as a *nahalah*—an inheritance—from God. In using this Hebrew word *nahalah*, Naboth reminded her that the land ultimately belonged to God, who had first given the land to his forefathers. Hence, it was not his to give up since his God-given duty was to care for it and to pass it on to his children. Jezebel was unhappy, however, and she arranged to have Naboth killed by calling false witnesses against him and accusing him of blasphemy against God for which the penalty was death by stoning. After his death, Jezebel instructed Ahab to take possession of the vineyard of Naboth "which he refused to give you for money" (1 Kgs 21:15, RSV). After these tragic events, Elijah visited King Ahab and told him that, because of what he had done, he would soon die and his blood would be lapped by the palace dogs.

The text drips with irony on many levels. Jezebel was the king's foreign wife who worshipped Baal, and Elijah the prophet was in a life-and-death struggle with the cult of Baal to preserve the worship of Yahweh under a king who had allowed the cult of Baal to prosper in Israel. The text recalls the origin of Israel as a people on whom was conferred a covenantal gift of good land on condition they worshipped the God who gave it them and lived justly in the land, observing the Ten Commandments, including the proscription of idolatry and the hallowing of the Sabbath, and so keeping themselves and the land holy. Ahab had compromised the worship of Yahweh; he had polluted the land with murder as well as erected altars to idols and hence, he would lose his inheritance. The text also carries a further meaning since Jezebel is said to wish to turn the vineyard into a vegetable garden. The Egyptians were great vegetable growers, and the Deuteronomist wrote of the time when the Israelites were slaves in Egypt that they were forced "to sow seed and water it with their feet, like a vegetable garden." But the land they received from God was not like Egypt: its hills were watered by rain from heaven, and hence it was a land which "the Lord your God cares for" (Deut 11:12).

We moderns no longer think that the rain comes from God, or that God lives above the sky. This is primitive thinking, pre-scientific thinking. But it carried with it a mythology not only of the relation of heaven and earth, but of the relation of people and land, of generation to generation, and of the law of the land, which was that the land could not be alienated from the families to whom God had originally given it. Hence in Israel, there was a jubilee provision that, when a family lost its land due to ill luck or poor farming practices, every fifty years the land was to return to the family that had originally owned it. The jubilee was designed to prevent intergenerational exclusion of the landless from the covenant community. It would also have had the effect of limiting land-related debt and land speculation of the kind that nearly destroyed the economy of the United States, the UK, and Europe in 2008. In effect, the jubilee meant that, when land was transferred from one party to another, what was transferred was the right to use the land until the next jubilee, but not the right to alienate it forever from the family whose ancestors received it as a divine inheritance.

In his encyclical on the environment, *Laudato Si'*, Pope Frances identifies private property as a core root of both the ecological crisis and the social crisis of dispossession of their ancestral lands and rights to food, water, and fresh air experienced by many indigenous peoples in the global South. Pope Frances explains that land theft—and the broader expropriation of the environment under the conditions of a global economic market rigged in favor of private corporations in the developed North—is contrary to the divine gifting of creation as the birthright of all the earth's peoples. Against this, the pope underlines a core doctrine of Catholic social teaching, that "the principle of subordination of private property to the universal destination of goods, and thus the right of everyone to their use, is a golden rule of social conduct."[1] And he adds that "the Christian tradition has never recognized the right to private property as absolute and inviolable, and has stressed the social purpose of all forms of private property."[2]

The forest in Sumatra has for millennia been inhabited by indigenous peoples who have built their villages out of timber, planted rice, and vegetables in small patches of land amidst the trees. Like most of the forest in the Indonesian archipelago, it was not formally "owned" in the Lockean and modern capitalist and "legal" conceptions of titled property ownership, but managed as a commons by the people. Commons management preserved this ancient forest until the late twentieth century so that not only is it peppered with small villages, schools, vegetable gardens, and mosques or churches, it is also home to orangutans, tigers, anteaters, and other wild inhabitants which continued to live in it alongside the human residents. But the land of Sumatra—like the land of Borneo, the other large tropical forest island that is burned every summer and shrouds the cities of Malaysia in haze from forest fires—has in the last thirty years gradually been transferred from communally managed forest into forest "concessions" which are delineated by the Indonesian Forestry Department and the Sumatran State government and sold to multinational plantation companies. The forest fires

1. Francis, *Laudato Si'*, 93.
2. Ibid.

that shrouded Malacca, Singapore, and Kuala Lumpur in the summer of 2013 were the worst haze incidents since the burning summer of 1998 when the whole region's economy collapsed as it was blanketed by thick, choking smoke from Borneo. But the government of Malaysia did not complain to the government of Indonesia, because the oil palm companies whose land was being burned in Sumatra were majority- or minority- owned by Malaysian government-owned plantation companies. The government of Singapore did complain to Indonesia, but Singapore too is complicit in the burning since many Indonesian corporations have changed their registration from Jakarta to Singapore to take advantage of its tax haven status and so avoid paying taxes on Indonesian land to the Indonesian government.

The land of the villagers of Sumatra and Borneo is being turned from communally owned land into capital for multinational corporations and their individual and corporate shareholding owners. The aim is to turn the land and what it has or will grow into marketable commodities: first, logged timber and then, palm oil which will be used as cooking oil, in cleaning products, or as biodiesel for vehicles to meet the growing demand for non-fossil transportation fuels. Regional and global demand for cooking oils, cleaning products, and biofuels are all growing. This, in part, reflects a population boom in Southeast Asia, India, and Africa, which shows no sign yet of abating. The population of Indonesia will surpass that of the United States in the next ten years. The population of the Philippines has trebled in the last forty years. At the same time, Europeans and North Americans are increasing their consumption of industrialized foods, cosmetics, and cleaning products containing palm oil. They are also converting a small margin of their transportation fuels to fuels derived from corn and oil palm to try to reduce the impacts of fossil fuels on the global climate, although in reality, the carbon footprint of transport fuels derived from agricultural land is as high as those derived from conventional oil and gas. And if the greenhouse gases emitted from burning forests, and subterranean peat fires and methane, are included then the footprint is much higher than oil or gas, which is why, when forest emissions are taken into account, Indonesia was the third highest greenhouse gas-emitting nation, per capita, in 2013. Running cars and trucks on food crops is a mistake, whether we are talking Amazonian soya, Illinois corn, or Indonesian palm oil. But it is more than a scientific error. It is unjust and sinful since it takes land out of small farmer, peasant, and indigenous ownership and use for food and shelter, and turns it into a commodity for consumption by the wealthy.

As with all ecological issues, the problem here is not population or consumption but population times consumption. Even with eight billion people, there will be sufficient fertile and well-watered land on the earth to produce enough food for all people to eat abundantly and not to be hungry. There will also be enough for ten billion people, but not if they all drive cars, fly in planes, and eat meat like the middle classes in the world's cities and like the majority of citizens in the developed North. The consumption of meat, fuel oils, cleaning products, cosmetics, and animal feeds is highest globally per capita in North America and Europe. But it is rising among elites and the middle classes in cities all around the world, including in Southeast Asia, which adopts a North American-style car-, plane-, and meat- dependent lifestyle. And the replication of this lifestyle is not happening by osmosis. It is instead part, as the pope argues in *Laudato Si'*, a consequence of "a consumerist vision of human beings encouraged by the mechanisms of today's globalized economy" and the quest for "short-term growth" at the expense of social and environmental justice for the poor, for future generations, and for all of God's creatures.[3]

The ruined forests of Southeast Asia have been turned by greedy individuals (working through the conventions of global capitalism) into personal wealth which, in the case of the former corrupt chief minister of Sarawak in Borneo, Abdul Taib Mahmud, resulted in a personal property portfolio worth $25 billion, with rental customers from Seattle to Sydney.[4] This is why I indicate in my title that there is a potential conflict between the political ecology of our God-given earth and global capitalism. It is not only tropical forests that are being stolen and turned into commodities for wealthy individuals and corporations to amass fortunes through ethically dubious international trades. It is also oceans, farmlands, rivers, subterranean minerals, and fuels, and even pollution in the atmosphere with the global market in "carbon credits" which the pope rightly criticizes.[5]

But the question arises, what do I mean by capitalism? Is a farmer who sells milk, butter, corn, and vegetables at a farmer's market from his own land and labor—and who employs machinery and farm workers to assist him—not a capitalist? Is a microbrewer who sells a hoppy, citrusy flavored pale ale of the kind now all the rage to outlets in a fifty-mile radius of his brewery not a capitalist? It helps in thinking about this problem to go back to the land. In Southeast Asia, communally owned and managed lands have gone through the process of commodification—and are still going through it—in just the last fifty years. In my country, England, the land was commodified first when much of it was stolen by Thomas Cromwell in the sixteenth century from the Catholic monasteries who had tilled and kept

3. Francis, *Laudato Si'*, 144, 178.

4. Straumann, *Money Logging*.

5. Francis, *Laudato Si'*, 171.

it well for many centuries, and in harmony with the needs of local communities and the replenishing powers of soils, trees, and rivers. These stolen lands were parceled up and conferred on the Crown, and much of them passed on to noble families in exchange for fealty to the Crown. After the English Civil War, the Crown and Parliament acted in a concerted fashion over three centuries through the Laws of Enclosure to steal much of the rest of the common fields and forests from the people of England and give it to themselves to raise sheep, animal feeds, and cereals for sale and use in the emergent industrial towns of Lancashire, London, and the Scots lowlands.[6]

This large-scale land theft, combined with intolerance of dissent both civil and religious, was the major motive for the emigration of hundreds of thousands of English, Irish, and Scots to North America in the eighteenth and nineteenth centuries. Here, they were allotted land they staked a claim to by fencing and working it as farmland. But of course the land was not empty. Like the common forests of Sumatra, or the monastic lands of England, it was previously the common home of indigenous peoples who used it for food and fuel, shelter, and clothing. And the new settlers did not always understand how to use the land. So there is the famous story of a peasant farmer and a native American who walks on his land and picks up a piece of recently ploughed sod and observes whimsically "wrong way up." The prairie was not used to being ploughed, and eventually, small settler farms in the Midwest provoked the dustbowl syndrome that led to many settlers losing their homes to banks and forced them back into penury and servitude in industrial cities such as this one, little different in misery and loss of dignity to the condition they or their grandparents or parents had sought to escape in England.

The original tragedy of the commons is not, as the United States academic Garrett Hardin has it in an essay of that title, that people are incapable of using and sharing nature in common without destroying her.[7] No, the original tragedy of the commons is the story of Naboth's vineyard writ large. Greedy people use the power of debt, of governance or kingship, or of inherited wealth and power, to claim too much of the earth and its products as their own personal fiefdom, their own private source of rent and capital. In so doing, they render the earth and its fruits inaccessible to others, even when others are in want of bread to feed their own children because of the loss of ancestral land, or a share in common forests and fields.

6. For a history of the English Enclosures, see Thompson, *Customs in Common*.

7. Hardin, "The Tragedy of the Commons," 1243–48; for a fuller critique, see Hauerwas, "Moral Limits of Population Control," 120–21, and Northcott, *Angel Directs the Storm*, 160–68.

As Francis says in *Laudato Si'*, at its root the ecological crisis is a *human* crisis, a social crisis, and not only a crisis of "nature" or the "environment." This is why the phrase "human ecology" was coined by a number of scholars in North America and Europe since the 1950s and was adopted in Catholic social teaching, first by John Paul II and now by Francis. In Christian ethical perspective, human ecology concerns "the relationship between human life and the moral law, which is inscribed in our nature and is necessary for the creation of a more dignified environment."[8] And this is why neglect of the moral law, such as the command "thou shalt not steal," not only harms other human beings but also the environment and other creatures. This ecological dimension of the moral law is not, however, a modern invention. On the contrary, as I have argued elsewhere, the Hebrew prophets and especially Jeremiah and Isaiah, clearly link land theft by the urban elites in the later Hebrew monarchies, and the failure of the rich to give the land its Sabbaths as the law commanded that the land had declining in fertility and suffered salinization before the Hebrews were forced into Exile.[9]

If land theft—including from the church as well as indigenous people—is the true historic root of the modern ecological crisis and the related economic system which turned land into rent and people's God-given vocation to till and replenish the earth into wage labor, then the third root is the growing technological powers of modern industrial humans. Modern humanity has acquired, in the last sixty years, such technological powers over the earth as to be able to determine what grows in most earth bioregions, what lives in the sea, and even what mix of gases is present in the earth's atmosphere. Human beings are now in charge of the planet's nitrogen and carbon cycles. So considerable have our powers become that earth scientists, geologists, and others propose that we have entered a new geological epoch which they called the Anthropocene.[10] Before this term was coined by the U.S. nuclear physicist Paul Crutzen, the U.S. Passionist monk and theologian Thomas Berry had also argued that humanity was entering a new geological time zone, but he called it—more radically—the "Ecozoic," since the choice of the term era indicates a much more earth-changing geological shift than epoch.[11]

Berry's term "Ecozoic" is intended to contrast with the Cenozoic era, which is the sixty-five-million-year geological era of earth history since the end of the avian dinosaurs in the Mesozoic era, the age of reptiles. The

8. Francis, *Laudato Si'*, 150.

9. Northcott, *The Environment and Christian Ethics*.

10. Crutzen, "The 'Anthropocene,'" 1–5.

11. Berry, *The Great Work*.

Cenozoic is the mammalian era in which evolved, ultimately, human beings who, for theologians and humanists, are the "crown" of creation/evolution as the first fully conscious—sensing, reasoning, planning, linguistic, and *spiritual*—beings who can shape cultural as well as ecological worlds in ways that transform pre-existing conditions and who, in many human cultures, have a consciousness of and seek to communicate with earth-transcendent gods, angels, and spirits. Anthropocene epoch or Ecozoic era? Most scholars have adopted the former epochal term. A few, such as Mary Evelyn Tucker and Satish Kumar, prefer Berry's nomenclature principally because the term "Anthropocene" may be said to underwrite an attitude of arrogance and domination over the future of life on earth of just the kind that is implicated in the ecological crisis.[12]

For Berry, mechanistic science and industrial capitalism have together de-spiritualized the Western view of earth and only a recognition of this fact—and a re-conscientization of all humans to the spiritual and material interconnectedness of all life, including us—will turn things around. The term "Ecozoic" implies that this new epoch involves not only a radical temporal break with the age of mammals, but also one in which the most conscious and powerful species must evolve to become newly aware of the symbiotic relations at the earth-system, as well as bioregional, level between human and mammalian flourishing and the biogeochemistry of the atmosphere, fields, forests, ice, oceans, rivers, rocks, and species of the earth.[13] Berry's Ecozoic era is eschatological, and it recalls the eschatology of Teilhard de Chardin, and arguably of St. John the Divine, in which recognition of the cosmic Christ as the Alpha and the Omega underwrites and advances a new vision and practice of paradise on earth, as the river of life flows from the newly sacralized cities through the trees "for the healing of the nations" (Rev 22:2) and waters all the earth. Whereas the term "Anthropocene" draws attention to increasing human power over the earth, and perhaps unhelpfully underwrites it, the term "Ecozoic" is more helpful because it implies that technologically empowered humans need a deep cultural, moral, and spiritual transformation to restrain these powers from wrecking the planet. "Ecozoic" is also helpful because it might be said to indicate that the change the earth is going through was preceded by the Incarnation of God in Christ in human, earthly life. As the pope puts it in *Laudato Si'*, in the Incarnation, Crucifixion, and Resurrection of Christ the divine intention to direct all creatures "towards fullness as their end" is revealed and all creatures "are

12. Kumar, "The Ecozoic Era," 1–2.

13. Berry and Swimme, *The Universe Story*, 67.

now imbued with his (Christ's) radiant presence."[14] Hence, the humanization of the cosmos is already anticipated in Christ. But this humanization will only facilitate the eventual redemption and fulfilment of the earth and her creatures in their journey towards union with the Creator when humans use the new powers that they have realized during the history of the church in such a way as to release from frustration the creatures waiting "with eager longing for the revealing of the sons of God" (Rom 8).

Whichever term we choose, both "Anthropocene" and "Ecozoic" underwrite the reality which is

1. Humanity has more power at its disposal than ever before, and currently these powers are degrading biodiversity and threatening a major shift in the climate which will end a unique ten-thousand-year period of climate stability and biodiversity maxima which, in turn, provided the ecological conditions for the emergence of human civilizations and world religions, including the conditions which have enabled us to pass on papyri, ritual objects, stories, and traditions across more than two thousand years and so sustain an intergenerational Christian faith.

2. The earth, whether she likes it or not, is now in human hands: the future of life on earth has been wrested from biological evolution. Humans, now and in the future, will decide which species live and die, what climate the earth will have and hence, for example, whether the three great and cooling Cryospheres of the Arctic, Antarctic, and Himalayan plateau will endure beyond the next two centuries. In their absence, as J. G. Ballard first imagined in his 1962 science fiction novel, *The Drowned World*, the earth will be inundated by sea level rise not seen in twelve thousand years, and it is unlikely the earth will cool again.[15] Ballard imagines that, in this world, an advantage is given to reptilian life again over mammals, and reptiles rapidly evolve in drowned cities and take over the drowned infrastructure left by departing humans.

I argue more fully elsewhere that the first priority for humans who are keen to reduce the growing destructiveness of global economic and industrial forces is to end fossil fuel extraction, and to end tropical and boreal deforestation. And the resources currently devoted to fossil fuel extraction and deforestation should be invested instead in

14. Francis, *Laudato Si'*, 100.
15. Ballard, *The Drowned World*.

1. infrastructure that requires less energy, such as cycle paths instead of roads, and buildings that store heat/cold and are naturally ventilated, instead of energy leaky homes, offices, and factories;

2. renewable energy production including wind, solar, tidal, hydropower, and biomass; and

3. land uses that favor the regrowth of forests on highlands over plantations for tropical oils, and that, on lowlands, favor horticulture, fruit growing and native bushes, and perennial grasses over animal rearing, and animal feed production.[16]

Much energy, if you will forgive the pun, has been put into the fossil fuel divestment movement here in the United States, led by 350.org, and Bill McKibben. But it is national governments, not economic corporations, that license fossil fuel extraction. National governments are political states and agencies governing, as we believe as Christians, the territories of their peoples under God. Since Christ, there is only one true Lord of the earth to whom one day "every knee shall bow": He is on the right hand of God, and all rulers exercise delegated authority from God under Christ, whether or not they recognize the significant limitations on their powers that this involves.[17] When national governments are functioning democracies, they also represent the combined "will of the people." And when asked, ordinary people—even here in Climate Denial Central–say that they would prefer to pass on a biodiverse, fertile, habitable planet to their children rather than one that is diminished in its beauty, biodiversity, and fertility. Who wants their grandchildren to inherit a planet where Sumatran tigers, polar bears, and anteaters only live in zoos, and myriad tropical bird species only survive in cages?

If these are the pragmatic policy priorities, the theological questions that precede them concern the origins of the errors that lead us to neglect these reparative paths in the present and into the near future, and the repair of these errors. If we look at the vision of human or "integral ecology" presented in *Laudato Si'*, first and foremost Francis puts the human duty to protect and care for the integrity of creation *and* the integrity of persons. Caring for creation is a duty intrinsic to humanity's vocation to till and protect the earth (Gen 1:28). But we are tilling too much and protecting too little: the balance between the areas of the earth we use to feed animals and people, to extract fossil fuels, and to dump wastes has shifted perilously,

16. See further Northcott, *A Political Theology of Climate Change.*

17. On the eschatological limitation of early powers under the Lordship of Christ, see O'Donovan, *The Desire of the Nations.*

such that we and our domesticated animals now use 70 percent of the day-to-day product of the life-giving forces of the sun on plants and hence, more than all other non-domesticated species put together, including even the fish in the ocean. We are also mining top soil and subterranean aquifers, and here in the Midwest, much good soil every year is eroded by poor farming practices and ends up in the Mexican Gulf having been transported there by the Mississippi.

The rebalancing of human intervention with the intrinsic flourishing of ecosystems—including wild lands and species not subjected to human uses—will and can only come by a reduction in human consumption. This means two things and not only one. First, it means we need to consume less energy, less fiber, less fish, less meat, less minerals, less paper, less timber, and less water. The careful construction of sustainable limits on the consumption of these things can only be addressed by democratic governance and regulation. We will not see reductions in fossil fuel mining and use if governments continue to license it, or in deforestation or soil erosion, if governments continue to license them and even subsidize them. But second—since the ecological crisis is about consumption *times* population—this also means we need to reduce the continuing growth in the human population. But here, I find a discordant note in the ecological implications of the teaching of the Catholic Church. When the bishops in the Philippines wrote about the ecological crisis in their islands in 1988, they said "it is crucial that people motivated by religious faith develop a deep appreciation for the fragility of our islands' life systems and take steps to defend the Earth. It is a matter of life and death."[18] They clearly thought that the finitude and fragility of the Philippines was threatened and, while they did not say it outright, there is no question that the extraordinary population explosion in the Philippines from just over twenty million in 1945 to eighty million in 2015 is partly responsible for the crisis.

Pope Frances lives in a city surrounded by a Catholic nation where, through artificial birth control and late marriage age, the birth rate is 0.8 per adult woman and population growth has dropped to below replacement. Italians are educated in and have access to artificial contraception methods. Most Filipinos are and do not, because of the power of the Catholic Church in those islands to control the school curriculum and even what may be sold in drug stores. The great majority of Italians are relatively wealthy by global standards. Most Filipinos remain poor. Refusing Filipinos education in how

18. Catholic Bishops' Conference of the Philippines, *What is Happening to Our Land?*

to control for family size ensures they will remain poor and their fragile islands even more ecologically threatened.

While Pope Francis in *Laudato Si'* notes that there may be regional imbalances in human population density which may exacerbate ecological problems, he refuses that continuing population growth is implicated in the environmental crisis globally.[19] And when he was in the Philippines in 2014, Francis praised the large families of many Catholics there despite the fact that, in many such families, finding food for all the children is a daily problem. The fact is that the Catholic Church's influence in the Philippines prevents access of the poor to contraception. And this is a grave injustice since rich professionals in Manila, just as in Italy, can and do use contraception and have smaller families.

The problem here is that there has entered into Catholic ethics, since the encyclical *Humanae Vitae,* an imbalance. There is a great deal in Catholic ethics and in papal encyclicals on the need to protect unborn human life, and to prevent sexual relations from occurring where children are not a possible outcome. But we hear much less in sermons, encyclicals, and from the magisterium, on the need to protect children that have already been born from pollution of the atmosphere they breathe, or erosion of the topsoil on which their futures depend. And we hear little on the need to restrain the personal fortunes of Catholic families, or to restrain their consumption of meat or plane tickets, or the size of their cars and houses. The magisterium is willing to prevent poor families in Catholic countries in the global South from controlling their family size. But it is much less willing to call on rich families, who do control their family size, to restrain their inherited wealth. Of course, the Catholic church cannot be held directly responsible for varying levels of development, and in sub-Saharan Africa, the Catholic Church remains by far and away the largest development agency, providing more schools, hospitals, clinics, and agricultural assistance schemes than all African governments combined. But even in Scotland, I have encountered the power of the Catholic church to prevent young people in poorer communities from having access to information about birth control in schools.

I also wonder if this imbalance in Catholic ethics has contributed to the tendency, in the Vatican and among theologians such as Cardinal Turkson, to continue to give air time to the tiny minority of physical scientists—most of them paid by the fossil fuel industries—who question humanity's role in destabilizing the climate and the Earth system more broadly. Turkson repeated this skepticism in a lecture in Maynooth in which he said

19. Francis, *Laudato Si'*, 50.

it is ultimately unimportant whether humanity is implicated in climate change.[20] But it is important! Humanity has acquired extraordinary powers over the planet, far beyond the powers of plant selection, of tilling the soil, and of naming of species that are described as part of the human vocation in Genesis 1–3. We have become a "godlike species" if not a "god species."[21] If the earth floods again as it did in the days of Noah, it will not be God, or a tilt in the planet in relation to the sun, which causes it, but the unrestrained powers of industrial humans.

It is notable that the nations that first legislated for environmental protection in the late nineteenth and early twentieth centuries were Protestant Christian majority nations like Britain, Germany, Sweden, and the United States. These nations were also the first in the modern era to embrace democratic governance. And there is a relationship between these two. In China today, it is rarely possible for children to see why traditionally the sky is said to be blue. It is almost never blue in China. This is not because of human or industrial development *per se*. China has made great strides in feeding and housing her people in the late twentieth century. Instead, as the documentary *Under the Dome* graphically reveals, it is because of the toxic smog produced in the main by the gargantuan state-owned energy enterprise, which continues to burn vast quantities of unwashed sulphurous coal to make electricity. The second and third largest point sources of the smog are the iron and steel works which make steel for a monopoly state-owned steel company (whose steel rusts in stock yards because no one wants it) and the cement factories which supply it on a vast scale to government-controlled builders who construct thirty-story apartment blocks that no one buys or lives in.[22] But there is no democracy in China, and so when the documentary went viral in the hours after its release, it was blocked from all ISPs by the Chinese government. Without democracy, the people cannot protest when their environment, air, food, and water make them and their children ill.

How are a lack of democracy and Catholic ethics connected? Well, Catholic ethics is governed by the Catholic hierarchy. The input of lay people into Catholic ethics is marginal because the post-Tridentine Catholic Church has had an undue belief in the need for authority and power in the church to be centralized in Rome and in the hierarchy in Rome, and above

20. Turkson, "Integral Ecology and the Horizon of Hope."

21. Lynas, *The God Species*.

22. Jing, *Qiong Ding Zhi Xia [Under the Dome]*. The dome(s) referred to in the title of this two-hour documentary are the air-filtered, enclosed sport-fields constructed by private schools in Beijing and other Chinese cities so the children of the rich can play sports without damaging their health. The film was viewed 200 million times in three days before internet access within China was blocked by the Chinese government.

all, in the pope. Italian Catholics may behave democratically and choose pharmaceutically to use birth control. But they do not influence the teaching of the magisterium.

I am an Anglican. We, of course, suffer from the opposite problem to the Catholic Church. If the leader of the Episcopal Church in the U.S. wishes to say we should not call Jesus Lord because it is unfair to women, there is nothing formally that the Archbishop of Canterbury can do about it. So, our communion is now riven with division over such matters. I am not holding out Anglicanism as the best alternate to Catholic communion! But I am suggesting that the ecological crisis, the growth in human power over the earth, and the growth in human numbers raise issues about Catholic ethics, including internal relations between rich and poor people in the Catholic Church, and the cult of leadership in the Catholic Church which, while it addresses the world in an encyclical, it ought also to address internally. And this is where the Messianic dimension comes in.

Christ was hailed as the Messiah by the first Jewish Christians, and the name *Christos* is Greek for Messiah in the Greek translation of the Jewish scriptures—the Septuagint—or what we call the Old Testament. But the Messianic King announced by the prophets—and above all, Isaiah—was not like other earthly kings. He would not rule by coercion, and he would not even "bruise a reed," words which are repeated in the gospels. Instead, his rule was to be a rule of self-sacrificial love, and this is how Christ lived, and died. He modeled a new form of leadership, authority, and power—the power of the weak hero, not the strong man; the power of Frodo and Hobbits, not Mordor and Sauron. This Messianic model of leadership produces in the political theology of Saint Paul a radical transvaluation of the then-regnant politics of empire through which the world was "turned upside down" by the early Christians. The mighty in their communities were, if not "put down from their thrones," at least restrained in the exercise of their powers, and the lowly were "lifted up," and the wealthy had to give away at least some of their wealth just to stay in communion with their poorer neighbors.

Messianism has an excellent record in environmental protection. John Muir was a weak Scots shepherd-prophet who persuaded a president to set aside and protect wild and beautiful land in Yosemite from industrial use in perpetuity, albeit in the process, the native people were evicted. Rachel Carson was not a strong woman physically. She was also as a writer threatened with being sued by the chemical industry; her book *Silent Spring* was prevented from being published for over a year, and she ultimately died of the cancer her book lay at the door of the chemical industries. But when her book was eventually published, its beautiful prose and forensic science led to legislation which enabled U.S. children to breathe less polluted air, drink less polluted water, and eat less chemically-laden foods. Restraints on power, restraint by the powerful of our growing earthly powers, are of the essence of what we need to do—morally, politically, scientifically, spiritually—to address and reverse earth-damaging levels of the exercise of industrial and technological powers over the planet. Such restraint—self-restraint—is intrinsic to the character of Christian Messianic politics. It does seem to me that, in his personal example, Pope Francis has made efforts symbolically to reduce the display and exercise of wealth and power that his office has acquired over the last few hundred years. So I take heart from this, and find hope in it.

My hope for *Laudato Si'*, and for the Catholic Church, is that the intrinsic connection between hierarchy and related concentrations of power and wealth among Catholics—as much as in the world beyond the church—will be seen as central to the environmental problem, and that Catholic parishes and their priests, along with other communities of faith, will begin to embrace a new kind of post-imperial and communitarian ecclesiology where the economic, ecological, and spiritual relations of God, people, and earth are front-and-center in the local gathering and polity of the church Sunday by Sunday, and in the organizations in the community which it sponsors. To that extent I find myself, somewhat to my surprise, much in sympathy with the heterodox geo-theology of Thomas Berry. From where he was sitting, under the great weight of Catholic hierarchy and orthodoxy, his was a deeply needed and well-targeted prophetic voice. I note that in a recently republished essay, he has this to say: "The Christian future, in my view, will depend above all on the ability of Christians to assume their responsibility for the fate of the earth."[23]

I am glad to say that I find that, here in Chicago, Christians have already been taking up this responsibility with some enthusiasm. The Christian nonprofit organization Faith in Place is the oldest faith-based conservation organization in the United States, so far as I can determine. It has a number of employees and offices and is working with congregations throughout Chicago and the state of Illinois to educate, enable, and stimulate Christian responsibility for the fate of the earth. It sponsors Interfaith Power and Light Illinois which encourages churches and local community groups to commission renewable power for their buildings and into the electric grid. It works to stimulate and educate local clergy around environmental care. It supports local food initiatives. It provides liturgical and scientific educational resources for local Christian groups. It provides

23. Berry, *Christian Future*, 35.

expertise on greening church buildings, old and new. But it is primarily a Protestant-led and a Protestant engaging organization, although of course Catholic parishes are welcome to engage with it.

In the Catholic Church in the United States, the greatest leadership on ecological responsibility both here in Illinois and across the country has been provided by Catholic religious sisters. My evidence for this claim is the wonderful book *Green Sisters* by Sarah McFarland Taylor, whom I met at last on Thursday when speaking at Northwestern University in Evanston, where she is based.[24] She shows in that book how the geo-theology of Tom Berry has stimulated thousands of religious sisters across the United States to redesign their ways of living, their mission, ritual, liturgy, and service to the community and the church around ecological responsibility and earth care. Berry calls this the "great work" of the Ecozoic era, and there is no greater testimony to the fitness of his vision to the mission of the Catholic church than the extraordinary range of earth-healing projects sponsored by religious sisters across the U.S. But the sisters, as Berry himself, experience constant pushback from priests and the hierarchy in this new understanding of the church's mission. This pushback is, of course, not unrelated to that experienced by the prophet Elijah when challenging the power of Ahab to steal Naboth's vineyard, and of Jezebel to falsely accuse him of blasphemy and murder him. In Brazil, Costa Rica, Ecuador, and Peru—all still predominantly Catholic countries—environmental activists are frequently murdered while trying to protect their forests, rivers, and species from ecologically rapacious logging, mining, and plantation companies.[25] Let us hope that *Laudato Si'* will empower priests and catechists in Catholic parishes to teach that it is a divine duty to protect the earth from ecological destruction, and enable Catholic priests and parishes to embrace ecological responsibility as a central part of the Christian mission to heal people and planet under God's heaven.

24. Taylor, *Green Sisters*.
25. Global Witness, *The Deadly Environment*.

19

An Eschatological Perspective on Our Hope for a Sustainable World

Reynaldo D. Raluto

Introduction

The series of deadly typhoons that hit the Philippines became the center of global news coverage. The tropical storm Sendong (international name: Washi) on December 16, 2011, violently claimed at least 1,268 lives in Mindanao-Visayas islands and destroyed around PhP 1.7 billion in infrastructure and agricultural produce.[1] The typhoon Pablo (international name: Bopha) on December 3, 2012, violently hit thirty-four provinces, left more than one thousand people dead, and displaced more than 6.2 million people. The estimated total cost of Pablo's damage in infrastructure, agriculture, and private property amounted to PhP 23 billion.[2] On November 6, 2013, the Super Typhoon Yolanda (international name: Haiyan) devastated the Visayas regions and some parts of Mindanao. As of April 17, 2014, the government agency reported a total of 6,300 dead; 28,689 injured; and 1,061 missing persons. This dreadful event left a total of PhP 89.6 billion worth of damages.[3] The extent of damages may lead one to think of an ecological apocalypse.

---

1. For a detailed report of the damage, see Bacongco, "The Path of Sendong," 17.

2. See "Situation Report on the Effects of Typhoon Pablo."

3. See Philippines Hurricane Yolanda Structural Assessment, "ASCE Philippines Hurricane Yolanda Post-Disaster Investigation."

The intersection of poverty and ecological issues in the above scenarios proves Pope Francis right when he says that we are facing today "one complex crisis which is both social and environmental."[4] The global concern for the challenges of ecological disasters and poverty is getting urgent today as these twin crises threaten our vision of a sustainable world. Aware of this urgency, this chapter tries to answer the question why many poor countries, like the Philippines, are highly vulnerable to nature-related calamities. What can our Christian faith offer to advance the hope for a sustainable future and transcend the temptation to despair? To answer these questions adequately, we need the analytical mediation of ecological sciences before proceeding to the theological interpretation in light of our eschatological vision of the final destiny of creation, which is the Kingdom of God.

1. The Philippine Experience of Ecological Disasters

The Philippines is beset by mutually reinforcing natural hazards and human-induced ecological disasters which are getting worse in the face of climate change. In 2012, the Philippines was the third most vulnerable to disaster risk in the world for the past years.[5] More recently, however, the *World Risk Report 2014* ranks the Philippines as second among countries which are most at risk worldwide.[6] Moreover, the latest risk analysis of Verisk Maplecroft affirms that out of one hundred cities alone with greatest exposure to natural disasters, twenty-one are located in the Philippines. Accordingly, "Natural hazard risk is compounded in the Philippines by poor institutional and societal capacity to manage, respond, and recover from natural hazard events." The Philippines is also considered high risk in part "due to entrenched corruption and high level of poverty."[7] Let us unpack this data by doing some ecological analysis.

1.1 The Threats of Natural Disasters

The new cosmological theory gives us a picture of a dynamically expanding and evolving universe.[8] Empirical evidence shows that galaxies and stars are constantly moving away from us and are receding from each other for about

---

4. Francis, *Laudato Si'*, 139.
5. Welle et al., "WorldRiskIndex 2012," 18–19.
6. Welle et al., "The WorldRiskIndex 2014," 39–50.
7. *Natural Hazards Risk Atlas 2015*.
8. On this account, see Davies, *God and the New Physics*, 17.

13.7 billion years. The Earth, which was formed out of the cosmic debris about 4.45 billion years ago,[9] has been in an irreversible stage of biogenesis. This planet is part of a "self-shaping cosmos," which has the power to destroy and to generate itself. This dynamism largely explains why we experience various cosmic disorders and chaos (entropy), which are deemed to be part of the cosmogenic process of a dynamically evolving universe.

Geological history shows that our planet had suffered five major occasions of mass extinction caused by naturally-occurring forces such as heavy volcanic activity and asteroid crashes.[10] Moreover, our planet has its wild and uncontrollable dimensions that "could render violence, storms, droughts, and general chaos."[11] To survive in this evolving planet, we have to "struggle for existence." We need "to participate creatively in the wildness of the world about us."[12] In other words, we have to learn how to dance with the wild rhythm of nature.

The Philippines is a country that has always been punctuated by the devastating forces of nature. Being situated within the Pacific Ring of Fire, the entire Philippine archipelago has been adversely affected by yearly occurrences of large-scale natural disasters throughout its geological history. Accordingly, the Philippines has about fifty volcanoes which expose the country to natural threats of earthquakes and tsunamis. Moreover, an average of twenty tropical cyclones hit the country every year, and about nine of them cross the land.[13] This symphony of natural calamities proves that Filipinos are not strangers to ecological disasters.

1.2 The Human-Induced Ecological Disasters

The natural hazards could be triggered by human factors. Our awareness of the human-induced catastrophes can help overcome our fatalistic attitude. Ecological tragedies are not God's will that must be passively accepted but serve as painful reminders to awaken us from our ecological slumber. To analyze their human causes, we need the analytical mediation of ecological sciences. Let us quickly highlight at least four interrelated human-induced ecological disasters.

9. For a more detailed account of the Earth's cosmic history, see Stewart and Lynch, *Earth: The Biography*, 32–39.

10. On this account, see Raup and Sepkoski Jr., "Mass Extinctions in the Marine Fossil Record," 1501–3.

11. Merchant, *Death of Nature*, 2.

12. Berry, *Great Work*, 51.

13. Perez, "Responding to the Challenges of the Rising Sea," 18.

1.2.1 Unsustainable Deforestation

Many of our present ecological crises could be associated with unsustainable deforestation. In 2005, the Food and Agriculture Organization (FAO) reported that the total forest area worldwide was 3.8 billion hectares, "which is approximately 30 percent of the global land area."[14] The rate of global deforestation between 1990 and 2005 averaged 14.5 million hectares per year. This alarming trend has been happening locally in the Philippines. In 2002, the Forest Management Bureau (FMB) reported that the country's forest cover was only 24 percent of its total land area.[15] This same agency claims that the Philippines needs at least 54 percent of forest cover to maintain its habitable condition.

Expectedly, being a "focal ecosystem," the destroyed natural forests would badly affect almost all other ecosystems. The FAO, a UN agency, reminds us that a severely damaged forest would not be able to deliver the expected ecosystems services, such as "the regulation of water regimes by intercepting rainfall and regulating its flow through the hydrological system; the maintenance of soil quality and the provision of organic materials through leaf and branch fall; the limiting of erosion and protection of soil from the direct impact of rainfall; modulating climate; and being key components of biodiversity both in themselves and as a habitat for other species."[16] Apparently, an extreme deprivation of the ecosystem services of the forests would eventually affect the community of life.

1.2.2 Soil-Related Tragedies

Unsustainable deforestation leads to soil-related ecological disasters like soil erosion and flash floods. It is well-established scientific knowledge that tree roots can, to a certain extent, control land degradation and soil erosion by means of slope stability and mechanical support to its soil. Studies show that 75 million tons of soil worldwide are eroded each year by wind and water due to the degraded state of the world's forests. In the Philippines, where roughly over 40 percent of the land area is degraded, the volume of soil lost through erosion is estimated to be "one meter deep over two hundred

14. Lindquist et al., *Global Forest Land-Use Change 1990 to 2005*.

15. On this account, see IBON Databank and Research Center, *The State of the Philippine Environment*, 4–5.

16. Lindberg et al., *Ecotourism and Other Services*, 3.

thousand hectares each year."[17] Soil erosion leads to siltation of many rivers and dams in the country.

It has been presumed that severe deforestation can easily turn the rainfall events into disastrous landslides and flash floods. This leads people to simply associate floods and landslides with deforestation. It has been claimed that this may be true only for small-scale catchments. For large-scale catchments, however, "there appears to be no scientific evidence for a connection" between upland deforestation and massive flooding in the lowland.[18] Many researchers have tried to falsify the long-held popular "sponge theory" on the grounds that it "fails the test of close scientific scrutiny."[19] Studies show that, as the forest soil becomes saturated by prolonged rainfall, "water no longer filters into the soil but instead runs off along the soil surface."[20] This largely explains the occurrence of flash floods and landslides. In other words, regulating a catastrophic large-scale flood is beyond the ecosystem services of the forests.

1.2.3 Social Vulnerability

In light of the above findings, reforestation would not necessarily solve the problems of disastrous floods and other soil-related calamities. Floods are considered a natural phenomenon that will always occur whenever there is an excess of water arising from large rainfall events. In this context, reforestation activities are urgent but not enough. To manage the detrimental effects of floods, we need to analyze the aspect of social vulnerability that aggravates the human-induced ecological disasters.

Let us highlight three interrelated causes of people's vulnerability to ecological disasters. One is poverty. The Philippines is a poverty-stricken country. In fact, it was the third poorest country in Southeast Asia in 2010.[21] The 2013 survey reveals that 10.7 percent of Filipinos have income below the food threshold. The poverty incidence among Filipinos in 2013 was estimated at 24.9 percent.[22] It cannot be denied that the poor unjustly suffer the worst effects of ecological disasters. "They have no other financial activities

17. "Down to Earth."

18. Phuong and van Dam, "Linkage between Forests and Water," 18.

19. Enters and Durst, "Questioning Long-held Beliefs," 11.

20. Center for International Forestry Research and Food and Agriculture Organization, Forests and Floods, 5.

21. See Asian Development Bank, "Poverty in Asia."

22. See National Assistance Coordination Board, "PSA: Poverty Incidence among Filipinos."

or resources which can enable them to adapt to climate change or to face natural disasters, and their access to social services and protection is very limited."[23]

The other cause of people's vulnerability is their hazardous location. With the growing population and the trend of urbanization, people tend to ignore the potential danger of residing in landslide hazard zones and areas that are naturally prone to flooding. Needless to say, the poor "are often left with the most hazard-prone lands, since these have the lowest market value and possess the greatest risks."[24] Their poverty forced them to build their homes beside waterways and other high-risk areas that naturally "obstruct, constrict, [and] deflect river flows."[25] Apparently, this inhuman condition is primarily an issue of efficient land-use and sustainable relocation. There should be proper land use, because we also need to relocate those who reside in hazardous places and flood-prone areas as part of our adaptation measures and disaster management.

Finally, the third cause of social vulnerability has something to do with the people's lack of disaster preparedness. As we have shown, with or without climate change, the Philippines is exposed and susceptible to both natural and human-made ecological disasters. With the advent of climate change, however, it is expected that "there will be more rain and it will happen more often and with more intensity."[26] Unfortunately, our present way of classifying extreme weather events is still based on the strength or speed of winds. Many of our people are not yet well-informed about new ways of disaster preparedness, such as how to prepare for the potential volume of rain brought about by the strong typhoons. All of this boils down to the issue of weak adaptation measures largely due to poverty and lack of ecological literacy.

1.2.4 Climate Change Phenomenon

In its November 2014 report, the Intergovernmental Panel on Climate Change (IPCC) unanimously affirmed that "The Earth is warming in the range of 0.5° C to 1.3° C."[27] Since 1880, it is said that the average surface temperature worldwide has gone up by about 0.8° C. The IPCC claims that climate change is anthropogenic, or caused by greenhouse gases (GHGs)

23. Francis, *Laudato Si'*, 25.

24. Ignacio, "ESSC's Seven Points."

25. Walpole and Yap, "Strategies for Disaster-Risk Reduction."

26. Walpole and Watkins, "Understanding Flooding Factors."

27. Pachauri et al., "Climate Change 2014 Synthesis Report."

produced by human activities. The current carbon dioxide (CO_2) levels are at 400 ppm, which is already exceeding the 350 ppm boundary.[28] This increase of GHGs is caused by severe deforestation which "accounts for 18 to 20 percent of climate change."[29] Forests have a "buffering effect" on the climate system as they sequester CO_2 from the delicate atmosphere.

The biggest challenge of our generation is to prevent the Earth's climate from rising more than 2° C, in order to avoid extreme and irreversible ecological disasters. One tragic effect is the loss of biodiversity, or "change in biosphere integrity." Alarmingly, this is one of the Core Boundaries which, according to the Stockholm Resilience Center's report, has already been crossed today.[30] The IPCC warns that "climate change will place up to 50 percent of biodiversity at risk and could cause the loss of as much as 88 percent of coral reefs in Asia in the next thirty years."[31] The Philippines has been identified as one of the thirty-nine biodiversity hot spots worldwide owing to the loss of at least 70 percent of its endemic species.[32]

Another alarming ecological consequence of climate change is the occurrence of severe meteorological events. The issue has been raised whether or not the formation of stronger and more frequent tropical typhoons today is necessarily part of the climate change phenomenon. According to prevailing scientific opinion, tropical storms are *likely* (i.e., have a probability of 66 percent or greater) to become both stronger and more frequent as the climate continues to warm.[33] Myles Allen, a climate scientist from the University of Oxford, pointed out that the latest assessment of the IPCC "stated explicitly that there is no clear evidence at present for any human-induced increase in tropic-wide cyclone frequency."[34] Accordingly, it still remains extremely difficult at this time for science to attribute specific weather events to climate change due to lack of sufficient data. In any case, this difficulty does not falsify the IPCC's finding that it is "extremely likely [i.e., 95 percent certain]" that the global phenomenon of climate change is "caused by the anthropogenic increase in greenhouse gas concentration" in the atmosphere.[35]

28. See "Planetary Boundaries."
29. "Speciocide."
30. "Planetary Boundaries."
31. Cited in "Speciocide."
32. See Diamond, *Collapse*, 486–525.
33. See Walsh, "Climate Change Didn't Cause Supertyphoon Haiyan."
34. Cited in Mathiesen, "Climate Change Aggravating Cyclone Damage."
35. Intergovernmental Panel on Climate Change, *Climate Change 2013*, 12–13.

2. Ecological Perspectives on Nature's Resilience and Sustainability

The foregoing ecological analysis leads us to raise questions about the planet's survival. Along this line, many ecological scientists emphasize the resilience of the Earth in the face of ecological crisis. Let us briefly revisit three ecological perspectives that explain how the Earth maintains its natural balance. They will affirm our vision of a sustainable world in the face of ecological disasters.

2.1 The Earth Has a Self-Regulating Capacity

Let us focus on two contemporary proponents of the self-regulating capacity of the Earth. One is the American plant ecologist Frederic Clements (1874–1945); the other is the English scientist James Lovelock (born 1919). Both scientists use the same term "organism" analogously and complementarily. On the one hand, Clements appropriated the ecological view that a "disturbed" nature has the innate capacity to heal and regulate itself. To support this view, he coined the term "plant succession" which proposed that, in the history of every "climax formation," there has always been "a series of invasions, a sequence of plant communities marked by the change from lower to higher life-forms."[36] The development of a climax community, which is analogous to the development of an organism into adulthood, "must progress from one stage to another, and finally must terminate in the highest stage possible under the climatic conditions present."[37] Clements, despite being criticized for his deterministic theory of succession,[38] was optimistic that the externally disturbed natural areas would always struggle to be able to recover naturally through the process of succession, which "must recur whenever proper conditions arise."[39] After all, according to him, it is the nature of plant formation to struggle to reach the stage of final equilibrium, which is the end point of the climax formation.

On the other hand, Lovelock sees the Earth as a complex system "comprising all of life and all of its environment tightly coupled so as to form a self-regulating entity."[40] His study of the tight interlocking between the

36. Clements, "Preface to Plant Succession," 40.

37. Ibid., 38.

38. See Gleason, "The Individualistic Concept of the Plant Association," 7–26.

39. Clements, "Preface to Plant Succession," 36. For a similar view, see Marsh, *Man and Nature*, 29.

40. Lovelock, *Healing Gaia*, 12.

living parts that form like a superorganism has led him to view the Earth as a *living planet*, making it "the largest living thing in the solar system,"[41] capable of maintaining the state of constancy (homeostasis) in the face of the changing external conditions. This is known as Gaia theory, which sees the Earth as having a self-regulative capacity to survive and to adapt in the face of external climatic changes.[42] He recalls that there were five major occasions of mass extinction in geological history, which proves that the Earth has the capacity to recover from *external* assaults.[43] Aware of this self-regulative capacity, he optimistically inferred: "What we are doing weakens her [the Earth] but is unlikely to destroy her."[44] For him, "it is hubris to think that we know how to save the Earth: our planet looks after itself."[45] Nevertheless, Lovelock considers "the Earth's declining health as our most important concern," because our very lives and welfare demand and depend upon a healthy Earth.

2.2 The Earth's Ecosystems Are Evolving to Reach Homeostasis

The view that the Earth is an "ecosystem" (or, ecological system) allows us to hope for a sustainable world order. The English ecologist Arthur George Tansley (1871–1955) coined the term "ecosystem" in 1935 to emphasize the view of nature as a "system" in a mechanistic sense. American ecologist Eugene Odum (1913–2002) borrowed Tansley's terminology and defined it as "[a]ny unit that includes all of the organisms (i.e., the 'community') in a given area interacting with the physical environment so that a flow of energy leads to clearly defined trophic structure, biotic diversity, and material cycles (i.e., exchange of materials between living and nonliving parts)

41. Lovelock, *Revenge of Gaia*, 21.

42. This is illustrated in his Gaian model of the white and black Daisyworld. On the explanation of this mathematical model, called Daisyworld, see Lovelock, *The Ages of Gaia*, 34–5, 43–4. Cf. Lovelock and Watson, "Biological Homeostasis," 286–89. Both authors clarified that the temperature regulation is an emergent property of the system that arises automatically as a consequence of feedback loops between biological organisms and their environment.

43. On this account, see Raup and Sepkoski Jr., "Mass Extinctions," 1501–3.

44. Lovelock, *Revenge of Gaia*, 77.

45. Lovelock, *Vanishing Face of Gaia*, 9. Along this line, many scientists also claim that the stuff about "saving the Earth" is nonsense, as the Earth does not need saving. "It's not the planet we should be worrying about. It's us." See Stewart and Lynch, *Earth*, 230.

within the system."[46] In Odum's holistic view, the Earth as a whole may be seen as an ecosystem.

The goal of an ecosystem is to reach the steady-state level of maturity that is called *homeostasis*. As an emergent property, homeostasis is the result of "the functional interaction of the [physical and biological] components"[47] of an ecosystem. The state of homeostasis basically affirms the celebrated Gestalt principle: a whole is greater than the sum of its parts. As Odum explains, the whole has "characteristics additional to the characteristics of the individuals composing them."[48] To put it differently, the forest is more than just a collection of trees. The ecosystem ecology proposes that *homeostasis* (and not deterioration or death) is the end point of the natural order. Similar to the superorganism perspective, it assumes that a "mature ecosystem" naturally lends self-regulation and resilience to the system. As a living system, an ecosystem has the characteristics of self-organization and self-generation. It has an inherent capacity to bring itself back into balance "whenever there is a deviation from the norm due to changing environmental conditions."[49] This creative dynamism "may include the emergence of new order at critical points of instability."[50] Thus, in the face of disasters, there is a reason to hope for a highly structured, ordered, regulated, and steady-state ecological system.

Despite the inherent capacity of the Earth's ecosystems to recover from external and human assaults, it should be emphasized that their self-regulative capacity has limits. The unsustainable exploitation of our planet's natural resources could paralyze the regular functioning of its ecosystems. The whole ecosystem will eventually collapse when the unsustainable exploitation goes beyond the limits. Given the extent of the present ecological damage, it is clear that the Earth badly needs our human assistance and intervention to restore its healthy condition.

2.3 The Coming of the Ecozoic Era

Another important ecological perspective is that of Thomas Berry (1914–2009), a North American Passionist Catholic priest and an ecological cultural historian who prefers to call himself a "geologian." Berry affirms that we are living in the Cenozoic Era, the biological era that started 65 million

46. Odum, *Fundamentals of Ecology*, 8.

47. Odum, *Ecology*, 34.

48. Odum, *Fundamentals of Ecology*, 146. [Emphasis in original.]

49. Capra and Luisi, *The Systems View of Life*, 355.

50. Ibid., 345–46.

years ago. The term "Cenozoic" came from the Greek root *kainos*, meaning "new," and *zoic*, meaning "life." As Berry explains, the Cenozoic (or, new life) is a "period when Earth and all its living forms . . . came into being."[51] This implies that biodiversity is the original nature of the evolving universe.

Berry argues that human beings have become a "devastating presence" on the planet as they falsely assume that nonhuman creatures are there solely for human use and benefit. He warns us that this anthropocentric attitude could lead to the extensive disintegration of the Earth's life systems, which could bring an end to the Cenozoic Era. This awareness pushed Berry to announce the coming of the "Ecozoic Era" characterized by "mutually enhancing" human-Earth relationships. To realize the dream of the Ecozoic Era, Berry highlights the extremely important "Great Work" that human beings must do to assist in its birth.[52] For this new period of creativity to come, almost every phase of the Ecozoic Era will require the human to speed up its coming.

Berry identifies many positive signs that the Ecozoic Era is emerging. One is our sensitivity to the natural world and conscious affirmation of the Earth as alive, which allows us to view the universe as "a communion of subjects rather than a collection of objects."[53] Another positive sign is our recognition of the sacredness of the universe, which overcomes the old dualistic view that falsely separates the sacred from the profane. In the Ecozoic Era, "the sacred community is the Earth community. The human community becomes sacred through its participation in the larger planetary community."[54] As participating members of the larger Earth community, human beings share in the single story and common destiny of the whole planetary community.

3. The Christian Hope for a Sustainable World

The foregoing ecological perspectives give us reason to hope for a sustainable world in the face of the present crisis. They challenge theologians to update their reflections on the eschatological destiny of creation. Let us deepen these ecological insights in light of the biblical vision of the kingdom of God. In this endeavor, we find the Brazilian theologian, Leonardo Boff, as a helpful dialogue partner. This choice is based on the fact that, being a Third

51. Berry, *Christian Future*, 69.
52. Berry, *Great Work*, 1–7.
53. Berry, *Universe Story*, 243.
54. Ibid., 257.

World theologian, Boff's locus of theologizing is similar to the Philippine context.

3.1 The Ecological Model of a Sustainable Society

Boff fully recognizes the importance of the notion of sustainability introduced by Lester Brown in the early 1980s. Boff defines sustainability as "the trend of ecosystems toward dynamic equilibrium sustained in the web of interdependencies and complementarities flourishing in ecosystems."[55] This affirms that sustainability is "a property of an entire web of relationships."[56] Boff, however, is skeptical of the vogue to integrate this ecological term into the dominant model of development, which he considers as largely responsible for the present ecological crisis. It can be recalled that the United Nations' celebrated notion of "sustainable development" refers to development that meets "the needs of the present without compromising the ability of future generations to meet their own needs."[57] For Boff, the term "sustainable development" is an "oxymoron" and remains "rhetoric and illusion"[58] in the context of the development model advanced by neoliberal capitalism. Boff believes that this prevailing economic development model, even as it exists in the so-called "diverse forms of capitalism,"[59] is incompatible with an ecologically sustainable society.

As an alternative, Boff embraces the vision of the "Earth Charter," which proposes the expression *sustainable lifestyle*. He explains that a lifestyle is sustainable when it "allows Earth, with its beauty and integrity and its abundant but limited resources, to meet the current needs of all humankind in a way that will allow Earth to reproduce itself, to regenerate itself, and to continue its evolution as it has done for four and a half billion years."[60] This entails that we should not simply conserve or allow nature to recover so that we can resume plundering it again. Boff argues that we need to liberate the Earth from this type of development paradigm which incurably plunders natural resources.

Implicit in Boff's notion of sustainability is the proposal to consider nature's ecosystems as models. As we have shown, the Earth—as an

55. Boff, *Cry of the Earth*, 66.

56. Capra and Luisi, *Systems View of Life*, 355.

57. World Commission on Environment and Development, *Our Common Future*, 43.

58. Boff, *Cry of the Earth*, 67.

59. On this account, see Renouard and Giraud, "Postface."

60. Boff, "Respect and Care," 44.

ecosystem—has an inherent ability to sustain life. An important character-istic of ecosystems is the *cyclical nature* of their ecological processes. As one may observe, "all organisms in an ecosystem produce wastes, but what is waste for one species is food for another, so that the ecosystem as a whole remains without solid waste."[61] This cyclical nature of an ecosystem is sim-ply missing in the prevailing "throwaway culture" of our modern economic production, which has been criticized by Pope Francis as deeply unsustain-able. Thus, for Pope Francis, if we wish to achieve a sustainable society, "the way natural ecosystems work is exemplary."[62] From ecosystems, we have to learn how to operate sustainably as a community of life.

3.2 The Coming of God's Kingdom and Our Hope for a Sustainable World

The Christian hope for a sustainable future is not simply based on scientific theories of the future of the cosmos. Boff sadly noted that many modern thinkers have a low regard for religious experiences which had their ori-gins in fantasy, in the realm of the imagination, and in the depths of desire. In response, Boff emphasizes the potential role of these human capacities in overcoming the oppressive forces of the present reality. Through their mediation, Boff argues, we are pushed not to accept passively "things as they are, but contest them, suspecting what is indeed true—that the real is much more than the apparently given."[63] These human capacities enable us to generate *utopia* (in its positive sense) that "does not conflict with real-ity" but rather discloses its "potential and ideal dimension."[64] The utopian dimension of reality gives us courage to resist the temptation to become resigned in the face of the present situation's contradictory state.

For Boff, the biblical notion of God's Kingdom may be described in utopian language as it perfectly summarizes everything for which a human being can hope.[65] To pray for the coming of God's kingdom is to activate what Boff calls the "most radical hopes of the heart," which longs for "the revelation of an absolute meaning that is to be realized by God in all of creation."[66] To highlight this ecological perspective of God's kingdom, Boff creatively retrieves its ancient Aramaic expression: *malkuta d'Alaha*, "an

61. Capra and Luisi, *Systems View of Life*, 354.
62. Francis, *Laudato Si'*, 22.
63. Boff, *Ecology and Liberation*, 59.
64. Ibid.
65. Cf. Matt 6:33.
66. Boff, *Lord's Prayer*, 61–62.

empowering vision . . . rooted in the presence of the divine in the cosmos." In other words, the kingdom of God is a divine presence of the "governing principles that guide the evolutionary process of the cosmos itself."[67] This ecological sense of God's kingdom needs to be retrieved.

From Boff's liberative perspective, our ecological vision of a sustainable world may be seen as part of the larger vision of the coming of God's kingdom. Arguably, this eschatological perspective on the promise of a sustainable world is our particular theological contribution to the ongoing discussion of the world's future. Like the numerous historical events of liberation, which will be fully realized in God's offer of salvation,[68] our present experience of the world's limited moments of sustainability may also be seen as a foretaste of the eschatological realization of God's kingdom. The Christian doctrine of continuous creation affirms this hope as it emphasizes the constant presence of a divine Creator who unfailingly sustains the evolving creation to its final destiny.

The biblical vision of the coming of God's kingdom does not necessarily negate the emerging cosmological theory that our expanding universe will either end in a massive fiery contraction (Big Crunch!) or die out in a general congealment and darkness.[69] On the contrary, many ecological theologians consider this speculation as an affirmation of the theological view of the common origin and destiny of all created realities, including human beings.[70] This theological view affirms that the scenario of a cosmic death in the future is part of the Christian hope for the renewal of the finite cosmos on "the last day." Nevertheless, the Christian hope for the potential survival of this finite universe is not based on scientific speculation but on the very character of the divine Creator who, in his mercy, has the power to "give life and breath back"[71] to the evolving cosmos. As one theologian puts it, "The Giver of life who created all beings out of nothing will still be there after devastation, holding fast to the beloved creation."[72] After all, our God is not only the creator of the cosmos but also its liberator and savior.

67. Boff and Hathaway, *Tao of Liberation*, 331.

68. On this account, see Boff, "Integral Liberation and Partial Liberations," 14–66.

69. On this account, see Hawking, *A Brief History of Time*.

70. For an excellent treatment of ecological eschatology, see Phan, "Eschatology and Ecology," 3–16.

71. 2 Macc 2:23.

72. Johnson, *Ask the Beast*, 221.

3.2 An Ecological View on Eschatology

Let us highlight two important features of Boff's ecological view on eschatology, which appropriates the insights of an evolutionary perspective in
view of overcoming the narrow view of anthropocentrism. On one hand,
Boff crucially departs from the dominant theological assumption that God
created a finished and perfect world. He argues that this view cannot be
supported by the emerging post-Darwinian evolutionary perspective of
modern sciences. To interpret the biblical story of creation with new eyes,
Boff embraces the view that "[t]he earthly paradise is what God intends,
and it serves as an image of contrast with the present reality, an image of the
time when all evil will be vanquished."[73] In this light, "Paradise is a prophecy
of the future projected back upon the past."[74] This interpretation highlights
the aspect of continuous creation, which affirms the unfinished process of
evolution until it arrives at its desired perfection in the new creation of all
things.

On the other hand, Boff strongly discards the predominant anthropocentric perspective on eschatology which unduly excludes nonhuman creatures from God's plan of salvation. Against this view, Boff repeatedly affirms
that the whole cosmos, and not only humanity, is destined by God to enjoy
eternal beatitude. He argues that the fate of humanity cannot be separated
from Earth, as they "make up *a single entity*."[75] For Boff, the essential one-
ness of human beings with the Earth is confirmed by the biblical truth that
"the Lord God formed [the human being] from the dust of the ground."[76]
Thus, being formed out of the Earth's dust (i.e., *humus* in Latin), *humans* do
not only essentially share common physical and chemical elements with all
other earthly creatures but are also "inseparably connected to the fate" of
the cosmos of which they are a part.[77] As their permanent home, the Earth
participates in the glorious transformation of humanity in the end time.

Boff's ecological theology invites us to see the coherence of our doctrine of creation and eschaton. He claims that "we are faced not with ter-
minal death but with the transfiguration of the cosmogenic process into
supremely ordered and vital new forms of life."[78] There is reason to "hope
that, as always happens in the evolutionary process, chaos will give birth

73. Boff, *Cry of the Earth*, 37.
74. Ibid., 37; cf. Mesters, *Eden*, 28–29.
75. Boff, *Cry of the Earth*, 14.
76. Gen 2:7.
77. Boff, *Cry of the Earth*, 14.
78. Boff, "Earth as Gaia," 26.

to a new and higher order, one that holds promise to all."[79] This cosmic dynamism resonates with the view of Jürgen Moltmann, who understands the biblical hope for the renewal of all things not as a creation out of nothing but as "a heightening and a giving of new form to what is already there."[80] This biblical hope for a new cosmic order gives light to our dream of a sustainable world and generates a utopia that sustains our struggle for "another possible world."

It is significant to note that the papal encyclical *Laudato Si'* emphasizes the ecological perspective on eschatology. This encyclical allows us to view the final destiny of created realities from a theocentric perspective. It affirms that "the ultimate destiny of the universe is in the fullness of God, which has already been attained by the risen Christ, the measure of the maturity of all things."[81] It teaches that the ultimate purpose of other creatures is not to be found in human beings but in God. It envisions that "[a]ll creatures are moving forward with us and through us towards a common point of arrival, which is God."[82] We are on a journey "towards the sabbath of eternity, the new Jerusalem, towards our common home in heaven."[83]

Conclusion

We have focused on the Philippines' experience of natural calamities induced by unsustainable human activities. In our ecological analysis, we emphasized the negative ecological effects of unsustainable deforestation on other ecosystems. However, we emphasized that reforestation is not enough. In the face of climate change, we also need to strengthen our adaptation measures as part of disaster management and preparedness.

Our exploration of the different ecological insights on sustainability pushed us to hope for a sustainable world in the face of the present ecological crisis. We considered them as helpful ecological insights to update our theological reflection on the eschatological destiny of creation. With Leonardo Boff, we deepened our ecological perspective on eschatology, which aptly expresses the coming of God's kingdom in utopic language and gives us hope for the desirable perfection in the new creation of all things. This biblical hope gives meaning to our ecological struggle for "another possible world," which is our human response to God's gift of salvation.

79. Boff, *Cry of the Earth*, xii.
80. Moltmann, "Is the World Unfinished," 411.
81. Francis, *Laudato Si'*, 83.
82. Ibid.
83. Ibid., 243.

Our faith in the eschatological future strengthens our hope in the face of the temptation to suffer helplessly or to surrender fatalistically to the forces of inhuman suffering. The truth is that those who opt to struggle are also willing to suffer and die rather than to embrace, hopelessly, the darkness of frustration and despair: "May our struggles and our concern for this planet never take away the joy of our hope."[84]

84. Ibid., 244.

Bibliography

Alcina, Ignacio Francisco. *History of the Bisayan People in the Philippine Islands: Evangelization and Culture at the Contact Period.* Translated and edited by Cantius J. Kobak and Lucio Gutierrez. Vol. 3. Manila: University of Santo Tomas Publishing, 2005.

"'Alfalfa George' is a Leader in a Missouri Farm Community, Besides Being a Priest." *Milwaukee Journal,* October 13, 1943.

Aglionby, John. "Four Times as Many Women Died in Tsunami." *The Guardian,* March 26, 2005. http://www.theguardian.com/society/2005/mar/26/internationalaidanddevelopment.indianoceantsunamidecember2004.

Agyeman, Julian, and Bob Evans. "Justice, Governance, and Sustainability: Perspectives on Environmental Citizenship from North America and Europe." In *Environmental Citizenship,* edited by Andrew Dobson and Derek Bell, 185–206. Cambridge, MA: MIT Press, 2005.

Amon, Siprianus. Eyewitness testimony in private report to JPIC-OFM Indonesia (Order of Friars Minor's Justice, Peace, and Integrity of Commission of Indonesia). February 2015.

Ángel, Augusto. *El Reto de la Vida—Ecosistema y Cultura: Una Introducción al Estudio del Medio Ambiente.* Bogotá: Ecofondo, 1996.

———. *La Fragilidad Ambiental de la Cultura.* Bogotá: Instituto de Estudios Ambientales (IDEA)–Editorial Universidad Nacional, 1995.

Aquinas, Thomas. *Summa Theologicae.* London: Blackfriars with Eyre & Spottiswoode, 1960.

Armstrong, Regis J., J. A. Wayne Hellman, and William J. Short, eds. *Francis of Assisi: Early Documents.* Vol. 1, *The Saint.* New York: New City, 1999.

———. *Francis of Assisi: Early Documents.* Vol. 2, *The Founder.* New York: New City, 2000.

Ashley, James Matthew. *Interruptions: Mysticism, Politics, and Theology in the Work of Johann Baptist Metz.* Notre Dame: University of Notre Dame Press, 1998.

Asian Development Bank. "Poverty in Asia: A Deeper Look." *Key Indicators for Asia and the Pacific 2014* (2014) 3–52. http://www.adb.org/sites/default/files/publication/43030/ki2014_0.pdf.

Australian Red Cross. "Largest Peacetime Evacuation as Typhoon Hagupit Hits Philippines." December 8, 2014. http://www.redcross.org.au/hagupit-evacuation.aspx.

Bacongco, Keith. "The Path of Sendong." *Our Mindanao.* Special Edition, 2:1 (February 2012) 17–18.

Bahnson, Fred, and Norman Wirzba. *Making Peace with the Land: God's Call to Reconcile with Creation.* Downers Grove, IL: IVP, 2012.

Bailey, Robert. "Oxfam Background Paper: The Right to Survive in a Changing Climate." Oxford: Oxfam International, 2009. https://www.oxfam.org/sites/www.oxfam.org/files/right-to-survive-changing-climate-background.pdf.

Bailey, Ronald. *Eco-Scam: The False Prophet of Ecological Apocalypse.* New York: St. Martin's, 1993.

Ballard, J. G. *The Drowned World.* London: Berkley, 1962.

Banco de la República. "Deuda Externa de Colombia" [Colombia's External Debt]." Subgerencia de Estudios Económicos, October 2014. *http://www.banrep.gov.co/sites/default/files/paginas/bdeudax_t_o.pdf.*

Bankoff, Greg. "Rendering the World Unsafe: Vulnerability as Western Discourse." *Disasters* 25:1 (2001) 19–35.

Baro, Mamodou, and Simon Batterbury. "Land-Based Livelihoods." In *Towards a New Map of Africa,* edited by Ben Wisner et al., 52–70. London: Earthscan, 2005.

Barrett Gross, Matthew, and Mel Gilles. "How Apocalyptic Thinking Prevents Us from Taking Political Action." *The Atlantic,* April 23, 2012. http://www.theatlantic.com/politics/archive/2012/04/how-apocalyptic-thinking-prevents-us-from-taking-political-action/255758/.

Barrientos, Stephanie, and Catherine Dolan. *Ethical Sourcing in the Global Food System.* London: Earthscan, 2006.

Bartolome, Peter. "The Land and the Spirit." Sermon for the Green Bay Convention. October 1946. NCRLC 5/2/26, National Catholic Rural Life Conference Records, Marquette Archives, Marquette University Raynor Memorial Libraries.

Basilio, Robert J. A., Jr. "The Ghosts of Yolanda." *BusinessWorld Online,* October 24, 2014. http://www.bworldonline.com/weekender/content.php?id=96594.

Bauckham, Richard. *The Theology of the Book of Revelation.* Cambridge: Cambridge University Press, 1993.

Beabout, Gregory R., et al. *Beyond Self-Interest: A Personalist Approach to Human Action.* Lanham, MD: Lexington, 2002.

Benard, Babatunde Bolaji. "Status of Mangrove Forest in the Niger Delta." In *Environmental Roundtable on the Status of Mangroves in the Niger Delta.* Port Harcourt, Nigeria: Centre for Environment Human Rights and Development, 2014.

Benedict XVI, Pope. "Address to the Bundestag—The Listening Heart: Reflections on the Foundations of Law." Reichstag Building, Berlin, September 22, 2011. https://w2.vatican.va/content/benedict-xvi/en/speeches/2011/september/documents/hf_ben-xvi_spe_20110922_reichstag-berlin.html.

——. *Africae Munus: Postsynodal Apostolic Exhortation of the Church in Africa in Service to Reconciliation, Justice and Peace.* Vatican City, 2011. http://w2.vatican.va/content/benedict-xvi/en/apost_exhortations/documents/hf_ben-xvi_exh_20111119_africae-munus.html.

——. *Caritas in Veritate: Encyclical on Integral Human Development in Charity and Truth.* Vatican City, 2009. http://w2.vatican.va/content/benedict-xvi/en/encyclicals/documents/hf_ben-xvi_enc_20090629_caritas-in-veritate.html.

——. "General Audience: Safeguarding of Creation." August 26, 2009. https://w2.vatican.va/content/benedict-xvi/en/audiences/2009/documents/hf_ben-xvi_aud_20090826.html.

——. "If You Want to Cultivate Peace, Protect Creation." Message for the Celebration of the World Day of Peace: January 1, 2010. Given in Vatican City, December 8, 2009. https://w2.vatican.va/content/benedict-xvi/en/messages/peace/documents/hf_ben-xvi_mes_20091208_xliii-world-day-peace.html.

———. "Message to Brazilian Bishops for the 2011 Brotherhood Campaign." February 16, 2011. https://w2.vatican.va/content/benedict-xvi/en/messages/pont-messages/2011/documents/hf_ben-xvi_mes_20110216_fraternita-2011.html.

———. "Message to Mr. Jacques Diouf, Director General of FAO, on the Occasion of World Food Day 2011." October 17, 2011. https://w2.vatican.va/content/benedict-xvi/en/messages/food/documents/hf_ben-xvi_mes_20111017_world-food-day-2011.html.

———. "Welcoming Celebration by the Young People: Address." Barangaroo, Sydney Harbor, July 17, 2008. https://w2.vatican.va/content/benedict-xvi/en/speeches/2008/july/documents/hf_ben-xvi_spe_20080717_barangaroo.html.

Benedict XVI, Pope, and Peter Seewald. *Light of the World: The Pope, the Church, and the Signs of the Times*. Translated by Michael J. Miller and Adrian J. Walker. San Francisco: Ignatius, 2010.

Bennagen, Ponciano. "Study on Indigenous Knowledge-Systems and Practices for Biodiversity Conservation." Unpublished study commissioned by the Butuan Office of Deutsche Gessellschaft für Internationale Zusammenarbeit, Butuan City, Philippines, March 11, 2013.

Berger, James. *After the End: Representations of Post-Apocalypse*. Minneapolis: University of Minnesota Press, 1999.

Berry, Thomas. *The Christian Future and the Fate of the Earth*. Edited by Mary Evelyn Tucker and John Grim. Maryknoll, NY: Orbis, 2009.

———. *The Great Work: Our Way into the Future*. New York: Bell Tower, 1999.

Berry, Thomas, and Brian Swimme. *The Universe Story: From the Primordial Flaring Forth to the Ecozoic Era: A Celebration of the Unfolding of the Cosmos*. New York: Harper Collins, 1994.

Berry, Wendell. *The Art of the Commonplace*. Washington, DC: Counterpoint, 2002.

———. "Discipline and Hope." In *A Continuous Harmony: Essays Cultural and Agricultural*. New York: Harcourt Brace Jovanovich, 1972.

———. *The Gift of Good Land: Further Essays Cultural and Agricultural*. San Francisco: North Point, 1981.

———. *The Unsettling of America: Culture and Agriculture*. San Francisco: Sierra Club, 1977.

———. "Whose Head Is the Farmer Using? Whose Head Is Using the Farmer?" In *Meeting the Expectations of the Land: Essays in Sustainable Agriculture and Stewardship*, edited by Wes Jackson et al., 18–32. San Francisco: North Point, 1984.

Biblia de Jerusalén. Bilbao: Desclée de Brouwer, 1976.

Bible, Seth A. *Pursuing Ecological Virtue: A Critical Analysis of the Environmental Virtue Ethics Models of Ronald Sandler, Louke Van Wensveen, and Philip Cafaro*. Ann Arbor, MI: ProQuest LLC, 2012.

Binkenfeld, Darryl L. "Deciphering Moral Landscapes in Agricultural Biotechnology." *The Annual of the Society of Christian Ethics* 17 (1997) 233–50.

Bjorner, Thomas B., et al. "Environmental Labeling and Consumers' Choice—an Empirical Analysis of the Effect of the Nordic Swan." *Journal of Environmental Economics and Management* 47 (2004) 411–24.

Blount, Brian. "Breaking Point: A Sermon." In *Lament: Reclaiming Practices in Pulpit, Pew, and Public Square*, edited by Sally A. Brown and Patrick D. Miller, 145–54. Louisville: Westminster John Knox, 2005.

Boersema, Jan. "Why Is Francis of Assisi the Patron Saint of Ecologists?" *Science and Christian Belief* 14 (2002) 51–77.

Boff, Leonardo. *Cry of the Earth, Cry of the Poor.* Translated by Phillip Berryman. Maryknoll, NY: Orbis, 1997.

———. *La Dignidad de la Tierra.* Vallalodid: Trotta, 2000.

———. "Earth as Gaia: An Ethical and Spiritual Challenge." *Concilium* 3 (2009) 24–33.

———. *Ecología: Grito de la Tierra, Grito de los Pobres.* Buenos Aires: Lohlé-Lumen, 1996.

———. *Ecology and Liberation: A New Paradigm.* Translated by John Cumming. Maryknoll, NY: Orbis, 1995.

———. "Integral Liberation and Partial Liberations." Translated by Robert Barr. In *Salvation and Liberation: In Search of a Balance between Faith and Politics*, edited by Leonardo Boff and Clodovis Boff, 14–66. Maryknoll, NY: Orbis, 1984.

———. *The Lord's Prayer: The Prayer of Integral Liberation.* Maryknoll, NY: Orbis, 1983.

———. "Respect and Care for the Community of Life with Understanding, Compassion, and Love." In *The Earth Charter in Action: Toward a Sustainable World*, edited by Peter Blaze Corcoran, 43–46. Amsterdam: KIT, 2005.

Boff, Leonardo, and Ambrosio Nguyen Van Si. *Sorella Madre Terra: Per una Dimensione Politica e Teologica dell'Ecologia.* Roma: Lavoro, 1996.

Boff, Leonardo, and Mark Hathaway. *The Tao of Liberation: Exploring the Ecology of Transformation.* Maryknoll, NY: Orbis, 2009.

Böhme, Gernot. *Die Natur von unsere Naturphilosophie in pragmatische Hinsicht.* Kusterdingen: Die Graue Edition, 2002.

Borchardt, F. L. *Doomsday Speculation as a Strategy of Persuasion: A Study of Apocalypticism as Rhetoric.* Lewiston, NY: E. Mellen, 1990.

Bovée, David S. *The Church and the Land: The National Catholic Rural Life Conference and American Society, 1923–2007.* Washington, DC: Catholic University of America Press, 2010.

Bracamonte, Nimfa, et al. "Social and Economic Aspects of the Agusan Marsh Key Biodiversity Area." In *Proceedings of the First Scientific Conference of the Agusan Marsh: Butuan City, Agusan del Norte, Philippines, 21–23 May 2007*, edited by Jurgenne H. Primavera, 83–97. Jakarta: Philippine Council for Aquatic and Marine Research and Development, 2008.

Bredin, Mark. "Ecological Crisis and Plagues (Revelation 11:6)." *The Biblical Theology Bulletin* 39 (2009) 26–38.

Brooks, Bradley. "In Brazil, Pope Francis Speaks Out on the Amazon, Environment, and Indigenous People." *The Toronto Star*, July 27, 2013. https://www.thestar.com/news/world/2013/07/27/in_brazil_pope_francis_speaks_out_on_the_amazon_environment_and_indigenous_people.html.

Brophy, Kathleen. "DRC's Largest Mine Was Just Sold. And DRC Got Nothing." *The Politics of Poverty: Ideas and Analysis from Oxfam America's Policy Experts* (blog). August 3, 2016. http://politicsofpoverty.oxfamamerica.org/2016/08/drcs-largest-mine-was-just-sold-and-drc-got-nothing/.

Brown, Oli, and Alec Crawford. "Climate Change and Security in Africa: A Study for the Nordic-African Foreign Ministers Meeting." Winnipeg: International Institute for Sustainable Development (IISD), 2009. http://www.iisd.org/pdf/2009/climate_change_security_africa.pdf.

Brueggemann, Walter. *The Land: Place as Gift, Promise, and Challenge in Biblical Faith.* 2nd ed. Minneapolis: Fortress, 2002.

————. *The Prophetic Imagination.* 2nd ed. Minneapolis: Fortress, 2001.

Buell, Frederick. *From Apocalypse to Way of Life: Environmental Crisis in the American Century.* London: Routledge, 1995.

Bunzl, Matti, and Rachel Havrelock. "From the Editors." *AJS Perspectives: The Apocalypse Issue* (Fall 2012) 3.

Burggraeve, Roger. "Humans Created and Called in the Image of God." In *Desirable God? Our Fascination with Images, Idols, and New Deities,* edited by Roger Burggraeve et al., 61–93. Leuven: Peeters, 2003.

————. "No One Can Save Oneself without Others: An Ethic of Liberation in the Footsteps of Emmanuel Levinas." In *The Awakening of the Other: A Provocative Dialogue with Emmanuel Levinas,* edited by Roger Burggraeve, 13–65. Leuven: Peeters, 2008.

————. "Responsibility Precedes Freedom: In Search of a Biblical Philosophical Foundation of Personalistic Love Ethic." In *Personalist Ethics: Essays in Honor of Professor Louis Janssens,* edited by Joseph A. Selling, 109–32. Leuven: Leuven University Press, Uitgeverij Peeters, 1988.

Burke, Christine E. "Globalization and Ecology." In *Earth Revealing—Earth Healing: Ecology and Christian Theology,* edited by Denis Edwards, 21–42. Collegeville, MN: Liturgical, 2001.

Cáceres, Alirio, et al. *Manual de Pastoral Rural y de la Tierra.* Conferencia Episcopal de Colombia. Bogotá: Secretariado Nacional de Pastoral Social–Cáritas Colombiana, 2007.

Caduto, Michael. *Guía para la Enseñanza de Valores Ambientales.* Madrid: Programa Internacional de Educación Ambiental UNESCO-PNUMA, 1996.

Cafaro, Philip. "Thoreau, Leopold, and Carson: Toward an Environmental Virtue Ethics." *Environmental Ethics* 22:1 (2001) 3–17.

————. *Thoreau's Living Ethics: "Walden" and the Pursuit of Virtue.* Athens: University of the Georgia Press, 2004.

Callicott, J. Baird, and Robert Frodeman. "Rio Declaration." In *Encyclopedia of Environmental Ethics and Philosophy,* 201–2. Detroit: Macmillan Reference, 2009.

Cannon, Terry, et al. "How Religion and Belief Influence Attitudes to Risk." In *World Disasters Report 2014: Focus on Culture and Risk,* 37–40. Lyon, France: International Federation of Red Cross and Red Crescent Societies, 2014. http://www.ifrc.org/publications-and-reports/world-disasters-report/world-disasters-report-2014/world-disasters-report-2014--chapter-2.

Capra, Fritjof, and Pier Luisi. *The Systems View of Life: A Unified Vision.* Cambridge: Cambridge University Press, 2014.

Carlsson, Fredrik, et al. "Consumer Benefits of Labels and Bans on GM Foods—Choice Experiments with Swedish Consumers." *American Journal of Agricultural Economics* 89 (2007) 152–61.

Carmon, Ziv, and Dan Ariely. "Focusing on the Foregone: How Value Can Appear So Different to Buyers and Sellers." *Journal of Consumer Research* 27 (2000) 360–70.

Carney, Margaret. "Naming the Earthquake: Franciscans and the Evangelical Life." *Cord* 56 (2006) 76–94.

Carrasquilla, Federico. *Escuchemos a los Pobres: Aportes para una Antropología del Pobre.* Bogotá: Indo-American Press Service, 2000.

Carson, Rachel. *Silent Spring*. Boston: Houghton Mifflin, 1962.

Castro, Lina V. "Assessing Vulnerabilities of Women and Children Exposed to Disaster: The Philippine Experience." Presentation at Fifth Global Forum on Gender Statistics, LVC/Aguascalientes, Mexico, November 3–4 2014. http://unstats. un.org/unsd/gender/Mexico_Nov2014/Session%207%20Philippines%20ppt.pdf.

"A Catholic Agricultural College." *The Wanderer* 29. July 1937. NCRLC Clipping Files 11/1/3, National Catholic Rural Life Conference Records, Marquette Archives, Marquette University Raynor Memorial Libraries.

Catholic Bishops' Conference of Japan. "Reverence for Life: A Message for the Twenty-First Century from the Catholic Bishops' Conference of Japan: January 1, 2001." http://www.cbcj.catholic.jp/eng/edoc/01life.htm.

Catholic Bishops' Conference of the Philippines (CBCP). *Catechism for Filipino Catholics*. Manila: ECCE Word and Life, 1997.

———. *What Is Happening to Our Land?* Tagaytay: CBCP, 1988.

Catholic Church. *Catechism of the Catholic Church*. New York: Doubleday, 1995.

———. *Gaudium et Spes: Pastoral Constitution on the Church in the Modern World*. Washington, DC: National Catholic Welfare Conference, 1965.

Catholic Cooperative Committee. *Catholic Churchmen and Cooperatives*. Huntington, IN: Our Sunday Visitor, 1944. [NCRLC 5/2/14, National Catholic Rural Life Conference Records, Marquette Archives, Marquette University Raynor Memorial Libraries.]

"Catholics Study Farm Problems." *Seattle Daily Times*, October 17, 1939.

Catton, William R. "Foundations of Human Ecology." *Sociological Perspectives* 37 (1994) 75–95.

Center for International Forestry Research and Food and Agriculture Organization. *Forests and Floods: Drowning in Fiction or Thriving on Facts?* Bogor Barat: Center for International Forestry Research, 2005.

Center for the Study of Language and Information at Stanford University. *The Stanford Encyclopedia of Philosophy*. Stanford, CA: Metaphysics Research Lab, 2005.

Chester, David K. "Natural Disasters and Christian Theology." Presentation at Faraday Institute for Science and Religion, St. Edmund's College, University of Cambridge, England, 2009. https://www.faraday.st-edmunds.cam.ac.uk/resources/FAR268%20Chester.pdf.

Christian Aid. *A Rich Seam: Who Benefits from the Rising Commodity Prices? January 2007*. London: Christian Aid, 2007.

Christiansen, Drew, and Walter Grazer. *And God Saw That It Was Good: Catholic Theology and the Environment*. Washington, DC: U.S. Catholic Conference, 1996.

Chryssavgis, John, ed. *On Earth as in Heaven: Ecological Vision and Initiatives of Ecumenical Patriarch Bartholomew*. New York: Fordham University Press, 2012.

Clements, Frederic. *Plant Succession: An Analysis of the Development of Vegetation*. Washington, DC: Carnegie Institution of Washington, 1916.

Climate and Development Knowledge Network (CDKN). *Managing Climate Extremes and Disasters in Africa: Lessons from the IPCC SREX Report*. London: CDKN, 2012. http://www.ifrc.org/docs/IDRL/-%20To%20add/ManagingClimateExtremesAfrica.pdf.

Cloke, Paul, and Justin Beaumont. "Geographies of Post-Secular Rapprochement in the City." *Progress in Human Geographies* 37 (2013) 27–51.

Collier, Paul. *The Bottom Billion*. New York: Oxford University Press, 2007.

"Colombia le ganó más terreno a la pobreza." *El País.* March 28, 2007. http://historico. elpais.com.co/paisonline/notas/Marzo282007/pobreza.html.

Conferência Episcopal Portuguesa [Portuguese Bishops' Conference]. Carta Pastoral: *Responsabilidade Solidária pelo Bem Comum* [Pastoral Letter: Joint Responsibility for the Common Good]. Lisbon: Conferência Episcopal Portuguesa, 2003.

Congress of Colombia. Law 1259 (December 19, 2008). http://www.alcaldiabogota.gov. co/sisjur/normas/Norma1.jsp?i=34388.

Cooper, Anderson. "New Official Death Toll from Typhoon Aftermath; New Fix for Obamacare? Interview with Senator Joe Manchin; New Official Typhoon Death Toll, 2,360." *CNN 360 Degrees* transcript. November 14, 2013. http://edition.cnn. com/TRANSCRIPTS/1311/14/acd.01.html.

Council for Scientific and Industrial Research. "Scientists Say Four of Nine Boundaries that Make Earth a Safe and Stable Place to Live, Crossed." January 21, 2015. http:// ntww1.csir.co.za/plsql/ptl0002/PTL0002_PGE157_MEDIA_REL?MEDIA_ RELEASE_NO=7526628.

Curtis, Helena, and N. Sue Barnes. *Invitation to Biology.* 5th ed. New York: W. H. Freeman, 2000.

Daly, Herman. "The Steady-State Economy: Postmodern Alternative to Growthmania." In *Spirituality and Society: Postmodern Visions,* edited by David Ray Griffin, 107– 21. Albany: State University of New York Press, 1988.

Daneel, Marthinus L. *African Earthkeepers.* Vol. 2, *Environmental Mission and Liberation in Christian Perspective.* Pretoria: University of South Africa Press, 1999.

———. "African Initiated Churches as Vehicles of Earth-Care in Africa." In *The Oxford Handbook of Religion and Ecology,* edited by Roger S. Gottlieb. Oxford: Oxford University Press, 2006.

Darr, Richard S. "Protestant Missions and Earthkeeping in Southern Africa, 1817– 2000." PhD diss., Boston University, 2005.

Darwin, Charles. *On the Origin of Species by Means of Natural Selection, or the Preservation of Favored Races in the Struggle for Life.* London: Oxford University Press, 1923.

Davies, Paul. *God and the New Physics.* London: Penguin, 1983.

Davis, Ellen. *Scripture, Culture, and Agriculture: An Agrarian Reading of the Bible.* Cambridge: Cambridge University Press, 2009.

Davis, Mike. *Planet of Slums.* New York: Verso, 2007.

Deane-Drummond, Celia. "A Case for Collective Conscience: Climategate, COP-15 and Climate Justice." *Studies in Christian Ethics* 24 (2011) 5–22.

———. "Environmental Sciences." In *Christianity and the Disciplines: The Transformation of the University,* edited by Oliver Crisp et al. London: Bloomsbury/T. and T. Clark, 2012.

———. "Joining in the Dance: Ecology in Roman Catholic Social Teaching." *New Blackfriars* 93:1044 (2012) 193–212.

———. "Technology, Ecology, and the Divine: A Critical Look at New Technologies Through a Theology of Gratuitousness." In *Just Sustainability: Technology, Ecology, and Resource Extraction,* edited by Christiana Z. Peppard and Andrea Vicini, 145– 56. Maryknoll, NY: Orbis, 2015.

Delavin, I. C. C. "PHL Slips in Gender Index Rank." *BusinessWorld Online,* October 29, 2014. http://www.bworldonline.com/content.php?section=TopStory&title=phl-slips-in-gender-index-rank&id=96810.

Delio, Ilia, et al. "Creation Care: A Return of Love for Love." *National Catholic Reporter*, December 5, 2008. http:// ncronline.org/news/creation-care-return-love-love.

Dessel, J. P. van. "The Environmental Situation in the Niger Delta." Internal Position Paper for Greenpeace Netherlands, February 1995.

De Tavernier, Johan. "Ecology and Ethics." *Louvain Studies* 19 (1994) 235–61.

Diamond, Jared. *Collapse: How Societies Choose to Fail or Succeed*. London: Penguin, 2005.

Dickenson, Colby. "Are the Only True Atheists Actually Theologians?" In *The Return of Apocalypticism*, edited by Hille Haker et al., 51–59. London: SCM, 2014.

Dickson, Gary, Marshall W. Baldwin, and Thomas F. Madden. "Crusades; The Fifth Crusade." *Encyclopedia Britannica*. https://www.britannica.com/event/Crusades/The-Fourth-Crusade-and-the-Latin-empire-of-Constantinople#ref1184383.

Diola, Camille. "1912 Reports on Tacloban Storm 'Killing' 15,000 Resurface." *PhilStar*, November 19, 2013. http://www.philstar.com/headlin es/2013/11/19/1258482/1912-reports-tacloban-storm-killing-15000-resurface.

Di Tommaso, Lorenzo. "Superflat Apocalypticism in the Internet Age." *Concilium* 3 (2014) 111–20.

Dittmer, Jason, and Tristan Sturm. *Mapping the End Times: American Evangelical Geopolitics and Apocalyptic Visions*. Farnham, UK: Ashgate, 2010.

Donaldson-Evans, Catherine. "Tsunami Animals: A Sixth Sense?" *FoxNews.com*, January 9, 2005. http://www.foxnews.com/story/2005/01/09/tsunami-animals-sixth-sense/.

Dorr, Donal. "'The Fragile World': Church Teaching on Ecology Before and By Pope Francis." *Thinking Faith*, February 26, 2014. http://www.thinkingfaith.org/articles/%E2%80%98-fragile-world%E2%80%99-church-teaching-ecology-and-pope-francis.

———. *Option for the Poor and for the Earth: Catholic Social Teaching*. Maryknoll, NY: Orbis, 2012.

Dourojeanni, Marc J., et al. *Amazonia Peruana en 2021: Explotación de Recursos Naturales e Infraestructuras: ¿Qué Está Pasando? ¿Qué es lo que Significan para el Futuro?* Lima: Sociedad Peruana de Derecho Ambiental (SPDA), 2010.

"Down to Earth." *Environmental Science for Social Change*, May 7, 2012. http://essc.org.ph/content/view/659/153/.

Doyle, Jack. *Riding the Dragon: Royal Dutch Shell and the Fossil Fire*. Boston: Environmental Health Fund, 2002.

Dube Dwilson, Stephanie. "The Strongest and Deadliest Hurricanes in History: Five Fast Facts You Need to Know." *Heavy*, October 23, 2015. http://heavy.com/news/2015/10/strongest-deadliest-hurricanes-mexico-united-states-patricia-galveston-katrina-sandy-linda-allen-damage-deaths-winds-mph-category-5/.

Dunlap, Thomas R. *Faith in Nature Environmentalism as Religious Quest*. Seattle: University of Washington Press, 2005.

Dussel, Enrique. *Ética de la Liberación en la Edad de la Globalización y de la Exclusión*. Mexico: Trotta, 1998.

Eaton, Leslie, and Cameron McWhirter. "An Unfinished Riff: New Orleans's Uneven Revival in Decade after Katrina." *The Wall Street Journal*, April 26, 2015. http://www.wsj.com/articles/the-new-orleans-economy-ten-years-after-katrina-1440628953.

Edwards, Denis. *El Dios de la Evolución: Una Teología Trinitaria*. Colección Presencia Teológica. Santander: Sal Terrae, 2006.

————. *Ecology at the Heart of Faith*. Maryknoll, NY: Orbis, 2006.

Edwards, Lucie. "Global Problems, African Solutions: African Climate Scientists' Perspectives on Climate Change." Waterloo, ON, Canada: The African Initiative and the Centre for International Governance Innovation (CIGI), 2013. https://www.cigionline.org/sites/default/files/ai_dp_7_0.pdf.

Eggemeier, Matthew. "Christianity or Nihilism? The Apocalyptic Discourses of Johann Baptist Metz and Friedrich Nietzsche." *Horizons* 39 (2012) 7–26.

Ehrlich, Paul R., and Anne H. *The Population Bomb*. Stanford: Stanford University Press, 1968.

————. "The Population Bomb Revisited." *The Electronic Journal of Sustainable Development* 1 (2009) 5–14.

Eklund, Rebekah. "Empires and Enemies: Re-reading Lament as Politics." In *Reading Scripture as a Political Act: Essays on the Theopolitical Interpretation of the Bible*, edited by Matthew A. Tapie and Daniel Wade McClain, 21–38. Minneapolis: Fortress, 2015.

Eleazar, Alma, et al. "Cultural Practices and the Realm of Meanings of the Lumad in Agusan on Gender, Reproductive Health, and Sexuality." Unpublished research, Fr. Saturnino Urios University, Butuan City, Philippines, March 2009.

Ellsberg, Robert. "Introduction." In *Dorothy Day: Selected Writings*, edited by Robert Ellsberg. Maryknoll, NY: Orbis, 2013.

Ellul, Jacques. *The Technological Society*. Translated by John Wilkinson. New York: Vintage, 1967.

Emanuel, Kerry. "Downscaling CMIP5 Climate Models Shows Increased Tropical Cyclone Activity over the Twenty-First Century." *Proceedings of the National Academy of Sciences of the United States of America (PNAS)* 110:30 (2013) 12219–12224. http://www.pnas.org/content/110/30/12219.full.pdf.

Enters, Thomas, and Patrick B. Durst. "Questioning Long-held Beliefs about Forests and Floods." In *Forests, Water, and Livelihood*, edited by Willemine Brinkman et al., 11–13. Bennekom: European Tropical Forest Research Network, 2005–2006.

Environmental Defense Fund (EDF). "Climate Change's Effects Plunder the Planet." http://www.edf.org/climate/climate-changes-effects-plunder-planet.

Ettel, Joseph. "I Am a Country Pastor." *Catholic Rural Life Bulletin* 3 (March 1940) 5.

European Commission on Climate Action. "Paris Agreement." http://ec.europa.eu/clima/policies/international/negotiations/future/index_en.

Evangelista, Patricia. "After Yolanda: The Barber of Guiuan." *Rappler*, November 23, 2013. http://www.rappler.com/video/44409-haiyan-the-barber-of-guiuan.

Farbotko, Carol, and Lesley Head. "Gifts, Sustainable Consumption, and Giving Up Green Anxieties at Christmas." *Geoforum* 50 (2013) 88–96.

"Farm Future Is Discussed: Catholic Parley on Rural Life Hears Talks by Three Leaders." *Milwaukee Journal*, October 13, 1943.

Feinberg, Matthew, and Robb Willer. "Apocalypse Soon? Dire Messages Reduce Belief in Global Warming by Contradicting Just-World Beliefs." *Psychological Science* 22 (2011) 34–38.

Fern, Richard L. *Nature, God, and Humanity: Envisioning an Ethics of Nature*. Cambridge: Cambridge University Press, 2002.

Fiddes, Paul. *The Promised End: Eschatology in Theology and Literature*. London: Wiley, 2000.

Fiedler, Maureen. "Faith Leaders March for Climate, Call for Fossil Fuel Divestment." *National Catholic Reporter*, September 26, 2014. http://ncronline.org/blogs/eco-catholic/faith-leaders-march-climate-call-fossil-fuel-divestment.

Fischetti, Mark. "Was Typhoon Haiyan a Record Storm?" *Scientific American*, November 12, 2013. http://blogs.scientificamerican.com/observations/2013/11/12/was-typhoon-haiyan-a-record-storm/.

Forum for the Future. *The Five Capitals Model: A Framework for Sustainability*. http://www.forumforthefuture.org/sites/default/files/project/downloads/five-capitals-model.pdf and http://www.forumforthefuture.org/project/five-capitals/overview.

Foster, John. *La Ecología de Marx: Materialismo y Naturaleza*. Barcelona: Intervención Cultural, 2000.

Fowler, Bertram. *The Lord Helps Those . . . How the People of Nova Scotia Are Solving Their Problems through Cooperation*. New York: Vanguard, 1938.

Francis, Pope. "Address at Second World Meeting of Popular Movements." Address given in Santa Cruz de la Sierra, Bolivia, July 9, 2015. http://w2.vatican.va/content/francesco/en/speeches/2015/july/documents/papa-francesco_20150709_bolivia-movimenti-popolari.html.

―――. "Address to the Bishops of Brazil." Address given on the occasion of the XXVIII World Youth Day in Rio de Janeiro, Brazil, July 28, 2013. https://w2.vatican.va/content/francesco/en/speeches/2013/july/documents/papa-francesco_20130727_gmg-episcopato-brasile.html.

―――. *Evangelii Gaudium: The Joy of the Gospel*. Washington, DC: U.S. Conference of Catholic Bishops, 2013. http://w2.vatican.va/content/francesco/en/apost_exhortations/documents/papa-francesco_esortazione-ap_20131124_evangelii-gaudium.html.

―――. "General Audience." St. Peter's Square, Rome, June 5, 2013. https://w2.vatican.va/content/francesco/en/audiences/2013/documents/papa-francesco_20130605_udienza-generale.html.

―――. "Homily for the Beginning of the Petrine Ministry." St. Peter's Square, Rome, March, 19, 2013. https://w2.vatican.va/content/francesco/en/homilies/2013/documents/papa-francesco_20130319_omelia-inizio-pontificato.html.

―――. "Homily for the Celebration of Palm Sunday." St. Peter's Square, Rome, March 24, 2013. http://w2.vatican.va/content/francesco/en/homilies/2013/documents/papa-francesco_20130324_palme.html.

―――. "Homily for 'Evangelium Vitae' Day." St. Peter's Square, Rome. June 16, 2013. http://w2.vatican.va/content/francesco/en/homilies/2013/documents/papa-francesco_20130616_omelia-evangelium-vitae.html.

―――. "Homily on the Occasion of the XXVIII World Youth Day." Copacabana, Rio de Janeiro, July 28, 2013. http://w2.vatican.va/content/francesco/en/homilies/2013/documents/papa-francesco_20130728_celebrazione-xxviii-gmg.html.

―――. *Laudato Si': On the Care for Our Common Home*. Vatican City, 2015. http://w2.vatican.va/content/francesco/en/encyclicals/documents/papa-francesco_20150524_enciclica-laudato-si.html.

Frasz, Geoffrey B. "Environmental Virtue Ethics: A New Direction for Environmental Ethics." *Environmental Ethics* 15 (1993) 259–74.

Freiman, Christopher. Review of *Environmental Virtue Ethics*, by Ronald Sandler and Philip Cafaro. *Ethics and the Environment* 11 (2006) 133–38.

Fromm, Erich. *On Being Human*. New York: Continuum, 1994.

Fukuyama, Francis. *The End of History and the Last Man*. New York: Avon, 1992.

———. *The Great Disruption: Human Nature and the Reconstitution of the Social Order*. New York: Free Press, 1999.

Galaz, Victor, et al. "Planetary Boundaries Are Valuable for Policy: Centre Researchers Reply to Criticism." Stockholm Resilience Centre, June 14, 2012. http://www.stockholmresilience.org/research/research-news/2012-07-02-planetary-boundaries-are-valuable-for-policy.html.

García, Alan. "El Perro del Hortelano contra el Pobre." *El Comercio*, March 2, 2008.

———. "El Síndrome del Perro del Hortelano." *El Comercio*, October 28, 2007. http://www.justiciaviva.org.pe/userfiles/26539211-Alan-Garcia-Perez-y-el-perro-del-hortelano.pdf.

———. "Receta para Acabar con el Perro del Hortelano." *El Comercio*, November 8, 2007.

García, María Isabel. "Economía-Colombia: Más pobres pero satisfechos." Inter Press Service, December 4, 2003. http://www.ipsnoticias.net/2003/12/economia-colombia-mas-pobres-pero-satisfechos/.

Gardner, Howard. *Mentes Flexibles*. Barcelona: Paidós, 2004.

Garrad, Gregg. *Ecocriticism*. London: Routledge, 2012.

Garvan, John M. *The Manóbos of Mindanao*. Washington, DC: U.S. Government Printing Office, 1941.

Gaspar, Karl. *Desperately Seeking God's Saving Action: Yolanda Survivors' Hope beyond Heartbreaking Lamentations*. Quezon City: Institute of Spirituality in Asia, 2014.

———. "To Speak with Boldness." In *Re-Imaging Christianity for a Green World*, edited by Randy J. C. Odchigue and Eric Genilo, 19–38. Quezon City: SVST/AdU: 2011.

Gatmaytan, Augusto. "The Hakyadan of Froilan Havana: Ritual Obligation in Manobo Religion." *Philippine Studies* 52 (2004) 383–426.

———. "Traditional Manobo Agriculture: Upland Rice Cultivation in the Upper Adgawan River." *Kinaadman: A Journal of the Southern Philippines* 20 (1–4) 1–52.

Gecaga, Margaret G. "Creative Stewardship for a New Earth." In *Theology of Reconstruction: Exploratory Essays*, edited by Mary Getui and Emmanuel Obeng, 28–49. 2nd ed. Nairobi: Acton, 2003.

George, Francis Cardinal. "Legislation Creating 'Same-Sex' Marriage: What's at Stake?" *Catholic New World*, January 6–9, 2013. http://www.catholicnewworld.com/cnwonline/2013/0106/cardinal.aspx.

Gifford, Terry. "Pastoral, Anti-Pastoral, Post-Pastoral." In *The Cambridge Companion to Literature and the Environment*, edited by Louise Westling, 17–30. New York: Cambridge University Press, 2014.

Glacken, Clarence. *Traces on the Rhodian Shore: Nature and Culture in Western Thought from Ancient Times to the End of the Eighteenth Century*. Berkeley: University of California Press, 1967.

Gleason, Henry. "The Individualistic Concept of the Plant Association." *Bulletin of the Torrey Botanical Club* 53 (1926) 7–26.

Gleason, Philip. *The Conservative Reformers: German-American Catholics and the Social Order*. Notre Dame: University of Notre Dame Press, 1968.

Global Witness. *The Deadly Environment: The Rise in Killings of Environmental Land Defenders*. London: Global Witness, 2014. https://www.globalwitness.org/en/campaigns/environmental-activists/deadly-environment.

Gnanakan, Ken. "Creation, Christians, and Environmental Stewardship." *Evangelical Review of Theology* 30 (2006) 110–20.

"The Golden Secret of Green Acres: Rural Life Pageant Expected to Draw Audience of 5,000." NCRLC 11/2/4, National Catholic Rural Life Conference Records, Marquette Archives, Marquette University Raynor Memorial Libraries.

Goldenberg, Suzanne. "U.S. Congressman Cites Biblical Flood to Dispute Human Link to Climate Change." *The Guardian*, April 10, 2013. http://www.theguardian.com/environment/blog/2013/apr/11/republican-biblical-flood-climate-change.

Gorringe, Timothy J. "On Building an Ark: The Global Emergency and the Limits of Moral Exhortation." *Studies in Christian Ethics* 24 (2011) 23–33.

Graham, Billy. *Approaching Hoofbeats: The Four Horsemen of the Apocalypse.* Waco, TX: Word, 1983.

Grant, Lindsey. "The Cornucopian Fallacies: The Myth of Perpetual Growth." *Futurist* 17 (1983) 16–22.

———. *TEF Report: The Cornucopian Fallacies.* Washington, DC: The Environmental Fund, 1982.

Greer, Jed, and Kenny Bruno. *Greenwash: The Reality of Corporate Environmentalism.* Manila: IBON Foundation, 1998.

Gregersen, Niels Henrik. *Incarnation: On the Scope and Depth of Christology.* Minneapolis: Fortress, 2015.

Gregory, Brad S. *The Unintended Reformation: How a Religious Revolution Secularized Society.* Cambridge, MA: Belknap Press of Harvard University Press, 2012.

Guzman, Edmundo Pacifico. "Creation as God's *Kaloob*: Towards an Ecological Theology of Creation in the Lowland Filipino Socio-cultural Context." Part Two, Doctoral dissertation, Katholieke Universiteit Leuven, 1995.

Haker, Hille, et al. *The Return of Apocalypticism,* London: SCM, 2014.

Hamlin, Christopher, and John T. McGreevy. "The Greening of America, Catholic Style, 1930–1950." *Environmental History* 11 (2006) 464–99.

Hamlin, Christopher, and Philip T. Shepard. *Deep Disagreement in U.S. Agriculture: Making Sense of Policy Conflict.* Boulder, CO: Westview, 1993.

Hancock, Philip, and Alf Rehn. "Organizing Christmas." *Organization* 18 (2011) 737–45.

Hannam, Peter. "Twin Typhoons Spin in the Pacific, Adding to Active Storm Season." *The Sydney Morning Herald*, August 17, 2015. http://www.smh.com.au/environment/weather/twin-typhoons-spin-in-the-pacific-adding-to-active-storm-season-20150817-gj12y5.html#ixzz3jbIEHdxp.

Haq, Gary, et al. *The Carbon Cost of Christmas.* Stockholm: Stockholm Environment Institute, 2007.

Harasta, Eva, and Brian Brock. "Introduction." In *Evoking Lament: A Theological Discussion,* edited by Eva Harasta and Brian Brock, 1–13. London: T. and T. Clark, 2009.

Hardin, Garrett. "The Tragedy of the Commons." *Science* 162 (1968) 1243–48.

Hardoon, Deborah. "Wealth: Having It All and Wanting More." Oxford: Oxfam GB, January 2015. https://www.oxfam.org/sites/www.oxfam.org/files/file_attachments/ib-wealth-having-all-wanting-more-190115-en.pdf.

Harris, David. "The Impact of Cultural and Religious Influences During Natural Disasters (Volcano Eruptions)." Earthquake-Report.com. September 27, 2012.

http://earthquake-report.com/2012/09/27/the-impact-of-cultural-and-religious-influences-during-natural-disasters-volcano-eruptions/.

Harrison, Peter. *The Bible, Protestantism, and the Rise of Natural Science.* Cambridge: Cambridge University Press, 1998.

———. "Having Dominion: Genesis and the Mastery of Nature." In *Environmental Stewardship: Critical Perspectives—Past and Present,* edited by R. J. Berry, 17–30. London: T. and T. Clark, 2006.

Hauerwas, Stanley. *Truthfulness and Tragedy: Further Investigations in Christian Ethics.* Notre Dame: University of Notre Dame Press, 1977.

Hawking, Stephen. *A Brief History of Time: From the Big Bang to Black Holes.* New York: Bantam, 1988.

Hawley, Amos. *Human Ecology: A Theory of Community Structure.* New York: Ronald, 1950.

Hayward, Tim. *Ecological Thought.* Cambridge, UK: Polity, 1994.

Heffernan, Teresa. *Post-Apocalyptic Culture: Modernism, Post-Modernism. and the Twentieth Century Novel.* Toronto: University of Toronto Press, 2000.

Helton, Shawn. "Philippines Typhoon Linked to 'Man-Made' Microwave Pulses." *Twenty-First Century Wire,* November 12, 2013. http://21stcenturywire.com/2013/11/12/philippines-typhoon-linked-to-man-made-microwave-pulses/.

Hendrix, Cullen S., and Sarah M. Glaser. "Trends and Triggers: Climate, Climate Change, and Civil Conflict in Sub-Saharan Africa." *Political Geography* 26 (2007) 695–71.

Hicks, Savannah. "Buen Vivir: An Old, but Fresh Perspective on Global Development." *IDEX: International Development Exchange* (blog), September 14, 2016. https://www.idex.org/blog/2016/09/buen-vivir-old-but-fresh-perspective-on-global-development/.

Holy See. "Position Paper: III Preparatory Committee Meeting of the United Nations Conference on Sustainable Development." Rio de Janeiro, June 13–15, 2012. http://www.vatican.va/roman_curia/secretariat_state/2012/documents/rc_seg-st_20120614_position-paper-rio_en.html.

Hope, Kempe Ronald. "Climate Change and Poverty in Africa." *International Journal of Sustainable Development and World Ecology* 16 (2009) 451–61.

Hull, Robert. "All About EVE: A Report on Environmental Virtues Today." *Ethics and the Environment* 10 (2005) 89–111.

Hunt, Arthur W. *Surviving Technopolis: Essays on Finding Balance in Our New Man-Made Environments.* Eugene, OR: Pickwick, 2013.

Hynes, Emerson. "'City Slickers' and 'Dumb Farmers.'" Des Moines, IA: National Catholic Rural Life Conference, 1940. [NCRLC 5/2/9, National Catholic Rural Life Conference Records, Marquette Archives, Marquette University Raynor Memorial Libraries.]

———. "Farm-Family-Prosperity: A Program for Restoring Rural Life to its Proper Orbit." St. Paul, MN: National Catholic Rural Life Conference, 1941. [NCRLC 5/2/10, National Catholic Rural Life Conference Records, Marquette Archives, Marquette University Raynor Memorial Libraries.]

IBON Databank and Research Center. *The State of the Philippine Environment.* 3rd ed. Quezon City: Ibon, 2006.

Ignacio, Andres. "ESSC's Seven Points in Disaster Risk Reduction and Climate Change Adaptation." Environmental Science for Social Change, February 5, 2013. http://essc.org.ph/content/view/779/153/.

Intergovernmental Panel on Climate Change (IPCC). *Climate Change 2013: The Physical Science Basis. Contribution of Working Group I to the Fifth Assessment Report of the Intergovernmental Panel on Climate Change.* Cambridge: Cambridge University Press, 2014. http://www.climatechange2013.org/images/report/WG1AR5_ALL_FINAL.pdf.

————. *Climate Change 2014: Impacts, Adaptation, and Vulnerability. Part A: Global and Sectoral Aspects. Contribution of Working Group II to the Fifth Assessment Report of the Intergovernmental Panel on Climate Change.* Cambridge: Cambridge University Press, 2015. https://www.ipcc.ch/pdf/assessment-report/ar5/wg2/WGIIAR5-PartA_FINAL.pdf.

International Energy Agency. "Global Energy-Related Emissions of Carbon Dioxide Stalled in 2014." March 13, 2015. http://www.iea.org/newsroomandevents/news/2015/march/global-energy-related-emissions-of-carbon-dioxide-stalled-in-2014.html.

Jackson, Wes. *Consulting the Genius of the Place: An Ecological Approach to a New Agriculture.* New York: Counterpoint, 2010.

Jahan, Selim, et al. *Human Development Report 2015: Work for Human Development.* New York: UN Development Program, 2015.

Jamieson, Dale. *Reason in a Dark Time: Why the Struggle Against Climate Change Failed—and What It Means for Our Future.* Oxford: Oxford University Press, 2014.

Janitch, Michael (Sincedutch). "Large Microwave Pulse Produces Two Tropical Storms in Asia Within Forty-Eight Hours." October 20, 2013. http://www.tatoott1009.com/2013/11/08/did-weather-weapons-make-the-typhoon/.

Jenkins, Willis. *Ecologies of Grace, Environmental Ethics, and Christian Theology.* Oxford: Oxford University Press, 2008.

Jing, Chai. *Qiong Ding Zhi Xia* [Under the Dome]. Directed by Chai Jing. 2015. Beijing: Chai Jing, 2015.

John Paul II, Pope. "Address to Conference on Environment and Health." Vatican City, March 24, 1997. https://w2.vatican.va/content/john-paul-ii/en/speeches/1997/march/documents/hf_jp-ii_spe_19970324_ambiente-salute.html.

————. *Centesimus Annus.* London: Catholic Truth Society, 1991.

————. "Centesimus Annus." In *12 Trascendentales Mensajes Sociales.* Bogotá: Secretariado Nacional de Pastoral Social de Colombia, 1996.

————. "Christifideles Laici." In *12 Trascendentales Mensajes Sociales.* Bogotá: Secretariado Nacional de Pastoral Social de Colombia, 1996.

————. *Dives in Misericordia.* Vatican City: Vatican Polyglot Press, 1980. http://www.vatican.va/holy_father/john_paul_ii/encyclicals/documents/hf_jp-ii_enc_30111980_dives-in-misericordia_en.html.

————. *Dominum et Vivificantem: On the Holy Spirit in the Life of the Church and the World.* Washington, DC: U.S. Catholic Conference, 1986. http://w2.vatican.va/content/john-paul-ii/en/encyclicals/documents/hf_jp-ii_enc_18051986_dominum-et-vivificantem.html.

————. *Ecclesia in Africa: The Church in Africa and its Evangelizing Mission Toward the Year 2000.* Washington, DC: U.S. Catholic Conference, 1996. http://

w2.vatican.va/content/john-paul-ii/en/apost_exhortations/documents/hf_jp-ii_exh_14091995_ecclesia-in-africa.html.

———. *Pastores Gregis*. London: Catholic Truth Society, 2003. http://w2.vatican.va/content/john-paul-ii/en/apost_exhortations/documents/hf_jp-ii_exh_20031016_pastores-gregis.html.

———. "Peace with God the Creator, Peace with All of Creation: Message for the Celebration of the World Day of Peace, January 1, 1990." Vatican City, December 8, 1989. https://w2.vatican.va/content/john-paul-ii/en/messages/peace/documents/hf_jp-ii_mes_19891208_xxiii-world-day-for-peace.html.

———. *Redemptor Hominis: Redeemer of Man*. Washington, DC: U.S. Catholic Conference, 1979. http://w2.vatican.va/content/john-paul-ii/en/encyclicals/documents/hf_jp-ii_enc_04031979_redemptor-hominis.html.

———. *Sollicitudo Rei Socialis*. London: Catholic Truth Society, 2003. http://w2.vatican.va/content/john-paul-ii/en/encyclicals/documents/hf_jp-ii_enc_30121987_sollicitudo-rei-socialis.html.

———. "Sollicitudo Rei Socialis." In *12 Trascendentales Mensajes Sociales*. Bogotá: Secretariado Nacional de Pastoral Social de Colombia, 1996.

Johnson, Dave. "A Study of the Animistic Practices of the Waray People of the Leyte-Samar Region of the Philippine." Master's thesis, Asia Pacific Theological Seminary, 2000.

Johnson, Elizabeth. *Ask the Beast: Darwin and the God of Love*. London: Bloomsbury, 2014.

Kairos Southern Africa. *South Africa Kairos Document 1985*. https://kairossouthernafrica.wordpress.com/2011/05/08/the-south-africa-kairos-document-1985.

Kakuchi, Suvendrini. "In Tsunami, Women Put Modesty above Survival." We News, February 23, 2005. http://womensenews.org/story/the-world/050223/tsunami-women-put-modesty-above-survival.

Kashimbo Kalala, Serge, et al. "Impact of Liquid Tailings of Chemical Plant of Africa (CHEMAF) in Activity on Groundwater Quality in the Area of Tshamilemba in Lubumbashi (Katanga/DR Congo)." *International Journal of Innovation and Scientific Research* 16 (2015) 448–64.

Katongole, Emmanuel. "Mission and the Ephesian Moment of World Christianity: Pilgrimages of Pain and Hope and the Economics of Eating Together." *Mission Studies* 29 (2012) 183–200.

———. *Stories from Bethany: On the Faces of the Church in Africa*. Nairobi: Paulines, 2012.

Katsouris, Christina, and Aaron Syne. *Nigeria's Criminal Crude: International Options to Combat the Export of Stolen Oil*. London: Chatham House, 2013.

Kearns, Laurel. "Saving the Creation: Christian Environmentalism in the United States." *Sociology of Religion* 57 (1996) 55–70.

Keenan, James F. *Virtues for Ordinary Christians*. Kansas City: Sheed and Ward, 1996.

Kelley, Kevin J. "U.S. Study Links Climate Change to Violent Conflict in East Africa." *The East African*, October 30, 2012. http://www.theeastafrican.co.ke/news/US+study+links+change+in+temperature+to+violent+conflict/-/2558/1606780/-/peo8cf/-/index.html.

Knapton, Sarah. "Professor Stephen Hawking: Disaster on Planet Earth is a Near Certainty." *The Telegraph*, January 19, 2016. http://www.telegraph.co.uk/news/

science/science-news/12107623/Prof-Stephen-Hawking-disaster-on-planet-Earth-is-a-near-certainty.html.

Knox, Peter. *AIDS, Ancestors, and Salvation: Local Beliefs in Christian Ministry to the Sick*. Nairobi: Paulines, 2008.

——. "Theology, Ecology, and Africa: No Longer Strange Bedfellows." In *Reconciliation, Justice and Peace: The Second African Synod*, edited by A. E. Orobator, 159–170. Maryknoll: Orbis, 2011.

Koné, Yéfanlan José-Mathieu. "Dynamics of Carbon Dioxide and Methane in the Mangroves of Vietnam, and the Rivers and the Lagoons of Ivory Coast. " Doctoral dissertation, University of Liège, 2008.

Koszarek, Thaddeus J. "Stewardship of the Land." In "Five Conferences for Rural Retreats for Farmers." Undated, late 1940s. NCRLC 1/1/61, National Catholic Rural Life Conference Records, Marquette Archives, Marquette University Raynor Memorial Libraries.

Kumar, Satish. "The Ecozoic Era." *Resurgence & Ecologist* 279 (2013) 1–2.

Lamoureux, Patricia, and Paul J. Wadell. *The Christian Moral Life: Full Discipleship for a Global Society*. Maryknoll, NY: Orbis, 2010.

Land, Philip S., et al. *Justice in the World: Synod of Bishops*. Vatican City: Pontifical Council for Justice and Peace, 1972.

Lane, Jan-Erik. "The Resolution of the Cornucopian-Ecologist Issue." *Archives of Business Research* 2 (2014) 87–93.

Laszlo, Ervin, and Allan Combs, eds. *Thomas Berry, Dreamer of the Earth: The Spiritual Ecology of the Father of Environmentalism*. Rochester, VT: Inner Traditions, 2011.

Latin American Bishops' Conference (CELAM). "Concluding Document: Aparecida—Fifth General Conference of the Latin American and Caribbean Bishops." Bogotá: CELAM, 2007. http://www.aecrc.org/documents/Aparecida-Concluding%20Document.pdf.

——. "Concluding Document: Medellín—Second General Conference of the Latin American and Caribbean Bishops, 1968." Bogotá: CELAM, 2002.

——. "Documento Conclusivo: Industrias Extractivas (Minería e Hidrocarburos), la Problemática de los Recursos Naturales no Renovables en América Latina y la Misión de la Iglesia" [Concluding Document: Extractive Industries (Mining and Hydrocarbons): The Problem of Nonrenewable Natural Resources in Latin America and the Mission of the Church]. International Seminar, Lima, Peru, June 14–16, 2011. http://omiusajpic.org/files/2011/07/Documento-conclusivo-Seminario-Internacional-sobre-industrias-extractiva.pdf.

Lattimore, Mark. *The Book of Job: A Biography*. Princeton: Princeton University Press, 2013.

Lee, Michael. *Bearing the Weight of Salvation: The Soteriology of Ignacio Ellacuría*. New York: Crossroad, 2008.

Leiserowitz, Anthony. "American Risk Perceptions: Is Climate Change Dangerous?" *Risk Analysis* 25 (2005) 1433–42.

Leiserowitz, Anthony, et al. *Global Warming's Six Americas 2009: An Audience Segmentation Analysis*. Yale University and George Mason University. New Haven: Yale Program on Climate Change Communication, 2009.

Leo XIII, Pope. *Rerum Novarum: Encyclical on Capital and Labor*. Vatican City, 1891. http://w2.vatican.va/content/leo-xiii/en/encyclicals/documents/hf_l-xiii_enc_15051891_rerum-novarum.html.

Lewis, Martin. "Science, Progress and the End of the Modern World." *Soundings* 75 (1999) 307–32.

Lichauco de Leon, Sunshine, and Calum MacLeod. "Philippines Sifting through Horror in Typhoon Haiyan." *USA Today*, November 11, 2013. http://www.usatoday.com/story/news/world/2013/11/10/typhoon-haiyan-philippines-vietnam/3488431/.

Ligutti, Luigi G., and John C. Rawe. *Rural Roads to Security: America's Third Struggle for Freedom*. Milwaukee: Bruce, 1940.

Lindberg, Kreg, et al. *Ecotourism and Other Services from Forests in the Asia-Pacific Region: Outlook to 2010*. Rome and Bangkok: Food and Agriculture Organization (FAO) of the United Nations, October 1997. http://www.fao.org/3/a-w7714e.pdf.

Lindquist, Erik J., et al. "Global Forest Land-Use Change: 1990 to 2005." Rome: Food and Agriculture Organization (FAO) of the United Nations, 2012. http://www.fao.org/docrep/017/i3110e/i3110e.pdf.

List, John A., and Jason F. Shogren. "The Deadweight Loss of Christmas: Comment." *American Economic Review* 88 (1998) 1350–55.

Locsin, Joel. "NDRRMC: Yolanda Death Toll Hits 6,300 Mark Nearly Six Months after Typhoon." LBG, GMA News, April 17, 2014. http://www.gmanetwork.com/news/story/357322/news/nation/ndrrmc-yolanda-death-toll-hits-6-300-mark-nearly-6-months-after-typhoon.

Lodge, David, and Christopher Hamlin. *Religion and the New Ecology: Environmental Responsibility in a World of Flux*. Notre Dame: University of Notre Dame Press, 2006.

Lohmer, Francis. "Keeping Them Up on the Farm." *Sunday Visitor*, October 11, 1942. [NCRLC Clipping Files 11/1/8, National Catholic Rural Life Conference Records, Marquette Archives, Marquette University Raynor Memorial Libraries.]

Lomborg, Bjørn. *Cool It: The Skeptical Environmentalist Guide to Global Warming*. New York: Vintage, 2007.

———. *How Much Have Global Problems Cost the World? A Scorecard from 1900 to 2050*. Cambridge: Cambridge University Press, 2013.

———. *The Skeptical Environmentalist: Measuring the Real State of the World*. Cambridge: Cambridge University Press, 2001.

———. *Smart Solutions to Climate Change*. Cambridge: Cambridge University Press, 2010.

Lotilla, Raphael. "Flashback: 1897, Leyte and a Strong Typhoon." *Rappler*, November 20, 2013. http://www.rappler.com/move-ph/issues/disasters/typhoon-yolanda/44062-leyte-1897-typhoon.

Love, Robert. "The Samahan of Papa God: Tradition and Conversion in a Tagalog Peasant Religious Movement." Doctoral dissertation, Cornell University, 1977.

Lovelock, James. *The Ages of Gaia: A Biography of Our Living Earth*. Oxford: Oxford University Press, 1995.

———. *Healing Gaia*. New York: Harmony, 1991.

———. *The Revenge of Gaia: Why the Earth Is Fighting Back—and How We Can Still Save Humanity*. London: Penguin, 2007.

———. *The Vanishing Face of Gaia: A Final Warning*. London: Penguin, 2009.

Lovelock, James, and Andrew Watson. "Biological Homeostasis of the Global Environment: The Parable of Daisyworld." *Tellus* 34 (1983) 286–89.

Lynas, Mark. *The God Species: How the Planet Can Survive the Age of Humans*. London: Random House, 2011.

Lyons, Kristen, et al. "The Darker Side of Green: Plantation Forestry and Carbon Violence in Uganda." Oakland, CA: Oakland Institute, 2014. http://www.oaklandinstitute.org/sites/oaklandinstitute.org/files/Report_DarkerSideofGreen_hirez.pdf.

Maathai, Wangari. *The Challenge for Africa*. New York: Anchor, 2009.

Macauley, David. *Minding Nature: The Philosophers of Ecology*. New York: Guilford, 1996.

MacIntyre, Alasdair. *After Virtue: A Study of Moral Theory*. 2nd ed. London: Duckworth, 1985.

Macy, Joanna. "Working through Environmental Despair." In *Ecopsychology: Restoring the Earth, Healing the Mind*, edited by Theodore Rosak et al., 240–59. New York: Sierra Club, 1995.

Magesa, Laurenti. *African Religion: The Moral Traditions of Abundant Life*. Maryknoll, NY: Orbis, 1997.

Maguire, Daniel, and Larry Rassmusen. *Ethics for a Small Planet: New Horizons on Population, Consumption, and Ecology*. Albany: State University of New York Press, 1998.

Mahé, Thuriane. "Are Stated Preferences Confirmed by Purchasing Behaviours? The Case of Fair Trade-Certified Bananas in Switzerland." *Journal of Business Ethics* 92 (2010) 301–15.

Mahecha, Germán Roberto. *Aproximación a los Rasgos de una Espiritualidad Ecológica*. Bogotá: Pontifical Xaverian University, 2008.

———. "Aproximación a los Rasgos de una Espiritualidad Ecológica." *Theologica Xaveriana* 169 (2010) 105–32.

———. "Dios y Biología: La Vida como Punto de Encuentro para el Diálogo entre Saberes." *Theologica Xaveriana* 150 (2004) 267–80.

Mahecha, Germán Roberto, et al. *Educación Ambiental: Reflexiones Epistemológicas y Praxiológicas*. Bogotá: Javegraf, 2008.

Malthus, Thomas. *Essay on the Principle of Population*. London: Liberty Fund, 2000.

Margalef, Ramón. *Ecología*. Barcelona: Omega S.A., 1986.

Margulis, Lynn, and Karlene Schwartz. *Cinco Reinos: Guía Ilustrada de los Phyla de la Vida en la Tierra*. Barcelona: Editorial Labor S.A., 1985.

Marlett, Jeffrey D. *Saving the Heartland: Catholic Missionaries in Rural America, 1920–1960*. DeKalb: Northern Illinois University Press, 2002.

Marsh, George Perkins. *Man and Nature: Physical Geography as Modified by Human Action*. Cambridge: Belknap, 1965.

Marx, Reinhard Cardinal. "An Archbishop's Perspective on the Future of Theological Ethics." In *Catholic Theological Ethics: Past, Present, Future*, edited by James F. Keenan, 275–81. Maryknoll, NY: Orbis, 2011.

Mary Charlotte, Sister, and Mary Synon, et al. *These Are Our Horizons*. Faith and Freedom VIII. New York: Ginn, 1945. [NCRLC 5/2/24, National Catholic Rural Life Conference Records, Marquette Archives, Marquette University Raynor Memorial Libraries.]

"Mass for Youth on Jocist Lines: Ancient Symbolic Rites Will be Re-Enacted at St. Cloud." *St. Cloud Register*. Undated 1940. NCRLC Clipping Files 11/1/6, National Catholic Rural Life Conference Records, Marquette Archives, Marquette University Raynor Memorial Libraries.

Massey, Doreen. *Space, Place, and Gender*. Minneapolis: University of Minnesota Press, 1994.

Mathiesen, Karl. "Climate Change Aggravating Cyclone Damage, Scientists Say." *The Guardian*, March 16, 2015. https://www.theguardian.com/environment/2015/mar/16/climate-change-aggravating-cyclone-damage-scientists-say.

Mauss, Marcel. *The Gift: Forms and Functions of Exchange in Archaic Societies*. New York: Norton, 1925.

Mbiti, John S. *African Religions and Philosophy*. London: Heinemann, 1969.

McCarthy, John. "Catholic Social Teaching and Ecology Fact Sheet." Rome: Society of Jesus Social Justice Secretariat, undated. http://sjweb.info/sjs/networks/ecology/CST_ENG.pdf.

McClean, Dennis. "Bieber Puts Spotlight on Disaster Zone Schools." United Nations Office for Disaster Risk Reduction (UNISDR), December 13, 2013. http://www.unisdr.org/archive/35866.

McDaniel, Jay. "'Where Is the Holy Spirit Anyway?' Response to a Skeptical Environmentalist." *Ecumenical Review* 42 (1990) 162–74.

McDonaugh, Sean. *The Greening of the Church*. Maryknoll, NY: Orbis, 1990.

———. *Passion for the Earth*. Ecology and Justice Series. Maryknoll, NY: Orbis, 1994.

McFague, Sallie. *The Body of God: An Ecological Theology*. Minneapolis: Augsburg Fortress, 1993.

McKechnie, Sally, and Caroline Tynan. "Social Meanings in Christmas Consumption: An Exploratory Study of UK Celebrants' Consumption Rituals." *Journal of Consumer Behaviour* 5 (2006) 130–44.

McKibben, Bill. *The Comforting Whirlwind: God, Job, and the Scale of Creation*. Grand Rapids: Eerdmans, 1994.

———. *Deep Economy: The Wealth of Communities and the Durable Future*. New York: Time, 2008.

Meadows, Donella H., et al. *Limits to Growth*. Potomac Associates. New York: Universe, 1972. http://www.donellameadows.org/the-limits-to-growth-now-available-to-read-online.

Meadows, Donella H., et al. *Limits to Growth: The Thirty-Year Update*. Burlington, VT: Chelsea Green, 2004.

Mellor, Leo. "The Lure of Wilderness." In *The Cambridge Companion to Literature and the Environment*, edited by Louise Westling, 104–18. Cambridge: Cambridge University Press, 2013.

Mendoza Alvarez, Carlos. "Eschatology and Apocalypse in Post-Modern Times." In *The Return of Apocalypticism*, edited by Hille Haker et al., 71–82. London: SCM, 2014.

Merchant, Carolyn. *The Death of Nature: Women, Ecology, and the Scientific Revolution*. San Francisco: Harper and Row, 1980.

———. *Ecological Revolutions: Nature, Gender, and Science in New England*. Chapel Hill: University of North Carolina Press, 1989.

Meredith, Martin. *The Fortunes of Africa: A Five-Thousand-Year History of Wealth, Greed, and Endeavor*. New York: Public Affairs, 2014.

Merton, Robert King. *Science, Technology, and Society in Seventeenth-Century England*. New York: H. Fertig, 1970.

Mesters, Carlos. *Eden: Golden Age or Goad to Action?* Translated by Patrick J. Leonard. Maryknoll, NY: Orbis, 1971.

Metz, Johannes B. *Faith in History and Society: Toward a Practical Fundamental Theology.* Translated and edited by J. Matthew Ashley. New York: Crossroad, 2007.

Michaels, Kenneth. "Oasis." *Rural Life News,* August 9, 1942. NCRLC Clipping Files 11/1/8, National Catholic Rural Life Conference Records, Marquette Archives, Marquette University Raynor Memorial Libraries.

Michel, Virgil. "Ownership and the Human Person." *The Review of Politics* 1 (1939) 155–78.

Midgley, Dominic. "Kidnap of the Tycoon's Tragic Grandson." *Express: Home of the Daily and Sunday Express,* July 8, 2013. http://www.express.co.uk/news/ uk/413215/Kidnap-of-the-tycoon-s-tragic-grandson.

Miller, Banks. "Ecology and the Post-Apocalypse." *Strange Horizons,* August 22, 2011. http://www.strangehorizons.com/2011/20110822/banks-a.shtml.

Miller, Patrick. "Heaven's Prisoners: The Lament as Christian Prayer." In *Lament: Reclaiming Practices in Pulpit, Pew, and Public Square,* edited by Sally A. Brown and Patrick D. Miller, 15–26. Louisville: Westminster John Knox, 2005.

Moe-Lobeda, Cynthia, and Daniel Spencer. "Free Trade Agreements and the Neo-liberal Economic Paradigm: Economic, Ecological, and Moral Consequences." *Political Theology* 10 (2009) 685–716.

Moltmann, Jürgen. "Is the World Unfinished? On Interactions between Science and Theology in the Concepts of Nature, Time, and the Future." *Theology* 114 (2011) 403–13.

Moody, Harry, and W. Andrew Achenbaum. "Solidarity Sustainability and Stewardship: Ethics across Generations." *Interpretations: A Journal of Bible and Theology* 68 (2014) 150–58.

Moore, Kathleen D. "The Truth of the Barnacles: Rachel Carson and the Moral Significance of Wonder." *Environmental Ethics* 27 (2005) 265–77.

Moran, Ashley McIlvain, et al. "Climate Change and Security in Africa: Clear Risks, Nuanced Impacts." GMACCC Paper No. 1, December 2014. The Hague: Institute for Environmental Security, 2014. http://www.envirosecurity.org/Climate_ Change_and_Security_in_Africa.pdf.

Morandini, Simone. "Reflections on the Relationship between Ecology and Theological Ethics." In *Applied Ethics in a World Church: The Padua Conference,* edited by Linda Hogan, 73–82. Maryknoll, NY: Orbis, 2008.

Moses, Paul. *The Saint and the Sultan: The Crusades, Islam, and Francis of Assisi's Mission of Peace.* New York: Doubleday, 2009.

Mumford, Lewis. *Technics and Civilization.* New York: Harcourt, Brace, 1934.

Murdoch, Iris. *The Good Apprentice.* New York: Penguin, 1985.

Muzaffar, Chandra. "Conclusion." In *Subverting Greed: Religious Perspectives on the Global Economy,* edited by Paul F. Knitter and Chandra Muzaffar, 154–72. Maryknoll, NY: Orbis, 2002.

Mwambazambi, Kalemba. "KÄ Mana Champion of the Theology of Reconstruction." In vol. 3 of *African Theology: The Contribution of the Founders,* edited by Benézét Bujo. Nairobi: Paulines, 2012.

Nagle, John Copeland. "The Evangelical Debate over Climate Change." *University of St. Thomas Law Journal* 5 (2008) 53–86.

Nash, James A. "Dimensions and Dilemmas of the Ecological Crisis: Exceeding the Limits." In *Loving Nature: Ecological Integrity and Christian Responsibility,* 40–63. Nashville: Abingdon, 1991.

National Administrative Department of Statistics of Colombia [Departamento Administrativo Nacional de Estadística (DANE)]. "Pobreza Monetaria Año Móvil Julio 2013–Junio 2014" [Monetary Poverty, July 2013–June 2014]. September 15, 2014. http://www.dane.gov.co/index.php/calidad-vida/pobreza/87-sociales/calidad-de-vida/5699-pobreza-monetaria-ano-movil-julio-2013-junio-2014.

National Assistance Coordination Board. "PSA: Poverty Incidence among Filipinos Registered at 24.9% as of First Semester of 2013." *Official Gazette*, April 29, 2014. http://www.gov.ph/2014/04/29/psa-poverty-incidence-among-filipinos-registered-at-24-9-as-of-first-semester-of-2013/.

"National Catholic Leaders Assemble." *Seattle Daily Times*, October 16, 1939.

National Catholic Rural Life Conference. *Manifesto on Rural Life*. Milwaukee: Bruce, 1939.

———. "Mechanization for the Small Farm." August 12, 1945. NCRLC Press Release 6/9/15, National Catholic Rural Life Conference Records, Marquette Archives, Marquette University Raynor Memorial Libraries.

———. "Program, NCRLC Annual Meeting, Jefferson City, Missouri, October 1941." NCRLC Clipping Files 9/4/1941, National Catholic Rural Life Conference Records, Marquette Archives, Marquette University Raynor Memorial Libraries.

———. "Resolutions, NCRLC Annual Meeting, Jefferson City, Missouri, October 1941." NCRLC Clipping Files 9/4/1941, National Catholic Rural Life Conference Records, Marquette Archives, Marquette University Raynor Memorial Libraries.

———. "Rural Life Summer Schools: Meeting of the Directors, October 1943." NCRLC 1.1/5/24, National Catholic Rural Life Conference Records, Marquette Archives, Marquette University Raynor Memorial Libraries.

———. "Rural Life Summer Schools: Program of the Collegeville Summer School." 1940, 1943. NCRLC 1.1/5/24, National Catholic Rural Life Conference Records, Marquette Archives, Marquette University Raynor Memorial Libraries.

National Catholic Rural Life Conference Records. NCRLC Clipping Files 11/1. Marquette Archives, Marquette University Raynor Memorial Libraries.

National Center for Charitable Statistics. "Profiles of Individual Charitable Contributions by State, 2011." Washington, DC: The Urban Institute's Center on Nonprofits and Philanthropy, 2013. http://nccsweb.urban.org/knowledgebase/showFile.php?file=bmNjczE1NDE=.

National Geographic News. "The Deadliest Tsunami in History?" January 7, 2005. http://news.nationalgeographic.com/news/2004/12/1227_041226_tsunami.html.

Natural Hazards: Risk Atlas 2015. Bath, UK: Verisk Maplecroft, 2015. https://maplecroft.com/portfolio/new-analysis/2015/03/04/56-100-cities-most-exposed-natural-hazards-found-key-economies-philippines-japan-china-bangladesh-verisk-maplecroft/.

Ndung'u, Nahashon W. "Environmental Management: Constraints and Prospects in Africa in the Twenty-First Century." In *Challenges and Prospects of the Church in Africa: Theological Reflections of the Twenty-First Century*, edited by Nahashon W. Ndung'u and Philomena Mwaura, 54–70. Nairobi: Paulines Africa, 2005.

Neira, Enrique. *La Cosmovisión de Teilhard de Chardin*. Bogotá: Pontifical Xaverian University, 2005.

Nelkin, Horthy, and Lori Andrews. "*Homo Economicus*: Commercialization of Body Tissue in the Age of Biotechnology." *Hasting Center Report* 28 (1998) 30–39.

Neussner, Olaf. "Assessment of Early Warning Efforts in Leyte for Typhoon Haiyan/ Yolanda." Deutsche Gesellschaft für Internationale Zusammenarbeit (GIZ) GmbH, 2014. http://www.preventionweb.net/english/professional/publications/v. php?id=36860.

Nichols, Alexander J. "Strategic Options in Fair Trade Retailing." *International Journal of Retail and Distribution Management* 30 (2002) 6–17.

Nicholls, Robert J., et al. "Coastal Systems and Low-Lying Areas." In *Climate Change 2007: Impacts, Adaptation and Vulnerability; Contribution of Working Group II to the Fourth Assessment Report of the Intergovernmental Panel on Climate Change.* Cambridge: Cambridge University Press, 2007. https://www.ipcc.ch/pdf/ assessment-report/ar4/wg2/ar4-wg2-chapter6.pdf.

Northcott, Michael S. *An Angel Directs the Storm: Apocalyptic Religion and American Empire.* London: I. B. Tauris, 2004.

———. "Artificial Persons against Nature: Environmental Governmentality, Economic Corporations, and Ecological Ethics." *Annals of the New York Academy of Sciences* 1249:1 (2012) 104–17.

———. *A Political Theology of Climate Change.* Grand Rapids: Eerdmans, 2013.

Nuss, Philip, and Matthew J. Eckelman. "Life Cycle Assessment of Metals: A Scientific Synthesis." *PLOS One* 9 (2014) 1–12.

Obeng, Emmanuel A. "Healing the Groaning Creation in Africa." In *Theology of Reconstruction: Exploratory Essays,* edited by Mary Getui and Emmanuel A. Obeng, 10–27. 2nd ed. Nairobi: Acton, 2003.

Obi, Edward Osang. "The Exploitation of Natural Resources: Reconfiguring Economic Relations toward a Community-of-Interests Perspective." In *Just Sustainability: Technology, Ecology, and Resource Extraction,* edited by Christiana Z. Peppard and Andrea Vicini, 223–30. Maryknoll, NY: Orbis, 2015.

———. "Oil Corporations' Private Ownership in South-South Nigeria in Light of the Universal Destination of Goods: Bringing Participative Ownership into the Global Public Goods Discourse." PhD diss., Katholieke Universiteit Leuven, 2009.

Odchigue, Randy J. C. "The Ecclesial Contribution to Sustainable Communities." In *Just Sustainability: Technology, Ecology, and Resource Extraction,* edited by Christiana Z. Peppard and Andrea Vicini, 171–81. Maryknoll, NY: Orbis, 2015.

———. "Recasting Christian and Cultural Resources for Environment and Sustainability." *Asian Horizons: Dharmaram Journal of Theology* 6 (2012) 274–77.

O'Donovan, Oliver. *The Desire of the Nations: Rediscovering the Roots of Political Theology.* Cambridge: Cambridge University Press, 1996.

Odum, Eugene. *Ecología.* Mexico City: Interamericana, 1987.

———. *Ecology: A Bridge between Science and Society.* Sunderland: Sinauer Associates, 1997.

———. *Fundamentals of Ecology.* 2nd ed. Philadelphia: W. B. Sanders, 1959.

———. *Fundamentals of Ecology.* 3rd ed. London: Holt, 1971.

Olopade, Dayo. *The Bright Continent: Breaking Rules and Making Change in Modern Africa.* Boston: Houghton Mifflin Harcourt, 2014.

Olupona, Jacob. "Religion and Ecology in African Culture and Society." In *The Oxford Handbook of Religion and Ecology,* edited by Roger S. Gottlieb, 268–74. Oxford: Oxford University Press, 2006.

O'Neill, John. *Ecology, Policy, and Politics: Human Well-Being and the Natural World.* London: Routledge, 1993.

Osorio, Flor Edilma. "Tierra y Territorio en las Dinámicas de Guerra y de Reconciliación" ["Land and Territory in the Dynamics of War and Reconciliation"]. Presentation at the Episcopal Conference of Colombia's Third National Reconciliation Conference. Bogotá, Colombia, May 23–25, 2005.

"Over 3,800 Catholic Students in Diocese Submit Entries in Rural Life Essay Contest." *Columbus Register*, October 28, 1949. NCRLC 11/2/4, National Catholic Rural Life Conference Records, Marquette Archives, Marquette University Raynor Memorial Libraries.

Oyebade, B. A., et al. "Quantitative Review and Distribution Status of Mangrove Forest Species in West Africa." *African Research Review* 4 (2010) 80–89.

Pachauri, Rajendra, et al. "Climate Change 2014 Synthesis Report." https://www.ipcc.ch/pdf/assessment-report/ar5/syr/SYR_AR5_FINAL_full.pdf.

Pachauri, Rajendra K., et al. *Climate Change 2007: Synthesis Report. Contribution of Working Groups I, II, and III to the Fourth Assessment Report of the Intergovernmental Panel on Climate Change.* Geneva: Intergovernmental Panel on Climate Change (IPCC), 2008. http://www.ipcc.ch/publications_and_data/publications_ipcc_fourth_assessment_report_synthesis_report.htm.

Pan Amazon Church Network (REPAM). *Informe Ejecutivo del Encuentro Fundacional Red Eclesial Pan-Amazónica REPAM.* Brasilia: REPAM, 2014. http://www.cpalsocial.org/documentos/104.pdf.

———. *Memoria del Encuentro Fundacional: 9 al 12 de Septiembre de 2014, Brasilia, Brasil.* Brasilia: REPAM, 2014. http://www.comboni.org/risorse/allegati/1266.pdf.

Paul VI, Pope. *Octogesima Adveniens.* Apostolic Letter from the Vatican, May 14, 1971. http://w2.vatican.va/content/paul-vi/en/apost_letters/documents/hf_p-vi_apl_19710514_octogesima-adveniens.html.

———. "Octogesima Adveniens." In *12 Trascendentales Mensajes Sociales.* Bogotá: Secretariado Nacional de Pastoral Social de Colombia, 1996.

———. *Populorum Progressio: On the Development of Peoples.* Washington, DC: Office of Public Services, U.S. Catholic Conference, 1967.

Pearlman, Jonathan. "Tsunami-Ravaged Aceh in Indonesia Now Faces Rising Islamic Fundamentalism." *The Telegraph*, December 25, 2014. http://www.asiaeu.com/asia/tsunami-ravaged-aceh-in-indonesia-now-faces-rising-islamic-fundamentalism-h109089.html.

Peerenboom, Jean. "Rev. Koszarek 'Practiced What He Preached.'" *Green Bay Press Gazette*, January 3, 2007.

Perez, Rosa. "Responding to the Challenges of the Rising Sea." In *Disturbing Climate*, edited by Jose Villarin, 17–24. Quezon City: Manila Observatory, Ateneo de Manila University, 2001.

Pertierra, Raul. *Religion, Politics and Rationality in a Philippine Community.* Quezon City: Ateneo de Manila University, 1988.

Petilla, Danny. "True Ghost Story from Leyte's Saintly Priest." *Inquirer.net*, November 2, 2014. http://newsinfo.inquirer.net/648274/true-ghost-story-from-leytes-saintly-priest#ixzz3UASAfTqk.

Phan, Peter. "Eschatology and Ecology: The Environment in the End-Time." *Irish Theological Quarterly* 62 (1996–97) 3–16.

Philippine Atmospheric, Geophysical, and Astronomical Services Administration (PAGASA). "Impacts of Climate Change." In *Climate Change in the Philippines*, 46–52. Quezon City: Department of Science and Technology–PAGASA, 2011.

http://dilg.gov.ph/PDF_File/reports_resources/DILG-Resources-2012130-
2ef223f591.pdf.

Philippines Hurricane Yolanda Structural Assessment. "ASCE Philippines Hurricane
Yolanda Post-Disaster Investigation." UNC Charlotte–The William States Lee
College of Engineering. http://physa.uncc.edu.

Phuong, Vu Tan, and Jinke van Dam. "Linkage between Forests and Water: A Review of
Research Evidence in Vietnam." *European Tropical Forest Research Network News*
45/46 (2005–2006) 16–19.

Pieper, Josef. *In Tune with the World: A Theory of Festivity*. South Bend, IN: St.
Augustine's, 1999.

Pilario, Daniel Franklin. "(Post)Apocalyptic Reflections from 'Ground Zero.'" In *The
Return of Apocalypticism*, edited by Hille Haker et al., 104–10. London, SCM,
2014.

"Planetary Boundaries: A Safe Operating Space for Humanity." Stockholm Resilience
Center.   http://www.stockholmresilience.org/download/18.6d8f5d4d14b3
2b2493577/1459560273797/SOS+for+Business+2015.pdf.

Pontifical Council for Justice and Peace. *Compendium of the Social Doctrine of the
Church*. Manila: Catholic Bishops' Conference of the Philippines, 2004.

Pontifical Council for Justice and Peace, and Marjorie Keenan. *From Stockholm
to Johannesburg: An Historical Overview of the Concern of the Holy See for the
Environment 1972–2002*. Vatican City: Vatican, 2002.

Poorthuis, Marcel. "The Prohibition of Idolatry: Source of Humanity or Source of
Violence?" In *Desirable God? Our Fascination with Images, Idols, and New Deities*,
edited by Roger Burggraeve et al., 39–60. Leuven: Peeters, 2003.

Porritt, Jonathon. "Capitalism as if the World Matters." *Jonathon Porritt:
Environmentalist & Writer* (blog), October 22, 2007. http://www.jonathonporritt.
com/blog/capitalism-if-world-matters.

———. *Capitalism as if the World Matters*. London: Earthscan, 2007.

Primavera, Jurgenne H., and Marcelino Tumanda Jr. "The Agusan Marsh: A Situationer
with Focus on Scientific Aspects." In *Proceedings of the First Scientific Conference
of the Agusan Marsh: Butuan City, Agusan del Norte, Philippines, 21–23 May 2007*,
edited by Jurgenne H. Primavera, 5–11. Jakarta: Philippine Council for Aquatic
and Marine Research and Development, 2008.

Primavesi, Anne. *From Apocalypse to Genesis: Ecology, Feminism. and Christianity*.
Tunbridge Wells, UK: Burns and Oates, 1991.

Principe, Kristine E., and Joseph G. Eisenhauer. "Gift-Giving and Deadweight Loss."
The Journal of Socio-Economics 38 (2009) 215–20.

Ratzinger, Joseph Cardinal. "Lo Splendore della Pace di Francesco." *30Giorni*, January
2002. http://www.30giorni.it/articoli_id_375_l1.htm.

———. "The New Covenant: A Theology of Covenant in the New Testament."
Communio: International Catholic Review 22 (1995) 633–51.

Raup, David, and John Sepkoski Jr. "Mass Extinctions in the Marine Fossil Record."
Science 215 (1982) 1501–3.

Real Academia Española. *Diccionario de la Lengua Española*. http://dle.rae.
es/?w=diccionario.

Recepcion, Andrew G. "The Filipino Transpersonal Worldview." *Asian Christian
Review* 1 (2007) 67–75.

Renouard, Cécile, and Gaël Giraud. "Postface." In *Twenty Propositions for the Reform of Capitalism* (20 Propositions pour Réformer le Capitalism). Paris: Flammarion, 2009. www.barchen.fr/20propositions/assets/postface_en.pdf.

Republic of Colombia, Ministry of Labor. Decree No. 2731 (December 30, 2014). http://www.mintrabajo.gov.co/normatividad-diciembre-decretos-2014/4118-decreto-2731-del-30-de-diciembre-de-2014.html.

Rigby, Kate. "Confronting Catastrophes: Ecocriticism in a Warming World." In *The Cambridge Companion to Literature and the Environment*, edited by Louise Westling, 212–25. Cambridge: Cambridge University Press, 2013.

———. *Dancing with Disasters: Environmental Histories, Narratives, and Ethics for Perilous Times*. Charlottesville: University of Virginia Press, 2015.

———. "Noah's Ark Revisited: (Counter-)Utopianism and (Eco-)Catastrophe." *Arena Journal* 31 (2008) 163–78.

Roa, Elnor. "Mercury Pollution: A Threat to Agusan Marsh." In *Proceedings of the First Scientific Conference of the Agusan Marsh: Butuan City, Agusan del Norte, Philippines, 21–23 May 2007*, edited by Jurgenne H. Primavera, 33–37. Jakarta: Philippine Council for Aquatic and Marine Research and Development, 2008.

Roca, Joaquín García. "Apocalyptic and Global Crisis." *Concilium* 3 (2014) 83–95.

Rockström, Johan. "Addressing Some Key Misconceptions." Stockholm: Stockholm Resilience Centre, 2009. http://www.stockholmresilience.org/research/research-news/2012-07-02-addressing-some-key-misconceptions.html.

Rockström, Johan, et al. "Planetary Boundaries: Exploring the Safe Operating Space for Humanity." *Ecology and Society* 14 (2009) 32. http://www.ecologyandsociety.org/vol14/iss2/art32.

———. "A Safe Operating Space for Humanity." *Nature* 461 (2009) 472–75. http://www.nature.com/nature/journal/v461/n7263/full/461472a.html.

———. "Supplementary Information." *Ecology and Society* 14 (2009) 1–22.

Rodrigues, Ana S. L., et al. "Boom-and-Bust Development Patterns across the Amazon Deforestation Frontier." *Science* 324 (2009) 1435–37.

Rodríguez, Leonardo. "Se Disparó la Igualdad: La Desigualdad entre Ricos y Pobres en Colombia Dejó de Ser Preocupante. Ahora es Aterradora." *El Espectador*, December 7, 2003.

Rodríguez, Stella. *Resiliencia: Otra Manera de Ver la Adversidad*. Colección Fe y Universidad 16. Bogotá: Pontifical Xavieran University, 2006.

Rosen, Elizabeth K. *Apocalyptic Transformation: Apocalypse and Postmodern Imagination*. Lanham, MD: Lexington, 2008.

Ross, Philippa. "Why Gender Disaster Data Matters: 'In Some Villages, All the Dead Were Women.'" *The Guardian*, September 8, 2014. https://www.theguardian.com/global-development-professionals-network/2014/sep/08/disaster-humanitarian-response-data-gender.

Ruffle, Bradley J., and Orit Tykocinski. "The Deadweight Loss of Christmas: Comment." *American Economic Review* 90 (2000) 319–24.

Rupp, George. "Religion, Modern Secular Culture, and Ecology." *Daedalus* 130 (2001) 23–30.

Ryan, John Charles. "Narrative Environmental Ethics, Nature Writing, and Ecological Science as Tradition: Towards a Sponsoring Ground of Concern." *Philosophy Study* 2 (2012) 822–34.

Ryan, Larry, and Ciara McCarthy. "An Analysis of Donation Rates at Christmas." Dublin: Behaviour and Attitudes, 2014. http://www.fundraisingireland.ie/assets/files/Fundraising%20Ireland%20Christmas%20Giving%20and%20Public%20Opinion%20Surveys%202014.pdf.

Salamon, Sonya. *Prairie Patrimony: Family, Farming, and Community in the Midwest.* Chapel Hill: University of North Carolina Press, 1992.

Sandler, Ronald. *Character and Environment: A Virtue-Oriented Approach to Environmental Ethics.* New York: Columbia University Press, 2007.

Sandler, Ronald, and Philip Cafaro. *Environmental Virtue Ethics.* New York: Rowman & Littlefield, 2005.

Scanlan, Michael. *The San Damiano Cross: An Explanation.* Steubenville, OH: Franciscan University of Steubenville, 2007.

Schaefer, Jame, and Tobias Winright. *Environmental Justice and Climate Change: Assessing Pope Benedict XVI's Ecological Vision for the Catholic Church in the United States.* Lanham, MD: Lexington, 2013.

Schaper, Donna. "Noah's Ark: A Symbol for a People's Climate March." *National Catholic Reporter,* September 16, 2014. http://ncronline.org/blogs/eco-catholic/noahs-ark-symbol-peoples-climate-march.

Schimek, William. Letter to Minnesota pastors. December 11, 1944. "Rural Retreat Materials." NCRLC 1/1/61, National Catholic Rural Life Conference Records, Marquette Archives, Marquette University Raynor Memorial Libraries.

———. "Retreats for Farmers." *Land and Home* 9 (1946) 5–7.

Schirber, Martin. "An Open Letter to Sisters." *Land and Home* 8 (March 1945) 8–9.

———. "Rural Life Schools—Reconversion." *Land and Home* 9 (March 1946) 1–2.

Schumacher, John N. "Syncretism in Philippine Catholicism: Its Historical Causes." *Philippine Studies* 32 (1984) 251–72.

Shapiro, Edward. "Catholic Agrarian Thought and the New Deal." *Catholic Historical Review* 6 (1979) 583–99.

Shaw, Bill. "A Virtue Ethics Approach to Aldo Leopold's Land Ethic." *Environmental Ethics* 19 (1997) 53–67.

Shellenberger, Michael, and Ted Nordhaus. *The Death of Environmentalism: Global Warming Politics in a Post-Environmental World.* New York: The Breakthrough Institute, 2004.

Sherwood, Angela, et al. "Resolving Post-Disaster Displacement: Insights from the Philippines after Typhoon Haiyan (Yolanda)." Washington, DC: Brookings Institution/International Organization for Migration, 2015. http://www.brookings.edu/~/media/research/files/reports/2015/06/15-philippines-typhoon-haiyan-displacement-solutions/resolving-postdisaster-displacementinsights-from-the-philippines-after-typhoon-haiyan-june-2015.pdf.

Silva, Cristina. "Philippines Typhoon Hagupit Update 2014: Thousands Stranded in Evacuation Centers." *International Business Times,* December 11, 2014. http://www.ibtimes.com/philippines-typhoon-hagupit-update-2014-thousands-stranded-evacuation-centers-photos-1749641.

Simon, Julian. *The Resourceful Earth: A Response to Global 2000.* London: Blackwell, 1984.

Sindima, Harvey. "Community of Life: Ecological Theology in African Perspective." In *Liberating Life: Contemporary Approaches to Ecological Theology,* edited by Charles Birch et al., 137–47. Reprint, Eugene, OR: Wipf and Stock, 2007.

Singh, Timon. "Vatican City Crowned the 'Greenest State in the World.'" *Inhabitat* (blog), October 12, 2010. http://inhabitat.com/the-vatican-city-is-the-greenest-state-in-the-world/.

"Situation Report on the Effects of Typhoon Pablo (NDRRMC)." *Official Gazette*, December 17, 2012. No pages. http://www.gov.ph/2012/12/17/situation-report-on-the-effects-of-typhoon-pablo-ndrrmc-december-17-2012-as-of-8-a-m/.

Sklair, Leslie. *Globalization, Capitalism, and Its Alternatives*. 2nd ed. Oxford: Oxford University Press, 2002.

——. *Sociology of the Global System*. 2nd ed. Baltimore: Johns Hopkins University Press, 1995.

——. *The Transnational Capitalist Class*. Malden: Blackwell, 2001.

Social Affairs Commission of the Canadian Conference of Catholic Bishops. "A Pastoral Letter on the Christian Ecological Imperative: 'You Love All that Exists . . . All Things are Yours, God, Lover of Life.'" http://www.cccb.ca/site/Files/pastoralenvironment.html.

Solnick, Sara J., and David Hemenway. "The Deadweight Loss of Christmas: Comment." *American Economic Review* 86 (1996) 1299–1305.

——. "The Deadweight Loss of Christmas: Comment." *American Economic Review* 88 (1998) 1356–57.

——. "The Deadweight Loss of Christmas: Reply." *American Economic Review* 90 (2000) 325.

"Speciocide." *Environmental Science for Social Change*, June 5, 2012. http://essc.org.ph/content/view/681/153/.

St. Francis Xavier University. *How St. F. X. University Educates for Action: The Story of the Remarkable Results Achieved by the Extension Department of St. Francis Xavier University, Antigonish, Nova Scotia*. New York: Cooperative League, 1935.

Stakeholder Democracy Network (SDN). *Communities Not Criminals: Illegal Oil Refining in the Niger Delta*. London and Port Harcourt, Nigeria: SDN International Secretariat and SDN Nigeria Secretariat, 2014. http://www.stakeholderdemocracy.org/wp-content/uploads/2015/04/CommunitiesNotCriminals.pdf.

Standard Bank. "Rise of the Middle Class in Sub-Saharan Africa." *Standard Bank Team* (blog), August 20, 2014. http://www.blog.standardbank.com/node/61428.

"Statement of the Conference, 'Churches for Water in Africa,' 21–25 May 2007, Entebbe, Uganda." Entebbe, Uganda: Ecumenical Water Network (EWN), 2007. https://www.oikoumene.org/en/resources/documents/wcc-programmes/justice-diakonia-and-responsibility-for-creation/climate-change-water/statement-of-the-conference-churches-for-water-in-africa.

Steffen, Will, et al. "The Anthropocene: Are Humans Now Overwhelming the Great Forces of Nature?" *Ambio: A Journal of the Human Environment* 36 (2007) 614–21.

——. "The Anthropocene: From Global Change to Planetary Stewardship." *Ambio: A Journal of the Human Environment* 40 (2011) 739–61.

Stewart, Iain, and John Lynch. *Earth: The Biography*. Washington, DC: National Geographic Society, 2007.

Stichnothe, Heinz, et al. "Carbon Footprint Estimation of Food Production Systems: The Importance of Considering Methane and Nitrous Oxide." *Aspects of Applied Biology* 87 (2008) 65–71.

Stockholm Resilience Centre. *Planetary Boundaries Research*. 2015. http://www. stockholmresilience.org/images/18.3110ee8c1495db74432676c/1421678696891/ PB_FIG33_globaia+16+Jan.jpg.

Stoll, Mark. *Protestantism, Capitalism, and Nature in America*. Albuquerque: University of New Mexico Press, 1997.

Stratman, Thomas B. "St. Francis of Assisi: Brother to All Creatures." *Spirituality Today* 34 (1982) 222–32. http://opcentral.org/resources/2015/01/12/thomas-b-stratman-st-francis-of-assisi-brother-to-all-creatures/.

Straumann, Lukas. *Money Logging: On the Trail of the Asian Timber Mafia*. Geneva: Bergli, 2014.

Sturm, Christoph Christian. *Christoph Christian Sturm's Betrachtungen über die Werke Gottes im Reiche der Natur und der Vorsehung auf alle Tage des Jahres*. Edited by Bernard Galura. 2 vols. Augsburg: Mon'schen, 1813.

———. *Sturm's Reflections on the Works of God, and His Providence throughout All Nature*. Philadelphia: Woodward, 1832.

Sucaldito, Milagros, and Olga Nuñeza. "Distribution of the Avifauna of Agusan March, Agusan del Sur, Philippines." In *Proceedings of the First Scientific Conference of the Agusan Marsh: Butuan City, Agusan del Norte, Philippines, 21–23 May 2007*, edited by Jurgenne H. Primavera, 51–68. Jakarta: Philippine Council for Aquatic and Marine Research and Development, 2008.

Suliman, Mohamed. *Ecology, Politics, and Violent Conflict*. New York: Zed, 1999.

Swyngedouw, Erik. "Apocalypse Now! Fear and Doomsday Pleasures." *Capitalism, Nature, Socialism* 24 (2013) 9–18.

Tawney, Richard H. *Religion and the Rise of Capitalism*. Harmondsworth, UK: Penguin, 1972.

Taxacher, Gregor. "God in Opposition: The Value of a Critique of Apocalyptic Reason." In *The Return of Apocalypticism*, edited by Hille Haker et al. London: SCM, 2014.

Taylor, Sarah McFarland. *Green Sisters: A Spiritual Ecology*. Cambridge, MA: Harvard University Press, 2009.

Teisl, Mario.F., et al. "Can Eco-Labels Tune a Market? Evidence from Dolphin-Safe Labeling." *Journal of Environmental Economics and Management* 43 (2002) 339–59.

"Tenke Fungurume Copper Mine DRC." March 11, 2011. Counter Balance: Challenging Public Investment Banks; "EIB Case Studies" Archives. http://www.counter-balance.org/tenke-fungurume-copper-mine-drc/.

Third International Synod of Bishops. "Concluding Document: Justitia in Mundo (Justice in the World)." November 30, 1971. https://www.cctwincities.org/wp-content/uploads/2015/10/Justicia-in-Mundo.pdf.

Thompson, Allen, and Jeremy Bendik-Keymer. *Ethical Adaptation to Climate Change: Human Virtues of the Future*. Cambridge: MIT Press, 2012.

Thompson, E. P. *Customs in Common: Studies in Traditional Popular Culture*. London: Merlin, 1991.

Thurow, Roger. *The Last Hunger Season: A Year in an African Farm Community on the Brink of Change*. New York: Public Affairs, 2013.

Thurow, Roger, and Scott Kilman. *Enough: Why the World's Poorest Starve in an Age of Plenty*. New York: Public Affairs, 2010.

"Tickets for Sale for Rural Life Pageant Nov. 6." *Columbus Register*, October 21, 1949. NCRLC 11/2/4, National Catholic Rural Life Conference Records, Marquette Archives, Marquette University Raynor Memorial Libraries.

Tilley, Terrence. *The Evils of Theodicy*. Washington, DC: Georgetown University Press, 1991.

Timberlake, Lloyd. *Africa in Crisis: The Causes, the Cures of Environmental Bankruptcy*. Philadelphia: New Society, 1986.

Tolan, John. "The Friar and the Sultan: Francis of Assisi's Mission to Egypt." *European Review* 16 (2008) 115–26.

———. *Saint Francis and the Sultan*. New York: Oxford University Press, 2009.

Totten, Sanden. "How Typhoon Haiyan Became So Powerful." Southern California Public Radio (SCPR), November 11, 2013. http://www.scpr.org/news/2013/11/11/40319/how-typhoon-haiyan-became-so-powerful/.

Tovar, Roberto. 1991. "La Última Esperanza." *Paz Verde*. TV Colombiana.

Tuazon, Rolando A. "Biotech Food, the Solution to World Hunger? A Socio-Ethical Consideration on the Introduction of Genetically Modified Organisms (GMOs) to Agriculture." *Hapag* 1 (2004) 93–139.

Turkson, Peter Cardinal K. A. "Integral Ecology and the Horizon of Hope: Concern for the Poor and for Creation in the Ministry of Pope Francis." Trocaire 2015 Lenten Lecture, Saint Patrick's Pontifical University, Maynooth, Ireland, March 5, 2015.

———. "Statement at the Summit of Heads of State and Government on the Millennium Development Goals." New York, September 20, 2010. https://holyseemission.org/contents//statements/55e34d33612193.11219189.php.

"Two Thousand Catholics at Conference." *Seattle Daily Times*, October 16, 1939.

"Uganda Population at Record 37 Million." *New Vision*, June 23, 2013. http://www.newvision.co.ug/news/644270-uganda-population-at-record-37-million.html.

Umehara, Hiromitsu, and Germelino M. Bautista, eds. *Communities at the Margins: Reflections on Social, Economic, and Environmental Change in the Philippines*. Quezon City: Ateneo de Manila University Press, 2004.

U.N. Department of Economic and Social Affairs (DESA). "Annex I: Rio Declaration on Environment and Development," in "Report of the United Nations Conference on Environment and Development (Rio de Janeiro, June 3–14, 1992)." August 12, 1992. A/CONF.151/26 (Vol. I). http://www.un.org/documents/ga/conf151/aconf15126-1annex1.htm.

U.N. Environment Program, United Nations Development Program, World Bank, and Inter Press Service. "Tierramérica." http://www.tierramerica.net.

U.N. Framework Convention on Climate Change (UNFCC) Handbook. Bonn: UNFCC Climate Change Secretariat, 2006. https://unfccc.int/resource/docs/publications/handbook.pdf.

U.N. General Assembly. "Declaration on the Right to Development: December 4, 1986 (Ninety-Seventh Plenary Meeting)." A/RES/41/128. http://www.un.org/documents/ga/res/41/a41r128.htm.

———. "The Future We Want: July 27, 2012 (Plenary)." A/RES/66/288.

———. "General Assembly Proclaims 22 April 'International Mother Earth Day' Adopting by Consensus Bolivia-Led Resolution." GA/10823. April 22, 2009. http://www.un.org/press/en/2009/ga10823.doc.htm.

———. "Special Subjects Relating to the Proposed Programme Budget for the Biennium 2012–13: December 24, 2011 (Committee 5)." A/RES/66/247.

————. "United Nations Regional Centre for Peace and Disarmament in Asia and the Pacific: December 2, 2011 (Committee 1). A/RES/66/56.

U.N. Office for Disaster Risk Reduction (UNISDR). "What Is Disaster Risk Reduction?" http://www.unisdr.org/who-we-are/what-is-drr.

U.N. World Commission on Environment and Development (WCED). *Report of the World Commission on Environment and Development: Our Common Future.* Oslo: United Nations WCED, 1987. http://www.un-documents.net/our-common-future.pdf.

Vatican Council II. *Dogmatic Constitution on Divine Revelation: Dei Verbum.* Boston: Pauline, 1966. http://www.vatican.va/archive/hist_councils/ii_vatican_council/documents/vat-ii_const_19651118_dei-verbum_en.html.

————. *Lumen Gentium: Dogmatic Constitution on the Church.* Boston: St. Paul Editions, 1965.

Veldman, Robin Globus. "Narrating the Environmental Apocalypse." *Ethics and the Environment* 17 (2012) 1–23.

Ventura, Luis. "El Clamor de los Pueblos y la Tierra Amazónica." Paper presented at "Redes Internacionales" REPAM Conference, Madrid, Spain, April 7, 2016.

Villar, Ruairidh, and Sophie Knight. "Haunted by Trauma, Tsunami Survivors in Japan Turn to Exorcists." *Reuters*, March 5, 2013. http://www.reuters.com/article/2013/03/05/us-japan-exorcist-ghosts-idUSBRE9240YZ20130305.

Vitug, Marites Dañguilan. "Forest Policy and National Politics." In *Forest Policy and Politics in the Philippines: Dynamics of Participatory Conservatism,* edited by Peter Utting, 11–39. Manila: Ateneo de Manila University Press, 2000.

Vucetich, John, and Michael Nelson. "Sustainability: Virtuous or Vulgar?" *Bioscience* 60 (2010) 539–44.

Waldfogel, Joel. "The Deadweight Loss of Christmas." *American Economic Review* 83 (1993) 1328–36.

————. "The Deadweight Loss of Christmas: Reply." *American Economic Review* 86 (1996) 1306–8.

————. "The Deadweight Loss of Christmas: Reply." *American Economic Review* 88 (1998) 1358–59.

————. *Scroogenomics: Why You Shouldn't Buy Presents for the Holidays.* Princeton: Princeton University Press, 2009.

Walpole, Pedro, and Julian Watkins. "Understanding Flooding Factors in the Cagayan Watershed." Environmental Science for Social Change, May 24, 2013. http://essc.org.ph/content/understanding-flooding-factors-in-the-cagayan-watershed/.

Walpole, Pedro, and Roberto Yap. "Strategies for Disaster-Risk Reduction." *Philippine Daily Inquirer*, December 25, 2011. http://opinion.inquirer.net/19817/strategies-for-disaster-risk-reduction.

Walsh, Bryan. "Climate Change Didn't Cause Supertyphoon Haiyan: But the Storm Is Still a Reason to Fight Warming." *Time*, November 11, 2013. http://science.time.com/2013/11/11/climate-change-didnt-cause-supertyphoon-haiyan-but-the-storm-is-still-a-reason-to-fight-warming/.

Walvord, John F., and Mark Hitchcock. *Armageddon, Oil, and Terror: What the Bible Says about the Future.* Carol Stream, IL: Tyndale House, 2007.

Walzer, Michael. *Thick and Thin: Moral Argument at Home and Abroad.* Notre Dame: University of Notre Dame Press, 1994.

Wapner, Paul. "Toward a Meaningful Ecological Politics." *Tikkun* 11.3 (May-June 1996) 21.

Ward, Leo. *Nova Scotia: The Land of Cooperation.* New York: Sheed and Ward, 1942.

Warner, Keith. "Retrieving Franciscan Philosophy for Social Engagement. *Cord* 62 (2012) 401–21.

Weaver, Matthew. "Refugee Crisis: EU Ministers to Discuss Binding Quotas." *The Guardian*, September 22, 2015. http://www.theguardian.com/world/live/2015/sep/22/refugee-crisis-eu-ministers-to-discuss-binding-quotas-live-updates.

Weber, Max. *The Protestant Ethic and the Spirit of Capitalism.* Translated by Talcott Parsons. New York: Scribner's, 1930.

Welle, Torsten, et al. "WorldRiskIndex 2012: Concept, Updating, and Results." In *World Risk Report 2012*, 18–19. Berlin and Bonn: Alliance Development Works and United Nations University–Institute for Environment and Human Security (UNU-EHS), 2012. https://www.ehs.unu.edu/file/get/10487.pdf.

———. "The WorldRiskIndex 2014." In *World Risk Report 2014*, 39–50. Berlin and Bonn: Alliance Development Works and United Nations University–Institute for Environment and Human Security (UNU-EHS), 2014. http://i.unu.edu/media/ehs.unu.edu/news/4070/11895.pdf.

Wensveen, Louke van. *Dirty Virtues: The Emergence of Ecological Virtue Ethics.* Amherst, NY: Humanity Books, 2000.

Werner, Eva-Maria. "Weg mit dem Überfluss." *Kontinente*, May/June 2015.

Westermann, Claus. *Genesis: A Practical Commentary, Text, and Interpretation.* Grand Rapids: Eerdmans, 1987.

Weston, Burns H. "The Theoretical Foundations of Intergenerational Ecological Justice: An Overview." *Human Rights Quarterly* 34 (2012) 251–66.

White, Lynn, Jr. *Dynamo and Virgin Reconsidered: Essays in the Dynamism of Western Culture.* Cambridge: MIT Press, 1973.

———. "The Historical Roots of the Ecological Crisis." *Science* 155 (1967) 1203–7.

Whitney, Elspeth. "Changing Metaphors and Concepts of Nature." In *Religion and the New Ecology: Environmental Responsibility in a World in Flux*, edited by David M. Lodge and Christopher S. Hamlin, 26–52. Notre Dame: University of Notre Dame Press, 2004.

———. "The Lynn White Thesis: Reception and Legacy." *Environonmental Ethics* 35 (2013) 313–31.

Wijkman, Anders, and Johan Rockström. *Bankrupting Nature: Denying Our Planetary Boundaries.* New York: Routledge, 2012.

Wildavsky, Aaron. *But Is It Really True? A Citizen's Guide to Environmental Health and Safety Issues.* Cambridge, MA: Harvard University Press, 1997.

———. *Searching for Safety.* Piscataway, NJ: Transaction, 1988.

Wilkinson, James. *Political Spirituality in an Age of Eco-Apocalypse: Communication and Struggle Across Species, Cultures, and Religions.* New York: Palgrave MacMillan, 2015.

Williams, Raymond. *The Country and the City.* London: Hogarth, 1993.

Winner, Langdon. *The Whale and the Reactor: A Search for Limits in an Age of High Technology.* Chicago: University of Chicago Press, 1986.

Winter, Gibson. *Liberating Creation: Foundations of Religious Social Ethics.* New York: Crossroad, 1981.

Witherington, Ben. *Revelation.* Cambridge: Cambridge University Press, 2003.

Woods, Michael J. *Cultivating Soil and Soul: Twentieth-Century Catholic Agrarians Embrace the Liturgical Movement.* Collegeville, MN: Liturgical, 2010.

World Commission on Environment and Development. *Our Common Future.* Oxford: Oxford University Press, 1987.

World Health Organization (WHO) Department of Gender, Women, and Health. "Gender and Health in Disasters." Geneva: World Health Organization, 2002. http://www.who.int/gender-equity-rights/knowledge/a85575/en/.

World Population Review. *Africa Population 2014.* October 19, 2014. http://worldpopulationreview.com/continents/africa-population.

World Resources Institute (WRI). "What is an INDC?" http://www.wri.org/indc-definition.

XE Currency Converter. "HNL to USD." November 17, 2016. http://www.xe.com/currencyconverter/convert/?Amount=1&From=HNL&To=USD.

Yan, Yunxiang. "The Gift and Gift Economy." In *A Handbook of Economic Anthropology*, edited by James G. Carrier, 246–61. Cheltenham, UK: Edward Elgar, 2005.

Yousafzai, Malala, with Christina Lamb. *I Am Malala: The Girl Who Stood Up for Education and Was Shot by the Taliban.* New York: Salarzai, 2013.

ZENIT. "Los Pobres, Víctimas del Cambio Climático." June 12, 2007. https://es.zenit.org/articles/los-pobres-victimas-del-cambio-climatico.

Zizioulas, John D. *Being as Communion: Studies in Personhood and the Church.* Crestwood, NY: St. Vladimir's Seminary, 1985.

Subject Index

between human life and moral
law, 292
in sustainability, 313
between theology and ecology,
165, 259
relativism, 198
Rerum Novarum, 14, 34, 36, 51
res extensa, 262, 264, 267
resource(s), 38, 54, 164n4, 185, 274
aquatic, 38, 82, 96, 137, 139,
164n4, 256
control of, 82, 102, 182
depletion of, 179, 228
destruction of, 220
distribution of, 40
earth's, 57, 66, 67, 94, 197, 202,
205, 205n35, 262, 313
energy, 38, 53, 57
exploitation of, 65, 82, 102, 189,
225
extraction, 183, 256, 266n74,
mineral, 142
natural, 15, 34, 36, 64, 96, 97, 98,
102, 102n5, 111, 112, 124,
131, 143n43, 262, 311, 313
nonrenewable, 36, 57, 94, 96,
114, 231
preserving, 231
scarcity of, 273
responsibility, 187, 189, 195
to the environment, 34, 42, 51,
54, 73, 84, 94–95, 104, 107,
132, 184, 185, 186, 196, 206,
208, 211, 227, 259, 261,
262–63, 265, 301
intergenerational, 257–59
moral, 132, 185, 186, 284–85
toward the poor, 256
shared, 99
restoration, 62
healing, 148, 186
dignity, 186
reterritorialization, 178
rights,
abuse of, 106
environmental, 86, 93, 110, 205
human, 43n40, 70, 76, 93, 94,
102, 104, 105, 106, 110

of indigenous peoples, 103,
200–201, 288
of the poor, 205, 250
Rio Declaration on Environment
and Development, 41–43
Rio de Janeiro, 41, 107, 119
Rio+20 Conference, 41, 119
ritualization of nature, 131
Rochdale principles, 25
Rome, 109–110, 152, 298
Rome's Pontifical Council for Justice
and Peace, 109–10
Royal Dutch Shell, 181

Sacred Scripture, 166
Sahel, 140, 144
Scandinavia, 26, 112
science,
on climate change, 18, 58, 99,
136, 149, 308
of ecology, 16, 50, 170n33, 304
and human survival, 179
in *Laudato Si'*, 59
modern, 316
and religion, 27, 258–59
scientific evidence, 45, 58, 118, 148,
149, 273, 306
scientism, 27, 55
sea level, 120, 140, 236, 294
Second Special Assembly for Africa
of the Synod of Bishops, 124
self-determination, 188, 201
Shell Petroleum Development
Company, 181
Siberia, 253, 264
Social Justice and Ecology
Secretariat of the Society of
Jesus's General Curia, 164
soil, 27, 29n63, 30, 82, 103, 164n4,
180, 225, 227, 230n24, 266,
291, 296, 298, 305–6
conservation of, 28–29
erosion, 23, 30, 163, 296, 305–6
poisoning, 68, 104
solar panels, 2
solidarity, 44, 48, 60, 79, 95, 124,
148, 150, 158, 169n30, 207,
248, 250

Scripture Index